The Nicene-Constantinopolitan Creed

πιστεύομεν εἰς ἕνα Θεὸν	Credo in unum Deum	We believe in one God,
πατέρα, παντοκράτορα,	Patrem omnipotentem;	the Father, the Almighty,
ποιητὴν οὐρανοῦ καὶ γῆς,	factorem coeli et terrae,	maker of heaven and earth,
ὁρατῶν τε πάντων καὶ ἀοράτων.	visibilium omnium et invisibilium.	of all that is, seen and unseen.
καὶ εἰς ἕνα κύριον Ἰησοῦν Χριστὸν,	Et in unum Dominum Jesum Christum,	We believe in one Lord, Jesus Christ,
τὸν υἱὸν τοῦ Θεοῦ τὸν μονογενῆ,	Filium Dei unigenitum,	the only Son of God,
τὸν ἐκ τοῦ πατρὸς γεννηθέντα	et ex Patre natum	eternally
πρὸ πάντων τῶν αἰώνων,	ante omnia saecula	begotten of the Father,
φῶς ἐκ φωτός,	Deum de Deo, Lumen de Lumine,	God from God, Light from Light,
Θεὸν ἀληθινὸν ἐκ θεοῦ ἀληθινοῦ,	Deum verum de Deo vero,	true God from true God,
γεννηθέντα, οὐ ποιηθέντα,	genitum, non factum,	begotten, not made,
ὁμοούσιον τῷ πατρὶ·	consubstantialem Patri;	of one Being with the Father.
δι᾽ οὗ τὰ πάντα ἐγένετο·	per quem omnia facta sunt;	Through him all things were made.
τὸν δι᾽ ἡμᾶς τοὺς ἀνθρώπους	qui propter nos homines	For us
καὶ διὰ τὴν ἡμετέραν σωτηρίαν	et propter nostram salutem	and for our salvation
κατελθόντα ἐκ τῶν οὐρανῶν	descendit de coelis,	he came down from heaven:
καὶ σαρκωθέντα ἐκ πνεύματος ἁγίου	et incarnatus est de Spiritu Sancto	by the power of the Holy Spirit
καὶ Μαρίας τῆς παρθένου	ex Maria virgine,	he became incarnate from the Virgin Mary
καὶ ἐνανθρωπήσαντα,	et homo factus est;	and was made man.
σταυρωθέντα τε ὑπὲρ ἡμῶν	crucifixus etiam pro nobis	For our sake he was crucified
ἐπὶ Ποντίου Πιλάτου,	sub Pontio Pilato,	under Pontius Pilate;
καὶ παθόντα καὶ ταφέντα,	passus et sepultus est;	he suffered death and was buried.
καὶ ἀναστάντα τῇ τρίτῃ ἡμέρᾳ	et resurrexit tertia die,	On the third day he rose again
κατὰ τὰς γραφάς,	secundum Scripturas;	in accordance with the Scriptures;
καὶ ἀνελθόντα εἰς τοὺς οὐρανούς,	et ascendit in coelum,	he ascended into heaven
καὶ καθεζόμενον	sedet	and is seated
ἐκ δεξιῶν τοῦ πατρός,	ad dexteram Patris;	at the right hand of the Father.
καὶ πάλιν ἐρχόμενον μετὰ δόξης	et iterum venturus est, cum gloria,	He will come again in glory
κρῖναι ζῶντας καὶ νεκρούς·	judicare vivos et mortuos;	to judge the living and the dead,
οὗ τῆς βασιλείας οὐκ ἔσται τέλος.	cujus regni non erit finis.	and his kingdom will have no end.
καὶ εἰς τὸ πνεῦμα τὸ ἅγιον,	Et in Spiritum Sanctum,	We believe in the Holy Spirit,
τὸ κύριον, καὶ τὸ ζωοποιόν,	Dominum et vivificantem,	the Lord, the giver of life,
τὸ ἐκ τοῦ πατρὸς ἐκπορευόμενον,	qui ex Patre Filioque procedit;	who proceeds from the Father and the Son.
τὸ σὺν πατρὶ καὶ υἱῷ	qui cum Patre et Filio	With the Father and the Son
συμπροσκυνούμενον καὶ συνδοξαζόμενον,	simul adoratur et conglorificatur;	he is worshiped and glorified.
τὸ λαλῆσαν διὰ τῶν προφητῶν·	qui locutus est per Prophetas.	He has spoken through the Prophets.
εἰς μίαν, ἁγίαν, καθολικὴν	Et unam, sanctam, catholicam	We believe in one holy catholic
καὶ ἀποστολικὴν ἐκκλησίαν·	et apostolicam ecclesiam.	and apostolic Church.
ὁμολογοῦμεν ἓν βάπτισμα	Confiteor unum baptisma	We acknowledge one baptism
εἰς ἄφεσιν ἁμαρτιῶν·	in remissionem peccatorum;	for the forgiveness of sins.
προσδοκῶμεν ἀνάστασιν νεκρῶν,	et expecto resurrectionem mortuorum,	We look for the resurrection of the dead,
καὶ ζωὴν τοῦ μέλλοντος αἰῶνος. Ἀμήν.	et vitam venturi saeculi. Amen.	and the life of the world to come. Amen.

Ancient Christian Doctrine

3

We Believe in the Crucified and Risen Lord

EDITED BY

Mark J. Edwards

SERIES EDITOR

Thomas C. Oden

IVP Academic

An imprint of InterVarsity Press
Downers Grove, Illinois

©2009 by Institute for Classical Christian Studies (ICCS), Thomas C. Oden and Mark J. Edwards

InterVarsity Press® is the book-publishing division of InterVarsity Christian Fellowship/USA®, a student movement active on campus at hundreds of universities, colleges and schools of nursing in the United States of America, and a member movement of the International Fellowship of Evangelical Students. For information about local and regional activities, write Public Relations Dept., InterVarsity Christian Fellowship/USA, 6400 Schroeder Rd., P.O. Box 7895, Madison, WI 53707-7895, or visit the IVCF website at <www.intervarsity.org>.

The Scripture quotations quoted herein are from the Revised Standard Version of the Bible, copyright 1946, 1952, 1971 by the Division of Christian Education of the National Council of the Churches of Christ in the U.S.A. Used by permission. All rights reserved.

Design: Cindy Kiple

Images: The Adoration of the Trinity, by Albrecht Dürer, at Kunsthistorisches Museum, Vienna, Austria. Erich Lessing/Art Resource, NY

ISBN 978-0-8308-2533-2

Printed in the United States of America ∞

InterVarsity Press is committed to protecting the environment and to the responsible use of natural resources. As a member of Green Press Initiative we use recycled paper whenever possible. To learn more about the Green Press Initiative, visit http://www.greenpressinitiative.org

Library of Congress Cataloging-in-Publication Data

Edwards, M. J. (Mark J.)
   We believe in the crucified and risen Lord/Mark J. Edwards.
     p. cm.—(Ancient Christian doctrine series; v. 3)
   Includes bibliographical references and index.
   ISBN 978-0-8308-2533-2 (cloth: alk. paper)
   1. Jesus Christ—Crucifixion—History of doctrines—Early church,
ca. 30-600. 2. Jesus Christ—Resurrection—History of
doctrines—Early church, ca. 30-600. 3. Nicene Crreed. I. Title.
   BT450.E39 2009
   232.96—dc22
                            2009011751

P 31 30 29 28 27 26 25 24 23 22 21 20 19 18 17 16 15 14 13 12 11 10 9 8 7 6 5 4 3 2 1

Y 36 35 34 33 32 31 30 29 28 27 26 25 24 23 22 21 20 19 18 17 16 15 14 13 12 11 10 09

To Alexander, Lucian and Jacob

Contents

Abbreviations

ACO	Augustine. *Confessions*. 3 vols. Commentary by James J. O'Donnell. Oxford: Clarendon Press, 1992.
ACV	Gustaf Aulén. *Christus Victor*. London and Toronto: Macmillan, 1931.
ACW	Ancient Christian Writers: The Works of the Fathers in Translation. Mahwah, N.J.: Paulist Press, 1946 .
AF	J. B. Lightfoot and J. R. Harmer, trans. *The Apostolic Fathers*. Edited by M. W. Holmes. 2nd ed. Grand Rapids, Mich.: Baker, 1989.
AGLB	*Aus der Geschichte der lateinischen Bibel*. Freiburg: Herder, 1957-.
ALSS	*Apollinaris von Laodicea und seine Schule*. Edited by Hans Lietzmann. Texte und Untersuchungen. Tübingen: Mohr, 1904. Reprint, Hildesheim: Olms, 1970.
ANF	A. Roberts and J. Donaldson, eds. Ante Nicene Fathers. 10 vols. Buffalo, N.Y.: Christian Literature, 1885 1896. Reprint, Grand Rapids, Mich.: Eerdmans, 1951 1956; Reprint, Peabody, Mass.: Hendrickson, 1994.
ASCG	Arnobius of Sicca. *Contre les Gentils*. Edited by Henri Le Bonniec. Paris: Les Belles Lettres, 1982.
CAO	*Clementis Alexandrini Opera*. Edited by Guliemi Dindorf. Oxford: Clarendon Press, 1869.
CASL	*Cyril of Alexandria: Select Letters*. Edited by Lionel R. Wickham. Oxford Early Christian Texts. Oxford: Clarendon Press, 1983.
CCL	Corpus Christianorum. Series Latina. Turnhout, Belgium: Brepols, 1953-.
CDL	Cyprian. *De Lapsis; and, De Ecclesiae Catholicae Unitate*. Text and translation by Maurice Bévenot. Oxford: Clarendon Press, 1971.
CHOO	*Cyrilli Hierosolymorum Archiepiscopi Opera quae Supersunt Omnia*. 2 vols. Edited by W. C. Reischl and J. Rupp. Munich: Lentner, 1848, 1860. Reprint, Hildesheim: Olms, 1967.
COGN	*The Catechetical Oration of Gregory of Nyssa*. Edited by James Herbert Srawley. Cambridge: Cambridge University Press, 1903. Reprint, 1956.
COJG	*The Commentary of Origen on Saint John's Gospel*. Edited by A. E. Brooke. Cambridge: Cambridge University Press, 1896.
CSEL	Corpus Scriptorum Ecclesiasticorum Latinorum. Vienna, 1866-.
DEC	Norman P. Tanner and Giuseppe Alberigo, eds. *Decrees of the Ecumenical Councils: From Nicaea I to Vatican II*. Washington, D.C.: Georgetown University Press, 1990.
DFS	*De Fide et Symbolo: Documenta Quaedam nec non Aliquorum SS. Patrum Tractatus.*

	Edited by Charles A. Heurtley. Edition 5a. Oxford: Parker, 1909.
ECC	Mark J. Edwards. *Constantine and Christendom*. Liverpool: Liverpool University Press, 2003.
ECTD	*Saint Ephrem's Commentary on Tatian's Diatessaron: An English Translation of Chester Beatty Syriac MS 709*. Edited by C. McCarthy. *Journal of Semitic Studies* Supplement 2. Oxford: Oxford University Press for the University of Manchester, 1993.
ELC	Eusebius, *Life of Constantine*. Introduction, translation and commentary by Averil Cameron and Stuart G. Hall. Oxford: Clarendon Press, 1999.
ELCEC	*The Earliest Life of Christ Ever Compiled from the Four Gospels: Being the Diatessaron of Tatian (Circ. A.D. 160) from the Arabic Version and Containi*. Translated by James Hamlyn Hill. Edinburgh: T & T Clark, 1894.
ELS	P. D. Baldi. *Enchiridion Locorum Sanctorum: Documenta S. Evangelii Loca Respicientia*. Jerusalem: Franciscan Printing Press, 1955. Reprinted 1982.
EOBO	*Eusebius: Das Onomastikon der Biblischen Ortsnamen*. Edited by Erich Klostermann. Hildesheim: Olms, 1966.
EPP	Mark J. Edwards, "Pauline Platonism: The Myth of Valentinus." *Studia Patristica* 35 (2001): 205-21.
GAP	J. Armitage Robinson and Montague Rhodes James. *The Gospel According to Peter and the Revelation of Peter: Two Lectures on the Newly Discovered Fragments Together with the Greek Texts*. 2nd ed. London: Clay, 1892.
GCCT	Alois Grillmeier. *Christ in Christian Tradition*. Translated by John Bowden. Atlanta : John Knox Press, 1975.
GCS	Die griechischen christlichen Schriftsteller der ersten Jahrhunderte. Berlin: Akademie-Verlag, 1897.
GNO	*Gregorii Nysseni Opera Sermones*. Edited by Ernestus Geberhardt. Leiden: E. J. Brill, 1967.
GNPA	*St. Gregory of Nazianzus: Poemata Arcana*. Translated by D. A. Sykes. Oxford: Clarendon Press, 1997.
GRB	Gildas. *The Ruin of Britain, and Other Works*. Edited and translated by Michael Winterbottom. Arthurian Period Sources 7. London: Phillimore; Totowa, N.J.: Rowman & Littlefield, 1978.
GT	"Gospel of Truth." Translated by Harold W. Attridge and George W. MacRae. In *Nag Hammadi Library in English*, pp. 38-51. Edited by James M. Robinson. 3rd rev. ed. New York: Harper & Row, 1988.
GTO	*Gregorii Turonensis opera*. Edited by Wilhelm Arndt and Bruno Krusch. Hanover, 1884-1885.
GTRNH	Bently Latyon, ed. and trans. *The Gnostic Treatise on Resurrection from Nag Hammadi*. HDR 12. Missoula, Mont.: Scholars Press, 1979.
HCTM	*Les Homélies Catéchètiques de Théodore de Mopsueste: Reproduction Phototypique*

	du ms. Mingana Syr. 561 (Selly Oak Colleges' Library, Birmingham). Edited by Raymond Tonneau and Robert Devreesse. Vatican City: Biblioteca Apostolica Vaticana, 1949.
HROH	*Hippolytus. Refutatio Omnium Haeresium.* Edited by M. Marcovich. Patristische Texte und Studien 25. Berlin: Walter De Gruyter, 1986.
HTAT	*The Treatise on the Apostolic Tradition of St. Hippolytus of Rome, Bishop and Martyr = [Apostolikē Paradosis].* Edited by Gregory Dix; reissued by Henry Chadwick. London: Alban Press; Wilton, Conn.: Morehouse, 1991.
HTCP	John Hick. *Theology's Central Problem.* Birmingham, U.K.: University of Birmingham, Publications Officer, 1968.
IOEP	*Interpretatio omnium epistularum Paulinarum per Homilias Facta.* Oxford: J. H. Parker, 1849 1862.
JBN	Josephus. *Josephs' Bible Notes = Hypomnestikon.* Edited by Robert McQueen Grant and Glen W. Menzies. Atlanta: Scholars Press, 1996.
JMAA	Justin Martyr. In *Die ältesten Apologeten.* Edited by E. J. Goodspeed. Göttingen: Vandenhoeck & Ruprecht, 1915.
LAE	U. M. Lang. "Anhypostatos-Enhypostatos, Protestant Theology and Karl Barth." *Journal of Theological Studies* 49.2 (1998): 630-57.
LCC	J. Baillie et al., eds. The Library of Christian Classics. 26 vols. Philadelphia: Westminster, 1953 1966.
LCL	Loeb Classical Library. Cambridge, Mass.: Harvard University Press; London: Heinemann, 1912-.
LEW	*Liturgies Eastern and Western; Being the Texts, Original or Translated, of the Principal Liturgies of the Church.* Edited by F. E. Brightman. Oxford: Clarendon Press, 1896.
MCOCM	*On the Cosmic Mystery of Jesus Christ: Selected Writings from St. Maximus the Confessor.* Translated by Paul M. Blowers and Robert Louis Wilken. Popular Patristics Series. Crestwood, N.Y.: St Vladimir's Seminary Press, 2003.
MID	Alister E. McGrath. *Iustitia Dei: A History of the Christian Doctrine of Justification.* Cambridge: Cambridge University Press, 1986.
MOPF	Melito of Sardis. *On Pascha and Fragments: Texts and Translations.* Edited by Stuart George Hall. Oxford: Clarendon Press, 1979.
MVCEP	*Marii Victorini Afri Commentarii in Epistulas Pauli ad Galatas, ad Philippenses, ad Ephesios.* Edited by Albrecht Locher. Bibliotheca Scriptorum Graecorum et Romanorum Teubneriana. Leipzig: Teubner, 1972.
NENH	*Nemesii Emeseni: De natura hominis.* Edited by Moreno Morani. Bibliotheca scriptorum Graecorum et Romanorum Teubneriana. Leipzig: Teubner, 1987.
NHLE	*Nag Hammadi Library in English.* Edited by James M. Robinson. 3rd rev. ed. New York: Harper & Row, 1988.

NHS   Nag Hammadi Studies Leiden: E. J. Brill, 1971-

NPNF   P. Schaff et al., eds. *A Select Library of the Nicene and Post Nicene Fathers of the Christian Church.* 2 series (14 vols. each). Buffalo, N.Y.: Christian Literature, 1887 1894; Reprint, Grand Rapids, Mich.: Eerdmans, 1952 1956; Reprint, Peabody, Mass.: Hendrickson, 1994.

OAD   *Optatus: Against the Donatists.* Translated by Mark J. Edwards. TTH 27. Liverpool: Liverpool University Press, 1997.

OBMLV   *The Oxford Book of Medieval Latin Verse.* Edited by F. J. E. Raby. Oxford: Clarendon Press, 1959.

OTP   *Origen. Treatise on the Passover; and, Dialogue of Origen with Heraclides and His Fellow Bishops on the Father, the Son and the Soul.* Translated by Robert J. Daly. ACW 54. Mahwah, N.J.: Paulist Press, 1992.

PCER   *Pelagius's Commentary on Paul's Epistle to the Romans.* Translated by Theodore De Bruyn. Oxford Early Christian Studies. Oxford: Clarendon Press, 1993. Reprint, 2002.

PDDN   Pseudo-Dionysius. De Divinis Nominibus. In *Corpus Dionysiacum I: Pseudo-Dionysius Areopagita. De Divinis Nominibus.* Edited by B. R. Suchla. Patristische Texte und Studien 33. Berlin: Walter De Gruyter, 1990.

PG   J. P. Migne, ed. Patrologiae cursus completus. Series Graeca. 166 vols. Paris: Migne, *1857 1886.*

PGV   *The Penguin Book of Greek Verse.* Introduced and edited by Constantine A. Trypanis with plain prose translations of each poem. Harmondsworth, U.K.: Penguin Books, 1971.

PL   J. P. Migne, ed. Patrologiae cursus completus. Series Latina. 221 vols. Paris: Migne, 1844 1864.

PLM   *Poetae Latini Minores.* Edited by Emil Baehrens and Friedrich Vollmer. 5 vols. Leipzig: Teubner, 1910-1914.

PO   Patrologia Orientalis. Paris, 1903-.

PS   *Patristic Studies.* Washington, D.C.: Catholic University of America Press, 1922-.

RIA   Hastings Rashdall. *The Idea of Atonement in Christian Theology* London : Macmillan, 1919

SC   H. de Lubac, J. Daniélou et al., eds. Sources Chrétiennes. Paris: Editions du Cerf, 1941-.

SAOS   *Saint Ambrose on the Sacraments.* Edited by Henry Chadwick. Chicago: Loyola University Press, 1960.

SIEL   *Sancti Irenaeit, Episcopi Lugdunensis, Libros Quinque Adversus Haereses [microform]: Textu Graeco in Locis Nonnullis Locupletato, Versione Latina cum Codicibus Claromontano ac Arundellano Denuo Collata, Praemissa de Placitis Gnosticorum*

Prolusione, Fragmenta Necnon, Graece, Syriace, Armeniace, Commentatione Perpetua et Indicibus Variis. Edited by W. Wigan Harvey. Cambridge: Typis Academicis, 1857.

STCEC   Holger Strutwolf. *Die Trinitätstheologie und Christologie des Euseb von Caesarea: Eine dogmengeschichtliche Untersuchung seiner Platonismusrezeption und Wirkungsgeschichte.* Göttingen: Vandenhoeck & Ruprecht, 1999.

TA   *Q. Septimi Florentis Tertvlliani Apologeticvs: The Text of Oehler.* Edited by John E. B. Mayor. Translated by Alex. Souter. Cambridge: Cambridge University Press, 1917.

TAW   William Thomson. *The Atoning Work of Christ Viewed in Relation to Some Current Theories.* London: Longman, Brown, Green and Longmans, 1853.

TCE   Theodoret of Cyrus. *Eranistes.* Critical text and prologomena by Gérard H. Ettlinger. Oxford: Clarendon Press, 1975.

TDI   Tertullian. *De Idololatria: Critical Text, Translation and Commentary.* Edited by J. H. Waszink and J. C. M. Van Winden. Supplements to Vigiliae Christianae 1. Leiden: E. J. Brill, 1987.

TP   *The Philokalia.* The complete text compiled by St. Nikodimos of the Holy Mountain and St. Makarios of Corinth. Translated and edited by G. E. H. Palmer, Philip Sherrard and Kallistos Ware. 4 vols. London: Faber and Faber, 1979-1995.

TTH   G. Clark, M. Gibson and M. Whitby, eds. Translated Texts for Historians. Liverpool: Liverpool University Press, 1985-.

INTRODUCTION

In a systematic theology, the doctrine of the person and work of Jesus Christ commences naturally with the nativity. It may seem paradoxical that a historical inquiry into the origins of Christology should begin with the resurrection. It was, however, Jesus himself who urged that his identity must remain hidden until the Son of man was risen from the dead. Three of the Evangelists at least regarded this as an event that lent itself to verification by the testimony of witnesses who knew Jesus before his death. It was, however, one who may never have known him in the flesh who became his apostle to the Gentiles, after encountering him in a form like that under which God had given the Law in Deuteronomy.[1] Thus Paul became a late witness to the mystery by which God had revealed the crucified malefactor to be his Son; when his own preaching quickened faith in the Gentiles this was to him the vindication of Abraham's faith that God would raise up many nations from the deadness of his loins.

The doctrines of the Trinity and the incarnation are not the second thoughts of Christendom after its encounter with Greek philosophy; on the contrary, they were forced on the church by its refusal to adopt the polytheism of the Greeks as a means of reconciling the sovereignty of God with the exaltation of Christ as Lord. The axiom that there is only one God entailed that the Christ who had proved himself immune to death must be more than another Hercules or Osiris. At the same time, if the plenitude of divinity is granted to him, while the title Son continues to distinguish him from the Father, it seems that the incarnate Lord is two as truly as he is one. But for the resurrection, there would have been no reason to argue for a union of two natures in the person of Christ, let alone for a dyad or triad in the Godhead. All that he had said and done in the course of his earthly ministry would have sat well enough with the character of a prophet who excelled such predecessors as Isaiah and John the Baptist only in power and closeness to God.

The resurrection, therefore, was the overture to Paul's teaching on the person and work of Christ when he addressed the Greek philosophers in Athens.[2] There he found that nothing could be proved by an unproved miracle, while at Corinth he discovered incredulity among Christians to whom nothing had been revealed except by hearsay.[3] The Gospels show that even Christ's disciples barely knew him for the same man, or a man at all, while those who had caused his death saw nothing and believed nothing. Thus it was the task of the first apologists

---

[1]Acts 9:3-9; Gal 1:15-16; 1 Cor 15:8.
[2]Acts 17:32.
[3]1 Cor 15:12ff.

to collate the visual testimonies, to show that the event was not only possible but natural and to demonstrate that while it is only God who can overcome death, it is only a man who can be said to have risen from it.

Reflection was inevitably carried back from the living Lord to the suffering man in any church that deemed them to be one person and did not (as some early teachers were said to do) propound a contrast between a mortal son of Mary and an angelic Christ from heaven. Every congregation represented in our New Testament maintained the integrity of the Redeemer. Even Paul, who disowned the knowledge of "Christ after the flesh,"[4] preserves our earliest narrative of the Last Supper and believes that it is Christ's descent from Abraham through David that enables the nations to enter the covenant through his resurrection.[5]

In the letter to the Hebrews, perhaps a commentary on Paul's teaching by a pupil, we meet a rudimentary doctrine of two natures: the captain of our salvation is tempted as we are in the flesh, yet at the same time has the power to frame a new bequest or covenant (*diathēkē*) that, when ratified by his death, supplants God's covenant with Israel.[6] Even this text, however, while it intimates that the man who is destined to rule the angels cannot be less than God, does not explain how a single person can unite two natures so disparate as divine and human. And it does not say whether the union occurred at the birth, the baptism or some other point in the earthly ministry. The deliberations of early Christian writers on these questions, which are regarded now as the nucleus of Christology, will be reviewed in the second part of this introduction.

In the third part I shall turn from the person of Christ to that work of his which is customarily regarded, in western Christendom at least, as the principal object of his coming. That Christ died for our sins was an axiom of all apostolic preaching. We shall see, however, that not all early Christians held that remission was secured by his death alone and that they offered a variety of glosses on the teaching of the New Testament, not a few of which look to modern eyes like seven-league strides from metaphor to myth. Our business in this volume is to read and not to judge—though we may be certain that, if judgment were to be rendered by all parties, the Fathers would combine to denounce the critical maneuvers that persuade us that the Scriptures do not mean what they plainly say, or did not say it in some hypothetical archetype or meant it for other times but not for ours.

The Resurrection

As Attested by the New Testament

In all writings of the New Testament that describe the resurrection, it is regarded as an event that admits of proof by testimony. At the same time, it fails to satisfy some of the usual tests for objectivity or for continuity of personhood. In Matthew's Gospel, Jesus appears in glory to his

---

[4]2 Cor 5:16.
[5]Rom 1:3; Gal 1:16-19.
[6]Heb 2:10; 4:15; 8:10; 9:15-18.

disciples and is worshiped in the act of recognition. Luke relates, by contrast, that his identity was concealed from two fellow travelers up to the moment of departure, while in the Gospel of John a female intimate takes him for the gardener by the tomb.[7] If his enemies never catch sight of him, that is because, as he has already declared in the same text, he returns only to his disciples; to them too he is invisible except when he comes among them, and on such occasions a locked door is no barrier. Lest he should be taken for a spirit, however, he eats with his disciples and displays the marks of his suffering. However, when Thomas says that he cannot believe until he puts his fingers in the wounds, we do not hear that anything more than the exhibition of Christ's hands and side was required to change his temper.[8] He acknowledges Jesus, not as a man restored to life but as Lord and God.[9] Likewise Saul of Tarsus, encountering Jesus for the first time on the Damascus road, salutes him as Lord before he learns his name.[10] In short, where he is taken for a man he is not recognized; where he is recognized he is perceived to be more than man.

To prove that a man was God, or the Son of God, is beyond the reach of any historical inquiry. Nor, so long as the skeptic can appeal to the uniformity of experience to show that the dead remain dead, will the apologist be able to persuade him that a miracle is more likely than a collective mirage, concerted deceit or premature interment. The apologist can, however, turn this trust in the uniformity of experience against the fantastic theory that the cult of Christ developed only by increments after a period during which he was revered as a human teacher. All analogy tells us that if Christ had not been worshiped from the beginning, he would never have been worshiped. It was never the custom to deify a Jewish teacher, or even to form a sect around his memory. The foremost Greek philosophers, though they left a school behind them, suffered no apotheosis except in poetry and metaphor. The majority of those who joined the pantheon after death in the ancient world were kings and emperors, and the honors accorded to them were often perfunctory in comparison with those that they had exacted or accepted during life. Anyone who likens the cult of Jesus to that of Alexander the Great or Julius Caesar should be ready to conclude that he was a deity before his death in the eyes of some contemporaries. Lucian, a pagan satirist, boasts that the posthumous cult of the charlatan Peregrinus was the product of his own conjuring; but if we are to believe this, we must also believe that the cult was born at Peregrinus's funeral and that the latter had enjoyed in life the ovations reserved for those whom the public took for gods on earth.

The Christology of the hypothetical sources of the New Testament is invariably lower than that of any extant testimony. When a forgotten document comes to light, it is always a relic of high Christology—a *Didache* or a *Gospel of Thomas*, never the modest Palestinian archetype that goes by the name of Q in speculation. In extant works that are confidently or colorably as-

---

[7]Mt 28:9-18; Lk 24:13-35; Jn 20:11-18.
[8]Jn 20:25-27.
[9]Jn 20:28
[10]Acts 9:5.

signed to Jewish authors, there is no trace of any gospel but the proclamation of Jesus Christ as Lord. We need not speak of Paul here, or the final chapter of Matthew. Those who set up James as the antithesis to Paul should be reminded that his Jesus is no crucified Galilean, no son of Mary, no carnal brother, but his Lord and the Lord of glory.[11] By common consent the loftiest Christology in the New Testament is that of the Apocalypse.

There is no consensus now that the high Christology is a proof of late composition. Perhaps it was the Greeks who first desired particulars of the earthly mission, but not (we may presume) before they had heard Paul's testimony to the resurrection. Even in the Gospel of Mark, where the powers of Christ are tempered by the natural limitations of humanity, it is not these limitations that the disciples fail to understand, but his miracles and his rising from the dead.[12] Scholars who regard all high Christology as docetic and therefore Greek (without examining the ancient sense of either word) have appealed to our meager records of the Ebionites, an Aramaic-speaking group who are sometimes thought, because they denied the virgin birth, to have owned no savior but the human Jesus. In fact, they are accused by ancient critics of impugning not the dignity of Christ but the intimacy of his union with the human Jesus, whom he was said to have anointed at his baptism and accompanied to the cross.[13]

As Attested by the Earliest Apologists

I have dwelled on these points because there are too many recent studies of the ancient world that raise the cry of docetism whenever they meet a Savior who transcends the finitude of his own humanity or indeed of our humanity. The term "docetic," coined from the Greek verb *dokeō* (I seem), was sparingly applied in the early church to those who held that the flesh of Christ was incorporeal or illusory. It is quite another thing to say that he manifested superhuman as well as human properties or that the body that he brought back from the grave was not in all respects identical with the vitiated legacy of Adam.

The laxity of modern use would leave Ignatius of Antioch in the same camp as his adversaries who, around 110 A.D., denied a body to the resurrected Jesus. Against them Ignatius quotes a saying of Christ to "those about Peter": "See, I am not an incorporeal daemon."[14] We infer that the *Gospel of Peter* was more familiar to him than that of Luke, who supplies the canonical parallel; elsewhere he relies primarily on a text akin to Matthew's Gospel, not without an occasional phrase that puts us in mind of John. The *Gospel of Peter* informs us that in Jewish accounts of the resurrection Jesus the man was supplanted by his angel, a position that may justly be styled docetic. Ignatius draws no contrast in his polemics between the docetists and a Judaizing party who, while shunning circumcision, kept the sabbath and refused to trust any statement in the gospel that was not

---

[11]Jas 1:1; 2:1.
[12]Mk 6:52; 8:21; 9:10.
[13]Irenaeus *Against Heresies* 1.26-12 assimilates their teachings to those of Cerinthus.
[14]*Epistle to the Smyrneans* 3; cf. Origen *On First Principles* 1, proem 10.

corroborated in the archives. The tart reply that "Jesus Christ is the archives" shows Ignatius to have been neither Jew nor God-fearer.[15] It is he, nonetheless, who insists on the humanity of the resurrected Christ as a vindication of his suffering in the flesh and as an incentive to fortitude in his elect. Why, he asks in the manner of Paul, do I bear these tribulations—why do I pray that they may end in death—if I do not hope to rise in the flesh that God has delivered to the lions? It is clearly the opinion of Ignatius that immortality has been granted to the flesh, not to an immaterial remnant of the body, or he would not have declared so frequently that the bread and wine of the Eucharist are the flesh and blood of Christ, and hence for worshipers a meal of faith and love.[16] For Jew as for Greek, resurrection in the present world was a paradox, but one that seemed to Christians to have been proved by the unconquerable sincerity of the first witnesses and verified in the faith of each new martyr.

Those who denied a corporeal resurrection were unable to receive the apostolic texts in the form that is now canonical. Marcion, for example, is supposed to have extorted a proof that the body of the risen Christ was a phantom from a text that reads, in all extant versions, "See, I am not a spirit."[17] Ignatius, as we have noted, turns a similar text against the docetic fallacy; yet his sacramental teaching seems to imply that the flesh that Christ imparts to his worshipers in the Eucharist is not of the same gross texture as the body in which he died.

Among Paul's professed disciples the Valentinians—glibly characterized as Gnostics and docetics in our textbooks—were perhaps the first to argue that in the resurrection flesh is not so much annihilated as swallowed up into eternity. The spiritual body is thus for them a refinement of the earthly domicile that, in Paul's view, can have no place in the kingdom. One Valentinian sect maintained that this was the habit in which Christ had performed his works before the crucifixion, while another held that he came to earth initially in the animal or psychic body that our souls are obliged to wear as the penalty of the fall.[18] A number of uncanonical gospels, not so readily classified as Gnostic, relate that even on earth Christ had the power to elude recognition or to make himself invisible. Such reveries may originate in the secret visit of Jesus to Jerusalem and the subsequent division of opinion as to his character, or possibly in the unexplained facility with which he evades the mobs who desired to stone him or make him king.

Clement of Alexandria, a knowledgeable critic of the groups that we now call Gnostic, does not seem to detect a heresy in the Valentinian teaching that the embodied Christ was already free from passion and did not take food or drink except to comply with the expectations of his neighbors. This is a bold, but not a wanton, inference from the numerous texts that fail to state

---

[15]*Epistle to the Magnesians* 9.

[16]See, e.g., *Epistle to the Smyrneans* 7; *Epistle to the Romans* 6; but the elements are not separable from the rite performed in the presence of the one congregation, nor is any vicarious sacrifice said to be performed.

[17]Lk 24:39.

[18]See especially the *Epistle to Rheginus*, which is not cited in this book, as it speaks only of the general resurrection. On the flesh of the embodied Christ, see Hippolytus *Refutation* 6.36.

that Christ partook of the food that he distributed or followed the dietary practices for which the Jews upbraided his disciples. It is not so easy to find canonical precedent for his anecdote that the flesh of the risen Christ offered no resistance to the hands of those who touched him;[19] but again he records it without disapprobation, and it is not a specimen of docetic teaching, since it is one thing to imagine flesh as subtle as air and another to refine that flesh to nothing.

Origen, Clement's younger contemporary in Alexandria, preferred to taste the word of God without such apocryphal seasonings. Persuaded as he was, however, that soul is no more separable from body than the spiritual from the literal sense of Scripture, he concluded that there is no regeneration of the inner person that leaves intact our gross and sinful members, the apostle's "body of death." The leavening of the body, like the eviction of vice and ignorance from the soul, will be completed only after physical death, and the end will be that, as soul becomes one with spirit, so body becomes in all respects obedient to soul. In the interim, however, when the form of the mortal body is transferred to the soul, the new body will resemble in texture and outward shape the one in which Christ appeared between his rising from the tomb and his ascension. If his only recorded appearances are to his disciples, that is not, as the pagan Celsus alleged, a symptom of their credulity or mendacity. It is a sign that it requires the eye of faith to discern a body that is no longer fattened by the deceitful contours of the flesh.[20]

Other representatives of the catholic faith were not prepared, however, to concede so much to the pagans or to stand in such proximity to the Gnostics. Irenaeus, almost alone of the early Fathers, argues that because it was always the plan of God to exhibit his perfect image in the incarnate Christ, the body participated in the image and likeness of God at the first creation.[21] Creation is thus an earnest of redemption, and the body that is mortal now is destined for immortality. The God to whose law Christ bowed when he came into the world is the God whose amnesty he proclaims to sinners by his rising from the dead. Had his body differed in quality from that of Adam, or had the risen body not been identical with the one that he surrendered to judgment, how was one to refute the claim of the heretics that the Law was not fulfilled but superseded in the gospel and that the Father whom Christ revealed was not the architect of our perishable world? Paul's argument that a seed must die in order to live is taken up in a text that has been attached to the works of Justin Martyr: so far from contradicting the natural course of the world, the resurrection is now declared to be the crowning instance of the law whereby the losses of winter are restored in spring. Clement of Rome, being less disposed to deny the miraculous character of the first resurrection, finds a unique though recurrent symbol of it in the rebirth of the phoenix from its ashes.

For Tertullian, the resurrection illustrates not a natural law but the power of the Creator

---

[19]*Hypotyposes* fragment 3, In Clementis Alexandrini Opera, vol. 3, pp 479-512, ed. Guliemi Dindorf (Oxford: Clarendon Press, 1869).

[20]See especially Origen *Against Celsus* 2.60-63.

[21]See especially *Against Heresies* 5.6.1; 5.16.1.

to suspend his own decrees. Since paradox is therefore the signature of divine activity, we can frame a new law—that whatever mundane experience declares to be impossible is not only possible but certainly true when revelation attributes it to God.[22]

Tertullian was aware of a certain Apelles, who had argued that Christ's flesh was of heavenly origin, a condensation of spirit.[23] The opponents who denied the resurrection were pupils of Marcion rather than Valentinus, and therefore they never canvassed the possibility that Christ's risen body was of a more subtle texture than the corpse. Thus for Tertullian, as for Irenaeus, it is the same thing to maintain the resurrection and to maintain that the risen body is of the same nature as the one derived from Mary. This was to become the presupposition of both dogmatic and apologetic literature.

Resurrection as Attested by the Fathers

Athanasius and his orthodox posterity were at pains to show from Scripture that the signs of death on the cross were incontrovertible, that the sojourn in the tomb was long enough to disarm the skeptic and that no charge of credulity or fraud can be laid against the witnesses to the resurrection.[24] The elusiveness of the resurrected body and its occasional defiance of the laws that curb mobility in the physical realm were not subjects of inquiry or disputation, though they did not cease to attract the sneers of pagans.

Even Augustine puts aside such problems when he weaves the epiphanies of the risen Jesus into one sequence in his *Harmony of the Gospels*. It is enough for him to argue that the "seeing" for which Thomas is praised includes the other senses; and we may be sure that to pilgrims in his flock, who had touched the stones of the empty sepulcher and seen the cross held up in pomp at Easter in Jerusalem, the resurrection was a self-evident fact of history.

To say otherwise would have been to assume—as is frequently assumed today, and not only by self-styled liberals—that the resurrection put an end to the intercourse between Jesus and the world. In many a book by an evangelical writer the "historical Jesus" takes his leave on Calvary, and the resurrection seems to function only as an apologetic cudgel. Have you no faith in miracles? Then disprove the resurrection. Do you doubt the divinity of Jesus? Then explain how he rose from the dead. Do you deny the efficacy of the cross? Then tell us what you make of the empty tomb. One need not think these arguments invalid to be conscious of their inadequacy to the teaching of the New Testament, where the resurrection is not a test by which believers prove their creed to outsiders but a summons to apostleship, the bedrock of communion in the body of Christ, the assurance that we are not still "in our sins" and the ripening mystery of a life "hid with Christ in God." Like the earthly ministry of Jesus, his resurrection sorts the faithful from the unfaithful. The world cannot perceive him, while to the eye of faith he is sometimes glorious,

---

[22]Note that at *On the Flesh of Christ* 5, the argument never takes the personal form—"I believe"—but only that of logical gradation: it is credible/certain/decorous because it is impossible/absurd.

[23]*On the Flesh of Christ* 1.

[24]*On the Incarnation* 21-26.

sometimes lowly, strange to some, familiar to others, a man to Thomas, a speaking light to Paul. In every guise, however, he is worshiped, and it is Paul's belief that the "name above all names,"[25] which has been vouchsafed to him by the Father, will be acknowledged in the last times by all creation. If this prophecy seldom finds an echo in the rites of Protestant churches, it can be argued that there is no proof in the New Testament that prayers were made to Christ except as private ejaculations of thanksgiving or intercession. The primitive church, however, held that if Christ was already exalted, there was no reason for the saints to withhold their testimony. A pagan magistrate, in the early years of the second century, records that at Christian gatherings in his province hymns were sung to Christ *ut deo*, "as a god."[26]

In a monotheistic cult there can be no more than one object of devotion. Christians were perhaps slow to draw the inference that the Son is God in the same sense as the Father. His commonest appellation in the New Testament is "Lord," the Greek equivalent for Yahweh in the Old Testament. Since, however, the term is regularly used of human masters, it cannot be assumed to signify that Christ is of the same substance, rank or nature as the Father, and it may mean only that the Father has delegated to him his privilege of command. A loftier claim has often been deduced from the addition of "my God" to "my Lord" in Thomas's homage to the risen Jesus; yet the qualification "my God" seems to ascribe to him an intermediate rank between true deity and a figure such as Moses, who was "god to Pharaoh"[27]—that is to say, the one who embodies all that Pharaoh is to know of God. The same locution—my God, rather than simply God—survives in the seven letters of Ignatius and is one indication of their early date.

Yet if the exalted Christ was God and Lord, he was also man. The Christ to whom the church prayed in Origen's day was, in his own words, of a different "matter" or "substrate" from the Father, and it is evident from his commentary on John that he means by this to assert the inseparability of the exalted Godhead from the manhood. A few years after Origen's death, the Antiochene bishop Paul of Samosata, who believed Jesus to have been an inspired man rather than God incarnate, was alleged to have replaced the name of Christ by his own in the hymns of his congregation. Eusebius of Caesarea, who supplies our earliest record of the condemnation of Paul in his native Antioch, was a warm admirer of Origen, though he may not have shared his opinion that the body of the saint is made more pliable to the spirit after death by a gradual lessening of its material density. The body of Christ he certainly believed to have survived his death, resurrection and ascension, for while he held that passages foretelling the enthronement of the Messiah in the Old Testament looked beyond David and his like, it was equally clear to him that they prophesied the enthronement of a man.[28]

While some Christian writers after Eusebius held that the manhood of the risen Christ was

---

[25]Phil 2:9.

[26]The authenticity of Pliny *Letter* 10.96 is now not commonly disputed.

[27]Ex 7:1.

[28]See the passage quoted from book 7 of the *Demonstration* in this volume.

so attenuated as to be barely visible even to the eye of faith,[29] there was none who denied that the Word had retained a body of a certain texture even in his ascent beyond the heavens. In accordance with the usage of Paul, they also held that Christ was bodily present in his church, while the greatest exegetes maintained that the believer who desires to know Christ on earth can know him as intimately as his first disciples through the humble and diligent reading of the Scriptures. All the words of Scripture, Origen says, are informed by the one Word who assumed body, soul and spirit for our salvation. Only because the incarnation was an event in history does the Christian now have the right to progress from the merely historical reading of the Scriptures to the higher and more timeless truths enshrined in its soul and spirit.

For Augustine, the written word is, like the incarnate Christ, the embodiment of love, and its sense is palpable only to those in whom that love has been awakened.[30] Again, the presence of Christ in the Eucharist is assumed by every Christian writer of this era, and while there are some who write as though this presence were symbolic or metaphorical, there are others, no less orthodox, who seem to consider the church as a place of sacrifice and the flesh and blood as real as the faith and love that they engender. "Body of Christ" is thus not a univocal expression in the early church, any more than in the Scriptures or in the liturgy and theology of our own day; nevertheless, it is clear that in one of its senses it denotes the corporeality that continues to be the peculiar and indefeasible attribute of the Word when he is recognized as God. The union of God and man in Christ, which is the subject of the Nicene-Constantinopolitan Creed's confession of salvation, was for the Fathers a presupposition of experience and worship, and not merely a theme for hermeneutic quibbling or for metaphysical prestidigitation.

Man and God

The Logos-Anthropos Pattern of Scripture and Tradition

The Fathers did not read the Bible as modern academics do, with the purpose of setting James against Paul, unpicking the threadwork of the Deuteronomist or excavating layers of redaction in the Gospels. Their task, as they believed, was to show that truth is one in all its expressions, and to this end they were prepared to borrow any tool of rhetoric, philosophy or scholarship that enabled them to banish the appearance of absurdity or discord from the text.

In the early twentieth century, it became fashionable to argue that one cannot acquire a term without acquiring the associated concept, and that as a result the Greek of the Fathers differed, without their knowing it, from the Greek that they purported to be interpreting in the Scriptures. One consequence is supposed to be that when Alexandrian Christians used the word *flesh*—the Alexandrians, *ex hypothesi*, being philosophers to a man—they cannot have meant by this the whole ensemble of human qualities or humanity in the mass, because this biblical sense was unknown to the philosophers. Hence they must mean body, and the Logos-sarx Christol-

---

[29]E.g., Gregory of Nyssa at the end of his letter to Theophilus.
[30]This is the theme of *On Christian Doctrine* 1.

ogy[31] that they embraced entails the denial of a human soul in Christ.

This Logos-sarx Christology is contrasted with a Logos-anthropos doctrine, which acknowledges the assumption of a human soul and a human intellect in the incarnation. It is something of a paradox that this Logos-anthropos model should be said to cohere more closely with the teaching of the New Testament, for, as Cyril of Alexandria pointed out, the New Testament teaches that the word became flesh and not that he became man. Furthermore, it is reasoning in a circle to deduce that because an author makes no allusion to a soul in Christ he is using *sarx* to denote the soulless body; his reticence might as easily be a consequence of his using *sarx* in the biblical sense, which renders mention of the soul redundant since it already comprehends all the vital functions of the person. When an author is known to have held the Platonic view that soul and body are different subjects, neither of which can lend its name to the other, failure to posit a human soul in Christ could be taken as evidence that he conceived the incarnation as nothing more than the animation of a body by the Word. But the most distinguished authors of this class, Apollinaris and Origen, expressly posit a soul as the seat of passion and sensibility in the Savior, and Origen at least is not disposed to use *sarx* as a synonym for body since, in contrast to modern critics of the Fathers, he was aware that they were *not* synonyms in the dialect of philosophers. There are indeed other Alexandrian writers, notably Cyril and Athanasius, who speak more freely of *sarx* than of soul in Christ. It should, however, be clear from our discussion that this may be a sign of nothing but their reluctance to use a term that was as protean in their time as it is quaint in ours.

The noun *psychē*, in that handful of Christ's sayings that declare it to be of more worth than the body, is commonly rendered "life" on some occasions, "soul" on others. In Paul the psychic is generally contrasted with the spiritual (*pneumatikos*), which is also the regular antonym of flesh. Flesh can be set against mind but not against soul, which is more properly its complement or correlative. To be soul, or to have a soul, is to derive one's life from Adam, while to be flesh, or inhabit flesh, is to be heir to Adam's sin. In Christ the two words part company, for, while we learn that the "likeness of sinful flesh" that veiled him on earth has now become the food of his worshipers, we hear nothing of his soul, except when he declares that he lays it down or that it is troubled to death. Soul and self are hardly to be distinguished here, but Christ employs the term that betokens the weakness, possibility and incertitude to which he surrendered in "becoming flesh."[32] Hence it is that in the earliest Christian reflections on the soul of Christ, it is always the seat of passion and sensibility, the bridge between the carnal and the spiritual, and never the source of wisdom, prophecy or righteous conduct.

Origen derives the noun *psychē* (wrongly) from another word that means "cold," and he infers that soul is spirit that has lost its ardor; the soul of Christ alone clung to the Word with undiminished love from the moment of creation, thus enabling his divine spouse to take on flesh

---

[31]See GCCT 162-442.
[32]Jn 1:14; 12:27; cf. Mt 26:38.

without its characteristic vices. For Origen, as for the Platonists, pure intellect cannot act on body except through the mediation of a third principle that reconciles the incorporeality of one with the passibility of the other.[33] The Word becomes one with the human spirit or intellect of Christ but is merely contiguous to his soul, so that when he is said to suffer a perturbation in spirit, it is not, in fact, in the spirit but in the soul that he feels the throes; the perturbation is nonetheless said to originate in spirit because it is only through his communion with the omniscient Word that Jesus the man is able to anticipate the horror of his death.[34] He sees as man what he foresees as God, and the affliction of his soul bears witness to the inseparability of the two natures.

Tertullian's treatise *On the Flesh of Christ* is more divisive, since his project is, by illustrating the weakness of Christ's soul, to prove that his flesh was not divine. Two sources of infirmity must therefore be distinguished: it is the soul that grieves for Lazarus, the flesh that thirsts at the well of the Samaritan.[35] Flesh is here synonymous with body, yet soul and body constitute one nature in Christ as in any other human being; in Christ alone, however, the defects of human nature are redressed by the miraculous knowledge, patience and fecundity in healing that pertain to him as God.

In merely collating evidence for the presence of two natures without pretending to ascertain how they work in concert, Tertullian commits none of the temerities that brought suspicion on Origen in the late third century. Origen was believed to have espoused a position akin to that of Apelles by attributing existence to the soul of Christ before the incarnation; however, it barely survives the union, since he maintains that it was absorbed into the Godhead as iron melts into an incandescent flame.[36] For all that, he is no monophysite, no dogmatic proponent of one nature in Christ, as passages can be found in which he assigns some acts and sayings to the divinity and others to the manhood, and he can sometimes write as though the Word were not properly the subject of the man's actions. Half a generation after his death, as we have noted, the infamous Paul of Samosata was convicted of suppressing prayers to Christ in the churches of Antioch and of teaching that the Savior was not God but a human plenipotentiary whose inspiration differed from that of the Hebrew prophets only in degree. This "psilanthropic" doctrine could assume the full humanity of Christ without the difficulty of reconciling two free centers of consciousness. A number of its adversaries appear to have concluded that in the one Christ there could be only one hegemonic principle, and that if Christ was to be God, the Word must therefore take the place of a human mind. This argument does not displace the passible soul, for no reputable opinion in the third century would have predicated grief or trepidation of the Godhead. But as the terms for mind and soul were seldom employed without confusion in Greek philosophy, and as Origen had clearly ascribed both a human soul and a human intellect

---

[33]*On First Principles* 2.6.3-4.
[34]*Commentary on John* 32.18.
[35]*Flesh of Christ* 9-11.
[36]*On First Principles* 2.6.3.

to Christ, it was alleged that he, like Paul of Samosata, had ascribed so much to the manhood as to leave no place for the Word.

While this charge was easily dispelled by his Caesarean apologists Pamphilus and Eusebius, we cannot be sure that either of them ascribed the deliberation and reasoning of the incarnate Christ to a human consciousness. However, there is little to support the common assertion that Eusebius substituted the Word for the human mind in Christ, since in the passage that is commonly thought to prove this, he is not speaking on his own behalf but offering a poisoned gift to his adversary Marcellus of Ancyra.[37]

From Athanasius to Gregory of Nazianzus

It is not until the fourth century that we hear of a theologian who dispensed with the appetitive and passible soul in Christ. Arius, who had been condemned in 325 for maintaining that the Word is divine by favor and not by essence, was alleged to have inferred that the higher element in Christ was as fallible as his humanity—that the Word himself, by virtue of his origin, was prone to sorrow, fearful of death and ignorant of the last day. It must be confessed that neither of our informants, Athanasius and Eustathius of Antioch, even notices that this tenet is inconsistent with the more securely attested position of Arius, that the Word, whatever his natural propensity, was preserved from sin and vagary by the will of God the Father.[38] The Word on earth, as Arius conceived him, had been endowed with perseverance, was unchangeable by divine fiat if not by nature and hence was not susceptible to grief or pain. It is possible that Athanasius, writing after Arius's death, has misunderstood his enemy. More probable, perhaps, is that, using the license that was granted to the author of a philosophical dialogue when he took a real personage as his interlocutor, he put into the mouth of Arius any speculation that he thought dangerous to faith.

The new seeds of catholic thought in Athanasius are more interesting to historians than the scarecrows that he set up to preserve them. No author before him had taught with such inexorable clarity that the acts of Christ belong to the Word because he employs the body as his organ in performing them, while the sorrow and fear are his because he suffers them in his flesh. Christ puts forth his hand as man and heals as God. His flesh is prone to suffering, and he suffers. Since the tribulations of the flesh include not only hunger and thirst but also his fear of death and his grief at the tomb of Lazarus,[39] "flesh" cannot be a synonym for body. It rather denotes the condition in which soul lacks strength to master the trials and perils that it inflicts on the body by its sins.

This distinction is Pauline; and if Athanasius seems at times to hold that the Word is properly superior to the flesh that is nonetheless proper to him, that too is no more than to say with

---

[37]Eusebius *Ecclesiastical Theology* 1.20.44-45, as interpreted by Strutwolf, STCEC 328-32. It would have been merely bewildering to the reader to include this in the present anthology.

[38]See Athanasius *Discourses Against the Arians* 1.5; *On the Synods* 16.

[39]*Discourses Against the Arians* 3.22-23.

Paul that the flesh is "I" and yet "not I."[40] It is easier, however, to maintain that part of the self remains unbruised by what it feels in another part than that we can be at once conscious and ignorant of the same matter. What would it mean to know when the end will be and yet not know it? Yet this must be the position of those who urge that Jesus' confession at Mark 13:32 ("none knows that day, not even the Son") touches only his knowledge as a man, while he remained omniscient as God. The title Son pertains to him (or so at least Athanasius holds) by virtue of his divinity, and the ancients never entertained the kenotic theory that he voluntarily curbed his knowledge in entering the womb. Athanasius was accordingly no more disposed than Origen to believe that Christ could be unaware as man of what he knew as God. But he argues that, because it is in the nature of the human mind to be finite, Christ elected to give an example of humility, of submission to the bounds that God has placed on his creatures, so that his listeners might not attempt to storm forbidden mysteries. Christ, in short, was practicing an economy, as Luke the Evangelist does when he declares that Christ grew in wisdom and stature.[41] This means not that the Word himself matured but that his Godhead became more patent to the world as he permitted the evidence of it to increase.[42]

This principle, that Christ for our sake sometimes speaks or is spoken of as a man among men, was endorsed by Epiphanius of Salamis in a defense of the Nicene faith against the "Arians."[43] Somewhat less inimical to the plain sense of Mark 13:32 is Basil the Great's conjecture that Christ was not so much disclaiming knowledge of the final day as owning that he possessed this knowledge only because he derived it from the Father.[44] Athanasius shows the same readiness to acknowledge the priority of the Father (not in essence, time or dignity but in order of generation) when he discovers in Christ's saying "The Father is greater than I" a testimony to his Sonship and not merely to his manhood.[45] Most champions of Nicea, however, argued that, as there is no subordination in the Godhead, we must refer these words to the manhood or more accurately to the willing abasement of the Son of God in his assumption of human form.

Such magnanimity is itself an exhibition of supernatural virtue. This would be even more true of Christ's obedience to death, were it not as much of a paradox to die and not to die as it is to know and not to know. References to the suffering of the Word in the passion of Christ are almost always circumlocutory and tentative in this era. When Apollinaris of Laodicea said openly that "God has died,"[46] he appeared to his contemporaries to be lapsing once again into that confusion of the two natures that was entailed or presupposed throughout his teaching on the person of Christ. No doubt he intended to say not that the Godhead was by nature prone to

---

[40]Rom 7:17-20.
[41]Lk 2:52.
[42]*Discourses Against the Arians* 3.52.
[43]*Ancoratus* 31.
[44]*Letter* 236.
[45]*Discourses Against the Arians* 1.58.
[46]Fragment 95 *ALSS* 221.

death but that the owner of the Godhead was identical with the man who had paid his debt to mortality—that is, the common person died in one of his two natures, while the other nature remained imperishable. Again, when Apollinaris styled Christ the man from heaven, his position was not, as his critics thought, that the flesh came from above, but that the Word came down and became the man who was consequently said to have done anything that could be predicated truly of the Word. Whatever is true of the God who is man is true of the man who is God. That is orthodoxy as we now conceive it, so long as due provision is made for the coexistence of two perfect natures in the one person. Since Apollinaris was perhaps the first to declare expressly that Christ was consubstantial in his deity with the Father and in his flesh with the human race, it might be thought that he met this standard. He failed because he held, without clear precedent in Scripture or tradition, that in this union of the two natures the Word supplants the human intellect. The human soul he appears to have left intact, though some of his adversaries do not distinguish soul from mind. The sinlessness and fortitude of Christ, however, seemed to him to bespeak the presence of a mind superior to that of any man in the fallen state. The Word, he opined, is joined to the flesh in just the same way as the inner man is joined to the outer man in any human individual. As it is the invisible, not the visible self, that constitutes human personhood, so in the person of Christ we see God bearing man and not man bearing God.

This, it was agreed on all sides, was heresy, yet the churchmen who combined to denounce the offender were not at one in their definition of the offense. To Gregory of Nazianzus it lay primarily in the exclusion of the mind from the economy of salvation. Echoing Tertullian's tract against Apelles, he lays down the rule that "what has not been assumed has not been healed." While Apollinaris could deny that he followed Apelles in ascribing celestial flesh to Christ, he could not deny that the mind was in need of healing, since he believed that all three elements in our nature had been corrupted by the Fall. He could, however, contest the premise that the regeneration of mind was the work of Christ in his incarnation, rather than (say) of the Holy Spirit after his resurrection. Would he have been more moved by the objection of Theodore of Mopsuestia, that if Christ was not fully man, the human race would have won no victory over Satan? Surely not, for even if he conceded that the binding of Satan was the principal object of Christ's ministry, he could argue that the victory was equally complete, and our deliverance equally sure, if the work was accomplished on behalf of humankind by God. Another of Theodore's arguments, that to substitute the Word for the human mind is to make him subject to vicissitude and passion, would have seemed to Apollinaris merely circular, since it assumes that an unfallen mind is as malleable as one enfeebled by the sin of Adam.

Modern readers are most impressed by Gregory of Nyssa, who contends that there is no merit in virtuous acts unless they are free, and that to take away Christ's human will is to take away his freedom. To this Apollinaris could reply that, on the contrary, the only acts that are truly free are those that proceed spontaneously from the nature of the agent. Only God, he would add, is naturally immune to all temptation, and the intercalation of a human mind would necessarily lead to sin unless that mind either coalesced with or was coerced by its divine partner. Gregory seems to seize the first horn of the dilemma in his letter to Theophilus, which concludes that the human nature in Christ is eclipsed by the Godhead, just as a drop of oil becomes invisible in the sea. Since the Stoic masters to whom he owed this simile believed that the oil nonetheless retains its character as oil, we need not suppose that Gregory's Christology disowns the human nature altogether.

The integrity of Christ is surely compromised, together with the liberty of his human will, in Theodore's account of his temptation. The Word, according to Theodore, leads Christ to the Jordan, where he receives the spirit in preparation for his conflict in the wilderness; thus the Word is his guide or mentor rather than his true or higher self. Theodore affirms elsewhere that the manhood is to the Word as a robe to a king,[47] and the bond appears to be no more intimate at the cross, to judge by a statement in a catechetical homily that the Word was in attendance at the man's death.

The condemnation of Apollinaris in 381 was a bill of attainder against the orthodoxy of any teaching that appeared to neglect the human soul in Christ. Since the great heresiarch had been apt to use the term "flesh" interchangeably with body, those who employed the term in its biblical sense were now required to add the unbiblical rider "not without a rational soul." Suspicion also fell on the term *Theotokos*, bearer of God, which had become a liturgical epithet of Mary, the mother of Jesus. Gregory of Nazianzus has the air of one who has captured the enemy's standard when he asks the Apollinarians what the *Theotokos* could have borne if, as they imagined, neither the Word nor his flesh had an origin in time.[48] A party in Constantinople, however, held that so long as the answer was "God," the Apollinarians had the better of the quarrel.

Uniting Two Natures in One Person as Required for Salvation: Ephesus to Chalcedon

A controversy arose between partisans of the *Theotokos* and those who espoused a new term, *anthrōpotokos*, "bearer of man." In 428, the new patriarch Nestorius disowned both titles, hoping to impose his own substitute, *Christotokos*, "bearer of Christ." Cyril of Alexandria denounced this innovation perhaps with unnecessary vehemence; Nestorius replied by branding him an Apollinarian, and both parties appealed to Rome. Though still acknowledged as the first see of Christendom, Rome was jealous of the prerogatives that Constantinople had granted to itself at the second ecumenical council in 381. Furthermore, the letters of Nestorius to Pope Celestine were boldly independent, contumelious to Cyril and still hostile to the term *Theotokos*. Celestine made common cause with Cyril, and at their instance the emperor Theodosius II summoned a council at Ephesus in 381. To Celestine and Cyril, the only purpose of this meeting was to secure the deposition or recantation of Nestorius, and the Roman bishop, declining to attend in person, told his representatives to treat Cyril's word as law.

---

[47]Syriac fragment from book 18 of the *Contra Eunomium*.
[48]*Letters* 101, 102.

Before the council, Cyril had addressed a second letter to Nestorius, which, receiving a stubborn answer, was quickly followed by a third. The second invoked the Nicene Creed of 325 to demonstrate that the Son of God is identical with the man who suffered under Pontius Pilate. Crediting Nestorius with the dictum, "I worship the one assumed for the sake of the one who assumed him," he pronounces this a blasphemy that makes two sons of Christ and an idol of his created manhood. The union, though ineffable and mysterious, may be said with confidence to be hypostatic, not, as Nestorius maintains, a mere conjunction of *prosōpa*. Cyril takes this term to mean mere appearance, though in a late work by Nestorius it appears to denote the concrete realization of a generic nature in the individual. Cyril's objection stands nonetheless, for Nestorius distinguishes the hypostatic union of his adversary from his own prosopic union, and it is hard to see how his own principles can even admit the latter. If the common *prosōpon* of Christ is to represent two natures, divine and human, then it flouts the definition of *prosōpon* that is laid down by Nestorius himself. If, therefore, this *prosōpon* is to be truly one, there must be a coalescence of the two natures that were hitherto instantiated in two distinct *prosōpa*; yet a mingling of the divine and human natures is the heresy that Nestorius has cast in the teeth of Cyril. The union of *prosōpa* is compared in one of his similes to the superimposition of two shields held by different warriors; if he could write thus around 450, he could easily have fallen, twenty years earlier, into a way of speaking that implied two Christs.

To his third letter, Cyril appended twelve anathemas, which he required his correspondent to endorse. The first was to fall on those who denied that the son of Mary was truly God, the fourth on those who allotted words or titles of the one Christ to distinct *prosōpa* or *hypostases*, the twelfth on those who refused to confess that God the Word had "tasted death" on the cross. Nestorius and his party countered these and the other nine with his own anathemas, distributing the anathemas of Cyril to the bishops of the east, who formed a party against Alexandria under John of Antioch. This party made its way so slowly to Ephesus, however, that the assembled bishops were forced or rather induced by Cyril to proceed without them. Arriving to find Nestorius deposed, they held their own conclave and deposed Cyril. Cyril replied in kind, but two years later he and John succumbed to the menaces of the emperor and agreed on a Formula of Reunion. It is commonly held that Cyril could not have ratified all its clauses in good faith had he been sincere in his condemnation of Nestorius. On inspection, however, all the hard sayings prove to have been as orthodox in Alexandria as in Antioch. The first sentence of the formula, for example, states that the body of Christ is the temple that he derived from the *Theotokos*. Cyril could accept this, though he had previously denied that the flesh of Christ could be called his temple, because the body, unlike the flesh, is not the whole man, and thus this metaphor does not entail that the whole man is a mere adjunct to the Word. Again it is often said that Cyril waived his fourth anathema when he endorsed the closing sentence of the formula, which assigns some works and sayings to Christ "according to his manhood" and others "according to his divinity." In fact, however, the formula and the anathema both preclude only the allocation of works and sayings to two *prosōpa* or *hypostases*, not the ascription of different works and sayings to the same person with respect to different natures. Finally, it is true that Cyril had not subscribed before this to the dictum that the Christ who is consubstantial with us in his manhood is consubstantial with the Father in his divinity; but neither had Nestorius, Theodore or John of Antioch, and if the phrase originates with Apollinaris, as the evidence cited above implies, it was evidently possible to uphold it without dividing the one hypostasis of Christ.

For all that—and notwithstanding the consistency with which Cyril affirms two natures in Christ in his writings after Ephesus—there were some who held that the Formula of Reunion had sacrificed truth to policy, diluting the resolutions of the council in 431. In 448, one zealot who maintained this position outside Alexandria, the Archimandrite Eutyches, was condemned by a synod in Constantinople. Bishop Flavian, who had tried in vain to persuade the accused that Christ was consubstantial with humanity in his flesh and with the Father in his divinity, was not hoping to right the balance between Nestorius and Cyril but to correct a misapprehension of Cyril's teaching; and it is certainly true that Eutyches found no precedent in Cyril for his teaching that the manhood of Christ was wholly swallowed up in his divinity. Nevertheless, Dioscorus, Cyril's nephew and successor in Alexandria, took the side of Eutyches, illegally convening a second council at Ephesus in 449. By violence rather than argument he secured the vindication of Eutyches and the deposition of Bishop Flavian, overruling the veto of two Roman visitors whose errand when they left Italy had been to add the authority of Pope Leo to Flavian's confutation of Eutyches. The letter that they were carrying, generally known as the Tome of Leo, drew its christological premises from Paul's letter to the Philippians, where we hear that Christ exchanged the form of God for that of a slave. Each form, according to Leo, retains its nature intact and unconfused, and each performs the work that is proper to it in every act of Christ. As in Athanasius, Christ puts forth his hand as man and heals as God; and while his birth and death unite his manhood with our fallenness, it is only by virtue of his being God that these events become medicines for our imbecility and sin.

Is this the doctrine of Ephesus? At the fourth ecumenical council, held in 451 at Chalcedon, partisans of Cyril alleged that if the two natures in Christ are both conceived as acting subjects, there is little to choose between Cyril and Nestorius. By the end of the council, however, it was generally agreed that Leo and Cyril taught the same Christology in different phrases and that this was a mean between the contradictory aberrations of Nestorius and Eutyches. Often praised today for having effected a compromise between the Antiochene and the Alexandrian schools, the council manifestly aimed at no such thing, for it canonized only Cyril's side of the correspondence with Nestorius and John of Antioch. It promulgated a definition in which the dominical titles were held to be equally true of the Word and of the man whom he became. As Cyril's forth anathema prescribed, it acknowledged only one *"prosōpon* or *hypostasis"* in the Savior. In affirming the double consubstantiality, it was consciously lifting a clause from Cyril's letter to John of Antioch. At the same time, it deferred to Rome in adopting the locution "in two natures," which in the east was supported only by defenders of Nestorius. The more Cyril-line "from two natures" had been ratified at the synod of 448, where Eutyches was chastised by Flavian, and may therefore be regarded as the Greek, not merely the Alexandrian, shibboleth. The definition also incorporated Leo's tenet that each nature performs the work proper to it. If, therefore, there was a compromise, it was not between Alexandria and Antioch but between the east and Rome.

It was not in Rome, however, but in Byzantium that the controversy flourished after 451 Among the Greeks there was no thought of amending or revising the thought of Cyril, but it was rare to find a disputant who denied that Christ, from his birth to his exaltation, was both human and divine. The Monophysites, or advocates of one nature in Christ, did not deny that the attributes of humanity and divinity co-existed in him without mixture or defect. They argued, however, that, since one person implies one nature in common speech, it is better to posit a single, hybrid nature in Christ than to speak obscurely of two. The Chalcedonian diphysites, or proponents of two natures, were as hostile to Nestorius as their adversaries, and as the victorious faction at the fifth ecumenical council in 553, they took occasion to condemn not only Theodore but also Theodoret and Ibas, who were also supposed to have entertained fissiparous christologies. The question to be settled outside the council of 553 was not whether Christ was a single person or whether he was both God and man but whether the nature that God assumed was the "enhypostatic" manhood of a single human being or the "anhypostatic" manhood of the species.[49] The eloquence and close reasoning of Leontius of Byzantium ensured that the first opinion would prevail. But now another question arose: if the Word became a human individual, assuming all the usual concomitants of individuality, does it follow that he acquired a second, human will in addition to the one that he had as God? At first it was thought heretical to answer in the affirmative, for how could there be two wills without two persons? At last, however, the Christian world, including Rome, endorsed the logic of Maximus the Confessor, who maintained that in Gethsemane two wills had been in conflict—the merely "gnomic" or deliberative faculty that Christ shared with other humans and the divine resolve to which his human will at last conformed.

The ratification of this dithelite view at the sixth ecumenical council entailed a posthumous judgment on the Roman Pope Honorius, who had lent his authority to the monothelite doctrine when it was almost a consensus. Pope Leo, wisely declining to investigate the consciousness of Christ, had been content to show how the conjunction of two natures had effected the salvation of the lower one. While the Chalcedonian definition added nothing to the bald statement of the Nicene Creed that Christ "came down for us and our salvation," it was never forgotten, either in the east or in the west, that even the subtlest understanding of Christ's person is valued only for what it tells us of his saving work. Conversely, as we shall see, it was no more possible for the Fathers to divorce the work from the person than to sever faith from love or to seek a benefit from the cross that was not prefigured by Christ's tribulation and victory in the flesh.

---

[49]LAE.

The Atonement

The meaning of the English word *atonement* was initially "causing two to be *at one*." There is nothing in the term to tell us which of the two effects the reconciliation. In modern use, however, it more often signifies restitution made to an injured party by the offender. When used of the work of Christ, it is commonly limited to his suffering on the cross, conceived as a sacrifice or punishment that blots out an affront to God.

This premise is characteristic of western thought, in which the load borne on the cross is held to consist of sins (*peccata*)—that is, of injuries to God that cannot be palliated as errors, infirmities, trespasses or shortcomings and that are therefore properly objects not of pity but of wrath. In the teaching of Anselm, God is the lord whose honor has been diminished by the rebellion of his creatures; to waive the satisfaction that the enormity of the crime demands would be to mar the order of the universe, yet the very imperfection of the transgressor makes him incapable of settling the account from his own resources.[50] No adequate recompense can be offered except in Christ, whose sinlessness as man is guaranteed by his indefeasible perfection as God the Word. In Protestant theology, the court supersedes the manor: God is now the judge who cannot overlook a wrong, and if he is to spare his guilty subjects, he must therefore inflict their punishment on an innocent volunteer.

To many western minds both theories are now unpalatable—the first because we think it a sign of greater magnanimity to overlook an insult than to requite it, the second because the same arguments that require us to inflict public retribution on the criminal also require that it be the criminal, and no one else, who suffers. If murder were still, as in Anselm's time, a civil tort redeemable by a payment to the family of the victim, it might be possible to argue that so long as the debt is paid, it does not matter who bears the cost. This avenue, however, is barred to modern theologians, who are consequently more disposed to deny both debt and penalty and to urge that the value of Christ's death lies not so much in any good that it achieves on our behalf as in the example of selfless love that it holds up for our imitation.[51] To know (it is said) that the body bruised by pain, injustice and want is always the body of God is to know that none of us suffers alone and none is exempt from suffering. This is at once a remedy for despair and an inducement to work together in relieving the world of its ills. If, however, the cross continues to be regarded as a means to the abolition of sin, it may be said to effect this not so much by making the sinner more acceptable to God as by making sin more painful and therefore less endurable to the sinner. Or if it is felt after all that sin must be not only abandoned but also forgiven, one may contend that it is God who annuls his own case against the sinner by vacating the bench and standing in the dock.

The modern gospel of suffering would have seemed morbid to the Fathers, since the terms that we render by "suffering" in English often served in Greek and Latin merely as antonyms to

---

[50]Anselm's *Cur Deus Homo* ("Why God Became Man") is briefly reviewed by Hastings Rashdall, RIA 350-57.
[51]RIA 357-62, sympathetically ascribes this view to Abelard.

words connoting action. It was not the physical tribulation of Jesus but his voluntary surrender to the forces of sin that constituted his "passion." At the same time, because the vulnerability of Christ's flesh did not result in any personal consent to sin, they held that the creaturely virtues of humility, temperance, fortitude and charity were perfected through this abnegation of power by the Creator. The apparent defeat of Christ was, in short, a victory—and a victory not merely over temptation but also over the tempter, to whom the ancient church conceded a just, though provisional, claim on all who refused obedience to God. Anselm's feudal reasoning, that a vassal can have no right to the property of his master, was refuted by experience in a world still thick with the images and shrines of pagan deities, whose thralls waged war on the Christian elect. Thus it should not surprise us that in patristic thought the discomfiture, reimbursement or deception of this dark suzerain is frequently regarded as the chief object of Christ's ministry and that the cross itself, if it has a special function in their theology, is less frequently imagined as an altar or a scaffold than as a ransom or a bait.

His Suffering for Us

Thus we read in Ignatius, "bishop of Syria" in the early second century, that the three divine stratagems hidden from the devil though the ages were the virginity of Mary, the birth of her child and his death on the cross.[52] In his birth he was the "word who proceeds from silence,"[53] in his death "true God,"[54] whose sinless blood continues to purge the waters of the font as they symbolically immerse the new believer.[55] The "sufferings that he underwent for our sake"[56] bore fruit on the cross and are imparted to the church through the bread and wine that the communicant receives as flesh and spirit, faith and love. This rite, performed in the presence of the bishop, draws the faithful together into the "place of sacrifice"—not a sacrifice that falls on a single victim and spares the onlookers but one that unites their mortal flesh with his, so that as they die, so they may rise again in Christ.[57]

Of the unrepeatable oblation of Christ himself we hear more in the letter ascribed to Barnabas, an older contemporary of Ignatius, in which it is said to have been foreshadowed in the mysterious expiation that the Israelites were required to perform through the sacrifice of the red heifer. The object of the rite, as in Ignatius, is that the blood of the beast may sanctify the worshiper, though of course it is only in Christ, not in the prototype, that the cleansing takes effect.[58] In other early texts we read that Christ took on our sufferings in order to relieve them and that his condemnation enabled us to repent and him to forgive. As in Paul's epistle to the

[52]*Epistle to the Ephesians* 19.
[53]*Epistle to the Magnesians* 8.2.
[54]*Epistle to the Ephesians* 7.
[55]*Epistle to the Ephesians* 18.2.
[56]*Epistle to the Smyrneans* 2.1.
[57]See *Epistle to the Trallians* 6; *Epistle to the Smyrneans* 8; *Epistle to the Philadelphians* 4.
[58]*Epistle of Barnabas* 5.1.

Philippians, salvation is accomplished through a career of meekness and humility,[59] and it is those who taste the afflictions of his life who imbibe the blessings of his death.

The devil is here excluded from the bargain in these accounts, and he is no more in evidence when Irenaeus—another bishop, writing about 180 A.D.—describes the offering as humanity's propitiation of God through a mediator.[60] This passage shows that Irenaeus cannot be invoked as an orthodox patron for theodicies that discard any notion of sacrifice or punishment and maintain that sin, being nothing more than ignorance or "epistemic distance," can excite the pity of God but not his wrath.[61] This was the position of the Marcionites, who opposed the law of retribution to the gospel of mercy and were in turn opposed by Irenaeus. It is true, however, that in his *Refutation of All Heresies* Irenaeus grounds his hope not on the death of Christ alone but on his obedience throughout life, which annuls the consequences of Adam's disobedience in Eden. This is not a merely forensic remedy, for his ministry recapitulates every phase of human life, displaying in fullness the image and likeness of divinity that are more feebly adumbrated in his creatures.[62] This he can accomplish because, as the Word of God, he created all humanity in its triple bond of body, flesh and spirit; and it is through his flesh and blood as these are made present in the Eucharist, that the risen Savior kneads humanity once again into a single body. The transgression of Adam, fatal though it was, was all the more readily healed because he had not received the perfect likeness of God and had therefore not been robbed of it; the heaviest punishment falls on his seducer, who, having ambushed the creature in infancy, is defeated in open conflict by the Creator. Gustaf Aulén, the Lutheran theologian, is therefore right to argue that in Irenaeus salvation is above all else a victory over Satan.[63] He is wrong, however, to seek the biblical origins of this theory in Colossians 2:14, where Christ is said to have made an open show of powers and principalities on the cross. That verse is never quoted by Irenaeus, and his own statements make it clear that the seat of battle is not Calvary but the wilderness, where Christ repels three overtures in succession with quotations from the Law.[64]

Bought with a Price

The true Irenaean theodicy, then, is not that of Hick or Aulén but of *Paradise Regained*. For a specimen of Christian thought in his own time that subordinates the ministry to the cross in the manner of Anselm and the Protestant Reformers, we must turn from Irenaeus to his bugbear Valentinus and his disciples. Valentinian theology, like that of Irenaeus, is a blend of John and Paul, but theirs remains tightly wound in allegory while he spins out a single thread.[65] His

---

[59]Phil 2:6-12.

[60]*Against Heresies* 5.17.1.

[61]The "Ireneaen theodicy" of John Hick (HTCP) is often mistaken for the teaching of the historical Irenaeus.

[62]*Against Heresies* 3.17.6; 3.30.

[63]ACV 33-51, esp. 48.

[64]*Against Heresies* 5.21.

[65]The following summary is based primarily on Irenaeus *Against Heresies* 1.1-2.

purpose was to instruct the unwary; theirs, it appears, was to intimate, with all the reserve and indirection proper to such high subjects, that the narrative that evolves for us in linear time is eternally prefigured in the mystery of the Godhead. For them, as for Ignatius, Christ is the Word who proceeds from silence; but the same revelation of the ineffable Father that was embodied in Jesus of Nazareth has been vouchsafed to all the ages or aeons in which the fullness or pleroma of the divine plan is accomplished. The personification of these aeons in myth betokens not so much plurality in God as the manifold working of his providence. In the last of the aeons, Sophia or Wisdom, we are shown the frailty, the overweening and the latent divinity of the human intellect. In her yearning to see what is hidden in the Father (or in some accounts, by striving to reproduce without a male consort), she infringes the bounds of nature and becomes subject to commotion and loss of form. Discord would have spread to the pleroma were it not for the institution of the cross as a limit or boundary. This new frontier is impassable to Sophia, just as the wisdom of the world is said to stumble at the cross (1 Cor 1:21-24).

Once we apply this gloss from Paul, the sequel in which Sophia is restored to form by Christ and the Holy Spirit, who have been produced by all the aeons in concert as the first fruits of the pleroma, hardly requires interpretation. Sophia's repentance is, however, preceded by the emission of a child, deformed as the product of feminine recklessness must always be, who proceeds to create his own world in imitation of the pleroma that he knows only at two removes. Sophia, represented now as bride and now as harlot, represents Israel in this parable, while the Demiurge, her abortive son, is the spirit of idolatry. The seven planetary archons are his first creation, then his coadjutors in the fashioning of a material universe from the tears of the contrite Sophia. These tears guarantee the presence of divinity in the world but are the sport of fate and ignorance until Sophia, assuming the masculine role in contradistinction to her effete and sterile progeny, implants a seed in the Demiurge that comes forth as Christ the Savior. His revelation of the true God incenses the human satellites of the Demiurge, who nail him to the cross, where he becomes once again the first fruits of the pleroma, this time for his elect on earth. Whether he is to be conceived as the bearer of a psychic or a pneumatic body, he quits this world for the aeon, or eternity, with all who embrace his teaching; nevertheless, this freedom from delusion and misery does not wholly release them from the material envelope that clothes them in the present world. While the Valentinian shunned the cosmos and belittled its creator, it was he, not the catholic follower of Paul, who regarded matter as a secretion of the Godhead, and it was he who, ignoring the caveats of the apostle,[66] promised a share in the life to come not to the body but to the flesh. I lay some weight on these points since it is commonly held that the sects whom we call Gnostic served as catalysts but never as contributors to the evolution of catholic formularies. This may be true of the Marcionites, who are said to have posited only a phantasmal incarnation and to have styled the resurrected Christ a spirit. Again there were teachers in the second century who conceived of the "inner man" as a luminous

---

[66]See especially 1 Cor 15:50: "flesh and blood cannot inherit the kingdom of God."

simulacrum of the heavenly Adam, while assigning the creation of his body to the archons.[67] Speculation of this kind barely admits of a Christology; but if it is Gnostic teaching, as our ancient witnesses tell us, it should be clear that Valentinus was no Gnostic. His scheme includes a fall and a restoration, a Johannine caesura between the world and God, a Pauline Christ who bridges it by his ministry on the cross. These elements of the catholic faith are more distinctly present in his thought than in that of Irenaeus. As Irenaeus insists, however, so long as he distinguishes the true Father from the Demiurge, he cannot grant what the New Testament plainly teaches—that the work of Christ is the consummation of promises given to Abraham by his maker and confided first to Israel then to the world in the law of Moses. Nor, when he read Paul's admonition, "You were bought with a price,"[68] could he say to whom the price was paid; the Father, not being the author of creation or the Law, could have had no claim, while it is hard to imagine a compact between the Demiurge and a Savior who had stolen into the world without his knowledge or consent.

To whom then is the price paid? The first answer was, to the devil, though it is not clear who first gave it. Hastings Rashdall cites a passage from Irenaeus that argues that it did not become the Word to employ coercion, even in undoing the coercion that had been practiced by "apostasy" on his own creatures.[69] Some peaceable transaction between apostasy and Christ is thus implied here. There follows an allusion to the redemption (*apolytrōsis*) of the creature by the blood of Christ, and since both terms mean literally a "buying back," the passage appears to Rashdall to describe a ransom paid by Christ to the one whom Irenaeus elsewhere styles "the apostate." Yet this is to set one theory against another, for if Satan had been vanquished in the wilderness, he would have been in no position to exact his fee on Calvary. There is no clear proof that the price is paid to Satan or that "apostasy" signifies anything but the spirit of compliance, which detains the captive even after the storming of the jail.[70] Satan is bound, but apostate humanity is not saved against its will. The price, if it must be paid, is perhaps received by God the Father, who, as we noted, is said elsewhere to have been propitiated by the death of Christ. At the same time, we ought not to lean too heavily on the literal meaning of the word *apolytrōsis*, which often signifies nothing more than rescue or deliverance, just as its English counterpart "redemption" seldom carries any notion of repayment except where something has been pawned.

Origen, by contrast, was not one to let a metaphor sleep in Scripture. If we are "bought with a price," he urged in his commentary on Romans, there must be one who pays and one who is paid; if one is God, the other must be the devil.[71] While he believed, with Irenaeus, that the first humans were endowed with the image of God but only a foretaste of the likeness, he took this

---

[67]See especially the *Apocryphon of John*.

[68]1 Cor 6:20.

[69]RIA 279, citing *Against Heresies* 5.2.1.

[70]For this interpretation, see TAW 156-57.

[71]*Commentary on Romans* (on Rom 2:13).

to mean that Adam and Eve had virtue enough to fall and reason enough to choose their own master. Hence it was by voluntary exchange, not lawless seizure, that the image of the devil was superimposed on that of God. In a closer approximation to Jewish teaching on the exodus,[72] Origen speaks of a release from servile bondage: in committing homicide, adultery or fraud we receive the coin of Satan, stamped, like that of Caesar, with his image and superscription. The currency that procures a change of master in both these parables is the blood of Christ, more precious than all that had hitherto been shed under the priestly dispensation. His sacrifice supersedes not only the offerings of the temple but also the rite of circumcision, customarily administered to Jewish males on the eight day of life. For those who are in Christ, the eighth is the day of resurrection and a new sabbath that rescinds the provisions of the Mosaic law.

Origen is aware, however, that lesser powers than Satan are said to have been deceived by Christ's dissimulation of his glory and to have forwarded his purposes unwittingly by bringing about his death. These rulers of the lower world did not perceive that the one whom they consigned to death had been consigned to them by God the Father for that very purpose;[73] hence it was that death, his would-be slayer, was overcome and the devil crucified in his turn. At the same time, the event may be understood as a propitiation of God the Father, the human soul of Christ performing the mediatorial function of the mercy seat in the temple.[74] The temple of Christ, however, is his body, of which Jew and Greek alike are called to be members; anyone may say of him what the speakers in Isaiah 53 say of the servant, that he bore our sins and iniquities in his own person. Christ, as the image of the invisible God, is therefore capable of amending Satan's work in every soul that has been created in that image. No soul was created otherwise, for the Father of the world was also the Father of Christ. The heretics are therefore wrong to suppose that a rational being can be robbed of the image except by its own free choice. Those who have been "conformed to his death" will share his triumph, receiving both forgiveness of sin and the promise of a sinless immortality.

The Melding of Reconciliation Metaphors

The cross now marks the crisis of a drama with many players. While it binds the devil, it does not make the guilty innocent, and it does not extinguish suffering. It cannot restore the image of God to a captive who is not conformed to the death of his liberator. Origen adds, in a newly discovered dialogue, that the Savior on the cross resigned his spirit to the Father, his soul to hades and his body to the tomb. Thus his Godhead shed the veil of flesh under which it had carried on its counterplot to the intrigues of the demons. Ignatius and the Gnostics had already explained the secrecy of this errand as a necessary ruse against the devil, while concealment is the goal of the incarnation once again in the orthodox, though not quite catholic, Hippolytus of Rome. This castigator of heresies holds that the object of the Word in assuming a body was to bathe

---

[72]See, e.g., *Homilies on Exodus* 6:9.
[73]*Commentary on Matthew* 12:28; cf. 1 Cor 2:8.
[74]*Commentary on John* 1:33; cf. Rom 3:24-25.

our mortal bodies in incorruption. Baptism is the means by which the elect receive the ablution, but we do not hear, as in Ignatius, that the water is hallowed by an aspersion of the blood of Christ. The divinity of the incarnate word enables him to forgive all sins, but he does not seem to require the cross as an instrument of pardon or redress. Even when we encounter an allusion to the ransoming of humanity by Christ's suffering, we hear of no peculiar efficacy in the sufferings of the cross, and the word *ransom* may be used without strict attention to its etymology.

Metaphors of sacrifice, punishment and restitution were therefore not so common as those that pictured birth and death as stratagems in a war against the enemies of God and his elect. At the beginning of the fourth century, Christendom found an earthly head in Constantine, who adopted the cross as his ensign after a vision.[75] The victories that established him as sole ruler of the empire put an end to the persecution and legal violence that had been the church's only relics of the crucifixion. This is the era in which the cross begins to figure in Christian iconography, and by the mid-fourth century an artifact purporting to be the holy rood was being displayed with great magnificence in Jerusalem. According to some conjectures, the empress Helena's "invention of the true cross" will have preceded the composition of Athanasius's famous treatise, *The Incarnation of the Word*, in which the cross, still represented more as a trophy than as an altar, bears paradoxical witness both to the manhood of the Savior and to the indestructible majesty of God.

It is because he is the image of God the Father—and hence consummately what humans are imperfectly—that Christ in Athanasius's scheme is the author of life to all whom Adam's fall involved in death. Through Adam's disobedience, which is both the cause and the archetype of all sin, the whole race had forfeited its immediate communion with God and was mired in error and corruption. Mortality was the inescapable price of sin, according to God's decree, which he himself could not revoke. If, then, he was to enjoy the eternal fellowship of his rational creation, he must either create anew or restore humanity from within. To accomplish the second object, a human being must live a sinless life not only on his own behalf but also on that of the whole posterity of Adam. Only the divine Word, the second person of the Trinity, who had created Adam in the image of God, could lead a life as man that was worthy of immortality and at the same time impart that life to all who were willing to hear his teaching and follow his example. If Christ is all of us, all of us who embrace him as a model are living his life rather than ours. It was nevertheless this very impeccability, this natural imperviousness to death, that led to the cross. No natural death can befall the Word of God, and he must therefore die by violence; at the same time the event must be a spectacle, to remove all doubt of his having truly died. His elevation on Calvary enables him to join battle with the demons who inhabit the air, while the spreading of his arms invites the world to share the fruits of his compassion. At the same time, the death of Christ is characterized, with a clarity not anticipated in any previous writer, as the repayment of a debt to an injured master, the propitiation of a wrathful deity by the sacrifice of an unpol-

---

[75]See further EPP.

luted victim. The reparation might be described as a substitution of Christ for his saints, were it not that he embraces in death all those whom he ennobles by his life. It is those who die with him who will partake of his resurrection; faith without works or sacramental fellowship is as incomplete as the cross would be if there were no rising from the tomb.

In a work that was almost certainly composed before this great essay by Athanasius, Eusebius of Caesarea had declared that Christ incurred the retribution for sins that were not his own, in accordance with Isaiah's prophecy of the suffering servant.[76] The event is conceived as a sacrifice that perfects and thus abolishes the piacular sacrifices of the old Law. At the same time, the cross is still God's engine against the tyranny and guile of his adversary, and "trophy" is the word used by Eusebius when, in his *Life of Constantine*, he reports the excavation of a relic that is sometimes thought to have been the same one that was subsequently exhibited in Jerusalem as the instrument of Christ's passion.[77] The theology with which Cyril of Jerusalem clothes this symbol in his homilies is rather lean, and neither sacrifice nor ransom seems to be an important feature of it. The latter notion is strongly repudiated by the author whom we know as Adamantius, while Gregory of Nazianzus doubts in one of his poems whether God has the right or the devil the will to exact the blood of Christ in payment for our sins.[78] Gregory of Nyssa's great *Catechetical Homily* couples the ransom theory with the old motif of deception: the devil voluntarily accepts the blood of Christ in compensation for the release of his captives, failing to see the God within the veil of flesh and therefore wrongly supposing that he will keep his prize forever. In another passage, Gregory imagines the cross as a baited hook; the metaphor is taken up by others, who, completing the analogy with Leviathan in the book of Job, surmise that the devil himself remains suspended on the barb.[79] Greek authors after this period add little but plethoric eloquence to aging metaphors; none of them embraces a theory of merely vicarious punishment or suffering, and none ascribes an efficacy to the death of Christ apart from his resurrection. As Gregory of Nyssa states most clearly, it is by his incorporation of all humanity into his flesh that he imparts the fruit and the fellowship of his sufferings to the saints. It is by his resurrection, and by our resurrection in him, that he consummates his victory over sin.

Latin was the language of legislation throughout the empire, and Latin theories of the atonement are characteristically forensic. The author whom we call Ambrosiaster declares that the devil forfeited both his liberty and his claim on Adam's seed when he unjustly made a sinless man his prisoner.[80] Augustine holds that sin has made us the property of the devil, but only because the God who is both the devil's master and ours approved the transfer. Humans are thus

---

[76]See *Proof of the Gospel* 10.1.19-24; 10.1.39-40. These passages, however, do not seem so innovative to me as they do to Rashdall, RIA 299-301.

[77]Eusebius *Life of Constantine* 3.30; ELC 283.

[78]Gregory of Nazianzus *Dogmatic Poems* 1.8.65-69.

[79]For these passages, see *Catechetical Homily* 22-24; for Leviathan, see Job 41:1.

[80]Ambrosiaster *Commentary on Colossians* 2:15. Rashdall, RIA 329, observes in citing this passage what he fails to observe in citing Irenaeus—that "the actual victory lies here in the temptation, and is quite independent of the cross."

simultaneously in the hand of Satan and under the wrath of God.[81] The oblation on the cross may be regarded now as a ransom paid to one and now as a debt enforced or a penalty inflicted by the other.[82] It is here that we see the origins of the Reformed view, for Augustine not only speaks of the execution as a punishment[83] but also omits to add that the suffering falls on us by incorporation or that the resurrection turns the expense to profit. Not all the Reformers, however, shared the indispensable premises of Augustine's theory, that everyone leaves the womb in a state of guilt arising not from his own malfeasance but from Adam's disobedience. It is this guilt, transmitted by another, that can be abolished only by another: what Christ blots out on Calvary is remitted for each believer at the font. Our own sins—products of that fleshly weakness that is also our common patrimony in Adam—must be effaced by penance, both before we profess our faith in baptism and whenever we fall again. A voluntary sin not expiated by the sinner would have been as incomprehensible to Augustine as a faith that merely saved but did no works. It is thus not strictly true that he presents the death of Christ as a vicarious reparation for all sin.[84]

It ought by now to be clear that the Fathers lived on the abundance of the Scriptures, and that, having such wealth at hand, the typical thinker of this period made few drafts on secular thought and fewer still on his own conceit. Christian theologians of our time who aspire to be evangelical or catholic can read almost any writer of the patristic age with profit, even those who failed to satisfy the exacting canons of the first five councils.[85] As the Fathers assumed the unity of the New Testament, so the Reformers and their medieval predecessors posited a consensus among the Fathers; all, in my view, were nearer to the truth than those who now speak of "competing Christianities" in antiquity. It seems to me that Christian thought was more diverse in dress than in substance even in the first and second centuries, while the conflicts of the fourth were all the fiercer because the combatants were aware that they were striving for possession of the same ground. My aim in this anthology has been to illustrate not only the trends that were then, as now, called catholic, but also the tenets of sectarians and experimental thinkers. If the catholic element preponderates, I submit that the reason is that it was catholic in fact as well as in name.

---

[81]*On the Trinity* 13.12.

[82]*On the Trinity* 13.15.

[83]See especially *Against Two Letters of the Pelagians* 4.4.

[84]See MID 28ff.

[85]Nicaea (325), Constantinople (381), Ephesus (431), Chalcedon (451) and Constantinople (553). These are the councils that have been regarded as normative in Anglican thought, and the last date may be said to coincide roughly with the extinction of Roman hegemony in the west and of paganism in the east. The majority of the excerpts in this volume are drawn from authors who wrote before 553, but some later materials are introduced where it seemed that the authors dealt more subtly with a topic that had been cursorily handled in earlier texts. The translations are the author's, unless otherwise noted.

WE BELIEVE IN THE CRUCIFIED AND RISEN LORD

FOR OUR SAKE

σταυρωθέντα **τε ὑπὲρ ἡμῶν**	crucifixus **etiam pro nobis**	*For our sake he was crucified*
ἐπὶ Ποντίου Πιλάτου,	sub Pontio Pilato,	*under Pontius Pilate;*
καὶ παθόντα καὶ ταφέντα,	passus et sepultus est;	*he suffered death and was buried.*
καὶ ἀναστάντα τῇ τρίτῃ ἡμέρᾳ	et resurrexit tertia die,	*On the third day he rose again*
κατὰ τὰς γραφάς,	secundum Scripturas;	*in accordance with the Scriptures;*
καὶ ἀνελθόντα εἰς τοὺς οὐρανούς,	et ascendit in coelum,	*he ascended into heaven*
καὶ καθεζόμενον	. sedet	*and is seated*
ἐκ δεξιῶν τοῦ πατρός,	ad dexteram Patris;	*at the right hand of the Father.*
καὶ πάλιν ἐρχόμενον μετὰ δόξης	et iterum venturus est, cum gloria,	*He will come again in glory*
κρῖναι ζῶντας καὶ νεκρούς·	judicare vivos et mortuos;	*to judge the living and the dead,*
οὗ τῆς βασιλείας οὐκ ἔσται τέλος.	cujus regni non erit finis.	*and his kingdom will have no end.*

HISTORICAL CONTEXT: The dispute that precipitated the Nicene Council of 325, where the original version of this creed was published, seemed at first to turn only on the question whether the Son was divine in the same sense as the Father and to have no consequences for Christian worship or the doctrine of salvation. It became apparent, however, that the person of Christ and his ministry could not be separated and that his power to save was intimately bound up with his divinity. The assertion that he was truly God proclaimed both his omnipotence and his sufficiency as Savior; at the same time, it intimated that the glory that he is capable of bestowing on the redeemed surpasses even that which human beings enjoyed in the state of innocence. While the creed as such does not make explicit reference to the earthly ministry of Jesus (his prophetic, teaching, healing work), the Scriptures do, and the Fathers reflected on it. Though it is not explicitly expressed in the Nicene Creed, the confession that Christ is tempted like we are yet is without sin is a crucial dimension of his true humanity, which the creed views as central to the affirmation of his incarnate lordship.

OVERVIEW: The incarnation was ordained from the beginning (IRENAEUS) and foreshadowed in Eden (CLEMENT OF ALEXANDRIA) and in Israelite history (HIPPOLYTUS). Nevertheless, it was hidden from Satan (IGNATIUS), being a remedy for the fall (LEO). This remedy could be effected only by a sacrifice (GREGORY OF NAZIANZUS), which redeems both body and soul (AUGUSTINE), because it involved both the body and the soul of the Word incarnate (THEODORE).

Prophecy is the surest test of Christ's divine commission (JUSTIN). MORE than one tribe bears witness to him (IRENAEUS), but in his ministry the substance ousts the shadow (BARNABAS). Our generation knows that another saw darkly (AMBROSE), and the prophets have seen their own words made good in Christ (ROMANUS). Christ was preceded by Elijah (JUSTIN), his death was foretold in Scripture (BARNABAS), and the lives of the apostles vindicate their testimony (ORIGEN). He increased in wisdom and stature, but only as man (ATHANASIUS). Even the growth of his human intellect was accelerated (AMBROSE), and the wise could perceive his Godhead even in infancy (METHODIUS). As the baptism was foreshadowed in prophecy (ARATOR, GREGORY THE GREAT), so the Baptist proclaimed the one who would make straight the way of the Lord (ORIGEN) and recognized him at the Jordan (CYRIL OF ALEXANDRIA).

Baptism delivered Christ from the law (THEODORE), though he was free of actual sin (ATHANASIUS) and any inherited stain (CYRIL OF ALEXANDRIA). Sinners have all the more reason to be baptized (AUGUSTINE). Christ baptizes not with water (ORIGEN), but with the Spirit (AUGUSTINE). The dove reveals the character of the Spirit (AUGUSTINE), while baptism prefigures death, for Christ as for his saints (TERTULLIAN).

Christ's temptation is prefigured in the affliction of the three children (EPHREM OF ANTIOCH, LEONTIUS) and effects the defeat of Satan (Irenaeus). The beasts and angels testify to his divinity (JEROME); so does his suffering (ATHANASIUS) and so, all the more, does his victory (CASSIAN). The divine nature nevertheless remains imperturbable (CYRIL OF ALEXANDRIA); he suffers in his human soul (AUGUSTINE), having assumed flesh like our own (TERTULLIAN). Hence too his temptations can be ours (MAXIMUS THE CONFESSOR, EVAGRIUS), and we can learn to imitate his fortitude (LACTANTIUS). The instrument of victory is love (MAXIMUS THE CONFESSOR). His death was voluntary (FAUSTINUS), his subordination being a means of revelation on

earth (ORIGEN) and no argument against his true divinity (ATHANASIUS).

Peter's confession at Matthew 16:16 is an antidote to error in his time, a pattern of faith in ours (ORIGEN). Our faith is grounded on the collective insight of the disciples (CYPRIAN), and Christ's rebuke to Peter shows that any individual's faith may err (JEROME). The transfiguration may be regarded as a symbolic epitome of Christ's saving mission (HILARY). It revealed to his disciples both his divinity (LEO) and the Holy Spirit (JEROME). A similar epiphany is vouchsafed to all who can rise above the carnal perception of Christ (ORIGEN).

The Redemptive Purpose of the Incarnation

GOD'S PLAN ALWAYS INCLUDED AN INCARNATION. IRENAEUS: There is one God and Father, whose voice is present to his creature from the beginning to the end, and our creaturely nature is manifestly revealed in the Gospel, so that there is no need now to seek any Father other than this one, or suppose that we have any creaturely nature apart from the one foretold and revealed by the Lord or that there is any other hand of God but the one that from the beginning to the end is fashioning us and making us fit for life, being present to his creature and perfecting it according to the image and likeness of God. But the time when this Word was made evident was the time when the Word of God was made man, making himself like human beings and human beings like himself, so that through the likeness which is that of the Son the human being may become precious to the Father. For in former times, it was indeed said that humans were in the image and likeness of God, but it had not yet been made evident. For up to this point the Word in whose likeness humans had been made was invisible, and for this reason humans also easily lost the likeness. When, however, the Word of God was made flesh, he confirmed both matters: he made evident the true image, becoming that which was his image, and he strengthened and restored the likeness, making humans like the invisible Father through the visible Word. AGAINST HERESIES 5.16.1-2.[1]

THE CROSS FORESHADOWED IN EDEN. CLEMENT OF ALEXANDRIA: Moses, as an allegory of divine wisdom, spoke of a tree of life planted in paradise, and paradise can be understood as the cosmos, in which all the products of his workmanship have their place. In this the Word too bloomed and bore fruit, having become flesh, and those who tasted of his goodness[2] he made alive, since he too has not become known to us without the wood.[3] In short, our life was hanged that we might have faith. STROMATEIS 5.11.72.[4]

THE INCARNATION FORETOLD IN THE BLESSING ON ISRAEL. HIPPOLYTUS: Jacob's stealthy appropriation of his father's blessing indicates that the Word of God was going to take flesh and assume the form of a slave, so that, having dissembled his identity through this, he might receive the blessing from the Father, imparting it also to us who believe in him. ON JACOB'S BLESSING 8.[5]

THE PLAN MATURED IN SECRET. IGNATIUS OF ANTIOCH: And the ruler of this world knew nothing[6] of the virginity of Mary, her childbearing or likewise of the death of the Lord— three mysteries crying aloud, though they were performed in the silence of God. TO THE EPHESIANS 19.[7]

THE INCARNATION WAS A REMEDY FOR THE FALL. LEO THE GREAT: The devil was exulting because humanity, deceived by his imposture, was in want of the divine bounty, and having been stripped of the gift of immortality, had submitted to the harsh sentence of death. Thus, by acquiring a partner in transgression, he had found a certain solace for his own evils,

and he believed that God too had been constrained by the principle of justice to change his resolve with regard to human beings, whom he had created in such honor. Hence it was necessary to adopt the economy of a secret plan, so that the unchangeable God, whose will cannot be estranged from his benevolence, might accomplish the original design of his paternal affection for us by a more secret act of grace; and that humanity, having been thrust into wrongdoing by the wiles of the devil, should not perish in defiance of God's intention. LETTER 128 (TO FLAVIAN) 3.[8]

THE NECESSITY OF SACRIFICE. GREGORY OF NAZIANZUS: When the Hebrews came to hold their law in dishonor, the whole human race at last gained its share in this great honor by the will of the eternal Father and the deeds of the Son. Christ, seeing that whatever heavenly portion he had deposited in the human body was being devoured by the evil that consumes the soul and seeing the crooked dragon rule over human beings, in order to raise up his own possession, no longer left the care of human disease to other physicians. . . .

But when he had been heralded by the brightly shining lamp of great light,[9] the lamp that preceded him at his birth and preceded him in his teaching, proclaiming Christ my God in the midst of the wilderness, then was he revealed and went as an intermediary to those people who were afar and those who were near, being a cornerstone joining both. He bestowed on mortals the twofold cleansing of the everlasting Spirit who purged the former evil born of flesh and made pure my human blood. For mine is the blood Christ my

---

[1]SC 153:214-16. [2]A pun on the words *christos* ("anointed") and *chrēstos* ("good"). The two words were pronounced identically at this period. [3]That is, of the cross, which now seems to be regarded as the tree of knowledge as well as the tree of life. [4]GCS 15:374-75. [5]PO 27:36. [6]See 1 Cor 2:7-8; 2 Cor 4:4. [7]AF 148. [8]DFS 209. [9]John the Baptist, but the subject of the omitted passage is the star of Bethlehem, which Gregory appears to regard as a correlated symbol.

Lord poured out, a ransom for primal ills, a recompense for the world. If I had not been a mutable, mortal man but of inflexible purpose, all I should have needed was the command of the great God to be caring for me, saving me and exalting me to great honor. But as it is, God did not create me a god but formed me prone to incline either way, an unstable being, and for this reason he supports me by many means. PERSONAL POEMS 8.[10]

CHRIST REDEEMS BODY AND SOUL. AUGUSTINE: When he says, "Through a man came death and through a man came the resurrection of the dead,"[11] what can he be understood to mean but the death of the body? After all, when he said this he was speaking of the resurrection of the body and was urgently and eagerly advancing arguments for it. What then is he saying here to the Corinthians: Through a man came death, and through a man the resurrection of the dead. For as in Adam all die so in Christ shall all be made alive?[12] Surely it is what he also says to the Romans, "Through one man sin entered into the world and through sin death."[13] The Pelagians[14] wish this death to be understood as that of the soul, not of the body, as if his words to the Corinthians, "through a man came death," meant something else. This they are prevented from taking to mean the death of the soul, because his subject was the resurrection of the body, which is opposed to the death of the body. Thus it was that death alone, not sin also, is mentioned as having been brought about by a man, because his subject was not righteousness, the opposite of sin; the subject was only the resurrection of the body, which is opposed to the death of the body. ON THE MERITS AND FORGIVENESS OF SINS AND ON INFANT BAPTISM 1.8.8.[15]

THE WORD ASSUMED FULL HUMANITY. THEODORE OF MOPSUESTIA: Had the divinity taken the place of a soul,[16] he would have suffered neither hunger nor thirst. He would not have grown weary, nor would he have had any need of nourishment. All that is due to the frailty of the body and to the fact that the soul cannot attain to satisfaction except by the means that are proper to it, in accordance with the law of nature that God has imparted to it. But the soul requires that the body should have all that is necessary to its subsistence, for if it lacks anything, not only is the soul unable to help it in any matter, but also the soul itself is vanquished by the infirmity of the body and compelled to flee it. Thus if the divinity fulfilled the role of a soul, it would necessarily fulfill that of the body also. In that case one could admit the justice of the beliefs entertained by certain heretics who contend that he did not assume a body and was visible only in seeming, that he was only a man in seeming and did not possess human nature but shared the condition of the angels. The divinity would have sufficed to accomplish the whole and to cause those who beheld him to believe that it was a real man that they saw— as was the case, by God's will, with the angels who appeared to Abraham. Now if the divine nature sufficed for all that, it was not necessary to assume a human nature that stood in need of redemption. . . . But that was not the will of God, who resolved instead to re-clothe and re-elevate fallen humanity—consisting of a body and a soul, immortal and rational— in order that "just as through one man sin entered the world, and through sin death, so the grace and the gift of God are poured out abundantly through the righteousness of a single man, Jesus Christ."[17] . . . It was not then only a body but a rational and immortal soul

---

[10]*GNPA* 42-46. [11]1 Cor 15:21. [12]1 Cor 15:21-22. [13]Rom 5:12. [14]Celestius, the mouthpiece of the heresy generally named after Pelagius, had maintained that Adam was always bound to die and thus that his sin was not the cause of his own or our mortality. [15]*CSEL* 60:9-10. [16]The position ascribed to the Arians, and to the otherwise orthodox Apollinaris, was that the Word took the place of a rational soul in Christ. Theodore's argument is that such a truncated humanity might have sufficed for revelation but not for release from sin. [17]Rom 5:12, 15.

that he needed to assume, and it was not only the death of the body that he had to abolish but that of the soul, which is sin. . . . Had sin not been eliminated, we would have remained, to our own destruction, mortals and sinners, for we are subject to vicissitude. And had we begun to sin again, we should have been once again subjected to punishment, and thus the power of death would have survived for our destruction. CATECHETICAL HOMILY 5.9-10.[18]

The Prophecies of the Incarnation

PROPHECY FULFILLED IS THE TOKEN OF DIVINE ACTIVITY. JUSTIN MARTYR: Hear what was said beforehand to show that Christ after having been born would escape the notice of the rest of humankind until he reached manhood—which indeed came to pass. There is this: "A child has been born to us, and a boy has been given to us, whose kingdom is on his shoulders."[19] This signified the power of the cross, on which he set his shoulders when he was crucified—a point that will become clearer as my argument proceeds. And again the same prophet says, "I have stretched out my hands to a disobedient and contentious people, to those who walk in a path that is not good. They seek judgment from me and presume to come near God."[20] And again in other words through another prophet it says, "Of themselves they pierced my feet and hands, and they cast a lot for my garment."[21] And David the king, who said this, suffered none of these things. Jesus, however, stretched out his hands, having been crucified by the Jews who contended with him and denied that he was the Messiah. Yes, they did indeed, as the prophet says, mock him by making him sit on the judgment seat and saying "Judge us."[22] As for "they pierced my hands and feet," that prefigured the nails that were hammered into his hands and feet on the cross. And after crucifying him, those who had crucified him cast lots for his robe and divided it among them. FIRST APOLOGY 35.1-8.[23]

MORE THAN ONE TRIBE OF ISRAEL HAD A SHARE IN CHRIST. IRENAEUS: Through them Christ was prefigured and made known and brought to birth. For he was prefigured in Joseph, while he was born of Levi and Judah after the flesh as king and priest. It was through Simeon in the temple that he was made known and through Zebulun he was believed on among the nations (for as the prophet says, "the land of Zebulon"[24]). And it was through Benjamin, through Paul, that he was glorified by having been proclaimed to the entire world. FRAGMENT 17.[25]

PROMISES ENTRUSTED TO ISRAEL WERE FULFILLED IN CHRIST. EPISTLE OF BARNABAS: Let us see then if the Savior's appearance through water and the cross was anticipated. As regards the water, it is written of Israel how they were not going to accept the baptism that brings remission of sins but were going to fabricate their own. For the prophet says, "Heaven be amazed and for this let the earth be struck with great horror, because this people has done two things, and they are evil. They have left me, the spring of life, and dug for themselves a ditch of death."[26] "Is not my sacred mountain Zion now a barren rock? For you shall be as a bird's nestlings that fly away and leave the nest void."[27] And again the prophet says, "I shall go before you, and I shall level the mountains, and the gates of brass I shall break to pieces, the iron bolts I shall shatter, and I shall give to you darkling treasures, hidden, invisible, that

[18]*HCTM* 111-15. [19]Is 9:6 (LXX). [20]Is 65:2; 58:2. [21]Ps 22:17-19, with omissions. [22]Allusion to the apocryphal *Gospel of Peter*, often cited in modern scholarship as a parallel to Jn 19:13. [23]*JMAA* 50. It is not clear whether Justin thought that these texts had already been adduced by apostolic writers. [24]Is 9:1, cited at Mt 4:13. [25]*SIEL* 487. [26]Jer 2:12, but in the imperative mood where the Septuagint is indicative. The second sentence was commonly cited against the adversaries of the church catholic. [27]Is 16:1, not quite corresponding to the Septuagint, and treated here as part of the same quotation. Barnabas may be citing a book of testimonies rather than consulting the text directly.

you may know that I am the Lord God."[28] And "you shall dwell in the high cave of a strong rock." Then, "His water is sure; you shall see the king with glory,"[29] and "your soul will meditate on the fear of the Lord."[30] And again in another prophet it says, "The one who does this is as a tree planted by the brooks of the waters, which will give its fruit in his season and its leaf shall not fall away, and all that he does shall go aright. Not so are the ungodly, not so, but they are like the chaff that the wind snatches away from the face of the earth. For this reason the ungodly shall not stand up in the judgment or sinners in the parliament of the righteous; for the Lord knows the way of the righteous, and the way of the wicked shall perish."[31] See how he allots the same significance to the water and to the cross. For his meaning is this: blessed are those who, having put their hope in the cross,[32] go down to the water. The words "in his season" allude to the reward. Now the meaning of "his leaves shall not fall away" is that every word that comes forth from your mouths in faith and love will be for an exhortation and hope to many. And again another prophet says, "And the land of Jacob is praised throughout the earth."[33] This means that he glorifies the vessel of his spirit. Then what does it say? "And there was a river flowing from the right, and from it sprang trees in season; and he who eats from them shall live forever."[34] The meaning of this is that we go down to the water full of sin and filthiness and come up bearing fruits in our heart, our hope and fear being now toward Jesus in the spirit. And "he who eats of them shall live forever" means that whoever hears these things being said and believes them, he will live forever. EPISTLE OF BARNABAS 11.[35]

KNOWLEDGE HAS NOW SUPERVENED ON PROPHECY. AMBROSE: The Lord's generation received testimony not only from angels and prophets, from shepherds and parents, but also from the aged and the righteous. Every age and both sexes, as well as the miraculous occurrences, build up faith: a virgin bears him, a barren woman gives birth, a dumb man speaks, Elizabeth prophesies, the magi adore, the one enclosed in the womb leaps for joy, the widow confesses him and the righteous awaits him. And the righteous man did well, as he sought the favor not for himself but for the people, desiring for himself release from the toils of his frail body but waiting to see the fulfillment of the promise. For he knew that blessed were the eyes that saw.[36] "Now," he says, "discharge your servant." See that the righteous, as though locked in the prison of his gross body, wishes to be dissolved that he may be with Christ— "for to be dissolved and to be with Christ is far better."[37] But he who wishes to be discharged must come to the temple, come to Jerusalem, take in his hands the Word of God and as it were enfold him in the arms of his faith. Then he will be discharged, that, having seen life, he may not see death. You observe that grace was liberally diffused in the Lord's generation and that prophecy was denied to unbelievers but not to the righteous. Note also that Simeon prophesies that Christ has come for the ruin and for the resurrection of a great many, that he may judge the deserts of the righteous and the wicked, and, as a true and righteous judge, allocate either torments or prizes to us in keeping with the character of our deeds. EXPOSITIONS ON THE GOSPEL OF LUKE 2.58-60.[38]

THE PROPHETS BEHELD THE FULFILLMENT OF THEIR OWN WORDS. ROMANUS THE MELODIST: Lifting his voice Zephaniah called

---

[28]Roughly, Is 45:2. [29]Both quotations from Is 33:16-17. [30]Ps 1:3, loosely corresponding to the Septuagint. [31]Ps 1:4-6, almost identical with the Septuagint. Barnabas does not seem to know that he has quoted consecutive verses in his last two citations or that one matches the Septuagint more closely than the other. [32]Presumably the tree prefigures the cross as well as those whom it delivers. See below, "Jesus' Suffering Predicted," pp. 72-74. [33]This text has not been identified. [34]Perhaps a loose reminiscence of Ezek 47:1-12. [35]AF 302-6. [36]Lk 10:23. [37]Phil 1:23. [38]CSEL 32.4:73-74.

to Adam, "This is the one whom you awaited until the day of resurrection, just as I foretold to you." And after him Nahum brought good news to the impoverished: "He has risen up from the earth, the one who breathes into your countenance, delivered from tribulation." And Zechariah shouted for joy, "Our God has come with your saints." And David made a psalm of blessing: "The Lord in his power has woken and as it were has risen from sleep." CANTICLE 25 [42], STROPHE 10.[39]

ELIJAH PREPARED THE WAY. JUSTIN MARTYR: Trypho replied, "It seems to me that those who say that he came to be as a human and became the Christ when he was anointed by way of election spoke more plausibly than you when you make these assertions of yours. For all of us, indeed, expect the Christ to be a human of human stock and Elijah to come beforehand to anoint him. But if this man is the manifestation of the Christ, he must certainly be regarded as a human of human stock; but from the fact that Elijah has not come, I prove that he is not the Christ."

And I in turn asked him, "Does not the word say through Zechariah that Elijah will come before that great and terrible day of the Lord?"[40]

And he answered, "Absolutely."

"If then the teaching forces one to admit that two appearances of Christ were announced as future events—one in which he will be revealed in suffering, ignominy and deformity, the other in which he will come in glory and as the judge of all, as has been demonstrated at many points in our previous conversation—shall we not deduce that the Word of God proclaimed the future advent of Elijah on that great and terrible day, that is, at his second coming? DIALOGUE WITH TRYPHO 49.1-2.[41]

CHRIST'S DEATH FORETOLD OPENLY IN SCRIPTURE. EPISTLE OF BARNABAS: For

God's Word makes them responsible for the beating of his flesh: "When they trample their own shepherd, then shall the sheep of the flock perish."[42] And he wished to suffer this, as it was necessary for him to suffer on a tree. For the one who prophesies of him says, "Spare my life from the sword." And "Pierce my flesh, for the assemblies of the wicked have risen against me."[43] And again he says, "See, I have set my back for smiting and my cheeks for blows, but my face I have set as a hard rock."[44] EPISTLE OF BARNABAS 5.12-14.[45]

THE APOSTLES' LIVES CONFIRMED THEIR TEACHING. ORIGEN: What need is there to tell how many persons, royal or private, are recorded in the Scriptures to have fared well or ill in accordance with their attention to prophecies or neglect of them? And if it is necessary to speak of people who were grieving for their childlessness but then became fathers or mothers, raising prayers of thanks for this to the Creator of all, one may read the account of Abraham and Sarah, whose child, when they were already old, was Isaac, the father of the entire Jewish race and of others beside. One may read the account of Hezekiah, who not only enjoyed a remission of his illness, as Isaiah had prophesied, but was also bold enough to declare, "From this time on I shall sire children who will proclaim your righteousness."[46] And in the fourth book of Kings the widow who played host to Elisha when, by the grace of God he had prophesied about the birth of a child, became a mother through Elisha's prayers. And countless too were the hardened infirmities that were cured by Jesus. And there were others who, having ventured to insult the Jewish cult at the

---

[39]SC 128:468. [40]While Mk 9:11-13 hints that the Baptist was Elijah, Justin would appear to have been aware of the Baptist's own disclaimer (Jn 1:21). [41]JMAA 147. [42]Zech 13:7. [43]Mingling Ps 22:20 with Ps 22:17 and inserting Ps 119:120, which, however, reads "pierce me with the fear of God." [44]Loosely quoting Is 50:6. [45]AF 286. [46]Is 38:19.

temple in Jerusalem, suffered what is written in the books of Maccabees.

Yet the Greeks will say that these are fables, though two whole races bear witness to their truth. Why not say this rather of the Greek myths than of these? It might be that one who collated the texts, so that he might not seem to act partially by accepting his own while disbelieving those of strangers, would say that among the Greeks such events were the work of demons, while among the Jews they were done either by God through the prophets or by the angels or by God through the angels, while among the Christians they were done by Jesus or by his power in the apostles. Come, let us lay them all side by side, and consider what resulted from the purpose of those who wrought them and see what good or harm (if either at all) accrued to those who enjoyed these pretended blessings. Surely he will see that the Jews were initially a philosophical race before they behaved insolently toward the divine, by whom they were abandoned because of their many vices. It will seem to him that the primitive Christians formed a strange league, under the influence of portentous and hortatory discourses, to abandon their ancestral ways and adopt those that were alien to their ancestors. In fact, if we are to form a probable opinion about this primitive league of Christians, we shall say that it is not plausible that the apostles of Jesus, unlettered and private men, were emboldened to preach Christianity to the human race by anything but the power dispensed to them and by the grace in their words that produced the aforesaid effects. Nor was it probable that those who heard them should depart from the immemorial ways of their ancestors, unless they had been impelled by some worthy power and portentous deeds toward customs so foreign and alien to those in which they had been reared. AGAINST CELSUS 8.46-47.[47]

Jesus' Growing in Wisdom and Stature

AN INCREASE IN THE STATURE AND WISDOM OF CHRIST'S HUMANITY. ATHANASIUS: As regards human beings, since they are creatures they are able to progress and increase in virtue. . . . But as for him, he is alone in the Father alone and does not come from him by progression but abides in him forever.[48] Increase, then, is for human beings; the Son of God, for his part, while no increase was possible for him since he was perfect in the Father, humbled himself for our sakes, so that in that humbling of his we might be able to grow all the more. Now, that growth of ours is nothing else than detachment from the visible and union with the Word himself, since that humbling of his consisted in nothing else than the assumption of our flesh. Thus it was not the Word, insofar as he was the Word, who increased, the one who lacked nothing, being the perfect offspring of the perfect Father; it was the rest whom he led into increase. Moreover, the word *increase* is used here in human fashion, once again because increase pertains to human beings. Indeed, the Evangelist, speaking with vigilant precision, has subjoined the term "stature" to "increase." Now he who is the Word and also God is not measured by stature, but stature belongs to bodies. Hence the increase takes place in the body; for as that increased, the manifestation within it of his divinity increased for those who saw. And the more his divinity was unveiled, the more that grace—in appearance that of a human being—increased for all human beings. AGAINST THE ARIANS 3.52.[49]

HE SET AN EXAMPLE OF JUVENILE OBEDIENCE. GREGORY OF NYSSA: For since in other humans the intellect in the young is imperfect and youth needs to be guided toward the good

[47]SC 150:274-78. [48]The real or notional adversaries who are called Arians in this treatise hold that the Logos is not divine and is therefore subject to the same laws that govern development in humans. [49]PG 26:432-33.

by the more mature, for this reason he is subject to his mother at the age of twelve years.[50] This is his way of showing that what is being perfected in stages rightly accepts subjection as a means of guidance toward the good until it attains perfection. ON THE SUBJECTION OF THE SON.[51]

HIS HIDDEN POWER WAS ALWAYS AT WORK. EPHREM THE SYRIAN: While he was increasing in wisdom and stature among the poor, from an abundant treasury he was nourishing all! While she that anointed him was anointing him, with his dew and his rain he was anointing all! HYMNS ON THE NATIVITY 3.[52]

HIS GROWTH EXCEEDED THE UNDERSTANDING OF HIS CONTEMPORARIES. AMBROSE: It was in his twelfth year, as we read, that the Lord began to engage in disputation. For this was the number of evangelists required for the preaching of the faith. Nor is it said redundantly that, having forgotten his parents after the flesh—though after the flesh he was certainly being filled with the wisdom and grace of God—he was discovered on the third day: this is an indication that on the third day of that triumphant passion of his he would be resurrected and present himself to our faith in a heavenly seat and with divine honor, having been supposed to be dead. "Why did you seek me? Do you not know that I have to be in my Father's house?"

There are two births in Christ, one paternal and one maternal. The paternal is the divine one, the maternal the one that involved a descent into human works and ways. And thus those episodes that are too high for his nature, his age or his education should not be rated among his human virtues but should be ascribed to his divine powers. Elsewhere his mother urges him on to a mystery, but here he resists his mother because she is still demanding what is human. In this case he is said to

have been twelve years old; in the other we learn that he had his disciples. You see that the mother had learned from her son to demand a mystery of him when he was more mature, though she was astonished by a miracle when he was younger. EXPOSITIONS ON THE GOSPEL OF LUKE 2.63-64.[53]

SIMEON KNEW HIM EVEN AS A BABY. METHODIUS: Once indeed the aged Simeon met the Savior, and received in his arms as an infant the Creator of the world and proclaimed him to be Lord and God. But now, even in the place of foolish elders, children meet the Savior as Simeon did, and instead of their arms strew under him the branches of trees and bless the Lord God seated on a colt, as on the cherubim, "Hosanna to the son of David."[54] . . . David in prophecy hid the spirit in the letter; children, opening their treasures, brought forth riches on their tongues. ORATION ON THE PALMS 5.[55]

Jesus' Baptism

THE BAPTISM IS FORESHADOWED IN PROPHECY. ARATOR: Christ is at hand, the one who, as all the oracles of the prophets sing, was to come as God under flesh, creating himself as he entered into the virgin's womb. Unravel whatever is hidden in your sabbaths: the prototypical figure you see to be brilliantly confirmed in the fold of the holy lamb, from whose fire the ancient prophets imbibed their sayings. First he gave speech, then came the beginning of his generation. John the Baptist, potent in virtue, exclaimed, "It is not I; behind me comes one the shoes of whose feet I am not worthy to touch or to loose the top of the humble latching that binds his lofty steps."[56] How well the voice of Paul intoned the code of baptism, mingling the old with the new! His

---

[50]Lk 2:51. [51]GNO 3.2:8. [52]NPNF 2 13:233. [53]CSEL 32.4:75. [54]Mt 21:15. [55]ANF 6:396. [56]Conflating Jn 1:20 with Mt 3:11.

letter does not cease to repeat this, teaching that "through the law our ancestors were illumined by baptism in the Red Sea under the name of Moses, when at the same time a rock followed them, for the rock was Christ."[57] What more do you ask for, you hardened race? See, in your own books the words ring out: "Be not slow in faith." Consider the miracles of the Sea, with their intimation of mystical gifts to come at the time of the cross, when Jesus impregnated the waters with his blood and from one wound in his side[58] came a stream that would impart the three gifts of life. APOSTOLIC HISTORY 2.71-92.[59]

THE BAPTISMAL PROMISE. GREGORY THE GREAT: For certainly the passage of the Red Sea was a figure of holy baptism, in which the enemies behind died, but others were found in front in the wilderness. And so to all who are bathed in holy baptism all their past sins are remitted, since their sins die behind them even as did their Egyptian enemies. But in the wilderness we find other enemies, since, while we live in this life, before reaching the country of promise, many temptations harass us and hasten to bar our way as we are wending to the land of the living. LETTER 11.45.[60]

THE BAPTIST FORETOLD CHRIST'S RIGHTEOUSNESS. ORIGEN: The way of the Lord is made straight[61] by two methods, that of contemplation, which runs smoothly in truth unmixed with lies, and that of practice, when, after the healthy contemplation of what our conduct ought to be, produces actions in harmony with sound reasoning about what our conduct ought to be. And so that we may more accurately understand the phrase "Make straight the way of the Lord," it will be opportune to set beside it what is said in Proverbs, "Turn not to the right hand or the left."[62] For the one who deviates in either direction has lost the right way and ceases to be worthy of further tutelage when he oversteps the straight

line of the track. . . . Let us, however, stand in the ways according to what is said by Jeremiah,[63] and having seen them let us ask after the everlasting paths of the Lord and let us see what is the good way and let us travel in it, as the apostles[64] urged, asking the patriarchs and the prophets about the everlasting paths of the Lord. It was by investigating and later understanding the written accounts of them that they saw the good way, Jesus Christ, who said, "I am the way," and they traveled in it. For the good way is that which leads the good person to the good Father—the person who brings forth good things from the good treasury and who is a good and faithful servant.[65] This way is narrow, and the carnal multitude cannot follow it, yet this way is burdened by those who are battling to travel along it, since it is not said to be a burden but to be burdened. For the one who burdens the living way, which feels the peculiarities of the wayfarer, is the one who has not unlatched his shoes from his feet[66] and has not sincerely accepted that the place in which he stands or on which he treads is holy ground. But it will lead him to life, to the one who said, "I am the life."[67] For the Savior, as the goal of every virtue, has numerous titles. For this reason the way is for the one who has not yet arrived at the end but is still progressing, and life is for the one who has put away all deadness. COMMENTARY ON JOHN 6.19.[68]

THE BAPTIST RECOGNIZED JESUS. CYRIL OF ALEXANDRIA: The one who leaped in his own mother's womb when the holy virgin was still

---

[57]Cf. 1 Cor 10:1ff., but Paul is speaking of the wilderness, not of the crossing of the Red Sea, which Arator here takes as a type of baptism. [58]Cf. Jn 19:34-35 with 1 Jn 5:8 on the three witnesses (Spirit, water and blood). Ambrose *Expositions on the Gospel of Luke* 10.48 states that the water is for cleansing, the blood for ransom, the spirit for resurrection. [59]CSEL 72:81-82. [60]NPNF 2 13:66. [61]See Jn 1:23; Is 40:3. [62]Prov 4:27. [63]Jer 6:16. [64]Probably a reference to the *Didache*, or Teaching of the Twelve Apostles, an early compilation of moral and liturgical precepts that continued to be regarded as a work fit to be read in churches until the fourth century. [65]See Mt 12:35; 25:21. [66]Ex 3:5. [67]Jn 14:6. [68]SC 157:206-8.

carrying the Lord in hers, the prophet before the birthpangs, the disciple in embryo, says of the Savior, "I did not know him."[69] And he speaks truly, for he does not lie. For whereas God knows everything of himself without teaching, the creation knows by teaching. But the Holy Spirit, dwelling in the saints, fills up what is wanting and vouchsafes his proper benefit to human nature—by which I mean the knowledge of things to come and the understanding of the hidden mysteries. Thus when the blessed Baptist says that he did not know the Lord, he is not speaking falsely in any way, but according to what is proper to humankind and the fit measure for a creature. For God alone he reserves the knowledge of all things, the one who through the Holy Spirit lights the way of human beings to the apprehension of the things that are hidden. It is greatly to our advantage for him to declare that he did not know Christ of himself but came primarily for the purpose of making him manifest to Israel, so that he might not seem to have rushed into testimony of his own accord or be regarded by some as the lackey of his own wishes, but rather as an agent of the divine economy and a minister of that counsel from above that had revealed to him "the Lamb that takes away the sin of the world."[70] In order, however, that the Jews might come more readily to belief in Christ the Savior and might have a notion of him that matched his dignity, he says that he knew him unwittingly, so that they might henceforth be aware of God the revealer, and, having shaken off their heaven-sent slumber of guilt, might after all receive his Word, estimating the dignity of the mighty one in proportion to the greatness which they saw in his servant. For to say that he had come so that he might make him manifest to Israel—how could this fail to indicate the office that fits a servant? COMMENTARY ON JOHN 2, PROLOGUE.[71]

CHRIST'S BAPTISM PREFIGURED OUR OWN.
THEODORE OF MOPSUESTIA: He advanced

to his baptism, therefore, to prefigure our own, and by this means he freed himself from the obligations of the Law. He gave a practical demonstration of the gospel, chose his disciples, inaugurated the teaching of a new doctrine and revealed the way of life, different from that which the Law enjoins, which was consistent with his doctrine. He taught that we should conduct ourselves accordingly toward our fellow believers[72] because we also, once baptized, hold up before the gaze of others a prefiguration of the world to come. We die with him in baptism,[73] and our resurrection is prefigured by his. CATECHETICAL HOMILY 6.11-12.[74]

CHRIST'S BAPTISM IS A REVELATION OF HIS SINLESS GODHEAD.
ATHANASIUS: When the Lord, as man, was cleansed in the Jordan, we were the ones who were cleansed in him and by him. And when he received the Spirit, we were the ones who became recipients of it through him. Thus it is that he was anointed merely with oil, like Aaron or David or all the rest, but in a different manner from all those who partake of him, with the oil of gladness. And he interprets this as the Holy Spirit through the prophet, saying, "The Spirit of the Lord is on me, because he has anointed me,"[75] as also the apostle said, "as God has anointed him with the Holy Spirit."[76] When, then, was this said to have happened to him, if not when, having come to be in flesh, he was baptized in the Jordan and "the Holy Spirit descended on him"?[77] Now consider, the Lord says that the Spirit will receive from me[78] and "I send him"[79] and to his disciples, "Receive the Holy Spirit."[80] Nonetheless, the one who, when he imparts to others, is spoken of as the Word and effluence[81] of the Father is said to have been sanctified at this point, because,

[69]Jn 1:31. [70]Jn 1:29. [71]PG 73:193. [72]Gal 6:10. [73]Rom 6:3. [74]HCTM 153. [75]Is 61:1. [76]Acts 10:38. [77]Mt 3:17. [78]Jn 16:14. [79]Jn 16:7. [80]Jn 20:22. [81]Jn 1:1; Heb 1:3.

once again, he had become man, and that which was sanctified was his body. AGAINST THE ARIANS 1.47.[82]

CHRIST WAS NOT BAPTIZED TO EXPUNGE AN INHERITED SIN. CYRIL OF ALEXANDRIA: The first man, being of earth and from the earth, had the option of doing good or evil residing in his own power and was master of his own propensity to one or the other. Carried away by baneful fraud and inclining to disobedience, he fell back into his mother the earth from whom he derived his nature, and mastered now by corruption and death, bequeathed the penalty to his race. And as evil increased in us and multiplied, our intellect within us falling further into vice, sin has become our king, and human nature from then on has been clearly bereft of the indwelling Holy Spirit. For, as it is written, "The Holy Spirit of Wisdom shall flee all fraud and will not inhabit a body beholden to sin."[83] Since, however, the first Adam did not preserve the grace that had been vouchsafed to him by God, God the Father destined for us the second Adam from heaven. For he sends his own Son, who in his nature is changeless and unalterable and wholly unacquainted with sin, in our likeness, in order that, just as through the first disobedience we became liable to divine wrath, so through the second we might both escape the curse and do away with the ills that proceeded from it. And when the Word of God became man, he received the Holy Spirit from the Father, as one of us, not receiving something peculiarly for himself; for he was the giver of the Spirit. He received it so that, as a human being who knew no sin, he might preserve it in his nature and implant in us again the departed grace. It was, in my view, for this reason that the holy Baptist added profitably, "I have seen the Spirit descending from heaven, and it remained on him."[84] For the Spirit flew away from us on account of sin, but the one who knew no sin became as one of us, so that he might accustom

the Spirit to remain in us, finding no occasion in him to depart or abscond. For us, therefore, through himself he receives the Spirit and renews in our nature the ancient blessing. COMMENTARY ON JOHN 2.1.[85]

CHRIST'S BAPTISM IS A PATTERN FOR SINNERS. AUGUSTINE: The Word that was made flesh was in the beginning and was with God as God.[86] Nevertheless, that participation of his in our lower condition, in order that we might participate in his loftier condition, occupied a certain mean even in the birth of his flesh. Thus, we were born in the flesh of sin, he in the likeness of the flesh of sin. We were born not only of flesh and blood but also of the will of man and the will of the flesh; he only of flesh and blood and not of the will of man or of the will of the flesh[87] but of God. And thus we come to death on account of our sin; he comes to death on our account without sin. Again, just as that lower condition of his in which he descended to us was not in all respects on a level with that lower condition of ours in which he found us, so that loftier condition of ours in which we ascend to him will not be on a level with that loftier condition of his in which we shall find him. For we shall be made children of God by his grace, but he was always the Son of God by nature. We who are converted at some point will cling to God as inferiors. He, never having turned away, remains equal with God.[88] We shall be partakers of eternal life; he is eternal life. He alone, therefore, remaining God even when made man, never had any sin, nor did he assume the flesh of sin, although he was from the flesh of sin on his mother's side. For in such measure as he assumed flesh, he either cleansed it in order to assume it or cleansed it by assuming it. His virgin mother conceived, not by the law

---

[82]PG 26:108-9. [83]Wis 1:5. [84]Jn 1:32. [85]PG 73:205, 208. [86]Jn 1:1, 14. [87]Meddling with the letter, if not with the spirit, of Jn 1:13. [88]Phil 2:6.

of the flesh of sin—that is, not by the motion of fleshly concupiscence—but by holy faith, being worthy that the sacred seed should come to be in her; thus he created the one whom he elected, he elected the one from whom he was created.[89] How much the more then should the flesh of sin be baptized to escape judgment, if the flesh that was without sin was baptized as an example for imitation! ON THE MERITS AND FORGIVENESS OF SINS AND ON INFANT BAPTISM 2.24.38.[90]

CHRIST DID NOT BAPTIZE WITH WATER.
ORIGEN: And in truth it was also a clear proof that their spirit bore the likeness of the serpent when they asked him maliciously, "Why then do you baptize if you are not the Christ or Elijah or the prophet?"[91] Since they imply that Christ and Elijah and the prophet baptize, while the voice of one crying in the wilderness has not received this authority, I would say to them, "You fellows, you put a hard question to the messenger sent before the face of Christ to prepare his way, when you know nothing whatever of the mysteries that belong to his position. For Christ himself, who is Jesus even if you do not wish it, did not baptize, though his disciples did, and he himself was the prophet also. And whence comes this belief of yours that Elijah will baptize the one who is to come? He did not baptize even the wood for the sacrifice in Ahab's time when they needed to be doused so that they might burn when the Lord appeared in the fire. For he told the priests do this, and not once only; for he says, 'Do it twice,' and when they had done it twice, again 'Do it a third time'; and when they had done it a third time. As for the one who did not baptize himself but left it to others to do this work, how was it his mission to baptize when he took up residence here in accordance with the words spoken through Malachi? Thus it is not Christ who baptizes with water but his disciples, while for himself he reserves the baptism in the Holy Spirit and

fire." COMMENTARY ON JOHN 6.23.[92]

CHRIST BAPTIZES IN THE SPIRIT. AUGUSTINE: It is asked whether those who were baptized at the time when it is written that the Lord baptized more people than John through his disciples[93] received the Holy Spirit; for it is said in another passage of the evangelist, "For the Spirit had not yet been given, as Jesus had not yet been glorified."[94] And there is a very easy answer to this—that the Lord Jesus, who even raised the dead, had it in his power to prevent them all from dying, so long as after his glorification (that is, his resurrection from the dead and ascent into heaven), they received the Holy Spirit. However, there comes to mind that thief to whom it was said, "Truly I say to you, this day you will be with me in paradise,"[95] when he had not received any baptism—even though Cornelius and those Gentiles in his company who had believed received the Holy Spirit even before they were baptized.[96] Yet I do not see how, without the Holy Spirit, that thief for his part was able to say, "Lord, remember me when you come into your kingdom."[97] For "no one says 'Lord Jesus,'" according to the apostle, "except in the Holy Spirit."[98] The fruit of this faith the Lord revealed, saying, "Truly I say to you, this day you shall be with me in paradise." Therefore, just as by the ineffable power and justice of God in his lordship, the thief who believed was deemed to have been baptized, and his free mind was held to have received what it had not been possible to receive in his crucified body: so also the Holy Spirit was given secretly before the glorification of the Lord. After the manifestation of his divinity, however, it was

---

[89]That is, from whom his flesh was created. Augustine, with all his catholic contemporaries, held that the virgin was free of sin and that she never had sexual intercourse with a man before or after the conception of Jesus; at the same time, this is one of a number of passages in which he intimates that she was not free of original sin. [90]CSEL 60:109-11. [91]Deut 18:15. [92]SC 157:224-26. [93]Jn 4:1-2. [94]Jn 7:39. [95]Lk 23:43. [96]Acts 10:44-47. [97]Lk 23:42. [98]1 Cor 12:3.

more manifestly given. And the meaning of the statement, the Spirit was not yet given, is that it had not yet so appeared that all might confess it to have been given. In the same way, the Lord had not yet been glorified in the human sphere, and yet his eternal glorification[99] was never interrupted. It is in the same way again that the actual disclosure of him in mortal flesh is said to have been his advent. In fact he came to the place where he already was, because "he came to his own, and he was in the world, and the world was made through him."[100] In the same way, then, as the advent of the Lord is understood to be the bodily disclosure, although before this disclosure he himself spoke in all the prophets as the Word of God and the Wisdom of God: so also the advent of the Holy Spirit is the disclosure of the Holy Spirit to these eyes of flesh, when the fire was seen to be parted above them and they began to speak with tongues.[101]

If indeed the Holy Spirit had not been in human beings before the visible glorification of the Lord, how was David able to say, "And take not your Holy Spirit from me"?[102] Or how were Elizabeth and her husband, Zacharias, filled so that they might prophesy, and Anna and Simeon too, since it is written of all of them that they were filled with the Holy Spirit when they uttered the words that we find in the Gospel?[103] Now the fact that God performs some operations secretly and others visibly through the visible creation is part of his providential government, by which all divine actions take effect at allotted points in space and time, with exquisite discrimination, even though divinity itself is not contained and does not migrate from place to place or display extension and variation over time. The Lord, after all, had the Holy Spirit with him in the man who clothed him when he came to John to be baptized, and yet after he had been baptized the Holy Spirit was seen to descend on him in the form of a dove.[104] In the same way, we should understand that before the manifest

and visible advent of the Holy Spirit, some of the saints were able to possess him secretly. ON EIGHTY-THREE VARIED QUESTIONS 62.[105]

THE DOVE IS AN APT SYMBOL. AUGUSTINE: Because Jesus came to give humans a demonstration of how to live, the dove appeared in order that he might symbolize that very gift that is attained by living well. Now each event occurred visibly in order that carnal observers might be weaned gradually by acts of grace from those things that are discerned with bodily eyes to those that are apprehended by the mind. For words are heard and pass away, yet those things that the words signify, when anything divine and eternally is described in speech, do not pass away likewise. ON EIGHTY-THREE VARIED QUESTIONS 43.[106]

CHRIST WAS BAPTIZED IN TOKEN OF HIS DEATH. TERTULLIAN: There is indeed for us a second washing, one and the same—namely that of blood, of which the Lord says, "I have a baptism to be baptized with"[107] when he had already been immersed. For he had come through water and blood, as John wrote,[108] that he might be immersed in water, glorified by blood. Accordingly he sent forth two baptisms from the wound in his stricken side,[109] that we might be called by water and chosen in blood. ON BAPTISM 16.[110]

Jesus Tempted As We Are

GOD'S SAINTS ARE REFINED BY TRIBULATION. EPHREM OF ANTIOCH: A likeness and prototype of the Son of God was presented beforehand in the furnace of the young men. For the human nature of those youths was almost wholly mingled with the activity and nature of the fire, while retaining both the bodily activ-

---

[99]Jn 17:5. [100]Jn 1:11; 1:10. [101]Acts 2:3-4. [102]Ps 50:13. [103]Lk 1:41–2:35. [104]Mt 3:16. [105]CCL 44A:132-34. [106]CCL 44A:64. [107]Lk 12:50. [108]1 Jn 5:6. [109]Jn 19:34-35. [110]CCL 1:290-91.

ity to walk around, moving and changing place, and the intellectual resolution to produce a hymn. The fire did not damage any of their bodily or psychic properties, but Azariah was perfect both in fiery and in human nature. In the same way we must also understand that in Emmanuel's case the fire of his divinity was commingled as a sort of breath of life with his soul and body, and, while he sanctified everything, he did not compromise any essential property of his soul or body. SERMON ON HIS BEING TEMPTED AS WE ARE.[111]

CHRIST DEFEATED SATAN IN THE WILDERNESS. IRENAEUS: Who then is the Lord God to whom Christ bears testimony—the one that no one is to tempt and whom all are bound to adore, serving him alone? Without the slightest doubt he is that same God who gave the Law. For these events were foretold in the Law, and it is through the pronouncement of the Law that the Lord makes his revelation, since it is indeed the Law from the Father that announces the Word of God. On the other hand, the apostate angel of God is confounded by his utterance, exposed for what he is and overcome by the Son of man in obedience to the command of God. For he had humanity in his power through having persuaded him in the beginning to flout the commandment of his maker; that power of his, however, is transgression and apostasy, and by these he put humanity in bonds. It was necessary that it should be once again through man himself that he conversely should be vanquished and bound with the very fetters by which he had bound humanity. Thus it was possible for humanity to be loosed and return to its Lord, renouncing those fetters—the fetters of transgression—by which it had been bound. Yes indeed, the binding of the devil was the loosing of humanity, for "none can enter the house of the strong man and steal his goods unless he has first bound the strong man."[112] . . . And thus he who had unjustly led humanity into captiv-

ity was himself justly led into captivity, and humanity, which previously had been led into captivity, was rescued from the power of his oppressor, in accordance with the compassion of God the Father, who took pity on his own workmanship and bestowed salvation on people, restoring their integrity through the word of God, that is, Christ. The purpose was that humanity should learn by experience that it receives incorruption not from itself but by the gift of God. AGAINST HERESIES 5.21.3.[113]

THE EPISODE REVEALS HIS DIVINE CHARACTER. JEROME: The beasts[114] are those that the Lord trod down with the foot of the gospel, when he trampled on the lion and the serpent. "And angels ministered to him." Not that it ought to appear a great and marvelous thing if angels were ministering to God, since it is no great thing for servants to minister to their Lord; all this, however, pertains to the man assumed. And he was with the beasts. God cannot be with the beasts,[115] but that flesh that is subject to human temptations—that body, that flesh that thirsted and hungered—this it is that is tempted and is victorious, and in this we are conquerors. HOMILIES ON MARK 2.9-19.[116]

SUFFERING PROVES THE TRANSCENDENT POWER OF GOD. ATHANASIUS: When the flesh suffered, the Word was not alien to it, as this is the reason why the suffering is said to be his. And when he divinely performed the works of the Father, the flesh was not alien to him, but again it was in this body that the Savior performed these acts. And that indeed is why, having become a man, he said, "If I do not the works of the Father, believe me not. But if I do them, and you believe not me, believe the

[111]Cited by Leontius of Byzantium (PG 86.2:2108). Ephrem was a celebrated defender of orthodoxy in the fifth century. [112]Mt 12:29; Mk 3:27. [113]SC 153:274-78. [114]Mk 1:13. [115]That is, no doubt, insofar as he is God. Such laxity would not have been tolerated in Nestorius. [116]CCL 78:460.

works in order that you may know that I am in the Father and the Father in me."[117] Manifestly, when there was need to cure Peter's mother-in-law of her fever,[118] he stretched forth his hand as a human act but arrested the disease by a divine one. And in the case of the man born blind,[119] it was a human act to wipe the spittle away from the flesh but a divine one to open his eyes by means of mud. And in the case of Lazarus,[120] his utterance, as a man, was that of a human voice, but it was divinely, as God, that he raised Lazarus from the dead. It was in this way that these acts were performed, revealing that he had a body in truth and not in mere seeming. It was indeed fitting for the Lord, having put on human flesh, to put this on in its wholeness, with the sufferings that belong to it, so that, just as we speak of his body as his own, so it may be said that what pertains to the body is his alone, even if it does not impinge on him in respect of his divinity. Had the body been another's, the sufferings too would have been said to be another's; if, however, the flesh is that of the Word (for "the Word became flesh"[121]), it is necessary also that the sufferings of the flesh should be said to be his, as the flesh belongs to him. . . .

And who would not marvel at this? And who would not concur that this is truly a divine matter? For if the works of the Word's divinity had not been performed through the body, humanity would not have been made divine. And again if the things that are proper of the flesh were not predicated of the Word, humanity would not have been wholly liberated from them. No indeed, had he held back even a little (as I said before), sin and corruption would still have dwelled in humanity, as in humans of former times. AGAINST THE ARIANS 2.32-3.[122]

THE DEVIL WAS CONFUTED BY HIS OWN WILES. JOHN CASSIAN: As for the devil, when he had tempted Jesus with deceit on every side and with every contrivance of his own

wickedness, what was it that he did not know but suspected, or what did he desire to know by temptation? What was it that had affected him so much? Was he seeking God in human lowliness? Surely he had not learned this from any previous record or ever known God to come truly in a human body? Certainly not; but it was by the evidence of great signs, by the experience of great deeds and by the voice of truth itself that he was forced to suspect and investigate the fact. Once already he had heard John say, "Behold the lamb of God, who takes away the sin of the world,"[123] and again the same man saying, "I ought to be baptized by you, and do you come to me?" Moreover, a dove descending from heaven and hovering above the head of the Lord had presented itself as a clear and manifest evidence of the God who had been proclaimed. A voice, too, sent from God without riddle or metaphor had affected him, saying, "You are my beloved Son; in you I am well pleased." And therefore, for all that he saw a man externally in Jesus, he subjected the Son of God to examination, saying, "If you are the Son of God, bid these stones become bread." . . . He was in no doubt that the thing was possible when he was in doubt as to whether it was so: he was anxious as to its truth, not confident of its impossibility. AGAINST NESTORIUS 7.11.[124]

THE DIVINE NATURE REMAINS IMPASSIBLE. CYRIL OF ALEXANDRIA: I think it quite insane to suppose that a "shadow of turning"[125] could occur with regard to the nature of the Word or that this admits of alteration; for it remains always what it is and has not changed, nor indeed could it ever change. And in addition we all confess that the nature of the Word is impassible, even if in his boundless wisdom he practices a mysterious economy and is seen to allot to himself those things that befall his

---

[117]Jn 10:37-38. [118]Mt 8:14. [119]Jn 9:14. [120]Jn 11:43. [121]Jn 1:14. [122]PG 26:389-93. [123]Jn 1:29. [124]CSEL 17:366-67. [125]Jas 1:17.

own flesh. It is of this nature, not that of the ineffable Godhead, that the all-wise Peter says Christ has suffered for us in the flesh. For in order that he might be believed to be the savior of the whole, he refers to himself the sufferings of his own flesh by an economic assimilation,[126] just as is proclaimed from the mouth of the prophet, as if from his: "I gave my back to beatings, my cheeks were for blows, my face I turned not from the shame of spitting."[127] LETTER 39.5-6, TO JOHN OF ANTIOCH.[128]

CHRIST SUFFERS BY POSSESSING A HUMAN SOUL. AUGUSTINE: Jesus was amazed; he experienced anger, sorrow, joy and countless other feelings, as well as those that betoken a simultaneous exertion of body and soul: such as the fact of his hunger, his sleeping, his sitting down in weariness after a journey, and others of this kind. Nor indeed is it possible for them to say that even in the Old Testament there is talk of the anger of God and his mirth and several motions of this kind and that it does not follow from this that God should be conceived as having a soul. These things are said in prophetic reveries, not in perspicuous narrative. For there is talk also of the members of God, of his hands and feet and eyes and countenance and the like: these sayings do not indicate that he has a body, or those that he has a soul. However, just as the narration of any episode in which reference is made to the hand, the head or any other member of Christ betokens his body, so too any reference, in narratives of the same tenor, to affections of his mind betokens his soul. It is absurd to believe the Evangelist when he relates that he ate and not to believe his assertion that he was hungry. Granted, it does not follow that everyone who eats is hungry—for we read that an angel ate, but we do not read that he was hungry—nor that everyone who is hungry eats: he may, for example, restrain himself by some exertion, or he may be in want of food or the power of eating. Nevertheless, when the Evangelist relates

both, both are to be believed, since he wrote of the occurrence and performance of each as though it were a record of real events. ON EIGHTY-THREE VARIED QUESTIONS 80.3.[129]

HIS FLESH WAS OF THE SAME NATURE AS OURS. TERTULLIAN: For you the prophets bear no testimony to his lowly mien, but his very passions and humiliations bear witness: whereas the passions proved his flesh to be human, the humiliations proved it to be of low degree. Or would anyone have dared to scratch his new body with the tip of a finger or to sully his face with spittle if this were not consonant with his dignity? Why do you speak of heavenly flesh when you have no evidence to apprise you of its heavenly origin? Why do you deny that it is earthly when you do have evidence to inform you of its earthliness? The devil finds him hungering, the Samaritan woman finds him thirsting, he weeps over Lazarus, shrinks from death—for as he says, the flesh is weak—and at last pours out his blood. These are heavenly traits, I suppose! But how, pray, would he have been despised or have suffered as he himself said, if there had been any lustre of heavenly nobility in that flesh? ON THE FLESH OF CHRIST 9.[130]

WE TOO CAN EXPERIENCE HIS TEMPTATIONS. MAXIMUS THE CONFESSOR: The demons either tempt us or arm against us those who have no fear of the Lord. They tempt us themselves when we withdraw from human society, as they tempted our Lord in the desert.[131] They tempt us through other people when we spend our time in the company of others, as they tempted our Lord through the

---

[126]That is, they were not his by nature but by an inscrutable condescension. Fourth-century Fathers frequently distinguish between the intrinsic nature of God and his nature or action in the economy, that is, the dispensation of grace. [127]Is 50:6. [128]DFS 203. [129]CCL 44A:236-37. [130]CCL 2:892-93. [131]The temptation of Christ coalesces here with the trials of the desert fathers.

Pharisees. But whichever line of attack they choose, let us repel them by keeping our gaze fixed on the Lord's example. SECOND CENTURY ON LOVE 13.[132]

THE THREE TESTS ARE A PARADIGM OF ALL TEMPTATION. EVAGRIUS OF PONTUS: The heart cannot be troubled except with the weapons of food, riches or glory . . . and in a word, a human cannot succumb to the devil unless he has been wounded beforehand by one of these assailants. Thus it was these three arguments that the devil brought before the Savior. First he urged him to turn the stones into bread, then he promised him the whole world if he would fall down and worship him, and thirdly he said that, if he would pay heed to him, he would be glorified by receiving no hurt from such a great fall. The Lord, showing himself greater than these things, commanded the devil to get behind him, teaching us also through this that, unless we despise these three arguments, it is not possible to drive away the devil. ON THOUGHTS 1.[133]

HIS TRIBULATIONS TEACH US NOT TO SPARE OURSELVES. LACTANTIUS: Should anyone say, "Your precepts are impossible," he can answer, "I do them myself, yet am clothed in flesh, whose nature is to sin. And I bear the same flesh, yet sin has no power over me." "It is hard for me to despise wealth, since one cannot live otherwise in this body." "Yet, while I too have a body, I fight against every appetite." "I cannot bear pain or death for the sake of justice, being frail." "Behold, death and pain have power in me, and I overcome the things you fear." DIVINE INSTITUTES 4.24.[134]

CHRIST'S WEAPON AND OURS IS LOVE. MAXIMUS THE CONFESSOR: He who loves Christ is bound to imitate him to the best of his ability. Christ, for example, was always confer-

ring blessings on people; he was longsuffering when they were ungrateful and blasphemed him; and when they beat him and put him to death, he endured it, imputing no evil at all to anyone. These are the three acts that manifest love for one's neighbor. If he is incapable of them, the person who says that he loves Christ or has attained the kingdom deceives himself. FOURTH CENTURY ON LOVE 55.[135]

He Turned His Face Toward Jerusalem

IN DEATH HE WAS VOLUNTARILY SUBORDINATE TO THE FATHER. FAUSTINUS: The heretics, as you point out, belittle the Godhead of the Son, everlasting and perfect as this is, with the saying, "The Father is greater than I."[136] But one must ask when it was that the Son said this: was it not when there was fulfilled in him what is written, "You have made him a little lower than the angels and have crowned him with glory and honor"? How he was made lower the apostle Paul, who had seen the third heaven, explains: "We see Jesus made lower than the angels by virtue of his mortal suffering; crowned with glory and honor that by the grace of God he might taste death on behalf of all."[137] "On behalf of all," he says, not "on his own behalf." Therefore, since he tasted death on behalf of all, what wonder if on behalf of all he was also made lower? Now the reason why he tasted death on behalf of all and not on his own was that, when all had been rendered guilty of sin, he himself was made man and was made liable to no sin that was his own. And see how this very fact—his being made lower by virtue of his mortal suffering and his tasting death on behalf of all by the grace of God—is interpreted by the wise Paul as a fitting act in what follows: "For it was fitting for him on whose account and

---

[132]TP 2:67. [133]SC 438:150, 152. [134]CSEL 19:374. [135]TP 2:107. [136]Jn 14:28. [137]Ps 8:6, with Heb 2:9-10, here attributed to Paul, as is the custom even in writers who do not assert his authorship of the letter. The Latin *ab angelis* may mean "by the angels" as well as "than the angels."

through whom are all things, having conducted many sons into glory, to be perfected through sufferings as the captain of their salvation."[138] ON THE TRINITY 35.[139]

THROUGH THIS SUBORDINATION THE DI-VINE CHARACTER IS MANIFEST. ORIGEN: Let us see fully what should be understood by the further saying that he is the image of the invisible God, so that through this we may also observe in what sense God is properly called the Father of his Son. And let us draw our first consideration from those things that, according to human custom, are commonly known as images. Sometimes the term "image" is applied to that which is commonly painted or sculpted in some material, that is, of wood or stone; sometimes the one who is born is said to be the image of him of whom he is born, since it is always the case that in the one who is born the traits of resemblance to the one who begot him appear without deceit. In my view the first example can be made to fit the one who was made human in the image and likeness of God[140] . . . while the image of the Son of God, of whom we are now speaking, invites an analogy along the lines of the second, inasmuch as he is the invisible image of the invisible God, just as according to the historical narrative we say that Adam's son Seth was his image. Thus indeed it is written: "And Adam begot Seth according to his own image and according to his own likeness."[141] This image also implies the unity of the Father and Son in substance and in nature.[142] For if all that the Father does the Son also does likewise,[143] the image of the Father is traced out in the Son insofar as the Son in this way does all things as the Father does, being born from him as if he were, so to speak, his will proceeding from his mind. . . .

But so that it may be better understood how the Savior is the figure of the substance or being of God,[144] let us use also an illustration. It neither fully nor precisely represents the matter of which we are speaking, but it should

be understood to have been adopted solely to explain how in emptying himself, the Son who was in the form of the Father is endeavoring to make plain to us the fullness of the Godhead through his very self-emptying.[145] Suppose, for the sake of argument, some statue were made of such magnitude that it covered the entire globe of the earth, exceeding everyone's power of contemplation because of its vastness, but then another statue were made resembling the first completely in the cast of the limbs and the lines of the face, in appearance and in matter but without being of such vast magnitude. The aim would be that those who were unable to contemplate and behold that vast statue could, by seeing this one, be sure that they had seen the other because it preserved, without any deviation, the lines of the members and face, the very appearance and the matter: it is by such a similitude that the Son, emptying himself of equality with the Father and showing to us the way of knowing him, is made the express figure of his substance. . . . But of course this analogy with statues, predicated as it is on material objects, is to be accepted for no other purpose than to show that the Son, enclosed for a very brief time in the form of a human body, was indicating the presence of the Father's vast and invisible magnitude in himself on account of his likeness in works and virtues, when he said to his disciples, "He who has seen me has seen the Father also," and "I and the Father are one."[146] And a like interpretation to this should be put on this other saying of his, "The Father in me and I in the Father."[147] ON FIRST PRINCIPLES 1.2.6, 8.[148]

---

[138]Heb 2:10. [139]CCL 69:336. [140]Gen 1:26. [141]Gen 5:3. [142]The Greek terms underlying the Latin which is all that remains to us were most probably *ousia* and *physis* (cf. *Commentary on John* 2.10). [143]Jn 5:19. [144]Properly, the character or impression of his hypostasis (Heb 1:3). [145]Phil 2:7; 2:6; Col 2:9. [146]Jn 14:9; 10:30. [147]Jn 10:38. [148]GCS 22:34-39. Since the lesser statue is the incarnate Christ, no evidence can be drawn from this passage that Origen subordinates the Son to the Father within the Trinity.

EVEN SUBORDINATION WOULD ENTAIL UNITY OF NATURE. ATHANASIUS: He for his part is the effulgence and the Word and the image and the Wisdom of the Father,[149] while contingent things of course occupy an order below the Trinity in servitude. Therefore the Son differs in kind and essence from the contingent order and is instead peculiar to the Father's essence and of one nature with him. And it was indeed for this reason that the Son himself did not say, "The Father is better than I," so that one might suppose him to be alien to the Father's nature. Instead, he said greater, not in any magnitude or in time but on account of his generation from the Father. But anyway, even in saying, "He is greater," he once again revealed the peculiar affinity of nature. AGAINST THE ARIANS 1.58.[150]

Peter's Confession

PREVENTING ERROR AND ENCOURAGING FAITH. ORIGEN: Observe, though, how it was that, because there were so many different opinions concerning Jesus among the Jews, that some, on unsound premises, said that he was John the Baptist (in the same way as Herod the tetrarch, who said to his sons, "This is John the Baptist; he himself has risen from the dead and this is why the powers are at work in him"[151]), whereas others said that the one now called Jesus was Elijah, having either undergone a second birth or having remained alive in the flesh from the first time to appear in the present age. And those who declared that Jeremiah was Jesus, rather than that Jeremiah was a type of Christ, perhaps based this opinion on what was originally said of Jeremiah but was not realized in the prophet but had begun to be realized in Jesus. God appointed him "for nations and kingdoms, to uproot and dig up and destroy and pull down and transplant,"[152] having made him to be a prophet to the nations to whom he had proclaimed the word. But those who said that he was one of the prophets entertained such a notion of him because of utterances in the prophets that seemed to have been addressed to them but had not been realized in their case.

Whereas the Jews, however, showed themselves worthy of the veil on their hearts by their false opinions about Jesus, Peter was no disciple of flesh and blood but had received the revelation of the Father in heaven. For his part he denied that Jesus was any of those persons whom the Jews supposed him to be but confessed that he was the Christ. And thus it was a great thing that Peter should say to the Savior, "You are the Christ," when this was not known to the Jews. But it was a greater thing that he understood him to be not only Christ but the Son of the living God. . . . But since we have said that those who pronounced Jesus to be John the Baptist, or one of the others who were suggested, spoke on unsound premises, let us substantiate this by saying that, had they chanced to be present at the baptism when Jesus came to John and John baptized Jesus or had they heard of it from anyone, they would not have said that Jesus was John. Nor, had they grasped the premises of Jesus' saying, "If you wish to receive him, this is Elijah, the one who is to come,"[153] and had heard this saying like those who have ears, would some have said that he was Elijah.[154] As to those who said that he was Elijah, had they known that the majority of the prophets adopted symbolic language concerning him, they would not have said that he was Elijah; nor, likewise, would others have said that he was one of the prophets. . . .

If we say what Peter did,[155] this having been revealed to us not by flesh and blood but by a light from the Father in heaven shining in our hearts, and become ourselves what Peter was, being blessed because we now have the same

---

[149]Heb 1:3; Jn 1:1; Col 1:15; 1 Cor 1:21-24; cf. Prov 8:22; Wis 7:25-26. [150]PG 26:133. [151]Jn 10:38. [152]Jer 1:10. [153]Mt 11:14. [154]Mt 16:14. [155]Mt 18:16.

cause of blessing as he did . . . it could be said to us also by God the Word, "You are Peter, and on this rock I shall found my church,"[156] and so on. For everyone is a rock if they imitate Christ, from whom those who drank from the spiritual rock that followed them were drinking.[157] And on every rock of this kind is built every teaching of the church and the corresponding way of life. For in each of the perfect, who possess in concert the words, the works and the thoughts that constitute blessedness, there is the church that God is building up. COMMENTARY ON MATTHEW 12.9-10.[158]

THE CHURCH IS GROUNDED ON THE UNANIMITY OF THE DISCIPLES. CYPRIAN:[159] The Lord speaks to Peter, saying, "I say to you that you are Peter, and on this rock I shall build my church, and the gates of hell shall not prevail against it. And I will give to you the keys of the kingdom of heaven, and whatsoever you shall bind on earth shall be bound also in heaven, and whatsoever you shall loose on earth shall be loosed in heaven."[160] And again after the resurrection he says to the same one, "Feed my sheep." On this one man he builds his church, and to him he commends his sheep. And although he confers an equal power on all the apostles after his resurrection and says, "As the Father has sent me, so I send you: receive the Holy Spirit. Those whose sins you remit, they shall be remitted to them, and those whose sins you retain, they shall be retained";[161] yet, so that he might make that unity manifest, he arranged by his own authority that the origin of this unity should proceed from one. No doubt the other apostles were, also as Peter was, invested with honor and power in an equal fellowship; but the beginning proceeds from unity, and the primacy is given to Peter, so that one church, one seat of Christ may be evident. ON THE UNITY OF THE CHURCH 4.[162]

EVEN PETER'S FAITH WAS COMPROMISED BY HIS IMPETUOSITY. JEROME: Straightway after his confession he heard from the Lord that it was his lot to go up to Jerusalem and then to suffer from the elders, the scribes and the rulers of the priests.[163] He did not want his confession to be undone, nor did he think that the Son of God could possibly be killed. Either he draws him into his embrace or he takes him apart lest he should be seen to remonstrate with his master in the presence of his fellow disciples. And he began to reproach him with the affection of one who loved him, choosing the words "Let this be far from you, Lord," or (as it is better expressed in the Greek), "be propitious Lord, this shall not be." He means it cannot be, and my ears cannot bear, that the Son of God should be killed. Turning to him the Lord says, "Get behind me, Satan";[164] you are a stumbling block to me. The meaning of Satan is enemy or opponent. He means, "Because you are speaking in opposition to my resolve, you deserve to be called an enemy." There are many who say that it was not Peter who was rebuked but the enemy spirit who was prompting the apostle to speak. To me, however, it will never seem that the errors of an apostle, proceeding from pious affection, could be of diabolic inspiration. COMMENTARY ON MATTHEW 3.135-52.[165]

The Transfiguration

THE TRANSFIGURATION WAS A FORETASTE OF ETERNAL GLORY. HILARY OF POITIERS: After six days, Peter, James and John are taken up with him and set their feet on a high mountain, and in their sight the Lord is transfigured and radiates splendor in the full condition of his own glory. In this kind of event the mo-

---

[156]Mt 16:18. [157]1 Cor 10:4. [158]GCS 40 (10):81-86. This translation blends the Greek and Latin versions, both of which appear to be corrupt. [159]Scholars are divided as to the authenticity of a longer version, which affirms the primacy of the Roman see. [160]Mt 16:18. [161]Jn 20:23. [162]CDL 60-62. [163]Mt 16:21. [164]Mt 16:23. [165]CCL 77:143-44.

tive, the number and the precedent are all to be observed. For after six days the condition of the Lord's glory is revealed; that is, the majesty of the heavenly kingdom is prefigured when six thousand years of time have elapsed. And the co-option of three reveals the future election of the people with their threefold origin in Shem, Ham and Japhet. As to the fact that, from the whole number of the saints, it is Moses and Elijah who are present, suggests that Christ in his kingdom is a mediator between the law and the prophets. For it is with these, the witnesses who proclaimed him, that he will judge Israel. At the same time, the purpose of the transfiguration was that we may learn that the glory of the resurrection is destined for human bodies. For even Moses had been present to view at a certain time. As for the Lord, he becomes brighter than snow and the sun—that is, refulgent in the splendor of heavenly light beyond our conceiving. When, however, Peter proposes that three tabernacles should be set up there, no answer is given, since it was not time for him to assume this glory permanently. COMMENTARY ON MATTHEW 17.2.[166]

IT WAS A LESSON TO THE DISCIPLES. LEO THE GREAT: Although they had learned that the majesty of God was in him, still they knew nothing of the power of that body of his where divinity was concealed. Then he had promised clearly and explicitly that "certain of the disciples there present would not taste death until they saw the Son of man coming in his kingdom,"[167] that is, in royal splendor, which (in a special manner pertaining to the manhood he had assumed) he wished to be visible to these three men. For, encompassed up to now in mortal flesh, in no way were they able to look at and see that ineffable and inaccessible vision of the divinity itself, which is saved for the clean of heart in eternal life.[168] . . .

He used this transfiguration chiefly that the scandal of the cross would be lifted from the hearts of the disciples and that the humil-

ity of his voluntary suffering would not upset the faith of those to whom the perfection of his hidden dignity had been revealed. But with no less foresight, the hope of the holy church was made firm, so that it might know with what sort of exchange the whole body of Christ was to be given and that the members might promise to themselves a sharing in the honor of the one who had shone as their Head.

The Lord had said, when speaking about the majesty of his coming, "Then the just will shine like the sun in the kingdom of their Father."[169] Blessed Paul the apostle assures us of the same thing when he says, "For I think that the sufferings of this time are not to be compared with the future glory that will be revealed in us." On another occasion the same apostle said, "For you have died, and your life is hidden with Christ in God. And when Christ your life appears, you also will appear with him in glory."[170] To strengthen the apostles and to advance them in all knowledge, yet another lesson came in this miracle. Moses and Elijah, meaning the law and the prophets, appeared speaking with the Lord, so that very truly in the presence of these five men, what was written might be fulfilled: "Among two or three witnesses, every word will stand."[171] What is more stable, what is more firm, than this saying in whose message the trumpets of the Old and of the New Testaments sound and with whose gospel teaching the records of the ancient pronouncements concur? The pages of both Testaments agree with one another, and the splendor of his present glory shows, manifest and clear, the one whom the preceding signs had promised under a veil of mystery. As blessed John says, "The Law was given through Moses; grace and truth have come through Jesus Christ."[172] SERMON 51.2-4.[173]

---

[166]PL 9:1013-14. [167]Mt 16:28. [168]Mt 5:8. [169]Mt 13:43; cf. Dan 12:2. [170]Col 3:3. [171]Deut 19:15; cf. 2 Cor 13:1. [172]Jn 1:17. [173]CCL 138A:298-300.

The Cloud Signifies the Spirit. Jerome: According to Matthew, the cloud was
luminous.[174] To me it seems that the cloud
was the grace of the Holy Spirit, which covers
the tabernacle and overshadows those within
the tabernacle. O Peter, who desired to make
three tabernacles,[175] behold the one tabernacle
of the Holy Spirit, which protects us equally.
Had you made tabernacles, those that you
made would have been human. Furthermore,
you would have made them such as to exclude
light and hold shadow. This cloud, however,
brilliant and overshadowing as it is, this one
tabernacle, does not shut out but holds the
sun of righteousness.[176] Homilies on Mark
5.231-39.[177]

All May Enjoy the Same Vision. Origen:
In my view, when they were led up by Jesus to
the high mountain and it was vouchsafed to
them alone to witness his transfiguration, the
statement that they were led up after six days
in the preceding words is not otiose. For since
it was in six days, a perfect number, that the
whole world, this perfect workmanship, came
into being, I therefore think that the statement
that Jesus took certain persons with him after
six days alludes to the one who transcends all

the objects of the world by no longer regarding
the things that are seen (for they are ephem-
eral) but now the things that are unseen, and
only the things that are unseen (because they
are everlasting). If then any one of us wishes
Jesus to take him and lead him up to the high
mountain, that a vision of his transfiguration
may be vouchsafed to him alone, let him tran-
scend the six days by no longer contemplating
the things that are seen or continuing to love
the world or the things in the world, or desiring anything that the world desires—meaning
the desire of the body and bodily wealth and
glory according to the flesh—or any of those
things that are wont to distract and divert the
soul from higher and better things, causing
it to descend and rest on the foppery of this
world in wealth and glory and the other desires
that are hostile to truth. For when you have
traversed the six days, as we have said, you will
celebrate a new sabbath, rejoicing on the high
mountain because you have seen Jesus transfigured before your eyes. Commentary on
Matthew 12.36.[178]

---

[174]Mt 17:5. [175]Mt 17:4. [176]Mal 4:2. [177]CCL 78:483. [178]GCS 40 (10):150-51.

HE WAS CRUCIFIED

σταυρωθέντα τε ὑπὲρ ἡμῶν	*crucifixus* etiam pro nobis	For our sake **he was crucified**
ἐπὶ Ποντίου Πιλάτου,	sub Pontio Pilato,	under Pontius Pilate;
καὶ παθόντα καὶ ταφέντα,	passus et sepultus est;	he suffered death and was buried.
καὶ ἀναστάντα τῇ τρίτῃ ἡμέρᾳ	et resurrexit tertia die,	On the third day he rose again
κατὰ τὰς γραφάς,	secundum Scripturas;	in accordance with the Scriptures;
καὶ ἀνελθόντα εἰς τοὺς οὐρανούς,	et ascendit in coelum,	he ascended into heaven
καὶ καθεζόμενον	sedet	and is seated
ἐκ δεξιῶν τοῦ πατρός,	ad dexteram Patris;	at the right hand of the Father.
καὶ πάλιν ἐρχόμενον μετὰ δόξης	et iterum venturus est, cum gloria,	He will come again in glory
κρῖναι ζῶντας καὶ νεκρούς·	judicare vivos et mortuos;	to judge the living and the dead,
οὗ τῆς βασιλείας οὐκ ἔσται τέλος.	cujus regni non erit finis.	and his kingdom will have no end.

HISTORICAL CONTEXT: All creeds of the fourth century affirmed the passion or suffering of Christ, and we may be reasonably certain that the same clause stood at the heart of earlier creeds. There would have been no cause to commemorate his death, let alone to "preach Christ and him crucified" had he not come to "give his life as a ransom for many." What may, however, surprise us is the absence in earlier versions of this creed of any allusion to the cross as the instrument of the Savior's death. It was only perhaps after Constantine had adopted the cross as his emblem that the manner of Christ's death, and not merely the death itself, assumed the significance that it now occupies in dogmatic exposition. The putative discovery of the true cross (by Helena, the mother of Constantine) led to the insertion of the word *crucified* in the liturgy of the Jerusalem church, where the relic was exhibited to admiring pilgrims in the late fourth century. Though the various defining titles of Christ are not explicitly rehearsed in the Nicene-Constantinopolitan Creed, the confession that Christ is the anointed one is explicitly presupposed in its confession of faith *in unum dominum Iesum Christum filium dei unigenitum*: "in

one Lord Jesus Christ, the only-begotten Son of God." Though previously looked at in volume 2 in relation to the person of Christ, this theme requires revisiting here in relation to the work of Christ. The confession that Christ is the teacher of the truth remains a crucial dimension of his work as the uniquely and definitively anointed one (Christ). While the creed as such does not make explicit reference to Christ's prophetic ministry, the Scriptures do, so in an effort to embrace major questions of classic Christian teaching, we include the discussion of Christ as prophet in this particular point of the sequence of the creed that speaks of his crucifixion. It is clear from this point forward in this volume we are speaking primarily of what the Savior does in his saving activity, having already established who he is, that is, his identity as truly God, truly human. In systematic terms we speak now of the work of Christ based on the person of Christ, which was fully discussed in volume 2. What he does can be done only by one who is who he is: truly God, truly human.

OVERVIEW: He was anointed from the creation (JUSTIN), as prophet, priest and king (EUSEBIUS). As Jesus means savior, so Christ means priest (CYRIL OF JERUSALEM). There are witnesses to his title throughout history (CYRIL OF JERUSALEM), yet some remain unconvinced (ORIGEN). Even to them the appellative "Christ" reveals his character (TERTULLIAN), and, while he dissembled for the sake of his disciples (ORIGEN), he underwent a visible anointing at his baptism (OPTATUS) that bore witness to the invisible anointing within the Godhead (GREGORY OF NYSSA). As the Israelite ceremonies testified to the anointing of Christ (ORIGEN), so chrism cements the believer in faith (GOSPEL OF PHILIP).

The prophet foretold at Deuteronomy is Jesus (ORIGEN), as John the Baptist acknowledged throughout his career (CYRIL OF ALEXANDRIA). He was foretold as prophet, priest and king (AUGUSTINE). The first two roles precluded marriage (METHODIUS); the royal office was the first to be honored during his life (TERTULLIAN), and its gradual consummation is prefigured in the three books of Solomon (ORIGEN). His teaching required no artificial trappings (LEONTIUS). He reciprocated the disdain of his own compatriots (CYRIL OF ALEXANDRIA), not being the first to suffer such dishonor (ORIGEN). He was destined, in fact, to suffer the greatest dishonor (HILARY), being the greatest of the prophets (AUGUSTINE). For all that, he did not despise his precursors (CYRIL OF ALEXANDRIA), any more than they despised sinners (GILDAS), and his preaching was of a piece with that of the Baptist (ORIGEN). As Christ's aim is to foster knowledge through love (MAXIMUS), so those who reject him prove themselves unworthy of love (HILARY). God can speak to the carnal mind only in parables (CLEMENT OF ALEXANDRIA), foreseeing our incomprehension (IRENAEUS) but adopting numerous modes of accommodation (THEODOTUS IN CLEMENT).

Prophecy is a kind of incarnation (CLEMENT OF ALEXANDRIA), and the Word is incarnate in Scripture (ORIGEN). The incarnation imparts three senses to Scripture, and every word in the canonical text is Christ (ORIGEN). The incarnate Word submits to the limitations of humanity in his professions of ignorance (EPIPHANIUS). Thus he exercises the mind of the interlocutor (EPIPHANIUS) and reveals that the source of all knowledge is the Father (BASIL). He also knows as man, but not by virtue of being man (GREGORY THE GREAT).

The healings fulfill the prophecies of the one God (JUSTIN) and bear witness to the divinity of his Son (ARNOBIUS OF SICCA). Christ surpasses every pagan god in his munificence and his power (ARNOBIUS OF SICCA). The Word acts under the laws of human nature (ATHANASIUS), yet the humanity and the divinity work as one (CYRIL OF ALEXANDRIA), though neither forfeits its natural properties (LEO). Christ is not mending the errors of an evil creator (TERTULLIAN) but glorifying the Father in his own works (IRENAEUS). Demonic possession is sometimes metaphorical (CLEMENT OF ALEXANDRIA) and even when real, seldom goes beyond delusion (MINUCIUS FELIX). Christ's exorcisms, however, reveal incomparable power (LEONTIUS) and fulfill the long-meditated plan of God (IGNATIUS). The demons' confession proves that the miracle is divine (TERTULLIAN).

The transformation of water into wine signifies regeneration (CYRIL OF ALEXANDRIA), sanctifying both natural vicissitude and marriage (AUGUSTINE). Christ reveals both his divinity and the triune nature of God (AUGUSTINE), and the transformation is completed in our own souls (MAXIMUS).

In the raising of Lazarus, Jesus proves his omniscience in thanking the Father for answering his prayer (ORIGEN). His apparent ignorance is a dissimulation of knowledge (AUGUSTINE, ORIGEN). The Son cooperates with the Father (ORIGEN) and shows his divinity by grieving at a distance (ORIGEN). Both the use of human intermediaries and the three days' delay enhance the cogency of the miracle (HIPPOLYTUS). The impotence of Lazarus represents bondage to sin (Augustine), while the wrappings that hamper him warn us that sin is not easily extinguished (Origen).

The feeding of the multitude looks back to the exodus and forward to the deliverance of the saints (Augustine). It foreshadows the Christian sacraments (Ambrose), but we must not forget that the manna was sometimes abused (Hilary).

Healings strengthen the faith of doubters (Cyril of Alexandria). They also serve as parables of redemption, and, while Bethsaida was a real place (Eusebius), the cure performed there prefigures the resurrection (Augustine). The angel is gone (John of Damascus), though it continues to stir the baptismal font (Tertullian). The man's carrying of his bed symbolizes the charity that supervenes on faith (Augustine).

Christ's miracles fulfill the plan of the Creator (Tertullian). He vindicates the sabbath by proving himself its Lord (Tertullian). The cure at Siloam illustrates the power of the revelatory and incarnate Word (Augustine); the day in which he works will endure as long as the present world (Augustine). While the priesthood of Christ is eternal (Gospel of Truth), it ennobles his manhood (Prosper) and is anticipated by that of the high priest Joshua (Eusebius), as well as by the captaincy of Joshua son of Nun (Origen). It hallows earthly ministry (Liturgy of St. James), while furnishing a lesson in constant obedience (Irenaeus). It is we, not Christ, who require sanctification (Augustine), and while his ministry does not dispense us from the summons to holiness (Chrysostom), it opens the door of eternal life (Ignatius).

The Christ[1]

THE ANOINTING TOOK PLACE AT THE CREATION. JUSTIN MARTYR: Father, God, Creator, Lord and Master are not names but designations taken from his benefits and works. But

his Son, the only one who is properly called Son, the Word who was his companion and his offspring before the creatures—this one, in the beginning when he created all things through him and set them in order, is called Christ because he was anointed and has set all things in order at the instance of his God. This name, too, is inscrutable in content, in the same way that the designation God is not a name but a notion of some unsearchable being implanted[2] in human nature. Jesus, by contrast, is the name of a man and a savior and has a meaning. For, as we have said before, he became a man, conceived according to the counsel of God the Father for the sake of believing humans and for the destruction of the demons. And this you are able to learn from what has happened before your eyes. For many of our people—the Christians—have healed many demoniacs throughout the whole world and in your own city, conjuring them in the name of Jesus Christ, the one crucified under Pontius Pilate, when all the conjurations, incantations and drugs of others had failed to heal them. Still they are healing them, confounding and chasing away the demons who hold human beings in thrall. SECOND APOLOGY 6.2-6.[3]

THE TITLE PERTAINS TO ALL THREE OFFICES AND BOTH COVENANTS. EUSEBIUS: It is now time to demonstrate that the name Jesus, and indeed the name Christ, have been honored of old by the God-loving prophets themselves. Moses was the first to make

---

[1]Though "Christ" is apt to function as a proper name in the New Testament, it is a title, the Greek equivalent of the Hebrew Messiah, or "the anointed one." Prophets, priests and kings were all supposed to receive this unction, and there is little evidence that Jewish contemporaries of Jesus expected all their offices to be united in one Messiah. Such an expectation is, however, presupposed in Johannine use of the term "Messias" (Jn 1:41; 4:26), in the confession of Peter (Mt 16:16 and other references) and in the malicious question of the high priest (Mt 26:63 and other references). [2]Here as elsewhere in Justin, the word *emphytos* may mean "implanted by teaching" rather than "innate" (cf. Jas 1:21 with *First Apology* 44 on the dissemination of knowledge through the prophets). [3]JMAA 82-83.

known the most venerable and glorious title "Christ." He handed down types of heavenly things and symbols and mystic images in accordance with the oracle that had said to him, "See, you shall make all things according to the type that has been shown to you on the mountain."[4] And when he blessed a human high priest with the greatest possible force, he styled him Christ. Yes, it is to this rank of high priest, which in itself excels every human institution, that he gives the honorific and glorifying name of Christ. In this way, therefore, Christ is commended by divine warrant.

And again the same man, by divine inspiration clearly foreseeing the appellation Jesus, dignifies this, too, with an exceptional provision. This name of Jesus had never been uttered among human beings until Moses made it known, and he conferred it first and solely on the man whom, by type and symbol, he knew to be the one who would succeed to rule over everything after his death. His successor had not at first made use of the appellation Jesus but had been called by another name, Auses, which had been given to him by his parents; Moses himself styles him Jesus, thus bestowing on him as an honor a name far more distinguished than any regal diadem, seeing that it was this very Jesus son of Nun who bore the image of our Savior, the only one who succeeded to rule over true and pure religion after Moses and the consummation of the symbolical worship that he had handed down. And Moses, one might say, conferred on two men who surpassed the whole people of his day in virtue and glory, the appellation of our savior Jesus Christ to their great honor—one the high priest, the other who was to be captain after him.

And after that the prophets plainly address Christ by name, at the same time witnessing presciently to the future combination of the Jewish people against him, as well as the calling of the Gentiles. At one time Jeremiah says, "The spirit before our face, Christ the Lord, has been taken up in their corruptions,

of whom we have said that we shall live in his shadow among the nations." Then David says in these words without disguise, "Why have the nations raged and the people imagined vanities? The kings of the world have made common cause and the rulers are gathered together for the same purpose, against the Lord and against his Christ."[5] Immediately after this it says, in the person of Christ himself, "The Lord has said to me, 'You are my son, this day I have begotten you. Ask it from me, and I will give you the nations for your inheritance and for your possession the ends of the earth.'"[6] It is therefore not only those who have been honored with the high priesthood, anointed[7] with manufactured oil for symbolic reasons, who have been adorned with the name Christ by the Hebrews; but kings also, who were themselves anointed by the prophets at God's behest and made as it were iconic Christs, since they themselves also bore in themselves the types of the regal and supreme authority of the one true Christ, the divine word ruling all.

And indeed we have heard that some of the prophets themselves, by their anointing, have become Christs typologically, since all of these men have their relation to the true Christ, the divine and heavenly word, he being the one high priest of all, the one king of the whole creation and the one lord of all the prophets of his Father. And the demonstration of this is that none of those anointed symbolically, whether priests or kings or prophets, had hitherto received divine virtue in such potency as had been shown to belong to our Savior and Lord Jesus, the one true Christ. ECCLESIASTICAL HISTORY 1.3.1-9.[8]

JESUS CHRIST IS SAVIOR AND PRIEST.
CYRIL OF JERUSALEM: Jesus Christ has two appellations, Jesus because he is savior and

---

[4]Ex 25:40. [5]Ps 2:1-2. [6]Ps 2:7-8. [7]The discussion presumes throughout that the reader will recognize the derivation of Christ from *chriō*, "I anoint." [8]SC 31:13-15.

Christ because of his priesthood. . . . Christ is a high priest as Aaron was in that it was not he who claimed for himself the glory of being high priest, but the one who said to him, "You are a priest forever after the order of Melchizedek." And in many ways Joshua the son of Nun, for when he began to rule the people, he began from the Jordan, and that was where Christ began to spread the gospel after his baptism. The son of Nun appoints twelve to divide the inheritance, and twelve are the apostles, harbingers of truth, whom Jesus sends out to the whole inhabited world. The one who bore the type saved Rahab the harlot, while the true one says, "Behold, the tax collectors and harlots go into the kingdom of heaven before you."[9] In the case of the man who bore the type, the walls of Jericho fell to a simple roar, and it was because of Jesus' saying that not one stone would be left on another that the temple of the Jews has fallen, in plain view for us.[10] Not that this assertion was the cause of its fall, but the cause of its fall was the sin of the lawless. CATECHETICAL LECTURE 10.11.[11]

WITNESSES TO THE TITLE ARE UBIQUI-TOUS. CYRIL OF JERUSALEM: That this Christ had come among them the Jews denied, but the demons confessed it. But David our ancestor was not ignorant of this and said, "I have prepared a lamp for my Christ."[12] Some have construed this lamp as the light of prophecy; others take the lamp to be the flesh assumed from the Virgin, according to the apostle's saying, "We have this treasure in earthen vessels."[13] Nor was the prophet ignorant of this when he said, "and announcing his Christ to humanity."[14] This Christ was known to Moses, to Isaiah, to Jeremiah also. None of the prophets was ignorant of him. And the demons, too, were cognizant of him, since he rebuked them, as the text says, "because they knew him to be Christ."[15] The chief priests were ignorant of him, and the demons confessed him. The chief priests were ignorant of him, and the Samari-

tan woman proclaimed him, saying, "Come, see a man who has told me all that I have done."[16] This is Jesus Christ, the high priest of future goods who comes among us and has given us a share in his title through his unstinting benevolence. For human kings hold this title of king without sharing it with other humans, but Jesus Christ, being the Son of God, has deigned to let us be known as Christians. CATECHETICAL LECTURE 10.15-16.[17]

JEWS, HERETICS AND SAMARITANS HAVE STILL TO LEARN THAT JESUS IS THE CHRIST. ORIGEN: You should know, however, that, just as Jesus arose from among the Jews, not only professing to be the Christ but proving it, so likewise one Dositheus arose from among the Samaritans, declaring himself to be the prophesied Christ. His followers, the Dositheans,[18] survive to this day, hawking about the books of Dositheus and relating fabulous tales about him as one who did not taste death but is still alive. So much then as to the literal sense. But there is also a heterodox teaching[19] which, standing by the spring of Jacob, which it takes for a well, uses this name of Christ, supposing it to be more perfect, and says, "When that one comes, he will announce all things to us."[20] But the one foreseen and hoped for appears to her, saying, "I am he, the one who speaks to you." COMMENTARY ON JOHN 13.27.[21]

THE TITLE PROCLAIMS HIS GOODNESS. TERTULLIAN:[22] As to the merits of names, if

---

[9]Mt 21:31. [10]An audience in Jerusalem would have seen that Jesus had permitted himself a hyperbole; the ruins of the temple survive to this day. [11]CHOO 1:274-76. [12]Ps 132:17. [13]2 Cor 4:7. [14]Amos 4:13 (LXX). [15]Lk 4:41. [16]Jn 4:29. [17]CHOO 1:280. [18]Possibly the same prophet whom the Samaritans call Dustan, he was reputed to have been the teacher of Simon Magus. [19]Origen takes the Samaritan woman to represent such heretics as the Cerinthians and Ebionites, who denied the identity of the heavenly Christ and the human Jesus. [20]Jn 4:25. [21]SC 222:120-22. [22]In Greek of the Roman period, the words *chrēstos* ("good") and *Christos* ("anointed") were often pronounced identically. Apologists could turn this phonetic accident to the advantage of the church under persecution.

there is any guilt in names or any ground of accusation in vocabulary, I hold that there is nothing to quarrel with in vocabulary or naming unless something has a barbarous sound, or a tone that is ominous or indecent or one that does not befit the speaker or please his audience. These are the crimes of vocabulary and naming, just as in diction and speech, barbarism is a vice, and so is grammatical error or a vulgar expression. But as to the denotation of the name Christian, it derives its sense from anointing. Even when you corrupt it, calling us Chrestians (for you are not absolutely certain even of the name), it receives from this, too, a sweet and benign inflection. Thus, as we are harmless, so the name of ours that you seize on is harmless, not uncouth to the tongue, not harsh to the ears, not bad for a person or odious to one's peers, but both a Greek word like others and one that is pleasant in sound and sense. AGAINST THE NATIONS 1.3.7-10.[23]

JESUS CONCEALED HIS ANOINTING TO SPARE THE DISCIPLES. ORIGEN: If the apostles, who were always with him, and had seen all the wonders that he performed and testified of his words that they were "words of eternal life,"[24] were offended in the night when he was handed over, what do you think that others who had heard before this that he was the Christ would have suffered? It was, as I think, to spare them that he enjoined this. Paul did likewise, when he announced Christ to the Athenians not as the Son of God but as a certain man, because they were as yet in an uninstructed state. COMMENTARY ON MATTHEW 12.17.[25]

HIS BAPTISM WAS A VISIBLE ANOINTING. OPTATUS: This, too, you must learn, whose voice it is that says, "Let not the oil of the sinner anoint my head."[26] . . . The voice is that of the Son of God, who at that time feared to encounter the oil of any sinner, that is of any human being, since no one is without sin save

God alone. The reason why his Son feared the oil of a human being was that it was indecent that God should be anointed by a human. Thus he begs the Father that he should not be anointed by a human but by God himself.

The Son therefore asks; let us see if the Father has agreed. This the Holy Spirit indicates plainly in Psalm 44, where he says to the Son, "Let God your Lord anoint you with the oil of exultation otherwise than your companions." His companions were the priests and kings of the Jews, who are well known to have been anointed severally by humans. But the Son was to be anointed by the Father, God by God according to the Son's prayer, so the promise of the Spirit was the Father's consummation in the Jordan. When the Son of God, our Savior, came there, he was revealed to John with these words: "Behold the Lamb of God, who takes away the sins of the world." He stepped down into the water, not because there was anything to be cleansed in God, but water had to go before the oil that was to come, in order to institute, direct and fulfill the mysteries of baptism. When he had been washed in John's hands, the order of the mystery succeeded, and the Father consummated what the Son had asked and the Holy Spirit had promised. AGAINST THE DONATISTS 4.7.[27]

BEFORE THIS HE RECEIVED AN INVISIBLE ANOINTING. GREGORY OF NYSSA: These destroyers of the Spirit's glory, who relegate him to a subject world, must tell us of what thing the unction is a symbol. Is it not a symbol of the kingship? And what? Do they not believe in the Only-begotten as in his very nature a king? People who have not once for all enveloped their hearts with the Jewish veil will not gainsay that he is this. If, then the Son is in his very nature a king and the unction is the symbol of his kingship, what in the way of a

[23]CCL 1:14. [24]Jn 6:68. [25]GCS 40 (10):108-9, which combines Greek and Latin versions. [26]Ps 140:5. [27]OAD 92.

consequence does your reason demonstrate? Why, that the unction is not a thing alien to that kingship and that the Spirit is not to be ranked in the Trinity as anything strange and foreign either. For the Son is King, and his living, realized, personified kingship is to be found in the Holy Spirit, who anoints the Only-begotten and so makes him the anointed and the king of all things that exist. AGAINST MACEDONIUS.[28]

CEREMONIAL UNCTION IN ISRAEL WAS A SHADOW OF SPIRITUAL ANOINTING. ORIGEN: Let us see what this unguent is composed of. "And the lord spoke to Moses," it tells us, saying, "Take for yourself the flower of choice myrrh, 500 shekels, and sweet cinnamon 250 shekels, and sweet calamus 250 shekels, and cassia 500 shekels using the shekel of the sanctuary, and oil from olives. . . ."[29] Now the spouse [in Solomon's Song] had heard the relation of this, but now she perceives the reason and truth in it. See then that those four ingredients in this unguent contained a type of the incarnation of the Word of God, who was compounded of four elements. In his body he bears the tokens of that myrrh of his death, which he undertook either as a priest for his people or as a groom for his bride. . . . As to the cinnamon, it is said to be spotless, no doubt on account of the church, which he causes to be spotless—free of spot, wrinkle or anything of this kind—by the washing of water. And calamus is also taken, because his tongue is like the pen of a scribe with rapid hand. . . . And that oil by which Christ is anointed, which is the unguent of the Holy Spirit, and the aroma of which the spouse now smells with wonder, is rightly called the oil of gladness, because the fruit of the Spirit is joy. COMMENTARY ON THE SONG OF SONGS I.[30]

THE ANOINTING MAKES THE CHRISTIAN. GOSPEL OF PHILIP: The chrism[31] is superior to baptism, for it is from the word *chrism* that

we have been called Christians, certainly not because of the word *baptism*. And it is because of the chrism that "the Christ" has his name. For the Father anointed the Son, and the Son anointed the apostles, and the apostles anointed us. One who has been anointed possesses everything. He possesses the resurrection, the light and the cross, the Holy Spirit. The Father gave him this in the bridal chamber; he merely accepted the gift. The Father was in the Son, and the Son is in the Father. This is the kingdom of heaven. GOSPEL OF PHILIP 74.[32]

The Expected One

JESUS, NOT THE BAPTIST, IS THE "ONE TO COME." ORIGEN: If the law and the prophets were until John, what else could we say that John was but a prophet? And that, too, is what his father, Zacharias, prophesied, saying in the fullness of the Spirit, "And you, child shall be called a prophet of the most high."[33] If he is also said by the Savior to be a prophet and greater than a prophet, how then, if he is a prophet, does he answer no when the priests and Levites ask him, "Are you the prophet?" To this we must say in reply that "Are you that prophet?" is not the same thing as "Are you a prophet?" We have observed the same distinctions when explaining how "God" differs from "a god" and "the Word" from "a word." Now it is written in Deuteronomy, "The Lord will raise up to you a prophet from your brethren like me. You shall listen to him, and every soul that does not listen to that prophet shall be eradicated from his people."[34] Thus there was an exceptional expectation of some prophet

[28]NPNF 2 5:321. [29]Ex 30:23. [30]GCS 33:98-100. [31]Anointing with oil, which followed baptism in the early church. In some modern churches it survives only vestigially in the rite of confirmation. [32]NHS 20:191 (translated by W. Isenberg). This gospel is generally held to be a product of the Valentinian school, which did not despise the sacraments, for all its supposed hostility to matter. [33]Lk 1:67. [34]Deut 18:15.

who in some way resembled Moses, in mediating between God and humankind and in receiving a new covenant from God that he handed on to his disciples. And the people of Israel ascertained of each of the prophets that none of them was the one who had been prophesied by Moses. Since they were in doubt as to whether John might possibly be the Christ, so also as to whether he might possibly be the prophet. Small wonder that, being in doubt over John, they did not grasp the point that Christ and the prophet were the same. For it is a consequence of that very doubt not to know that Christ is the same as the prophet. COMMENTARY ON JOHN 6.15.[35]

THE BAPTIST'S QUESTION IMPLIES NO DOUBT. CYRIL OF ALEXANDRIA: The Baptist introduced a strange and novel regime, pursuing a course of life that was uncongenial to others and not to be embarked on by any chance comer. Thus, as was perfectly natural, he was much admired by the Jews. . . . Yet when the Lord to whom he bore witness seemed to have forsaken the worship according to the Mosaic law, introducing in its place the regime of the gospel (or rather refashioning into truth the things that were in type and shadow), the Baptist did not escape recrimination, since those who reasoned foolishly were persuaded that he was an ally of one who was subverting the lawful discipline. . . . Subsequently they were obliged to love him as one who was suffering for the Law and became more ready to believe the things that he preached. Thus it was laid on the Baptist that both the goodwill of the Jews and the unbelief of the stiff-necked would accrue to him. But since he was a partaker of the Holy Spirit and had been filled with the gift of prophecy even from his mother's womb, he sought—while he was contemplating the naked sword of the tyrant and his own inexorable death—to reinforce the faith of his disciples in Christ the Savior. And his earnest desire was that they would know plainly,

without any wavering, that this is the one who is expected to come for the salvation of all. Yet he makes a pretense of ignorance, so that when he has expressed belief, his disciples also may be forced to keep pace with him in belief. For only a mind in labor with a great conceit of itself would have chosen to be guided by its own counsels rather than by those of the master. THESAURUS ON THE TRINITY 11.[36]

The Three Offices

THE THREE OFFICES ARE UNITED IN THE PSALMS. AUGUSTINE: "Yet am I set by him as a king on Sion, his holy hill, preaching his decree."[37] This is clearly spoken in the person of the very Lord our Savior Christ. But if Sion signifies, as some interpret, beholding, we must not understand it of anything rather than of the church, where daily is the desire raised of beholding the bright glory of God according to that of the apostle, "but we with open face beholding the glory of the Lord."[38] Therefore, the meaning of this is, "Yet am I set by him as king over his holy church," which for its eminence and stability he calls a mountain. . . .

"The Lord has said to me, 'You are my son, today have I begotten you.' "[39] Although that day may also seem to be prophetically spoken of, on which Jesus Christ was born according to the flesh, and in eternity there is nothing past as if it had ceased to be, nor future as if it were not yet, but present only, since whatever is eternal always is: yet as "today" intimates presentness, a divine interpretation is given to that expression, "Today have I begotten you,"[40] whereby the incorrupt and catholic faith proclaims the eternal generation of the power and wisdom of God, who is the only-begotten Son.

"Ask of me and I shall give you the nations for your inheritance."[41] This has at once a temporal sense with reference to the manhood that

[35]SC 157:194-96. [36]PG 75:169. [37]Ps 2:6. [38]2 Cor 3:18. [39]Ps 2:7. [40]Ps 2:7. [41]Ps 2:8.

he took on himself, who offered up himself as a sacrifice in the stead of all sacrifices, who also "makes intercession for us."[42] Thus the words "ask of me" may be referred to all this temporal dispensation that has been instituted for humankind, namely, that the "nations" should be joined to the name of Christ and so be redeemed from death and possessed by God. EXPOSITIONS OF THE PSALMS 2.5-7.[43]

THE CONJUNCTION OF PRIESTHOOD AND PROPHECY ENTAILS CELIBACY. METHODIUS: First of all we must examine why, when so many prophets and righteous persons taught and performed so much, none of them either celebrated or embraced virginity. It was reserved to the Lord alone to be an ambassador for this discipline, since he alone taught us to pass from the human to God. For it was fitting for this high priest and arch-prophet to be also known as the prince of virgins. SYMPOSIUM OR BANQUET OF THE TEN VIRGINS 1.4.[44]

HOMAGE WAS PAID TO HIS KINGSHIP AT BIRTH. TERTULLIAN: Once the sign of his unprecedented birth had been reported, immediately after the sign a new order of child is proclaimed, one that is to eat honey and butter.[45] Nor certainly does the sign consist in his being unacquainted with malice—for that is also a trait of childhood—but in his future acceptance of the power of Damascus and the spoils of Samaria against the kings of the Assyrians. If you observe the measure of his age and consider the meaning of the prophecy, then you will certainly concede to the Gospel the truth that you have hitherto denied to it,[46] and the prophecy is understood as soon as its fulfillment is announced. Let those eastern magi remain after all, endowing Christ, in the freshness of his infancy, with gold and incense,[47] and the infant will receive the spoils of Damascus without battle or arms. For besides what all know—that the power of the east, that is, its force and vigor,

generally burgeons in gold and spices—David says of that dower of gold that there shall be given to him of the gold of Arabia, and again kings of the Arabs and Saba shall offer gifts to him; and Damascus was formerly part of Arabia . . . while the spoils of Samaria are the magi themselves, since they had recognized him and honored him with gifts, worshiping him like a god and king on the testimony of their token and guide the star,[48] they were made the spoils of Samaria, that is, of idolatry, by their faith in Christ. AGAINST MARCION 3.13.5-8.[49]

HIS KINGSHIP IS PREFIGURED IN THAT OF SOLOMON. ORIGEN:[50] Who then is Solomon, that is, the peaceable one like our Lord Jesus Christ, who was made for us the wisdom of God and the righteousness of God?[51] Well, in the first book of Proverbs, when he imbues us with teachings for mortal life, he is said to be king in Israel, not yet in Jerusalem. Even if we are said to be Israel on account of our faith, we have not, however, reached the point where we can see the heavenly Jerusalem. But when we have advanced, and reach the point where we mingle with the church of our ancestors that is in heaven, and, after resolutely dispelling the concerns of the old and natural person, become aware that the heavenly Jerusalem is our heavenly mother: then indeed Christ is made for us the Ecclesiast and is said to reign not only in Israel but also in Jerusalem. But when we have reached the perfection of all things and every rational creature is united with him as his perfect bride, because through his blood he has caused not only things on earth but also things in heaven to be at peace—then he is called

---

[42]Heb 7:25. [43]CCL 38:4-5. [44]SC 95:62. [45]Is 7:14-15. [46]Addressing Marcion, who had denied the veracity of the Gospel of Matthew. [47]Mt 2:10. [48]Mt 2:9. [49]CCL 1:524-25. [50]Origen contends that, as readers make their way through the three books of Solomon (Proverbs, Ecclesiastes and the Song), they will acquire by degrees a deeper understanding of this human type of Christ. [51]1 Cor 1:30.

simply Solomon, when he has handed over the kingdom to God the Father, putting down every principality and power.[52] COMMENTARY ON THE SONG OF SONGS, PROLOGUE.[53]

Christ as Teacher

CHRIST WAS BY NATURE A TEACHER. LEONTIUS OF BYZANTIUM: "How does this man know letters, without having learned letters," says the Jew at John 7:15. Does the teacher of letters need these aids? Does he need to go to a school, as a lathe for his tongue? Does he, the distiller of wisdom, need an education? . . . If you wish to ponder the imponderable, say first how he gave sight to the man born blind. . . . All that he did was to anoint the blind man's eyes with mud. Yet mud blinds even those with sight and does not give sight to the blind. Even so, you Jews, he healed the one born blind without medical art, manifesting his freedom in the exercise of his divine power. And it was just the same here: without rhetorical myth making or sophistical complication, without poetical vanities or astronomical babbling, he taught those who were present; as also in the case of the blind man those present were meant to learn that this is the one who took clay from the earth and fashioned Adam as the first human. And therefore, after such an impressive lesson, they would become vividly aware that this is the one who said through the prophet, "Open your mouth, and I will fill it."[54] PENTECOST SERMON 1.[55]

FAMILIARITY BRED CONTEMPT IN HIS OWN COUNTRY. CYRIL OF ALEXANDRIA: The Evangelist is required to say, as an explanation of his detour, that Jesus himself testified that a prophet has no honor in his own country.[56] For we are by nature disposed to think nothing of what is familiar, even if it is great and honorable. And the Savior, for his part, did not see fit to reap from them the honors that were due to him, as if he were a man of the vainglorious and self-aggrandizing type, but he was well aware that for those who give no thought to the duty of honoring their teacher even the word of faith would not be pleasant or acceptable. Quite reasonably, then, he passes them by, not deigning to expend idle labors on those who received no good of it and thus gratify those who held him in contempt. COMMENTARY ON JOHN 2.5.[57]

THE PROPHETS HAD BEEN DISHONORED BEFORE HIM. ORIGEN: The prophets are dishonored first in having been persecuted by the people, as history relates, and secondly in that their prophecies were not believed by the people. For if they had believed Moses and the prophets, they would have believed Christ, too, when he represented to them that the consequence of believing Moses and the prophets is to believe in Christ and that those who do not believe in Christ do not believe in Moses. Furthermore, just as the one who sins is said to dishonor God by his transgression of the Law, so when one fails to believe in the prophets, the prophet is dishonored by his disbelief in the one who is prophesied. COMMENTARY ON MATTHEW 10.18.[58]

GREATER DISHONOR AWAITED HIM. HILARY OF POITIERS: The Lord received no honor from his own people.[59] For all the wonder aroused by that the astuteness of his teaching and his mighty works, they nonetheless refused to judge truly in their faithlessness. For they do not believe that it is God who performs these works in a man. Indeed, they go so far as to name his father, his mother, his brethren and to cast something of a slur on his father's craft. Yet clearly here was the son of the artificer who overcomes iron with fire, roasting

---

[52]1 Cor 15:28. [53]GCS 33:84. [54]Ps 81:10. [55]PG 86.2:1984. [56]Jn 4:44. To the Fourth Evangelist, his own country is Judea (cf. Jn 1:11); in Mk 6 it is Galilee. [57]PG 73:332. [58]GCS 40 (10):23. [59]See Mt 13:57.

the mighty world entire in his judgment and fashioning the whole mass into every product of service to humans. That is, he fashions the unformed matter of our bodies into the diverse operations of the limbs and into every practice that brings everlasting life. It is this, then, that gives offense to all, and in the midst of all those remarkable deeds that he was performing, it was the look of his body that moved them. To them the Lord replied that a prophet is not without honor except in his own country,[60] because it was in Judea that he was going to suffer humiliation even to the cross. And because the might of God acts only among the faithful, he abstained from all works of divine might on account of their incredulity. COMMENTARY ON MATTHEW 14.1-2.[61]

JESUS IS THE GREATEST OF THE PROPHETS. AUGUSTINE: The woman says to him, "Sir, I perceive that you are a prophet."[62] The husband[63] has begun to come but has not yet arrived. She thought the Lord a prophet. And a prophet indeed he was, for he says of himself, "A prophet is not without honor save in his own country."[64] Again it is said of him to Moses, "I shall raise up a prophet for them from among their brethren, one like you."[65] Like, that is, in the form of his flesh, not in royal pre-eminence. Therefore, we do find the Lord Jesus styled a prophet, and thus the woman does not err greatly. TRACTATES ON THE GOSPEL OF JOHN 15.23.[66]

YET HE DOES NOT DISHONOR HIS PREDECESSORS. CYRIL OF ALEXANDRIA: See again what economy the Savior practices in this matter. He had had occasion to speak much and at length about the holy Baptist, for he exploded the opinion that made it seem reasonable to do him an injury. By saying instead that he possessed something more than a prophet, he was showing his hearers that John was admirable and worthy of great love. Then he adds to this that no one greater has ever arisen among

those born of women. Having, however, set him up as an exemplar of the highest virtue that dwells in those born of women, he sets against this the greater good—that is, the one who has lately laid hold of the kingdom and has been reborn as a child of God through the Spirit. His intention was that partakers of the kingdom should seem all the more estimable by comparison with the admiration that accrued to John from an inferior distinction and that some might press on more ardently to seize it when they took the measure of its superabundant beauty from the honor paid to John. THESAURUS ON THE TRINITY 11.[67]

HE IMITATES A LINE OF PROPHETS. GILDAS: Noah had no mind to exclude his son Ham from the ark or from table fellowship, for all his writings on the art of magic;[68] Abraham did not shun Aner and Eshcol in his defeat of the five kings.[69] Isaac did not refuse to share his table with Abimelech, Ahuzzath and Phicol the captain of the troops, but after meat and drink they struck a compact together.[70] Jacob was not afraid to hold intercourse with his sons, though he knew that they were worshiping idols. Joseph did not refuse to share the table and cup of Pharaoh.[71] Aaron did not exclude the idolatrous priests of Midian from his table.[72] In the same way Moses peaceably enjoyed bed and board with Jethro. And our Lord Jesus Christ did not shrink from dining with publicans, so that he might save all sinners and harlots. LETTERS, FRAGMENT 1.[73]

NO ANTITHESIS OUGHT TO BE DRAWN BETWEEN JOHN AND JESUS. ORIGEN: Heracleon, treating somewhat pejoratively of John and the prophets, says that the word is the

---

[60]Mt 13:57. [61]PL 9:996. [62]Jn 4:19. [63]Augustine takes Christ as the husband whom the woman disclaims at Jn 4:17. [64]Lk 4:24. [65]Deut 18:18. [66]CCL 36:159-60. [67]PG 75:173. [68]Ham's sin (Gen 9:22) is eclipsed here by an apocryphal tradition. [69]Gen 14:9-13. [70]Gen 26:26-31. [71]Gen 41:46. [72]Ex 18:12. [73]GRB 143. Gildas seems to be denying the utility of excommunication.

Savior, but what is apprehended through John in the wilderness is voice, and the whole order of prophets is an echo. But one should say in reply to him that, just as if the trumpet gives an uncertain sound, no one is prepared for war, and the one who possesses knowledge of mysteries or prophecy without love is sounding brass or a tinkling cymbal, just so, if the prophetic voice is nothing but an echo, how is it that the Savior refers us to the prophets, saying, "Search the Scriptures, since in them you think to have eternal life." [74] . . .

And on what principle, if the prophets did not have love and were therefore sounding brass or tinkling cymbals, does the Lord, as these people assume, send us back to their echo, as though they would be of benefit? COMMENTARY ON JOHN 6.20.[75]

Jesus' Use of Parables

CHRIST'S TEACHING FOSTERS KNOWLEDGE THROUGH LOVE. MAXIMUS THE CONFESSOR: The whole purpose of the Savior's commandments is to free the intellect from dissipation and hatred and to lead it to the love of him and one's neighbor. From this love springs the light of active holy knowledge. FOURTH CENTURY ON LOVE 56.[76]

THOSE WHO REJECT HIM TELL THEIR OWN PARABLE. HILARY OF POITIERS: He spoke not to the multitude but to his disciples[77] and gives to them a testimony that matches their understanding of the parables. They are surely the ones whom he compares to himself under the name of the householder, in that they have embraced the teaching from his own treasury of the new and the old. These he dubs on account of their knowledge, because they have understood the things that he has brought forth—the new and the old being those that are in the gospel and the Law. Both belong to one householder, and issue from one treasury. COMMENTARY ON MATTHEW 14.1.[78]

GOD SPEAKS ONLY SYMBOLICALLY TO THE MULTITUDE. CLEMENT OF ALEXANDRIA: This great mass judges not with a view to truth but in accordance with its own pleasures. And it could not take pleasure in anything except what is like itself, in the measure of its own blindness and deafness. It possesses no understanding or the dauntless and quick-eyed vision of the contemplative soul, which the Savior alone imparts. It is as with those who, being uninitiated in rites or unskilled in the dances, not yet being pure or worthy of holy truth, are obliged to stand outside the divine chorus, unstrung, disordered and stolid. For we judge spiritual matters spiritually, and for this reason the way of occultation, a mode of speech indispensable to us, truly divine and absolutely holy, laid up in the inner sanctum of truth, was symbolized by the Egyptians through what are called their sanctuaries, and by the Hebrews through the veil, through which no unsanctified person was allowed to pass. By this is meant one not dedicated to God and circumcised from the passions in his heart. For would you have the impure lay hold of what is pure? . . . In the Psalms, in fact, the parabolic character of all our Scriptures is frankly asserted: "Hear my law, my people, incline your ear to the words of my mouth, I shall open my mouth in parables, I shall utter dark sayings from the beginning."[79] STROMATEIS 5.4.19, 25.[80]

EVEN THE MISUNDERSTANDING OF THE PARABLES IS FORESHADOWED. IRENAEUS: Long before when Balaam said this in a parable he received no recognition; and now Christ, being present and fulfilling this prophecy, is not believed. Thus he says, foreseeing this with wonder, "Alas, alas, who will live when God does these things?"[81] FRAGMENT 15.[82]

---

[74]Jn 5:39. [75]SC 157:210-12. [76]*TP* 2:107. [77]Mt 13:51-52. [78]PL 9:996. [79]Ps 78:1-2. [80]GCS 15:338-39, 341. [81]Num 24:23 (LXX). [82]*SIEL* 486.

THREE CATEGORIES OF SAYING MAY BE DISTINGUISHED. CLEMENT OF ALEXANDRIA: The Savior taught his apostles the first things figuratively and mystically, the next parabolically and enigmatically, the third clearly and nakedly when they were alone. EXCERPTS FROM THEODOTUS 66.[83]

ALL REVELATION MAY BE DESCRIBED AS AN INCARNATION. CLEMENT OF ALEXANDRIA:[84] And the "Word became flesh,"[85] not only when he became a man in his appearing, but even in the beginning when the changeless Word became the Son, not in essence but by circumscription. And again he became flesh in his operation through the prophets. And the Savior is called the child of the changeless Word. . . . Because of which, the statement that he "took the form of a slave"[86] refers not only to the flesh in which he appeared but also to his essence that comes from the material substrate. And this essence is a slave, insofar as it is passable and acts as a substrate to the active and sovereign cause. EXCERPTS FROM THEODOTUS 19.[87]

THE WORD ACCOMMODATES HIMSELF TO OUR CONDITION IN THE SCRIPTURES. ORIGEN: Remaining the Word in essence, he suffers none of the things that the body or soul suffers, but condescending now and then to the one who lacks the capacity to look on the rays and the brightness of his being, he becomes as it were flesh, speaking in bodily form, until the one who has received him, being elevated little by little by the Word, is able even to behold what I venture to call his preeminent form. AGAINST CELSUS 4.15.[88]

SCRIPTURE CONTAINS THREE SENSES. ORIGEN:[89] The Scripture is constituted, as it were, of the visible body, the soul within which lends itself to conception and comprehension, and the spirit which, as it were, involves the "types and shadows of things celestial." So, then, having called on the one who has framed the body,

soul and spirit in the Scripture—the body for those before us, the soul for us and the spirit for those who shall inherit eternal life in the age to come . . . we shall discover not the letter but the soul[90] in the present instance. HOMILIES ON LEVITICUS 5.2.[91]

EVERY WORD OF SCRIPTURE IS CHRIST THE WORD. ORIGEN:[92] The whole Word of God, the Word in the beginning, is not much speaking, for he is one word, not words. For there is one word, comprising a multitude of visions, each vision being a part of the entire Word. But any tidings apart from this are full of digression and even a sort of hiding, even if they purport to be words about the truth, and—to adopt a rather paradoxical manner of speaking—there is no Word in them but each is a word. PHILOKALIA 5.4.[93]

The Bounds of Jesus' Knowledge[94]

CHRIST AT TIMES DISOWNS KNOWLEDGE OR APPEARS TO MANIFEST IGNORANCE. EPIPHANIUS: As a man he asks, "Where have

---

[83]GCS 17:128. He is quoting a Valentinian author. [84]It is not clear whether Clement or the Valentinian Theodotus is speaking here. The author appears to believe that the Word accepted limitation and the title Son, but without any change of essence, in order to administer a world outside the Godhead. When he appeared on earth, he acquired a new essence through his assumption of a body. [85]Jn 1:14. [86]Phil 2:8. [87]GCS 17:112-13. [88]SC 136:220. [89]The discovery of two senses in Scripture higher than the bodily or historical sense is possible only because of the threefold incarnation of the Word. If this were not true literally, we should have no right to read Scripture allegorically. The bodily sense, though the lowest, is as indispensable to our salvation as the historical embodiment of Christ. [90]The soul of Scripture, often styled the moral sense by interpreters of Origen, enables the reader to understand his place in the scheme of providence. [91]GCS 29:334. [92]Throughout this passage, Origen plays on the fact that the Greek word *logos* denotes not only speech but also sense and reason. He also sets the word *epangelia* ("tidings") against its antonym *apangelia* ("hiding"). [93]SC 302:290. [94]None of the Fathers anticipates the modern kenotic theory, according to which the second person of the Trinity temporarily surrendered his omniscience when he took flesh. Instead they maintain that he honored the limits of creaturehood by displaying the ignorance proper to a human.

you laid Lazarus?" and of the woman with the haemorrhage, "Who touched me?"[95] And of those who were looking for him, "Whom do you seek?"[96] As a man he even asks the disciples, "Who do they say that I, the Son of man, am?" and further he says, "How many loaves of bread have you with you?"[97] . . . He who is wisdom and teaches knowledge to humans, the one who planted the human ear and made human beings fit for speech, the one who made the tongues of the mute loquacious—this one submitted for our sake to all these things, so that he might be entirely faithful to the human nature that has been dispensed to us, without relinquishing his character as truth. ANCORATUS 31.[98]

THE PURPOSE OF THIS ECONOMY MAY BE TO STIR THE INTELLECT. EPIPHANIUS: "Who do they say that I, the Son of man, am?" he says.[99] The reason for his acknowledging himself as son of man here is to prevent their thinking that he is asking them about what cannot be seen. Now they say Elijah, Jeremiah and John the Baptist. "Who do you say that I am?" "You are the Christ, the son of the living God," says Peter. And at once he blesses him. You see, he was not asking in ignorance but wished to show that the teaching that proclaims the true son to the church is from the Father. His purpose was to press Peter into saying what he had learned from the Father. ANACORATUS 39.[100]

HE KNOWS ALL BY VIRTUE OF THE FATHER'S KNOWLEDGE. BASIL OF CAESAREA: With regard to Mark, who seems plainly to exclude the Son from the knowledge, this is my opinion. No one has knowledge; neither the angels of God nor even the Son possess it, if the Father has it not. That is, the cause of the Son's knowing is from the Father. And this reading will not appear forced to one who listens with goodwill, because the word *alone* is not added,[101] as in Matthew. LETTER 236.[102]

KNOWLEDGE FROM HIS FATHER, SUSCEPTIBILITY FROM HIS MOTHER. GREGORY THE GREAT: The Only-begotten, being incarnate and made for us a perfect man, knew indeed in the nature of his humanity the day and hour of the judgment, but still it was not from the nature of his humanity that he knew it. What then he knew in it he knew not from it, because God, made man, knew the day and hour of the judgment through the power of his deity. Similarly at the marriage, when the Virgin Mother said that wine was wanting, he replied, "Woman, what have I to do with you? My hour is not yet come."[103] For it was not that the Lord of the angels was subject to the hour, having, among the things that he created, made hours and times; but because the Virgin Mother, when wine was wanting, wished a miracle to be done by him, it was at once answered to her, "Woman, what have I to do with you?" As if to say plainly, "That I can do a miracle comes to me of my Father, not of my mother." For he who of the nature of his Father did miracles had it of his mother that he could die. This is why also, when he was on the cross, he acknowledged his mother, whom he commended to the disciple, saying, "Behold your mother."[104] He says, then, "Woman, what have I to do with you? My hour is not yet come." That is, "In the miracle, which I have not of your nature, I do not acknowledge you. When the hour of death shall come, I shall acknowledge you as my mother, since I have it of you that I can die." And thus the knowledge that he had not of his humanity, whereby he was with the angels a creature, this he denied that he had with the angels, who are creatures. The day,

---

[95]Jn 11:34; Lk 8:45. [96]Jn 18:4. [97]Mt 16:13; Mk 6:38. [98]PG 43:73. [99]Mt 16:13. [100]PG 43:88. [101]Mt 24:36 allots this knowledge to the Father alone but does not expressly deny it to the Son. Mark denies it to the Son, yet does not add that the Father alone possesses it. Hence both authors mean that, while the Father and Son both have the knowledge, the Son has it only by virtue of the Father's knowing. [102]LCL, Basil 3:394. [103]Jn 2:4. [104]Jn 19:27.

then, and the hour of judgment he knows as God and man, but for this reason, that God is man. LETTER 10.39.[105]

Jesus' Teaching Through Miracles

CHRIST'S HEALINGS WERE FORETOLD. JUSTIN MARTYR: As to the prophecies that our Christ would heal all diseases and rouse the dead, listen to what was spoken.[106] Here is the passage: "At his advent the lame shall leap like a hart, and the tongues of the mute will be loosed. The blind shall see, and the lepers shall be cleansed, and the dead shall rise and walk about."[107] And that he did this you may learn from the Acts produced under Pilate.[108] And as to the prophetic Spirit's foreshowing his destruction, together with that of those who hoped in him, listen to what was spoken through Isaiah. Here is the passage: "See how the righteous perishes and no one lays it to heart. And the righteous are destroyed, and none takes account. From the sight of the unrighteous the righteous is removed and shall be at peace; his tomb has been raised in the middle."[109] FIRST APOLOGY 48.1-6.[110]

HIS DIVINITY IS MANIFEST IN THE POWER OF HIS WORKS. ARNOBIUS OF SICCA: Was he a mortal, or one of us, when distempers, illnesses, fevers and the other torments of the body fled his authority, his mere voice, though he used only popular and everyday expressions? Was he one of us when that race of demons who live buried in our entrails was unable to bear his presence and his aspect and was so dismayed by the new power that it yielded the possession of our limbs? Was he one of us, when foul eruptions were banished abruptly in obedience to his command, leaving a peaceful mixture of humors in the infected entrails? Was he one of us, whose light touch stayed emissions of blood and prevented the spilling of fluid? Was he one of us, when the somnolent waves of dropsy fled his touch,

when that corrosive fluid shunned him and swelling entrails contracted with healthy dryness? Was he one of us who bade the lame walk (finding it possible to extend their crippled arms as they loosened the ingrained immobility of their members) and those whose limbs were paralyzed to rise up (even carrying their mattresses, which had but lately been borne on the shoulders of others) and those who had been deprived of sight to see (beholding the sky and the light of day even when they had been born without eyes)? I ask again, was he one of us when once with a single intercession he healed a hundred, or more than this, who were afflicted by diverse infirmities and illnesses; when the enchafed and raging sea became calm at the mere sound of his voice; when the blasts of wind and the tempests abated; when he passed securely on foot through the deepest waters? Or when he trampled the back of the sea, to the stupefaction of the waves, as nature itself accepted service under him, or when he satisfied the five thousands who were following him with five loaves—amassing fragments to fill a dozen baskets to capacity, lest the incredulous and hard-hearted should take this for an illusion—was he one of us? Was he one of us, who bade souls that had long been exhaled from the body to return, and those who had been hidden away to come forth from their burial places and to be extracted from the undertaker's vestments after the third day of their interment? Was he one of us who saw clearly what each person was thinking, and the content of their tacit meditations in the silence of the heart? Was he one of us, who had but to make one utterance to be heard among diverse peoples using widely different languages, each thinking that he was employing the everyday phrases of their own tongue? Was he one of us, when, having communicated the practices

[105]NPNF 2 13:48. [106]That God foretold the miracles is proof that he, not Satan, was the author. [107]Is 35:5; Mt 11:6. [108]An apocryphal text, of which little now remains. [109]Is 57:1-2. [110]JMAA 59-60.

of a particular religion to his own followers, he forthwith filled the whole world with them, proving both how great he was and who he was by the magnitude of his fame? Was he one of us, who, when his corpse had been buried, disclosed himself on the morrow to countless people, speaking and hearing speech, teaching, correcting and admonishing, and furthermore (lest they should think themselves deceived by vain imaginings) proving his identity once and again and many times more in familiar conversations? Was he one of us who even now appears to the most righteous, those without blemish, not in vain dreams but through the outward form of pure simplicity; whose name when heard drives out pernicious spirits, forces silence on the prophets, leaves the diviners without a client, caused the acts of overweening priestcraft to miscarry, not (as you say) by the dread of his name but by the privilege of superior power? AGAINST THE NATIONS 1.45-46.[111]

No Pagan God Is So Prodigal in His Benefits to the Sick. ARNOBIUS OF SICCA: You compare the gifts of health that other deities have bestowed with those of Christ. How many thousands of the sick do you wish us to show you, how many sufferers from wasting illnesses, who have received no physic whatsoever? They have passed as suppliants through all the temples, grovelled before the faces of the gods, they have worn away the very thresholds with their kisses. Aesculapius,[112] the very donor of health, as they aver, they have wearied with prayers and importuned with the most wretched petitions as long as life was left to them. Do we not see that some die with their woes, others grow old with excruciating illnesses, others have begun to suffer more deadly ills after they began to wear out their nights and days with continuous prayers and hopeful devotions. So what is gained by displaying one or another who may perchance have been cured, when so many thousands

have had none to succor them? And yet all the shrines are teeming with the wretched and the unhappy! Or will you perhaps assert that the gods gave aid to the good but disdain the misfortunes of the wicked? Christ, by contrast, gave succor equally to the good and to the wicked. This man drove no one away who sought his help in harsh adversity against the malignant attacks of fortune. For this is the hallmark of true deity, as of regal power, not to withhold benevolence from any, not to calculate who deserves much or little. It is natural frailty that makes a person a sinner, and it is, therefore, not his own will but God's judgment that renders him eligible. To say that the gods give aid to the meritorious in their struggles is to put what you say in jeopardy and lay it open to doubt. It could just as well be thought that he who is made whole has been healed by chance, whereas one who is not could be thought to have failed to rid himself of his condition not because he has received his deserts but because the gods were weak. AGAINST THE NATIONS 1.49.[113]

Nor Can Any God Equal Him in Power. ARNOBIUS OF SICCA: I do not ask, I do not demand to know, what god brought aid to whom at what time or what broken frame he restored to health: all I wish to hear is whether this god, without the instrumentality of any matter—that is, of any medicine—ordered the illnesses to fly away from human bodies at his touch; whether his mere command both put an end to the distemper and caused the bodies of the invalids to return to their proper condition. For it is well known that Christ was accustomed, either by laying his hand in the region of the ailment or by the simple authority of his voice, to open the ears of the deaf, drive blindness in rout from the eyes, give

---

[111]ASCG 170-72. [112]Son of Apollo and patron of physicians, to whom a host of miraculous healings was ascribed in the ancient world. [113]ASCG 174-75.

speech to the dumb, relieve paralysis in the joints, restore to cripples the power of walking, to heal by his word and command alone the eruptions, fevers, dropsies and all the other species of distemper that the cruelty of whatever power it is has desired that human bodies should suffer. Was the like ever done by any of the gods who according to you have given aid to those in sickness and peril? AGAINST THE NATIONS 1.48.[114]

Miracles and the Two Natures

CHRIST SUBMITS TO HUMAN LIMITATIONS IN HIS MIRACLES. ATHANASIUS: This is obvious to all, that ignorance pertains to the flesh, while the Word himself, insofar as he is the Word, knows everything even before his birth. For it is neither the case that when he became man he ceased to be God or that since he is God he shuns what is human. God forbid! The truth is rather that, being God, he assumed flesh for himself, and being in flesh he made the flesh divine. For just as it was in the flesh that he asked his question,[115] so it was in the flesh that he raised the dead man. And he proved to all that he who revives the dead and calls back the soul is all the more aware of the secrets of all things and knew where Lazarus was laid. But he asked a question: yes, this too the most holy one of God did—the one who endured all things for us—in order that, having thus taken our ignorance on himself, he might confer on us the knowledge of that one true father of his[116] and of himself as the one sent on our account for salvation: no grace could be greater than this. AGAINST THE ARIANS 3.38.[117]

THE HUMANITY IS UNITED WITH HIS DIVINITY. CYRIL OF ALEXANDRIA: There are some who say that we should admit no fellowship between the flesh of the Only-begotten and his divinity or between the divinity and the flesh in his working of miracles. Some say that it was God the Word, not the man, whose call

roused Lazarus from the tomb,[118] and that it was not God who grew weary in his journey[119] but the assumed man, and that this was the one who hungered and thirsted, was crucified and died. These people, we say, have gone completely astray from the truth and do not know the mystery of his economic union with the flesh. For we do not say that there were two sons or two Christs, but one Christ and Son, who on the one hand is God the only-begotten, born before every age and time from God the Father, his substantial Word, and on the other hand is the very same one who was born in flesh from the Virgin in the last age of the world. For all that, let them not divide him double-mindedly or foist on us two sons but confess him as one and the same, as the Word of God become man, and predicate everything of him, words and deeds alike. For since the same one was at the same time God and man, he speaks both what befits God and what befits humans, and likewise his acts are both human and divine. Now when they confess a single Son and Christ and Lord, they will stop dividing him ignorantly and splitting him in two, so as to conceive of one Son who is severally and peculiarly the Word from God the Father and another Son again who, as they say, is severally and peculiarly the assumed man. For this is not what we say or what we believe; rather, we believe that being God the Word became flesh, that is, a man, not ceasing to be God but indeed remaining what he was unchangeably and without alteration, while participating in flesh and blood, as it says in Scripture.[120] And this flesh that was united to him and became his own we affirm to have been ensouled with a rational soul. ANSWER TO TIBERIUS 5.[121]

NEITHER HUMANITY NOR DIVINITY IS COMPROMISED. LEO THE GREAT: Each

---

[114]ASCG 173-74. [115]Jn 11:34: "Where have you laid him?" [116]See Jn 17:3. [117]PG 26:404-5. [118]Jn 11:43. [119]Jn 4:6. [120]Heb 2:14. [121]CASL 154.

form[122] does what is proper to it in conjunction with the other, the Word obviously performing that which belongs to the Word, while the flesh accomplishes what belongs to the flesh. One of these blazes with miracles, the other succumbs to injuries. And just as the Word does not withdraw from equality with the Father's glory,[123] so the flesh does not surrender its natural affinity with us. For he is one and the same, as we must say again and again—the true Son of God and the true Son of man. He is God inasmuch as "in the beginning was the Word, and the Word was with God and the Word was god";[124] he is man inasmuch as "the Word was made flesh and dwelt among us."[125] He is God inasmuch as all things came to be through him, and without him was nothing made."[126] He is man inasmuch as he is "made of a woman, made under the law."[127] The birth of the flesh is a manifestation of his human nature; the childbearing of the virgin is an index of divine power. The infancy of the little child is shown forth in the lowliness of his cradle; the greatness of the Most High is proclaimed in the songs of the angels. The one whom Herod impiously set out to slay is in feature like humanity; yet he whom the magi delight to worship on their knees is Lord of all. At the time when he came to the baptism of John his harbinger—with the aim of avoiding concealment, as his divinity was concealed in a veil of flesh—the voice of the Father, thundering from heaven, declared, "This is my beloved Son, in whom I am well pleased." And likewise, when the devil's cunning tempted him as a man, the angels paid their devoirs to him as God. To hunger, to thirst, to grow weary and to sleep, are evidently human traits; but to satisfy five thousand people with five loaves and to dispense living water to the Samaritan, the drinking of which vouchsafes to those who imbibe it that they will never thirst again, to walk with unfailing step upon the back of the sea, and to level the billowing waves with a rebuke to the storm—this beyond all ques-

tion is divine. And just as, therefore—to leave many things aside—it does not belong to the same nature to mourn a dead friend at the prompting of compassion and to rouse the same man by the summons of one's voice at a distance from his four-days' tomb; or to hang on the cross yet, having turned day into night, to inspire a trembling in all the elements; or to be transfixed by nails and to open the doors of paradise to the faith of a robber: thus it does not belong to the same nature to say "I and the Father are one"[128] and to say "the Father is greater than I."[129] For although in the Lord Jesus Christ there is a single person, of God and of man, there is one origin of the humiliation common to both, and one of the common glory. For from us he derives that humanity that is less than the Father and from the Father that divinity that is equal to the Father. LETTER 128 (TO FLAVIAN) 4.[130]

HE IS NOT GREATER THAN THE FATHER. TERTULLIAN: See, there are some of those imbecilities and frailties of the Creator in Christ, since for my part I consent to attribute ignorance to him. Allow it to me against the heretic.[131] He was touched by the woman who suffered the issue of blood and did not know by whom. "Who touched me?" he said.[132] And notwithstanding the protests of his disciples, he persisted in his expressions of ignorance: "Someone has touched me." And as evidence he asserts this: "for I felt that power has gone forth from me." What does the heretic say? Did he know her identity? Then why did he speak as though ignorant? No doubt that he might provoke a confession, that he might

---

[122]That is, the form of God (Phil 2:6) and the form of a servant (Phil 2:8). [123]Phil 2:6. [124]Jn 1:1. [125]Jn 1:14. [126]Jn 1:4. [127]Gal 4:4. [128]Jn 10:30. [129]Jn 14:28. [130]DFS 210. [131]Marcion had maintained that the Creator of the world was inferior to Christ and that he governed by his own purblind notion of justice. Augustine undertakes to show that if Christ's professions of ignorance can be palliated, so can that of God, who is in any case God the Word (Gen 3:9). [132]Mk 5:31.

put her fear to the test. And so it was that he inquired of Adam as though he were ignorant, "Adam, where are you?"[133] Thus you have the Creator acquitted along with Christ, and Christ made equal to the Creator. AGAINST MARCION 4.20.7-8.[134]

HIS MIRACLES ALWAYS REDOUND TO THE GLORY OF THE CREATOR. IRENAEUS: Now God gave his precept to Adam through the Word: for Adam heard, it says, the voice of the Lord God.[135] Rightly then his Word says to a man, "Your sins are forgiven you":[136] the very same one against whom we sinned in the beginning bestows forgiveness at the end. Now if we had violated the precept of some other being, then the other one who said "Your sins are forgiven you" was neither good nor truthful nor just in this respect. For how was he just if he gave from what was not his own? Or how was he just, if he stole what belonged to another? How indeed were sins truly forgiven, if it was not he against whom we sinned who bestowed forgiveness, "through the bowels of God's pity, in which he worked on us"[137] through his Son?

For this same reason, when he had healed the paralytic, "the populace seeing this," says Matthew 9:8, "gave thanks to God, because he had given such power to humans." What God was it then that the bystanders glorified? Could it have been that figment of the heretics, the unknown Father? How, pray, did they glorify one who was wholly unknown by them?[138] It is therefore patent that the one whom the Israelites glorified was the God proclaimed by the law and the prophets, who is the Father of our Lord. And on this account he taught people, by the signs that he performed in their sight, to give glory to God. AGAINST HERESIES 5.17.1-2.[139]

Exorcisms

POSSESSION MAY BE A DISEASE OF THE HUMAN FACULTIES. CLEMENT OF ALEXAN-

DRIA: When the passions that are in the soul are called spirits, this does not mean spirits of power. A man in passion is called a legion of demons, but only for the purpose of exhortation. For it is the soul itself that accommodates vice by turns, one species after another, and then it is said to have taken in demons. PROPHETIC EXTRACTS 46.[140]

DECEIT IS THE CHIEF ACTIVITY OF DEMONS. MINUCIUS FELIX: There are lying spirits, vagabonds, who have lost their heavenly strength, weighed down by earthly imbecilities and desires. These spirits, therefore, once they have lost the simplicity of their own natures under an overwhelming load of vices, do not cease to alleviate their woe by damning others as they have been damned, to instill corrupting error (being corrupt themselves) and, estranged as they are from God, to separate others from God by promoting corrupt religions. . . . They slip in under statues and images and by their own afflatus secure authority such as belongs to a god, as now and then they inspire prophets or lodge in shrines, or occasionally animate internal fibers [of slaughtered beasts], direct the flight of birds, regulate lots and produce oracles shrouded in falsehoods. For they are at once the deceivers and the deceived, in that while they are ignorant of the plain truth, they will not damn themselves by confessing what they know. OCTAVIUS 26.1; 27.1.[141]

EXORCISMS REVEAL SUPERHUMAN POWER.[142] LEONTIUS OF BYZANTIUM: Do you say, Jews, that he has a demon, when your father the devil could not endure to see him? No longer, I say, having strength to bear the one who

---

[133]Gen 3:9. [134]CCL 1:595-96. [135]Gen 3:8, 10. [136]Mt 9:2; Lk 5:20. [137]Lk 1:78. [138]As Marcion claimed, distinguishing the just but benighted Creator of the world from the unknown Father of Jesus Christ. [139]SC 153:222-26. [140]GCS 17:149-50. [141]LCL, Minucius Felix 394, 396. [142]What we know of pagan exorcisms before the time of Christ can be said in three words: there were none. Of Jewish exorcism we have more evidence, but almost all of it from the New Testament.

had invisibly struck that legion, he made the truth public, crying openly, "What have we to do with you, Jesus of Nazareth? Have you come before the time to torment us? I know who you are, the Son of God."[143] In burning pain the demon vindicates him, and you, his beneficiaries, pronounce that the Lord is possessed by demons? To whom did the legion of demons say, "If you cast us out, grant us that we may enter into the herd of swine"? Was it to Solomon, the founder of Jerusalem, or to Christ, who holds all things together in his hand?

But the demon-loving Jews will reply immediately, "What of it? Was not Solomon absolute master of the demons? Did he not shut them all as one together in one place? Do they not fear him to this day? O Jews, you adepts of demons, these arguments that you advance are futile, for only the Lord Jesus has bound the strong man with power and spoiled him of his goods.[144] For Solomon not only failed to master the demons as a king, but toward the end, having been corrupted, was himself mastered by them. For in his besotted passion for polygamy, ruined by the works of the devil, ran whinnying among a herd of foreign women like a horse lusting for mares, he defiled the chamber of divine knowledge.[145] For having abandoned the God of his ancestors, to whom he had built the temple, he constructed dark chambers for idols. How then was he the master of demons when he was their slave? **Pentecost Sermon 1.**[146]

The Overthrow of Satan Commences with the Incarnation. Ignatius of Antioch: Hidden from the ruler of this age were the virginity of Mary and her childbirth, likewise also the death of the Lord[147]—three mysteries that cry aloud, though performed in the silence of God. How then was he manifested to the ages? A star shone in heaven, greater than any star: its brilliance was ineffable and its novelty caused astonishment, while all the other stars, together with the sun and moon, became a cho-

rus to this star,[148] and the star itself in its surpassing brilliance was greater than all. And they were confounded: from where came this thing so new, so unlike them? By this all magic and every evil spell was done away; ignorance was abolished, the ancient kingdom was destroyed as God was manifest in human form to bring the newness of life everlasting. And he assumed the kingdom that God had prepared for him. Thus all things were agitated in concert, for what was planned was the annihilation of death. **To the Ephesians 19.**[149]

The Demon Is Forced to Acknowledge His Conqueror. Tertullian: Let a person who is agreed to be troubled by demons be brought on the spot before your tribunal, and, when he is charged to speak, he will as freely confess the truth, that he is a demon, as he will elsewhere lyingly style himself a god. Likewise, let any one of those who are supposed to be under some divine visitation be brought forth . . . and if the demons do not confess themselves to the Christian, not daring to lie, spill the blood of that shameless Christian on the spot. **Apology 23.**[150]

The Transformation of the Wine

The Miracle at Cana Sanctifies Birth and Signifies Rebirth. Cyril of Alexandria: Opportunely he proceeds next to the beginning of his miracles, even if he seems to have been called to it without design. For a celebration was being held after a wedding—a

---

[143]Cf. Mt 8:29; Mk 5:7. [144]Mt 12:29. [145]An allusion to the mystical reading of the Song of Songs. Legends of Solomon's trafficking with demons were already known to Jews at the time of Christ and may have prompted his statement, in the wake of the controversy about Beelzebub, that a greater than Solomon is here (Mt 12:42). [146]PG 86.2:1979-80. [147]See 1 Cor 2:8; 2 Cor 4:4. The themes of silence and dissimulation were pervasive in Gnostic literature of the generation following Ignatius, as was the notion that God worked out his plan through a series of "ages" under the visible hegemony of obtuse angelic powers. [148]See Job 38:7 [149]AF 148. [150]TA 80.

decorous one, we may be quite sure—and the Savior's mother is present, while he, having also been invited, comes with his own disciples—more to work miracles than to join the festivities, though in addition to this he means to hallow the beginning of human generation. This we say so far as concerns the flesh. For it was necessary, as he was recapitulating[151] of human nature, entirely remolding it into a better condition, that he should not only dispense his bounty to those who had already been called into existence but also make grace available also for those yet unborn, hallowing their emergence into being. And now hear a third explanation of this act. It has been said to woman by God, "In pains you shall bear children."[152] How then were we to shake off this curse, how else were we to avoid reprobate marriages? This, too, our Savior resolved in his love of humanity. He, who is the mirth and joy of all, honored the marriage by his presence, so that he might banish the ancient malediction on childbearing. For "if anyone is in Christ, he is a new creation. And the old things have passed away," as Paul says, "and the new have come."[153] He comes, then, with his own disciples, to the marriage; for it was necessary that eager spectators of his marvels should be with the miracle worker, to take in what was accomplished as a sort of nourishment for the faith that was in them. But when the wine failed the guests, his mother called the good Lord to exhibit his wonted love of humanity, saying, "They have no wine." For she is urging him to perform a miracle, as one who has it in his power to do whatever he will.

"What have I to do with you, woman? My hour is not yet come." This too was an excellent saying that the Savior devised for our sake. For it was not right to go precipitately into action, or spontaneously as though to be seen as a miracle worker, but to approach this task reluctantly even when called and to meet a need rather than gratify the spectators. Moreover, the good issue of our desires seems to be somewhat more gratifying when it is not bestowed all at once on those who ask but is put off so that our hopes are ennobled by a short delay. Here as elsewhere Christ shows that the honor that we owe to our parents is of the highest by undertaking, out of reverence for his mother, what he had declined to do. COMMENTARY ON JOHN 2.1.[154]

IT HALLOWS A NATURAL LAW AND A HUMAN MYSTERY. AUGUSTINE: A dead man rose, and people wondered; so many are born every day, and no one wonders. If we consider more shrewdly, it is more of a miracle that that which had not existed should exist than that that which has existed should live again. It is, after all, the same God, the Father of our Lord Jesus Christ, who through his own Word does all these things and rules what he has created. The former miracles he did through the Word in his presence, the latter miracles he did through his own Word incarnated and made man on our account. As we wonder at what was done through Jesus the man, let us be amazed at what was done through Jesus as God. Through Jesus as God the heaven and the earth were made, the sea and the whole array of heaven, the wealth of the land, the fertility of the sea. All these things that lie before our eyes were made through Jesus as God. And we see these things, and if his own Spirit is in us, we admire them sufficiently to praise the designer and are not so turned to the works that we are turned away from the designer, setting our faces, as it were, toward what he has made and setting our backs against him who made it. . . .

All flesh is corruptible; it melts into rottenness unless it is held, as it were, by the seasoning of the soul. But this it has in common with the soul of the brute; more wonderful are those

---

[151]The Greek word *anakephalaioō* ("recapitulate," Eph 1:10) had been used since Irenaeus to describe the summing up of all humanity in Christ. [152]Gen 3:16. [153]2 Cor 5:17. [154]PG 73:224-25.

attributes that I spoke of, which belong to mind and intellect, where the human being is actually renewed in the image of him in whose image he was made. What will this force of the soul be when this body too has put on incorruption and this mortal has put on immortality? If it can do this through corruptible flesh, what will it be able to do through the spiritual body after the resurrection of the dead? Yet, as I have said, this soul of wondrous nature and substance is an invisible thing, known only to intellect, and nevertheless this too was made through Jesus as God, since he is the Word of God. "All things were made through him, and without him nothing was made."[155]

When, therefore, we see such great things done through Jesus as God, why do we wonder when water is turned into wine by Jesus the man? For he was not made man in such a way as to lose his Godhead.[156] As the man accrued to him, God was not lost. Thus the one who did this was the very one who made all those. Let us not, then, be amazed that God did it, but let us feel love because he did it among us and for our restoration. For there is something in the very event that gives a sign to us. I believe that it was not without cause that he came to the wedding. Leaving aside the miracle, there is something of a mystery and a sacrament hidden in the very event. Let us knock that he may open[157] and may make us drunk with invisible wine, since we too were but water, and he has made us wine making us wise;[158] for our wisdom is to have faith in him, when we were formerly unwise. And it may belong to that same wisdom, with honor to God, with praise of his majesty and with love for his overwhelming compassion, to understand what was effected in this miracle.

The Lord came by invitation to the wedding. What wonder if he came into that house for a wedding, when he came into this world for a wedding? For if he did not come for a wedding, he has no bride here. And what is it that the apostle says? "I have made you fit to present as a chaste virgin to one husband, Christ."[159] What is this fear of his lest the virginity of the bride of Christ be corrupted by the cunning of the devil? "I fear," he says, "lest, just as the serpent led Eve astray with his cunning, so your minds may be suborned from the simplicity and chastity which are in Christ."[160] Here, then, he has a bride whom he redeemed by his own blood and to whom he gave the Holy Spirit for a pledge. He rescued her from servitude to the devil, he died on account of her trespasses, he rose again for her justification.[161] Who will offer so much to his bride? Whatever beauties of the earth people may offer—gold, silver, precious stones, horses, estates, farms, spoils—would anyone offer his own blood? No, for if he has given his blood to his bride, there will be no one to take her to wife. The Lord, however, dying with impunity, gave his blood for her whom he was to have when he rose again, having already joined her to himself in the womb of the virgin. For the Word is the bridegroom and human flesh the bride, and the same one is equally Son of God and Son of man. From the place where he was made the head of the church—that womb of the virgin Mary, his bridal chamber—he came forth like a bridegroom from his own chamber, as the Scripture foretold: "And he himself, coming forth like a bridegroom from his own chamber, rejoices as a giant to run a race."[162] He came forth from the chamber like a bridegroom and came by invitation to a wedding. Tractates on the Gospel of John 8.1-4.[163]

HIS WORDS TO HIS MOTHER INDICATE HIS DIVINE CHARACTER. AUGUSTINE: By a certain sacramental grace, he appears not to

---

[155]Jn 1:3. [156]A clear denial of the kenotic theory, which maintains that the divine properties of the Word were laid aside in the incarnation. [157]Mt 25:11. [158]The Latin word also means to have taste; both the pun and the frequent repetition of the same term are characteristic of the homiletic manner in Augustine. [159]2 Cor 11:2, 3. [160]2 Cor 1:22. [161]Rom 4:25. [162]Ps 19:6. [163]CCL 36:82-84.

acknowledge the mother from whom he came forth as a bridegroom and to say to her, "What have I to do with you, woman? My hour is not yet come."[164] What does this mean? Was it his purpose, in coming to a wedding, to teach contempt for mothers? Surely the one whose wedding he had come to was taking a wife for the purpose of siring children and surely wished to be honored by those whom he hoped to sire. Had Jesus therefore come to the wedding in order that he might deprive his mother of honor, when it is for the sake of having children, whom God commands to honor their parents, that one celebrates a wedding or takes a wife at all?[165] . . .

Why then does the son say to his mother, "Woman, what have I to do with you? My hour has not yet come"? Our Lord Jesus Christ was both God and man. Insofar as he was God, he had no mother; he had one, insofar as he was man. She was, therefore, the mother of his flesh, the mother of his humanity, the mother of the weakness that he assumed for our sakes. But the miracle that he was about to do he was going to do by virtue of his divinity, not by virtue of his weakness; by virtue of being God, not by virtue of his natal weakness. But the weakness of God is stronger than human beings. Thus his mother demanded a miracle; he, who was on the point of performing a divine work, said, as it were—as though he did not acknowledge his human conception—"It was not you who gave birth to that in me which performs a miracle, you did not give birth to my divinity; but because you gave birth to my weakness, it will be time for me to take notice of you when that very weakness shall hang on the cross." For that is the meaning of "my hour is not yet come." For then it was that he took notice of her, though of course he had always known her. Even before he had been born from her he had known his mother by predestination; yes, even before he himself created as God, he knew the one through whom he himself would be created as man. But at a

certain hour, there was a mystery in his not acknowledging her, and at a certain hour that had not yet come there was a mystery in his acknowledging her again. TRACTATES ON THE GOSPEL OF JOHN 8.5, 9.[166]

THE TWO OR THREE MEASURES SIGNIFY THE TRINITY. AUGUSTINE: When the Father and Son are named, two measures are named, as it were; when, however, the Holy Spirit is understood along with them, three measures. Thus it is not said that the some vessels held two measures and others three but that all six held two or three measures.[167] It is as though it were to say, "Even when I say two, I wish the Spirit of the Father and the Son to be understood along with them; and when I say three, I affirm the Trinity itself more plainly."

And so whoever names the Father and the Son ought also to understand here the love, as it were, between Father and Son, which is the Holy Spirit. . . .

But there is another interpretation that is not to be overlooked, and I shall declare it. Let each choose what pleases him; what is provided we do not take away. For the table is the Lord's, and it is not for a servant to defraud the guests, least of all when they are so famished as your signs of hunger imply. The prophecy that was handed down from ancient times pertained to the salvation of all nations. Moses was sent, indeed, only to the people of Israel, and through him the Law was given to that people alone, and the very prophets were from that people and the very allocation of times was reckoned with respect to that same people, so that the vessels too are said to be "for the purification of the Jews." For all that it is patent that that prophecy was also addressed to other nations, seeing that Christ was hidden within it, and in him all nations are blessed as

---

[164]Jn 2:4. [165]Omitted is a digression in which Augustine refutes those who argued from this passage that Christ was not the son of Mary after the flesh. [166]CCL 36:84, 87. [167]Jn 2:6.

was promised to Abraham when the Lord said, "In your seed shall all nations be blessed."[168] It was not understood, however, because the water had not yet been turned to wine. TRACTATES ON THE GOSPEL OF JOHN 9.7-9.[169]

A SYMBOL OF INWARD REGENERATION. MAXIMUS THE CONFESSOR: When the Logos of God became man, he filled human nature once more with the spiritual knowledge that it had lost; and, steeling it against changefulness, he deified it, not in its essential nature but in its quality. He stamped it completely with his own Spirit, as if adding wine to water so as to give the water the quality of wine. For he becomes truly man so that by grace he may make us gods. SECOND CENTURY OF VARIOUS TEXTS 26.[170]

The Raising of Lazarus

JESUS' PRAYER IS ANSWERED BEFORE HE UTTERS IT. ORIGEN: As one who had been heard in matters that he had in mind only but had not yet brought forth in prayer, he says, "Father, I give you thanks because you have heard me."[171] Thus he was on the point of praying for the resurrection of Lazarus, and the only good God and Father,[172] anticipating his prayer, heard what was about to be said in his prayer. For these things, in the hearing of the multitude standing around him, the Savior renders thanks instead of a prayer, doing two things at the same time: he both gives thanks for his success in the case of Lazarus and brings about faith in the multitude standing around him. He wished them to accept that he had taken up residence in the present life at the commission of the Father. Now he knew that he had been heard, since he saw that the soul of Lazarus had been restored to his body, having been sent up from the place of souls.[173] For it is not to be imagined that the soul of Lazarus was present to his body after its departure, and that being close at hand, it instantly

heard Jesus crying out and saying, "Lazarus, come forth." If someone indeed supposes this to be true of the soul of Lazarus and entertains the absurd position that the soul, when quit of the body, remains close by it, let him say how Jesus was heard by the Father while the body of Lazarus remained dead, yet the soul (as one of those who say this would opine) remained close by the body even while separated. For we could endorse this only by saying that Jesus would not have been heard when he was about to be heard because the soul was still dwelling in the body. The circumstances were much the same, in my opinion, when he raised the daughter of the ruler of the synagogue,[174] having prayed concerning this. He prayed that the soul would return and make its dwelling again in the body. Whether or not such was also the case with respect to the widow's son on the bier,[175] you may inquire for yourself, so that you may arrive at a general conclusion for these passages, for such lengthy excursions are not to my present purpose. Now it may be that one so great as Jesus saw the very soul of Lazarus being brought already either by those appointed for these purposes or by the mere will of the Father when he had given ear to Jesus, and when he saw it pass through the place where the stone had been taken away, he said, "Father, I give you thanks because you have heard me." But since he had prayed also before this for countless other things and had succeeded, for this reason he gives thanks not only with regard to Lazarus but also with regard to the previous occasions. As to Lazarus he declares, "Father, I give you thanks," and as to

---

[168]Gen 22:18. [169]CCL 36:94-96. [170]*TP* 2:193. The last sentence alludes to Athanasius *On the Incarnation* 54.3; the language of deification should be interpreted by reference to Jn 10:34-35 and Ps 82:6. [171]Jn 11:41. [172]See Mk 10:18; Jude 25. [173]*Apokatastasis*, or "restoration," is Origen's term for the end designed for us by God; as is clear from the present passage, this does not entail the return of the soul to a disembodied state. Origen's belief that the souls of the just are detained in hades is supported by appeal to 1 Sam 28:8ff. in his brief treatise *On the Sorceress*. [174]Lk 8:55. [175]Lk 7:12.

the previous occasions, "I knew that you hear me always"; and all this, he says, I have said for the sake of the multitude standing around, that they may believe that you have sent me. Commentary on John 28.6.[176]

He Dissembles His Knowledge Because God's Plan Is Inscrutable. Augustine: As for his question, when he says, "Where have you laid him?"[177] I consider this to signify his calling of us, which takes place in secret; for his calling of us is secretly predestined. It is to illustrate this mystery that the Lord asks a question as though he were ignorant, just as the apostle says, "That I may know, as I also am known."[178] Or it may be because in another place the Lord represents himself as not knowing sinners, saying, "I know you not." That was the meaning of Lazarus's burial, since in his regimen and commandments there is no sin. Of a piece with this question is the one in Genesis, "Adam, where are you?"[179] because he had sinned and had hidden his face from God. This secrecy is represented by this burial, so that when Lazarus dies he is the image of the sinner, and when buried he is the image of one who is hidden from the face of God. On Eighty-Three Varied Questions 65.[180]

God Cannot Be Ignorant. Origen: As for the words "Where have you laid him,"[181] you need not be surprised that these are said as though in ignorance. For the Scripture predicates ignorance not only of the Savior but even of the Father in the text, "If one among you thinks he is spiritual, let him know that what I write to you is of God; but if one knows not, he is not known."[182] He asks, "Where have you laid him," as he also bids his disciples release the dead.[183] Fragments on John 83.[184]

The Miracle Is the Common Work of Son and Father. Origen: Now my question is whether Jesus fulfilled the words "I go that I may wake him," which he added to the remark,

"Our friend Lazarus has fallen asleep."[185] My conjecture is that he did so in crying out with a loud voice when he said, "Lazarus, come forth." For it might be said, not without reason, that the great voice and the cry were the cause of his waking.[186] And it seems possible, if need be, to demonstrate that it was in this that the words "I go that I may wake him" were fulfilled, rather than that the Father, on hearing the prayer of the Son, caused the soul to return to the body of Lazarus as it lay in his tomb. For one might say that the Father, having heard the Son's prayer, raised up Lazarus from the dead, while the Son, when he cried out in a great voice saying, "Lazarus, come forth," fulfilled what he had announced beforehand, "I go that I may wake him." And one who construes it in this way will distinguish the sayings "Lazarus our friend has fallen asleep" and "Lazarus has died." He will say that "I go that I may wake him" corresponds to the saying "Lazarus has fallen asleep," while there is no saying "I go that I may raise him up" corresponding to "Lazarus has died." But one who resolves this apparent difference and grants that the raising of Lazarus from the dead was the common work of the Son who prayed and the Father who heard him, will cite the Lord's words to Martha when he said, "I am the resurrection and the life."[187] And he will add the saying, "For as the Father wakes the dead and makes them alive, so the Son makes alive those whom he will."[188] Commentary on John 28.9.[189]

Even His Grief Betrays His Divinity. Origen: When he was at a distance from the tomb, he was vexed in spirit.[190] But when he comes near to the corpse, he is no longer vexed in spirit but represses the vexation within himself. Thus it is written, inwardly vexed, he

---

[176]SC 385:80-84. [177]Jn 11:34. [178]1 Cor 13:12. [179]Gen 3:9. [180]CCL 44A:147-48. [181]Jn 11:34. [182]1 Cor 14:37-38. [183]Jn 11:35. [184]COJG 291-92. [185]Jn 1:11. [186]Jn 11:43. [187]Jn 11:25. [188]Jn 5:21. [189]SC 385:96-98. [190]Jn 11:33.

comes to the tomb. And again he rebukes the passion, so that we may know that he became a man unchangeably, as we are. There was the cave and the stone lay across it; for Lazarus had been laid not in some built tomb but in one carved out in the rock.[191] And possibly the words "Woe to those who build sepulchers and tombs"[192] were spoken on this account. For houses and a ship are what ought to be built, and whatever there is that may be of use to the living. Then he says, "Take away the stone." Since the cave was a tomb, he did not put his own hand to the stone but bade others, who were suited to the task, to take it away. By contrast, Jacob himself had to take hold of the obstacle at the mouth of the well in Genesis[193] that hindered the sheep from drinking. . . . In short, it was necessary for Jacob to approach the well himself, but for Jesus only to stand outside the tomb. COMMENTARY ON JOHN, FRAGMENT 84.[194]

DETAILS ADD TO THE COGENCY OF THE MIRACLE.

HIPPOLYTUS: What need was there to weep for one whom he was going to raise before long? Jesus wept as an example to us of sympathy and humanity to one's own kind. Jesus wept in order that he might give the lesson of weeping with those who weep in deeds rather than in words. "Jesus wept." He wept but did not grieve. To be without tears he rejected as harsh and inhuman, but addiction to grief he eschewed as base and unmanly. Rather, he wept, giving sympathy its due place. He comes to the cave and contemplates the stone lying across the tomb. He orders the Jews standing by to roll away the stone, from the mouth of the cave. Now this is the man who says, "If you have faith like a grain of mustard seed, you will say to this mountain, 'Get up and throw yourself into the sea, and that will come to pass for you.' "[195] How, Jesus, are you now unable to roll away the stone? "No," he says, "it is not as being unable that I do this, but so that they may not suppose the miracle to be an illusion. I command the Jews themselves to roll away the stone with their own hands, leaving the greatest sign to myself, so that they may become witnesses of the signs that I perform." ON LAZARUS.[196]

EVEN THE DELAY ADDS TO THE PROBATIVE FORCE OF THE MIRACLE.

HIPPOLYTUS: What necessity was there for the Lord to wait after hearing the news and not to go at once to the one who was sick? Undoubtedly, he tarried after Lazarus's death in order that in the death greater faith might accrue to those who beheld his miracles. . . . Can you not bring the dead to life even where you are? "But, if I am absent, the Jews will not acknowledge the grace; for perhaps when he has risen, they will suppose that Lazarus has come to life again by some stroke of fortune. Therefore, I myself go to be there, so that in my presence they may become eyewitnesses of the miracles that I perform, and, receiving grace from me, may be brought to steadfast faith." ON LAZARUS.[197]

THIS MIRACLE IS AT ONCE PARABLE AND FACT.

AUGUSTINE: Although we hold with full belief to the resurrection of Lazarus as related in the evangelical history, I nonetheless have no doubt that it also signifies something allegorically. Nor when events are allegorized do they cease to be believed in as events, as is the case when Paul explains that the two sons of Abraham are allegorically the two covenants.[198] Therefore, let us take Lazarus in the tomb to be in allegory the soul overwhelmed by earthly sins—that is, the human race, which the Lord in another place represents as a lost sheep,[199] for the liberation that he says he has come down, leaving the other ninety-nine in the hills. ON EIGHTY-THREE VARIED QUESTIONS 65.[200]

---

[191]Jn 11:38. [192]Lk 11:47. [193]Gen 29:10. [194]COJG 292. [195]Mt 17:20. [196]GCS 1.2:224-25. [197]GCS 1.2:217. [198]Gal 4:22-24. [199]Mt 18:12. [200]CCL 44A:147.

THE WRAPPINGS THAT HAMPER LAZARUS ARE A PARABLE FOR US. ORIGEN: Now you must know that even now there is many a Lazarus who, after enjoying the friendship of Jesus, grows weak and dies, tarries in the tombs and the place of the dead, dead among the dead, then after this is made alive by the prayer of Jesus and emerges from the tomb to the world outside it at the call of Jesus with his great voice. . . . You must think of a man as being in the underworld when after having received knowledge of the truth and been enlightened, tasting the heavenly gift and becoming a partaker of the Holy Spirit, having tasted indeed the good word of God and the powers of the age to come, he departs from Christ and runs back to the life of the unconverted. When, therefore, Jesus comes on behalf of such a one to his tomb, then standing outside it makes his prayer and is heard, praying that his voice and his words may be imbued with power, he cries out in a great voice, calling the one who has been such a friend to him to that which lies without the life of the unconverted, their tomb and cell. And in the case of one who follows Jesus one sees that he in a sense is such a one when he comes out on account of Jesus' voice but is still bound and swathed in the bands of his own sins: although he lives by virtue of his repentance and his heeding of Jesus' voice, he has nonetheless not yet rid himself of the bonds of sin and is, consequently, unable yet to walk on his feet with freedom, or even to be his own man in matters indifferent, because his feet and his hands are bound with the grave clothes that bind the dead. And because of the deadness within him, not only is such a one bound hand and foot, but also his vision is obscured and circumscribed by ignorance. Jesus has resolved that he shall not only continue to live in the tomb, but this man's bonds, as was said above, prevent him from living when he has come to the outside of the tomb. And because, inasmuch as he is bound, he cannot emerge from the tomb, Jesus says to those who are able to help him, "Release him, and let him come." My view is that when such a one came out of the tomb, he had not assented to the word of conversion after sinning but was still too weak to live according to Christ, because the progressive, productive and contemplative powers of his soul were still constrained; and he was still bound hand and foot by the grave clothes, and his vision was circumscribed by the headcloth.[201] But when Jesus had spoken to those who were able to release him, then through the command of Christ as Lord—"Release him, and let him come"—his hands and feet were loosed, and the veil that lay on his vision was put away; then he walks such a path as to be himself one of those who recline with Jesus.[202] COMMENTARY ON JOHN 28.7.[203]

The Feeding of the Multitude

THE FEEDING MAY BE INTERPRETED TYPOLOGICALLY. AUGUSTINE: The five loaves of barley with which the Lord fed the multitude on the mountain[204] signify the old law. This is either because it was given to those who were not yet spiritual but still carnal—that is, devoted to the five senses of the body, the multitude itself amounting to five thousand people—or else because the Law was given through Moses, and Moses wrote five books. And in being loaves of barley they aptly signify either the Law itself—which was given in such a way that the vital nourishment of the soul was hidden under corporeal symbols, just as the heart of the barley is hidden under a very tenacious husk—is the populace, which was not yet stripped of carnal desire, which clung to their heart like the husk. In other words, they were not yet circumcised in heart—so much so that even the threshing of tribulation,

---

[201]In his *Commentary on John* 28.8, Origen likens this to the veil across the face of Moses (Ex 34:33; 2 Cor 3:13-15). [202]Jn 12:2. [203]SC 385:86-92. [204]Jn 6:1ff.

when they were led through the wilderness for forty years, did not cause them to put off the carnal envelope when the true sense was revealed, just as barley is not divested of the enveloping husk on the threshing floor. And thus the Law was appropriately given to that populace.

As for the two fish, which gave a sweet savor to the loaves, they seem to signify the two characters by whom that populace was ruled, so that their own counsels were moderated by them. These, of course, were the characters of the king and the priest, to whom also the hallowed rite of anointing pertained. It was their duty never to be broken or depraved by the winds and tides of the populace and frequently to break through the violent discords of the multitude as though through adverse waves, occasionally resigning, as conscience demanded, what had been entrusted to them, and generally conducting themselves, as they governed the turbulent populace, like fish in a stormy sea. Now these two characters foreshadowed our Lord, for it was he alone who sustained both characters, fulfilling both not figuratively but in the proper sense. For Jesus Christ is our king, having given us an example of fighting and conquering, taking on our sins in his mortal flesh and never succumbing to the enemy's temptations, however seductive or fearful, then at last divesting himself of the flesh to make a show of principalities and powers, triumphing over them in his own person. And thus by that same leader we are delivered from the burdens and labors of our present pilgrimage as though from Egypt, and the sins that pursue us are drowned when we escape them by the sacrament of baptism.[205] And so long as we live in hope of that promise that we do not yet see, we are as it were led through the desert, consoled by the word of God in Scripture as they were consoled by the manna from heaven. And we trust that by that same leader we can be led into the heavenly Jerusalem as into the promised land, receiving there eter-

nal salvation under his kingship and tutelage. Thus our Lord Jesus Christ is shown to be our king. At the same time, he is also our priest for eternity after the order of Melchizedek,[206] having presented himself as burnt offering for our sins and enjoining a rite analogous to this sacrifice as a memorial of his own passion, so that what Melchisedek presented to God we now see to be presented throughout the world in the church of Christ. . . .

And likewise that second feeding of the populace,[207] which was performed with seven loaves, is rightly understood to allude to the preaching of the new covenant. For it is not said by any of the Evangelists that these loaves were of barley, as John said of those five. This feeding with seven loaves, then, alludes to the grace of the church, which is known by that famous sevenfold operation of the Holy Spirit.[208] And thus it is not written that there were two fishes in this case, as in the old law where two alone were anointed, the king and the priest, but several fish—that is, the first who believed in the Lord Jesus Christ and were anointed in his name and were sent to preach the gospel and to weather the turbulent sea of the present age, so that, as Paul the apostle says,[209] they might act as ambassadors for the great fish, that is, for Christ. Nor in that multitude were there five thousand people, as in that other one where those who received the law carnally (that is, were devoted to the five senses) were signified, but four thousand instead, a number that signifies spiritual persons, because of the four virtues of the mind by which one lives spiritually in the present life—prudence, temperance, courage and justice. The first is the knowledge of what things

---

[205]Emerging from the font, the believer leaves his sins behind, as the Israelites left Pharaoh's host behind in the waters of the Red Sea. [206]Heb 6:20; Ps 110:4. [207]Mk 8:1-9 and other references. [208]Is 11:2. [209]2 Cor 5:20. Christ was often symbolized in Augustine's time by the Greek word *ICHTHUS* ("fish"), which served as an acronym for *Iēsous Christos Theou Huios Sōtēr* ("Jesus Christ, God's Son, Savior").

are to be desired or shunned, the second the restraint of our craving for things that bring temporal pleasure, the third constancy of mind in the face of temporal adversity, the fourth—diffused through all the rest—the love of God and one's neighbor.[210]

Furthermore it is reported that women and children were excluded from the reckoning of the five thousand and the four thousand.[211] To me this seems to have the purpose of apprising us that among the people of the old covenant there were some too weak to fulfill the righteousness that is according to the Law (the righteousness in which the apostle Paul says that he persevered without blemish), and others again who were easily seduced into the veneration of idols. Both characteristics—that is, weakness and error—are adumbrated by the terms "women" and "children." . . . And thus neither in the old covenant nor in the new are such people counted in the number; on the contrary, both the five thousand in one place and the four thousand in another are said to have excluded women and children. On Eighty-Three Varied Questions 61.1-2, 4-5.[212]

The Miraculous Feedings Prefigure the Sacraments. Ambrose: Consider which is nobler, the food of angel or the flesh of Christ, which is the body of life. The one was manna from heaven; the other is above the heavens. Where that was heavenly, this belongs to the Lord of heaven. That was liable to corruption if kept for another day; this was a stranger to all corruption, and if anyone tastes it with reverence it will be impossible for him to experience corruption. For the Israelites water flowed from the rock; you have blood from Christ. They were satisfied with water for the occasion; the blood washes you for eternity. The Jew drinks and thirsts; for you, once you have drunk, thirst will be impossible. And that was in shadow, this is in truth. On the Mysteries 8.48.[213]

The Manna Was Both a Blessing and a Temptation. Hilary of Poitiers: Now this also must be considered, that the manna is given to try them, to discern, by each person's observance of the law, whether he is apt to follow the precepts of God. For thus it is written: "God said to Moses, 'Behold, I shall rain down bread from the heavens for you, and the people shall go out and collect it, one day at a time for that day, that I may test them to see whether they are walking in my law or not.' "[214] Of the flesh, meanwhile, it is said, "In the evening you shall eat in flesh, and in the morning you shall be filled with bread." By flesh, then, is signified the meal at evening, and by bread the satisfaction of appetite in the morning. Thus so far as concerns the flesh, the point is that the people remained in the wilderness, detained by their habitual desire, for they desired the fleshpots of Egypt. This flesh they consume in the evening, which means that they are unfaithful to God and unwilling to wait on his promises until the end of the age (which is what evening signifies) because they indulge the desires of the world (which are frequently signified by Egypt). Thus it was that the people had this flesh once only, that we might learn that it was given not for their needs but to indicate the presence of a type. In the manna, however, there is a testing, for through it the people are tested as to whether they will be obedient to God—that is, whether they will be worthy to receive the true bread from heaven. And what this testing means we must discover from the sequel.

It is found in the morning, for this time of the heavenly food is that of the Lord's resurrection. The same quantity is provided for every age and sex, which is incongruous with regard to human nature—for when does the same amount suffice for a child and for a

---

[210]These were the four cardinal virtues of pagan philosophy, justice being regarded in Plato's *Republic* as the virtue that regulates the other three. [211]Mt 14:21; 15:38. [212]CCL 44A:120-22, 126-28. [213]CSEL 73:109-10. [214]Ex 16:4.

grown man?—whereas with regard to our spiritual archetype it is quite proper that the heavenly bread should be dispensed equally to all. Its working is not piecemeal—for to those who understand, we are speaking of a sacrament—and there is no surfeit for any of the great, no lack for any of the less, since all of course are satisfied equally by the food that they have consumed piecemeal. By contrast, those which are gathered in excess and are left over in the morning suffer maggots and putrefaction. This intimates, not obscurely, that when people gather more than they need, beyond the dispensation of heaven and the teaching of the Spirit, the results are noisome in content, that is, corrupted from the truth. And they seethe with demonic vices—that is, are heaving with maggots—in the warmth of the sun; that is, they will be liquidated when Christ, who is the sun of righteousness,[215] returns for judgment. ON THE MYSTERIES 39-40.[216]

The Healings

MIRACLES OF HEALING ASSIST WEAK FAITH. CYRIL OF ALEXANDRIA: The nobleman[217] approaches him as one with power to heal but does not yet perceive him to be God by nature. "Lord" he calls him indeed but does not yet ascribe to him the true measure of lordship. For in that case he would at once have implored him as a suppliant, not by any means to walk with him to his own home and approach the invalid youth in his company, but much rather to drive away the illness that had afflicted him with an authoritative commandment, worthy of God. For what need was there for him to be in the presence of the sick man when it was easily within his power to restore him even at a distance? And is it not profoundly ignorant to suppose of him that he is stronger than death, and yet to have no notion that one so full of god-like strength is properly God? While the mind remains obstinate in error, the miraculous is stronger

than the word that calls them to faith. For this reason the Savior declares that they have more need of wonders so that they may be easily taught to change for their own advantage and to acknowledge that he is God by nature. The nobleman is certainly somewhat inclined to understanding, but he speaks like a child in his request for a favor and babbles weakly without perceiving it. For his petition would have been most fittingly presented if he had believed not only that Christ has power when present but also that he is fully able to work even at a distance. As it is, his words and actions are incongruous, since he is begging for power that befits God but does not think that as God he fills all things, or even that he will prove stronger than death, though he urges him to exert his power over one who is all but vanquished; for the youth was on the point of death.

This is how a believer should have come to him, but Christ, we see, does not strive with our ignorance. On the contrary, as God, he is liberal even to those who stumble. Notwithstanding all that the man has failed to do, he teaches him what he ought to have found miraculous even had he done it, revealing himself at once as a teacher of the loftiest virtues and as the provider of goods that are prayed for. For in the word *go*, faith is implied, and in "your son lives" the fulfillment of his desires is expressed, with a certain great authority, worthy of God. One command of the Savior heals two souls, for he causes an unwonted faith to work in the nobleman, while he snatches the youth from bodily death. Who was healed before whom it is very difficult to say, for both, in my view, were healed at the same juncture, when the illness was relieved at our Savior's bidding. The servants who came to meet him announced the cure of the youth and at the same time disclosed the rapid effect of the

---

[215]Mal 4:2. [216]SC 19:136-38. [217]Jn 4:47ff. The rebuke to the nobleman at Jn 4:48 has puzzled scholars; Cyril assumes that it is the desire to witness the healing that gives offense.

divine commandments. This was a manifest part of the plan of Christ, as he strengthened the diffident master in faith by the prompt fulfilment of his hope. COMMENTARY ON JOHN 2.5.[218]

THE CLEANSING OF THE LEPER IS AN EPITOME OF SALVATION. HILARY OF POITIERS: A leper is at hand. He begs to be made clean and is made pure at a touch by the power of the Word.[219] He is commanded to be silent, yet to show himself to the priest and to offer the gift that Moses required to serve as a testimony. In the leper, then, is exhibited the healing of the multitude who hear and believe and come down from the mountain with the Lord. They are sullied with the foul defilement of the body, and on hearing the proclamation of the kingdom, they beg to be healed. They are vouchsafed a touch of the body, they are healed by the force of the Word, and so that this salvation may not be offered more than it is sought, silence is commanded and they are bidden to show themselves to the priests. This is so that he may be seen to have been announced beforehand in the Law by deeds and works and that the force of the Word may be perceived in those matters in which the Law was weak. The one who is made pure is also to offer to God a trophy of the salvation that he has received, but that gift is not to be from his ancestors: that same person, having been cleansed of the filth of bodily sins, must undertake the sacrifice to God, because the precepts by Moses in the Law were not efficacious but declarative. COMMENTARY ON MATTHEW 7.2.[220]

BETHSAIDA[221] WAS KNOWN TO OBSERVERS IN THE FOURTH CENTURY. EUSEBIUS: Bethsaida is a fishpool in Jerusalem, which is also called the sheep pool. Initially it had five porticoes. And now, in the place where it appears, there are two lakes, one of which is filled by the annual rains, while the water in the other is seen to be strangely empurpled—bearing a trace, as they declare, of the victims who of old were purified there. And this, too, is the reason for its being called the sheep pool, because of the sacrifices. ONOMASTICON.[222]

THE INVALID IS A PARADIGM OF MORTALITY. AUGUSTINE: It should not be a wonder when God performs a miracle, for it would have been a wonder had a mortal performed it. We should rather rejoice than wonder, and rather because our Lord and Savior Jesus Christ was made a man than because as God he wrought divine works among humans. For what he did for the sake of humanity matters more to our salvation than what he did among humans, and his healing of the vices of the soul matters more than his healing of sicknesses in the bodies of those who were going to die. But because the soul did not recognize the one by whom it needed to be healed and had eyes in the flesh that enabled it to witness bodily actions but did not yet have sound eyes in the heart that would enable it to recognize God in hiding, he did what could be seen, so that the soul might be healed by means that could not be seen. He entered a place where there was a great multitude of the sick, the blind, the lame, the withered. Being a physician both of souls and of bodies, and one who had come to heal all the souls of those who were going to believe, he chose from the sick one whom he would heal as a demonstration of unity. If we consider his work with mean intelligence—as it were with human insight and sagacity— and as touching only his power, he did not achieve anything great; and even as touching his benevolence, he did little. So many were lying there, and he cured one, when he could have raised them all by a single word. What, therefore, should we understand if not that the chief question for that power and goodness was how much instruction souls would draw

---

[218]PG 73:332-33. [219]Mt 8:1-4. [220]PL 9:954-55. [221]Bethesda (Jn 5:2); also rendered as Beth-zatha. [222]EOBO 58-59.

from his acts with regard to their everlasting salvation, rather than how much bodies deserved with regard to their temporal health?[223] For it is at the end, at the resurrection of the dead, that bodies will obtain that true health that we await from God. Then that which lives shall not die; that which is healed shall not suffer illness; that which is filled shall not hunger or thirst; that which is renewed shall not grow old. In the present world, however, in those acts of our Lord and Savior Jesus Christ, the eyes of the blind are opened, but closed by death, and the hampered limbs of cripples are dissolved by death. In short, whatever healing mortal limbs have received in the temporal realm, it has failed at the end; whereas the soul that has believed has made the passage to eternal life. It was, therefore, to the soul that will believe, whose sins he had come to remit, abasing himself to heal its sicknesses, that he gave this great sign in his healing of the sick man. The deep mystery contained in this work and sign I shall explain to you according to my abilities, so far as God deigns to grant this, while you attend and assist my weakness with your prayers.

Many times, as I recall, I have treated of this fishpool, surrounded by five colonnades, where there lay a great multitude of this sick; and for many of my audience what I am about to say will be not so much a lesson as the repetition of one. But it is not at all beside my purpose even to repeat what is familiar, so that those who were not familiar with it may receive instruction, while those who were may be strengthened. As being familiar, then, they should be lightly and briefly expounded, and without redundant emphasis. That fishpool and that water seem to me to have signified the Jewish people. That peoples are signified by the names of waters the revelation of John teaches us openly, where many waters are shown to him and when he asks what they are he receives the answer that they are peoples.[224] Thus that water, that is, that people, was

fenced around by the five books of Moses as though by five porticoes. Those books, however, exposed the sick without healing them; for the Law convicted sinners, yet did not pardon them. Thus the Law without grace created criminals, who when they confessed were liberated by grace. For this is what the apostle says: "For had a law been given that was able to give life, then certainly righteousness would be from the Law."[225] Why then was the Law given? He continues, saying, "And Scripture has concluded all are under sin, that the promise through faith in Christ Jesus might be given to those who believe." What could be more obvious? Have not these words made plain to us both the five porticoes and the multitude of the sick? . . .

How, then, was it the case that they were healed in that troubled water when they were not able to be healed in the porticoes? For the water was seen to be troubled all of a sudden, and the one who troubled it was not seen. Even if you believe that angelic power was the regular cause of this, it does not follow that there was no mysterious signification in it. After the troubling of the water, one who could would put himself in and would be healed alone; but whoever put himself in after this one would act in vain. What, then, is the meaning of this, if not that the one Christ came to the Jewish people and by doing great works and teaching useful lessons he troubled sinners, troubling the water by his presence, and made them the instruments of his passion? But he troubled them secretly: "For if they had known, they would never have crucified the Lord of glory."[226] To go down into the troubled water is thus to have humble faith in the passion of the Lord. There one was healed signifying unity; after that, whoever came was not healed, for

---

[223] The Latin word *salus* means both "health" and "salvation." The Arminian hypothesis that God offers grace to those whose acceptance of it he foresees is rejected in later works on the grounds that it leaves too much to the human will. [224] Rev 17:15. [225] Gal 3:21-22. [226] 1 Cor 2:8.

whoever was outside the unity was incapable of being healed. TRACTATES ON THE GOSPEL OF JOHN 17.1-3.[227]

A CHURCH SUCCEEDED THE ANGEL. JOHN OF DAMASCUS: You may rejoice, sheep pool, now that you are the most hallowed precinct of the mother of God. You may rejoice, sheep pool, as the ancestral lodging of the queen. You may rejoice, sheep pool, for of old you were the fold of the sheep of Joachim, while now you are the heaven-imitating church of the spiritual flock of Christ. There was a time when once a year this place received the angel of God, who troubled the spring and healed but one, relieving him of the disease that oppressed him; now, however, it holds the plenitude of the heavenly powers, who hymn with us the Mother of God. HOMILY ON THE NATIVITY 1.11[228]

THE ANGEL RETURNS IN THE FONT. TERTULLIAN: If it seems a new thing that an angel should enter the waters, an example of what was to come went before: an angel entered the waters of the fishpool in Bethsaida and troubled them. Those who were complaining of invalidity watched for this, because if anyone went down there before the rest, the bathing became an end to his complaint. This medicine for the body was a figurative omen of a spiritual medicine, on the principle that carnal events are always anticipatory figures of spiritual events. And accordingly, with the universal advance of the grace of God, the angel and the waters received new powers. Where they cured the infirmities of the body, they give medicine to the spirit. Where they brought about temporal health, they now renew eternal health. Where they delivered one in a year, they now daily deliver whole peoples, having blotted out death through the washing away of transgressions. Obviously, when the guilt is taken away, the punishment, too, is taken away. Thus humanity is restored to God in the likeness of him who had been previously

in the image of God—the image belongs to the one who was fashioned, the likeness to eternity. For it recovered that Spirit of God which, though it received it at that time by insufflation,[229] it subsequently lost through transgression. It is not that we attain to the Holy Spirit in the water but that once our ways have been mended by the angel we are prepared for the Holy Spirit. Here also a figure went before: for just as John was the harbinger of the Lord, preparing his ways, so also the angel who presides at baptism makes the ways straight for the Spirit of God, once the abolition of sins that faith solicits has been conveyed under the sign of the Father, the Son and the Holy Spirit. ON BAPTISM 5-6.[230]

THE MAN'S BED REPRESENTS OUR NEIGHBOR. AUGUSTINE: This sick man is cured by the Lord who is present; but what does he say to him first? Do you wish to be healed? He replies that he has no man by whom he may be put into the pool. Truly a man was necessary to that man for his healing, but it was that man who is also God. "For there is one God, and also one mediator of God and humanity, the man Christ Jesus."[231] Thus the man who was needed had come; why then was the healing deferred? "Rise," he says, "take up your bed, and walk." Three things he says, "Rise, take up your bed, and walk." "Rise," however, was not a command to work but the working of health. Yet he gave two commands to the healthy man: "take up your bed, and walk." I ask you, why was it not enough to say "walk"? Or in any case why was it not enough to say "rise"? For when

---

[227]CCL 36:169-71. [228]PG 96:677. [229]Like Origen (*On First Principles* 3.6.1), Tertullian believes that the likeness of God (Gen 1:26) is distinct from the image and a guarantee of eternal life. With Irenaeus (*Against Heresies* 5.6.1), he also holds that this likeness is conferred by the Holy Spirit, which (in contrast to his teaching elsewhere) he here believes to have been infused into Adam's nostrils (Gen 2:7). Whether Adam fully possessed the likeness that he is said to have lost, rather than the promise or foretaste of it, is not clear in this passage, any more than at Irenaeus *Against Heresies* 5.16. [230]CCL 1:281-82. [231]1 Tim 2:5.

he had risen in a state of health, he would not have remained in the place. Surely he had risen in order to depart. It also strikes me that he gave two precepts though he found less than two men lying there, as though in requiring two things he effected less. How, then, are we to discover in these two commands of the Lord those two precepts of charity that are signified? "Take up your bed," says he, "and walk." What those two precepts are, brethren, remember with me; for they ought to be very familiar and should not come into your minds only when you recollect them but should never be erased from your hearts. Consider it at all times your absolute duty to love God and your neighbor: "God with your whole heart, with your whole soul, with your whole mind, and your neighbor as yourself."[232] This at all times you must consider, must think on, must keep in mind, must perform, must fulfill. Love of God is first in the order of instruction, but in the order of performance, love of neighbor is first. For the one who enjoined this love on you in two precepts did not commend your neighbor to you first and then God, but first God, then your neighbor. You, however, since you do not yet see God, deserve that you should see him by loving your neighbor. . . . But so far it is obscure and an explanation is needed, I think, as to why the love of neighbor is commended in the taking up of the bed. Otherwise, it might perhaps offend us that the neighbor is commended through a blockish and senseless object. Let not the neighbor be angry if he is commended to us through an object that lacks soul and feeling. Our Lord and Savior Jesus Christ is described as the cornerstone so that he might make himself a foundation for two.[233] He is also called the rock, from which the water flowed; and the rock was Christ.[234] What wonder, then, if Christ was the rock, that the neighbor should be wood? Not, however, just any kind of wood, in the same way as that was not just any kind of rock, but one from which water flowed out for the thirsty; and not just

any kind of stone, but that of the corner, which served as the junction of two walls approaching from opposite directions. Likewise, you should not regard your neighbor as just any kind of wood, but a bed. What is there in a bed, I pray you? What, except that in sickness that man was carried on a bed, but in health it was he who carried the bed? What was it that the apostle said? "Bear one another's burdens, and thus you will fulfill the law of Christ."[235] The law of Christ, then, is charity, and charity is not fulfilled unless we carry one another's burdens. "Bearing each other in love," he says, "intent on preserving the unity of the Spirit in the bond of peace."[236] When you were sick, your neighbor carried you; you, having been made healthy, must carry your neighbor. Bear one another's burdens, and thus you will fulfill the law of Christ. So you will fill up what was lacking for you.[237] But when you have taken him up, do not stay: walk. By loving your neighbor and taking thought for your neighbor, you make a journey. And where do you make your journey, if not to the Lord God, to him whom we are bound to love with the whole heart, the whole soul, the whole mind? For we have not yet reached the Lord, but our neighbor we have with us. Carry, therefore, the one with whom you walk, that you may come to him with whom you desire to remain. TRACTATES ON THE GOSPEL OF JOHN 17.7-9.[238]

Miracles and the Law

THE HEALING OF THE PARALYTIC FULFILLS A PROPHECY. TERTULLIAN: A paralyzed man is also healed,[239] and in a crowd at that, with the people looking on. For as Isaiah says, "The people shall see the exaltation of the Lord and the glory of God."[240] What exaltation and what glory? "Be strengthened, feeble hands

---

[232]Lk 10:27. [233]That is, for Jews and Gentiles; Eph 2:14-20. [234]1 Cor 10:4. [235]Gal 6:2. [236]Eph 4:2-3. [237]Col 1:24. [238]CCL 36:174-75. [239]Mk 2:1-12; Jn 5:1-9. [240]Is 35:2.

and feeble knees; this will be the paralysis. Be strengthened, and do not fear." The repetition of "be strengthened" is not redundant, nor does he add to no purpose "and do not fear," since with the restoration of limbs he was also promising renewal of powers: Arise and take up your bed. He promised renewal also of mental vigor, so that he would not fear those who were about to say, Who is to forgive sins but God alone? Thus you see fulfilled a prophecy of a particular healing and of the things that followed the healing. Likewise you must acknowledge that Christ is the one who remits sins in the same prophet: Since, he says, amid many he shall forgive their sins and our transgressions he himself bears away.[241] . . . Therefore you must first deny that the Creator was ever indulgent to trespasses, and your next task is to show that he never prophesied such a thing of his own Christ. Then, no doubt, you will prove that thesis of yours—a new benevolence in a new Christ, so long as you have proved that he was neither the Father's peer nor prophesied by the Father. But anyway, whether the remission of sins is the business of one who is said not to be keeping toll of them or absolution the business of one who does not even exercise condemnation, and whether it could be proper for one to pardon a sin when he is not the injured party—having addressed these points already, I prefer to mention them here rather than handle them again. AGAINST MARCION 4.10.1-2, 4-5.[242]

CHRIST HONORED THE SABBATH OF THE CREATOR. TERTULLIAN: With regard to the sabbath too I observe at the outset that this question could not arise had Christ not proclaimed himself "lord of the sabbath."[243] For there would have been no controversy as to his reason for breaching the sabbath if it had been his duty to breach it. And it would have been his duty to breach it if it had pertained to another God, and no one would have been surprised at his doing what was proper for

him. Thus the reason for their wonder was that it was not proper for him to proclaim God the Creator and to violate his sabbath. And, in order that we may settle all primary questions, and not bring up the same things in reply to every opposing argument that relies on some new teaching of Christ, this stipulation will hold good throughout—that where there is controversy concerning the novelty of some teaching, it is because there had so far been no novelty or controversy in what was said of God. Nor can it be retorted that Christ gave sufficient proof of another deity by the very novelty of his teaching in each instance, when it was agreed that the very novelty, foretold by the Creator, was not to be wondered at in Christ. Undoubtedly he ought first to have revealed another God, and after that introduced his rule, since it is God who gives authority to the rule, not the rule to God—though obviously it may be the case that Marcion did not acquire such perverse arguments from a teacher, but his teacher through the arguments. The rest of what concerns the sabbath I explain as follows. If Christ overthrew the sabbath, he did so in keeping with the Creator's example, seeing that the ark of the testament, carried around for eight days, including the sabbath, during the siege of the city of Jericho, breached the sabbath "by working"—as those believe who think the same thing about Christ, not knowing that neither Christ nor the Creator in fact breached the sabbath, as we shall now prove. Nonetheless, the sabbath was in fact broken at that time through Joshua, in order that this also might be later referred to Christ. Even if he vented his hatred on the most solemn day of the Jews, as not being the Christ of the Jews, he acknowledged the Creator at the same time by his hatred of the sabbath, as being the Christ of the Creator, as

---

[241]Is 53:4, 12. He goes on to cite Is 1:18, Mic 7:18ff. (LXX); 2 Sam 12:13; 1 Kings 21:29; 1 Sam 14:45; Ezek 33:11. [242]CCL 1:562-63. [243]Mk 2:28.

he was acting in accordance with his exclamation through the mouth of Isaiah, Your new moons and sabbaths my soul hates.[244] Now, in whatever way this was said, we know none the less that in a case of this kind a sharp defense must be made against a sharp assault.

And now I proceed to discuss the actual circumstances in which Christ's rule appeared to breach the sabbath. His disciples were starving on that day; they had plucked ears of wheat with their hands and rubbed off the husk, and in making food they had violated the holy day. Christ excuses them and is held guilty of Sabbath breaking; the Pharisees accuse him, and Marcion derives a quibble from the grounds of the controversy (if I may toy a little with the truth about my Lord)—the written word and the intention alike. For the excuse is derived both from the Scripture of the Creator and from the intention of Christ, the precedent being furnished by David's entrance into the temple on the sabbath, where he boldly broke the showbread and made food.[245] For he too remembered that this privilege had been conceded from the very first sabbath on which this day was instituted—I mean a pardon for hunger. For when the Creator had forbidden the hoarding of manna for two successive days, he allowed this on the Friday alone, so that the holiday of the following sabbath might be relieved from hunger by the preparation of food on the previous day. It was well then that the Lord acted on same motive in his breach of the sabbath—if they insist on that term. And it was well that he expressed the Creator's desire on the sabbath by the distinctive mark of not fasting.[246] In sum, then, he would indeed have breached the sabbath if he had ordered his disciples to fast on the sabbath against the true sense of Scripture and the will of the Creator. But since he does not robustly defend his disciples but excuses them, since he advances human need as a sort of mitigation, since he upholds the honor of the sab-

bath more in keeping it free from sorrow than in breaching it, since he puts David and his companions on a level with his disciples both in blame and in pardon, since he is happy to accept what the Creator concedes, since it is this precedent that enables him to be so benign: how then can he be foreign to the Creator?

Following this, the Pharisees watch to see if he performs healings on the sabbath, so they may accuse him—surely as a Sabbath breaker, not as the apostle of a new god. It seems indeed that I shall insist on this one fact everywhere, that nowhere is there a proclamation of another Christ. But as for the Pharisees, they were wholly mistaken about the sabbath, not perceiving that it prohibited works on the holy day only provisionally, and only under a certain aspect. For when he said of the sabbath day, "You shall not do any work of yours on it," he said "of yours" to make it apply to the human work that each person pursues as his craft or trade, not to divine work. Now the work of healing or preservation is proper not to humanity but to God. And so it is that he says again in the Law, "You shall not do any work on it, save that which is done for every soul"[247]—that is, with the aim of delivering the soul. For the work of God can also be done through a human for the saving of a soul, though it is from God; and that is what Christ was going to do, since he was also God. It is therefore because he wishes to lead them to this understanding of the Law that after the restoration of the withered hand he demands of them, "Is it permitted to do good on the sabbath, or not? To deliver a soul or to destroy it?" His purpose was that, in sanctioning such labor as he was about to perform on behalf of the soul, he would let them know what works the law of the sabbath prohibits—namely,

---

[244]Is 1:14. [245]1 Sam 21:2, though in this text there is no allusion to the sabbath. [246]Tertullian, who considered the fasts of the "psychic" or catholic church too lax, nonetheless observes the principle that Sunday is not a fast day, even in Lent. [247]Ex 20:19.

human ones—and what works it enjoins— namely, the divine ones that were to be done for every soul.

He was called Lord of the sabbath because he protected the sabbath as his own. Yet even had he breached it, he would have been in the right, since he who instituted it is all the more lord of it. But he wholly refrained from destroying it in his capacity as Lord, so that from this it might also be apparent that the sabbath was not breached by the Creator either when the ark was carried around Jericho. For this work of God also was of the kind that he had enjoined, being ordained on behalf of the souls of his people who were in a critical state of war. And if, however, he did profess hatred for sabbaths elsewhere, saying "your sabbaths," he considered that they were human, not his own, when the people, glutted with pleasures, celebrated them without fear of God, loving God with their lips, not their heart. But to his own sabbaths, that is, whatever was done according to his rule, he gave a different character, declaring subsequently through the same prophet[248] that they were true, delightful and not to be profaned. And so neither did Christ wholly abrogate the sabbath, and he observed its law both in the earlier instance, when in the case of his disciples he worked on behalf of their souls, conceding to them the solace of food in their hunger, and in the present one, where he cures a withered hand. Everywhere he insists that he had come not to break the Law but to fulfil it, even if Marcion has stopped his mouth with this utterance. For he fulfilled the Law also in this instance when he interprets its conditions, when he brings to light the difference between works, when he does that for which the law of the sabbath holiday makes an exception, when by his own benefactions he hallows the sabbath day even more, hallowed as it already was by the Father from the beginning. This he did by dispensing the divine benefits that an adversary would have reserved for the other days, so that he

would not adorn the sabbath of the Creator or render to the sabbath the works that are due to it. If it was on this day that Elisha the prophet restored the dead son of the Shunamite to life, behold, Pharisee, and you, Marcion, that it was at one time the Creator's part to do good on the sabbath, to deliver the soul and not to destroy it, and that Christ introduced nothing new that did not stem from the Creator's example, his clemency, his compassion, even his promise. For in this instance too he effects a particular healing that was prophesied:[249] feeble hands grow strong, just like the feeble limbs of the paralytic. AGAINST MARCION 4.12.[250]

Light to the Blind

RECAPITULATING THE ENTIRE WORK OF THE LOGOS. AUGUSTINE: The astonishing and wondrous deeds of our Lord and Savior Jesus Christ consisted both in works and in words; in works, inasmuch as he performed them, and in words, inasmuch as they were signs. If then we consider what is signified in this deed, that blind man is the human race; for this blindness afflicted the first man through his sin, and it is from him that not only our mortality but also our sinfulness arises. For if blindness is unbelief and belief is enlightenment, whom will Christ find to be faithful when he comes? After all, the apostle, born into the race of the prophets, says, "We too were once by nature children of wrath, like the rest."[251] If children of wrath, then children of retribution, children of punishment, children of hell. How could he speak of nature, but that when the first man sinned, vice overran our nature? And if vice overran our nature, every human being is born blind in intellect. For if he sees, he has no need of a guide; if he has need of a guide and one to enlighten him, he is consequently blind from his natal hour.

---

[248]Is 58:13; 56:2. [249]See Is 35:3. [250]CCL 1:568-72. [251]Eph 2:3.

The Lord came: what did he do? He enjoined a great mystery. He spat on the ground, he made mud of his own spittle, because "the Word was made flesh."[252] And he anointed the eyes of the blind man. He was anointed, and he did not yet see. He sent him to the fishpool that is called Siloam. Now it was the Evangelist's part to draw our attention to this name, and he says "which means sent." Who it was that was sent you know well: for had he not been sent, none of us would have been released from sinfulness. He therefore bathed his eyes in that fishpool whose name means sent and was baptized in Christ. Thus, when he baptized him, as it were, in himself, that was when he enlightened him; if so, when he anointed him, he perhaps made him a catechumen. There are indeed various other ways of expounding and treating the deeps of such a great mystery, but let this be enough for your charity.[253] You have heard a great mystery. Ask a person, "Are you a Christian?" The response is "I am not," if that person is a pagan or a Jew. But should it be "I am," you go on asking, "A catechumen or a believer?" If the answer is "a catechumen," that person is anointed but not washed. But from where comes the anointing? Ask, and you get a response; ask of that person "in whom do you believe?" and the very fact of being a catechumen prompts the reply, "In Christ." See now, I am addressing both catechumens and believers. The catechumens are also listening to this. But it is not enough for them that they are anointed; let them hasten to the bath if they would have light. TRACTATES ON THE GOSPEL OF JOHN 44.1-2.[254]

CHRIST WILL WORK UNTIL THE DAY OF JUDGMENT. AUGUSTINE: What is this that he says?[255] If no human being is without sin, can the parents of this blind man possibly have been without sin? Surely he could not have been born without original sin or failed to add anything in the course of life? Is it that his eyes were sealed and consequently made little study of worldly desire? How many evils the blind commit! What evil does the evil mind abstain from, even if the eyes are sealed? He could not see, but he knew how to think and perhaps to covet something that, being blind, he was unable to secure; but in his heart he could be judged by the inspector of the heart. If therefore his parents had sin, then he had sin; why did the Lord say "neither this man sinned nor his parents," if not with regard to the matter on which he was being questioned—his being born blind? Yes, his parents had sin, but it was not this actual sin that caused him to be born blind. If then the sin of the parents was not the cause of his being born blind, why was he born blind? Hear the master's teaching: he seeks one who believes in order to make him understand.[256] He stated the cause of that man's being born blind: "It is not that this man sinned," he says, "or his parents, but that the works of God might be manifested in him."[257]

Then what follows? "I must work the works of him who sent me while it is day. . . The night comes when none can work."[258] Not even you, Lord? Is that night so powerful that even you cannot work in it, though night is your work? For I think, Lord Jesus—no, I do not think, I believe and affirm—that you were there when God said, "Let there be light; and there was light."[259] For if he did it with a word, he did it through you. And so it is said, "All things were made through him, and without him was nothing made."[260] God made a division between the light and the darkness; the light he called day and the darkness he called night.[261] What is that night in which none can work when it comes? Hear what the day is, and then you will understand what the night is. How are we to learn what is the day? He says,

---

[252]Jn 1:14. [253]Charity, in Augustine's view, is the test of truth in the exposition of Scripture. [254]CCL 36:381-82. [255]Jesus says, "Neither this man sinned nor his parents" (Jn 9:3). [256]One of Augustine's favorite verses is "If you will not believe, neither shall you understand" (Is 7:9 LXX). [257]Jn 9:3. [258]Jn 9:4. [259]Gen 1:3. [260]Jn 1:3. [261]Gen 1:4-5.

"So long as I am in the world, I am the light of the world." See then, he himself is the day. He bathes the eyes of the blind man in day that he may see the day. . . . But for how long is he in this world? Do we think, brethren, that he was here at that time and now is no longer here? Well, if that is what we think, that dread night in which no one can work came already after the ascension of the Lord; but if that night came after the ascension of the Lord, from where came all those great works of the apostles? . . . What then? What shall we say of that night? When will it be that no one will be able to work? That is the night of the ungodly, that night will be theirs to whom it is said at the end, "Depart into eternal fire, which has been prepared for the devil and his angels."[262] Yes, it is night that is spoken of, not flame, not fire; but hear that it is also night. He says of a certain servant "bind his hands and feet, and cast him into outer darkness."[263] Let everyone therefore work as long as he lives, so that he will not be overtaken by that night in which no one can work. Presently it is possible for faith to work through love;[264] and if we work in the present, here is the day, here is Christ. TRACTATES ON THE GOSPEL OF JOHN 44.3-6.[265]

The Priesthood of Christ

CHRIST WAS A PRIEST FROM BEFORE THE CREATION. GOSPEL OF TRUTH: He is completely ineffable to the All, and he is the confirmation and the hypostasis of the All, the silent veil, the true high priest, the one who has the authority to enter the Holy of Holies, revealing the glories of the Aeons and bringing forth the abundance to fragrance. . . . He is the one who revealed himself as the primal sanctuary and the treasury of the All. GOSPEL OF TRUTH 25-26.[266]

THE PRIESTHOOD SUBLIMATES CHRIST'S HUMANITY. PROSPER OF AQUITAINE: If we understand "before the dawn"[267] of the

birth of the Savior in the Virgin's womb, it is undoubtedly by virtue of this that he is a priest forever, after the order of Melchisedek. For insofar as the Lord is born of the Father, co-eternal and equal to the one who begot him, he is no priest. . . . "You are a priest forever"[268] means, "your priesthood does not lapse, nor will your pontificate be curtailed as the line of Aaron came to an end. There will be no end to your priesthood, but after the order of Melchisedek"—that is, in accordance with the mysteries that were revealed through him— "it will abide forever." EXPOSITION OF PSALM 109.4.[269]

HIS PRIESTHOOD IS FORESHADOWED IN THAT OF JOSHUA.[270] EUSEBIUS: Quite naturally, then, that Joshua who bore the image of the truth in himself also puts on filthy clothes,[271] and the devil is said to oppose him and to stand at his right, seeing that Jesus our true Savior and Lord came down to our captivity, taking our sins on himself and wiping away the human defilement even as he bore his ignominious sufferings on account of his humane love for us. For which reason Isaiah says, "He bears our sins."[272] PROOF OF THE GOSPEL 4.17.16.[273]

PRIESTHOOD SYMBOLIZED IN JOSHUA'S SUCCESSION TO MOSES.[274] ORIGEN: If we do not understand what it was for Moses to die, we shall not discern what it is for Jesus to reign. If then you consider Jerusalem overthrown, the altar desolate, no sacrifice anywhere—neither a burnt offering nor a libation—nowhere a priest, nowhere a high

---

[262]Mt 25:41. [263]Mt 22:13. [264]Gal 5:6. [265]CCL 36:382-84. [266]GT 483. [267]Ps 110:3, which also reads "from the womb of the morning." The numbering of the Psalms in patristic texts diverges from ours by one in most cases. [268]Ps 110:4. [269]CCL 68A:61-62. [270]The name Joshua is the Hebrew prototype of Jesus and belonged to a high priest at the time when the Jews returned from Babylon. [271]Zech 3:4. [272]Is 53:4. [273]GCS 23:198. [274]Josh 1:1. For this captain of hosts as the forerunner of Jesus, see Heb 4:8.

priest, nowhere a ministry of Levites: when you see that all these things are at an end, say that Moses the friend of God is dead. If you see that no one comes three times a year into the sight of God, that none offers gifts in the temple or slits the throat of the Passover lamb, none eats the unleavened bread or offers firstfruits or dedicates the firstborn: when you see that none of these rites is performed, say that Moses the servant of God is dead. When, however, you see that the nations enter into faith, that churches are raised, that altars are not sprinkled with the blood of beasts but hallowed with the precious blood of Christ; when you see the priests and the Levites dispensing not the blood of goats and bulls but the Word of God through the Holy Spirit, then say that Jesus has succeeded to Moses and obtained the primacy, not that Jesus the son of Nave[275] but Jesus the Son of God. When you see that Christ our Passover has been sacrificed for us and we eat the unleavened bread of sincerity of truth; when you see in the church the fruits of the good soil bearing thirtyfold, sixtyfold and a hundredfold, that is, widows, virgins and martyrs; when you see that the seed of Israel is increased from those who are born not of blood nor of human will but of the will of God;[276] and when you see the children of God, who had been dispersed, forming one congregation; when you see the people of God keeping the sabbath not by resting from their common business but by resting from the business of sin: say that Moses the servant of God is dead and that Jesus the Son of God has obtained the primacy. HOMILIES ON JOSHUA 2.1.[277]

HIS PRIESTHOOD CONSECRATES THAT OF THE EARTHLY CELEBRANT. LITURGY OF ST. JAMES:

The priest, consecrating the gifts, says, "Holy are you, king of the ages, Lord and giver of all holiness; holy too your only-begotten Son our Lord Jesus Christ, through whom you have made all things; and holy your Spirit, the all-holy, who searches all things and your depths, O God. Holy are you, almighty, omnipotent, benevolent, dread, compassionate, and moved to the utmost on account of your creation. You have humanity from the earth in your image and likeness, you did bestow on him the enjoyment of paradise, and when this one had transgressed your commandment and fallen, you did not overlook or abandon him in your benevolence, but as a compassionate father you did school him, summoning him through the Law and guiding him through the prophets. And after that you did send out into the world none other than your only-begotten Son, our Lord Jesus Christ, that when he came he might renew and awaken his own image. Having come down from heaven and taken flesh from the Holy Spirit and Mary the virgin, the mother of God, he lived in the human world and discharged the whole economy of salvation for our race. As the sinless one prepared to undergo his willing and life-giving death on behalf of us sinners, in the night when he was given up—or rather gave himself up—for the sake of the life and salvation of the cosmos."

Then the priest, holding the bread in his hand, says, "Taking the bread in his unsullied and blameless and immortal hands, looking up to heaven and showing it to you, God the Father, he gave thanks and sanctified it, then broke it and gave it to his holy disciples and apostles, saying . . . "

The deacons say, "For the forgiveness of sins and everlasting life." LITURGY OF ST. JAMES.[278]

TRUE PRIESTHOOD IS SERVICE TO GOD, WHEREVER PERFORMED.

IRENAEUS: To those who arraigned his disciples when they plucked ears of corn and ate them on the sabbath, the Lord said, "And have you not read this, which David did when he was hungry, how he entered into the house of God and ate

---

[275]More familiar to us as Joshua the son of Nun. [276]See Jn 1:13. [277]SC 71:116-18. [278]LEW 51.

the showbread, giving it also to those who were with him, though it was not lawful for any to eat it but the priests?"[279] He was excusing his disciples through the words of the Law and intimating that priests are permitted to do as they will. Now David was an appointed priest before the Lord, notwithstanding the persecution that Saul carried on against him. For every righteous king[280] has the rank of priest. All the apostles of the Lord are priests, however, inheriting neither fields nor houses but constantly serving the altar of the Lord. Of these Moses said in Deuteronomy, in his blessing of Levi, "The one who has said to his own father and his own mother, 'I do not know you,' and has not known his brothers, relinquishing his children—this one has kept your precepts and maintained your covenant."[281] But who are those who have abandoned father and mother,[282] abjuring all close ties on account of the Word of God and his covenant, if not the Lord's disciples? AGAINST HERESIES 4.8.3.[283]

CHRIST SANCTIFIES HIS PEOPLE. AUGUSTINE: Now it could be asked how they were already not of the world if they were not yet sanctified in truth;[284] or if they already were so, why he should request that they should be. Could it be that while they are sanctified, they advance in that sanctification; and that this is not without the help of God's grace, but he sanctifies their progress as he sanctified the beginning? That is why the apostle also says, "He who has begun a good work in you will make you perfect for the day of Christ Jesus."[285] And so the heirs of the new covenant are sanctified in truth, the sanctifying procedures of the Old Covenant being shadows of this truth. And when they are sanctified in truth, they are certainly sanctified in Christ, who said truly, "I am the way, the truth and the life."[286] . . . When he had said, "and for their sake I sanctify myself,"[287] he added immediately "that they may be sanctified in truth," so that we should understood that what

he meant by this was that they should be sanctified in him. TRACTATES ON THE GOSPEL OF JOHN 108.2, 5.[288]

HIS OFFERING DOES NOT RELEASE HIS PEOPLE FROM ALL ADVERSITY. CHRYSOSTOM: What does "I sanctify myself"[289] mean? "I offer you a sacrifice." Now all sacrifices are called holy, and the name "holy things" applies particularly to those that are reserved for God. Of old the sanctification was effected typologically by the sheep, but now by the truth without typology. Therefore he says, "that they may be sanctified in your truth," meaning "for I at once dedicate them to you and present an offering." He says this either because this is what is happening to their head or because they also were being sacrificed. For it says "present your bodies as a living sacrifice, holy."[290] Again, we were "counted as sheep for the slaughter."[291] And he makes them a sacrifice and an oblation without their dying; for it is clear from the sequel that "I sanctify" refers to his own sacrifice. HOMILIES ON JOHN 82.1.[292]

HIS PRIESTHOOD IS FOR US THE DOOR TO THE KINGDOM. IGNATIUS OF ANTIOCH: Excellent were the priests,[293] but more excellent still the high priest to whom was entrusted the Holy of Holies, the only one entrusted with the hidden things of the Lord. He is the door to the Father,[294] through which enter Abraham, Isaac and Jacob, with the prophets and the apostles and the church. All these things enter into the unity of God. But in the gospel

---

[279]Lk 6:3-4. [280]This phrase survives in a late Greek citation. The Latin, from which the rest is translated, says here "every righteous person has the rank of priest." Since this is the doctrine of the New Testament, the Latin may be closer to the Greek original. [281]Deut 33:9. [282]See Mk 10:29 and other references. [283]SC 100:472-74. [284]Jn 17:19. [285]Phil 1:6. [286]Jn 14:6. [287]Jn 17:19. [288]CCL 36:616-18. [289]Jn 17:19. [290]Rom 12:1. [291]Ps 44:22; cf. Rom 8:36. [292]PG 59:443. [293]It is clear that the high priest in this passage is Christ, but it is not clear whether the other priests are servants of a fallen altar, nominal priests of Israel in the author's time or Christian ministers. [294]Jn 10:7.

there is something exceptional, the appearing of the Savior, our Lord Jesus Christ, his passion and his resurrection. For to him were directed the proclamations of the beloved prophets, and the gospel is the consummation

of incorruptibility. All things together are excellent, if you believe in love. To THE PHILADELPHIANS 9.[295]

[295]*AF* 182

UNDER PONTIUS PILATE

σταυρωθέντα τε ὑπὲρ ἡμῶν	*crucifixus etiam pro nobis*	*For our sake he was crucified*
ἐπὶ Ποντίου Πιλάτου,	***sub Pontio Pilato,***	***under Pontius Pilate;***
καὶ παθόντα καὶ ταφέντα,	*passus et sepultus est;*	*he suffered death and was buried.*
καὶ ἀναστάντα τῇ τρίτῃ ἡμέρᾳ	*et resurrexit tertia die,*	*On the third day he rose again*
κατὰ τὰς γραφάς,	*secundum Scripturas;*	*in accordance with the Scriptures;*
καὶ ἀνελθόντα εἰς τοὺς οὐρανούς,	*et ascendit in coelum,*	*he ascended into heaven*
καὶ καθεζόμενον	*sedet*	*and is seated*
ἐκ δεξιῶν τοῦ πατρός,	*ad dexteram Patris;*	*at the right hand of the Father.*
καὶ πάλιν ἐρχόμενον μετὰ δόξης	*et iterum venturus est, cum gloria,*	*He will come again in glory*
κρῖναι ζῶντας καὶ νεκρούς·	*judicare vivos et mortuos;*	*to judge the living and the dead,*
οὗ τῆς βασιλείας οὐκ ἔσται τέλος.	*cujus regni non erit finis.*	*and his kingdom will have no end.*

HISTORICAL CONTEXT: No religion older than Christianity can attach a precise or secure date to its founder. For Christians it was part of the original proclamation that the Savior had suffered and risen in their sight, and thus at a date that could be recorded. Early pagan witnesses reaffirm the unanimous testimony of the Gospels, that Christ's executioner was Pontius Pilate, procurator of Judea from A.D. 26 to 36. Acts had been fabricated under his name in the first three centuries of the Christian era, first on behalf of the church and then in the interest of its persecutors. It was even said that the Senate possessed a letter in which he accounted for his proceedings. Since he was one in a line of provincial governors and the servant of an emperor who was not the first of his dynasty, the historical allusion shows that the death of Christ is the consummation of an evolving plan and not, as some Gnostic groups maintained, the gratuitous incursion of a hitherto idle deity into a world that he had no part in creating. Furthermore, the wide and rapid diffusion of the gospel in the first century was made possible by the Roman unification of the Mediterranean world.

OVERVIEW: The event of Jesus' crucifixion cannot be doubted (CYRIL OF JERUSALEM). Calvary was a well-known site in early Christian memory in Jerusalem (CYRIL OF JERUSALEM). Christian faith is subject to historical verification (AUGUSTINE). The date of Pilate's tenure is correctly reported in the canonical Gospels (EUSEBIUS). Pilate testified to the innocence of Christ (CHRYSOSTOM). Even pagan witnesses can be summoned, along with investigators of paranormal phenomena who have ascribed foreknowledge to Christ (ORIGEN).

An Event in History

CALVARY WAS A CONSPICUOUS SITE IN EARLY CHRISTIAN JERUSALEM. CYRIL OF JERUSALEM: There are many valid testimonies of Christ, beloved. . . . The holy wood of the cross, which is seen among us to this very day, bears testimony and, through those who in their faith have plucked bits from it, has filled almost the whole inhabited world. . . . And this holy Golgotha that stands over us bears visible testimony . . . showing up to the present how through Christ the stones were shattered on that occasion; the sepulcher nearby where he was laid, and the stone laid across the door, which up to the present day lies by the sepulcher. He stretched out his hands on the cross that he might embrace the farthest reaches of the inhabited world; for this Golgotha is the midmost point of the earth. This is not my assertion; it is a prophet who says,[1] "You have wrought salvation in the midst of the earth."[2] CATECHETICAL LECTURE 10.19; 13.39; 13.28.[3]

THE EVENT AND ITS SIGNIFICANCE CANNOT BE DOUBTED. CYRIL OF JERUSALEM: This man was truly crucified for our sins; should you wish to deny this indeed, you are refuted by this visible place, this blessed Golgotha in which we are now assembled on account of the one who was crucified here. And step by step the whole inhabited world has subsequently been filled with the glory of the wood of the cross. Now he was crucified not for sins of his own but so that we might be delivered from the

sins that pertain to us. And he was despised by the rest of humanity and buffeted like a man, yet he was recognized as God by the creation. For the sun, seeing its Creator in ignominy, trembled and faded, unable to bear the sight. CATECHETICAL LECTURE 4.10.[4]

EVEN PAGAN WITNESSES CAN BE SUMMONED. ORIGEN: Celsus thinks that the earthquake and the darkness are merely portentous. We have made our defense regarding these to the best of our ability above, laying the account by Phlegon's report that these events occurred at the time of the Savior's passion. AGAINST CELSUS 2.59.[5]

PHLEGON ASCRIBED FOREKNOWLEDGE TO CHRIST. ORIGEN: Celsus could have accepted or conceded "the happy issue of Christ's foreknowledge of what would befall him" and taken the same view that he took in the case of the miracles, which he declared to have been produced by sorcery. He could at least have said that many have known what would befall them from divination, through greater birds or lesser birds, through sacrifices or horoscopes. But this he declined to concede as though it were too much, whereas, having accepted that the miracles were performed, he thinks it possible somehow to disparage them with an allegation of sorcery. Phlegon,[6] however, in the thirteenth or fourteenth book (I think) of his Chronicles did in fact grant Christ the foreknowledge of some future events, mingling these as reports about Jesus with those about Peter, and bore witness that the things spo-

---

[1]This use of the psalm is specious, but we can acquit Cyril of ignorance if we assume that by "the earth" he means the great continent that now comprises Asia, Europe and Africa. It was commonly assumed in his time that the earth is a perfect sphere. [2]Ps 74:12. [3]As collated in *ELS* 624-25. [4]*CHOO* 1:100. [5]SC 132:422. [6]A connoisseur of miracles at the turn of the second century. The matter cited by Origen, however, is unlikely to have been collected by a pagan author, and if the thirteenth and fourteenth books were not apocryphal, we must assume that Phlegon was a believer, or at least an admirer of Christians.

ken of occurred as Jesus had said. AGAINST
CELSUS 2.14.[7]

**CHRISTIAN FAITH IS SUBJECT TO HISTORI-
CAL VERIFICATION.** AUGUSTINE: The name
of the judge[8] needed to be added so that the
time might be known. Furthermore, when that
burial of his is an object of belief, mention is
made of a new monument that would testify
to his future resurrection to newness of life, as
the virgin womb testified to his forthcoming
birth. For just as in that monument no other
dead person was buried either before or after,
so in that womb no other mortal creature was
conceived, before or after. ON FAITH AND THE
CREED 11.[9]

**DATE OF PILATE'S TENURE CORRECTLY
REPORTED.** EUSEBIUS: The same Josephus
shows in the eighteenth book of his *Antiquities*
that Pontius Pilate received charge of Judea in
the twelfth year of the reign of Tiberius (this
man having succeeded to the universal empire
after Augustus had maintained his rule for
fifty-seven years) and that he remained there
for a full ten years, almost up to the death of
Tiberius.[10] This clearly refutes the forgery of
those who handed down accounts of today and
yesterday, which are inimical to our Savior, for
the date in the marginal note at the beginning
exposes the deceit of the forgers. The presumptuous acts that accompanied the saving
passion are here assigned to the fourth consul-
ship[11] of Tiberius, which fell in his seventh
year, though it has been shown, if Josephus is
to be taken as a witness, that Pilate was not yet

set over Judea. ECCLESIASTICAL HISTORY 1.9.[12]

**PILATE TESTIFIED TO THE INNOCENCE OF
CHRIST.** CHRYSOSTOM: What does Pilate
say? Do you not hear all the things that these
people say against you? For his desire was
to release him when he had made a defense.
Now when he answered nothing, he devised
another stratagem. What was this? Their
custom was to release one of the condemned,
and by this means he attempted to have him
pardoned. Do you see how the order of things
was overturned? For the custom was that the
people should make the request on behalf of
the condemned and that the ruler should grant
it. But here the opposite came to pass, and the
governor puts the request to the people. Not
even so are they mollified, but they rage all the
more like beasts, and when they cry out they
are intoxicated with the passion of jealousy.
HOMILIES ON MATTHEW 86.1.[13]

---

[7]SC 132:324. [8]Pontius Pilate, whose name appears in the
Apostles' Creed on which Augustine is commenting, though not
in the Nicene Creed of 325. [9]CSEL 41:14-15. [10]Josephus *Jewish
Antiquities* 18.2.2. Tiberius succeeded in A.D. 14 and died in 37,
so that the dates assigned to Pilate are 16/17–26/27. The reign of
Augustus is dated not from the year 27 B.C., in which he received
this title, but from 43 B.C., the year in which he formed a govern-
ing triumvirate with Lepidus and Antony. [11]The reference is
to a book called the *Acts of Pilate*, published as an antidote to
the Gospels by the persecutor Maximinus Daia (305–312). The
consuls were the two chief magistrates of the Roman Republic,
and two were appointed every year even after all power had been
vested in the emperor. The latter periodically assumed the office
himself to maintain the appearance of republican forms. [12]SC
31:34. [13]PG 58:764.

HE SUFFERED DEATH

σταυρωθέντα τε ὑπὲρ ἡμῶν	crucifixus etiam pro nobis	For our sake he was crucified
ἐπὶ Ποντίου Πιλάτου,	sub Pontio Pilato,	under Pontius Pilate;
καὶ παθόντα καὶ ταφέντα,	**passus** et sepultus est;	**he suffered death** and was buried.
καὶ ἀναστάντα τῇ τρίτῃ ἡμέρᾳ	et resurrexit tertia die,	On the third day he rose again
κατὰ τὰς γραφάς,	secundum Scripturas;	in accordance with the Scriptures;
καὶ ἀνελθόντα εἰς τοὺς οὐρανούς,	et ascendit in coelum,	he ascended into heaven
καὶ καθεζόμενον	sedet	and is seated
ἐκ δεξιῶν τοῦ πατρός,	ad dexteram Patris;	at the right hand of the Father.
καὶ πάλιν ἐρχόμενον μετὰ δόξης	et iterum venturus est, cum gloria,	He will come again in glory
κρῖναι ζῶντας καὶ νεκρούς·	judicare vivos et mortuos;	to judge the living and the dead,
οὗ τῆς βασιλείας οὐκ ἔσται τέλος.	cujus regni non erit finis.	and his kingdom will have no end.

HISTORICAL CONTEXT: What the ancients mean by suffering (Gk *pathos*) is passivity, the antonym of activity and the characteristic state of matter as opposed to mind. The statement that Christ suffered, then, invites us not to dwell on his physical afflictions but to admire the magnitude of his condescension, since, although he was "in the form of God," he voluntarily accepted the infirmity and subjection to hostile forces that are unavoidable for his mortal creatures. To say not only that he was crucified but also that he suffered is to insist on the reality of his body against the Gnostic or docetic claim that the incorporeal God cannot truly partake of our condition; against the Arian doctrine that it was possible for Christ to share our creaturehood because he was himself a creature, this clause has been so worded as to make it clear that the subject of the crucifixion and the attendant suffering was "true God from true God."

OVERVIEW: The gravity of the Fall entails a compensatory suffering in the incarnate God (ATHANASIUS). In his self-abnegation he

becomes feminine (CLEMENT OF ROME). We have no word for love that conveys the magnitude of his sacrifice (PSEUDO-DIONYSIUS), for divine love is as sublime as God (CYRIL OF ALEXANDRIA) and all the more inscrutable because it is freely given (AUGUSTINE). The curse of the hanged man in Scripture foreshadows the cross (JUSTIN). He is the suffering servant foretold by Isaiah (JUSTIN). His noble pains (EUSEBIUS) are anticipated by all the prophets (CLEMENT OF ROME). The man Jesus is the martyr lamb assumed by the priestly Word (EUSEBIUS). The water and blood of his death look forward to baptism and martyrdom (RUFINUS OF AQUILEIA).

Allegorical readings of the entry into Jerusalem are grounded in the historical detail (EPIPHANIUS). Thus the discrepant accounts of the cleansing of the temple may imply that Christ performed this action twice (AUGUSTINE) but also warrant our taking one account allegorically, to symbolize the expulsion of vice from the soul (ORIGEN). In this act he reveals his sonship (CYRIL). In his procuring of the two mounts, which is a historical event

(AUGUSTINE), we may discern a foreshadowing of the eschatological harvest (ORIGEN).

Jesus' washing of the disciples' feet demonstrated that while they had already received the baptism of John (TERTULLIAN), they were still in need of a spiritual purification (ORIGEN). In this ministry, Christ's eternal status as plenipotentiary of the Father became apparent (ORIGEN), and a new rite was established for the church (AMBROSE). Christ celebrated his last Passover in foreknowledge of his death (HIPPOLYTUS). By his acts he upholds the Law (CHRYSOSTOM) but rebukes formality in devotion (ORIGEN). As the bread is real, so is the body that it signifies (TERTULLIAN).

Christ's toleration of Judas's betrayal is a proof of his magnanimity (CHRYSOSTOM). Even his fear originates in divine prescience (ORIGEN). So long as Christ kept his secret, it was possible for Judas to repent (CHRYSOSTOM), but in the end he was exposed (EPHREM). The fall of Judas recapitulates that of Adam (ORIGEN). God's foreknowledge does not limit human freedom (ORIGEN). Peter, for example, was able to learn from his own temerity (CHRYSOSTOM).

Christ's weeping in Gethsemane, while it reveals his humanity, does not diminish his Godhead (AMBROSE). His trial fulfilled a prophecy (JUSTIN), and he set an edifying trial for his disciples (CHRYSOSTOM). While his struggle is evidence of a human will (MAXIMUS), it is possible that he feared more for his companions than for himself (HILARY) or that he shrank from ignominy rather than death (ORIGEN). His modern disciples commemorate his afflictions (EGERIA); the violence of his original disciples, thought excusable, was misguided (CHRYSOSTOM).

The conspiracy of Caiaphas and Annas betrays the corruption of the Jews (EUSEBIUS). GOD revenged himself on both Caiaphas and Herod (PRUDENTIUS, JUSTIN). By his silence Christ fulfilled the Scriptures (JUSTIN), while when he spoke it was to convict the high priest

from his own mouth (ORIGEN). Although he submitted to buffeting in fulfillment of prophecy (ORIGEN), he received the unconscious homage of his persecutors (JEROME).

The superscription King of the Jews attests his eternal kingship (AMBROSE). The divided garments prefigure the gathering of the elect, while the seamless robe proclaims the unity of the church (AUGUSTINE). In the thief at the cross we see every sinner (AMBROSE, LEO). The words to Mary and John are Christ's last testament and are recorded by the Evangelist as his own testament (AMBROSE). Christ exhibits superhuman fortitude on the cross (CHRYSOSTOM), while his solidarity with the Father is proved by the darkness and his cry of dereliction (CHRYSOSTOM). The words "It is finished" express at once a sense of consummation (AMBROSE) and a submission to his appointed suffering (CHRYSOSTOM).

The Significance of the Suffering

THE FALL WAS REDRESSED BY AN ACT OF CONDESCENSION. Athanasius: It was not worthy of God's goodness that the things that had come into being through him should fall into corruption, through the fraud that the devil had practiced. It would, moreover, have been of all things the least seemly that the workmanship of God should pass from the sight of humans, either through their own negligence or through the fraud of the devil. But when rational beings had suffered corruption and such works had been destroyed, what was God to do in his goodness? Should he leave the corrupt to their own resources and allow death to take them its subjects? Then what need was there for them to have come into being in the first place? For they ought rather not to have come into being than to have been abandoned to destruction once they had come into being. For negligence in God would have been evidence of weakness, not of goodness— the more so if, having created, he had winked

at the destruction of his work than if he had not created humans in the first place. For if he had not created there would have been no one to impute weakness to him, but once he had created and caused it to come into existence, it would have been quite absurd to give his work to destruction, particularly in the sight of the one who had created it. Thus it behooved him not to let human beings be carried off by corruption, because this would have been unseemly and unworthy of God's goodness.

But while it was in order that this should happen, there were facts on the other side that set against this, as a matter of principle for God, that God should be seen to have been true in his decree concerning death. For it would be absurd that through his help and sustenance in our cause, God the Father of truth should be seen to lie. What then ought to happen in this case, or what ought God to do? Should he exact repentance from humans for their transgression? For one might say that this was worthy of God, saying that just as they became liable to corruption through their transgression, so through their repentance they should once again come to a state of incorruption. But repentance would not have secured this matter of principle for God. For he would still remain untrue if human beings had not been made subject to death. Nor does repentance call us back from our natural urges but merely restrains from sinning. If, then, there had been only a delinquency and no consequences, repentance would have been a fine thing. But if, when once transgression had taken hold, humans were made subject to natural corruption and had been deprived of the boon of being in the image, what else ought to happen? Or what was required to bring about such a boon and revocation but the same one who in the beginning had made the universe from that which was not—God the Word? For it lay with him to bring the corruptible to incorruption and to uphold the overriding matter of principle for the Father.

For being the Word of the Father, superior to all other agents, he was accordingly the only one who was able to renew the universal creation, the only one equal to suffering for the sake of all and acting as an ambassador to the Father concerning all things.

For this reason, the incorporeal and incorruptible and immaterial Word of God becomes present in our sphere, though in fact he was not far off before, for no portion of the creation remains empty of him. He has filled all things, all while remaining beside his own Father. Nevertheless he becomes present, condescending by his humane love toward us and by apparition. He saw that the race of rational beings was perishing; he saw that the threatened penalty of transgression was imposing corruption on us and that it was absurd for the law to be relaxed before it had been fulfilled. He saw also what an unfitting corollary it was that the things that he himself had created should be obliterated; and he saw the exorbitant wickedness of humans, how they had augmented it little by little and rendered it unbearable to themselves. He saw also that the chastisement of all human beings was terminating in death. Pitying our race and taking compassion on our weakness, condescending to our corruption without undergoing subjection to death, so that what had come into being would not perish and God's work in respect of humans would not become void, he assumes for himself a body, and this not alien to ours. For he did not wish to come to be in a body by regular means, nor did he wish only to appear. For had he wished only to appear, he would have been able to manifest his divinity through some other and higher medium. No, he assumes ours, and this not by regular means but from an unsullied and undefiled virgin without experience of a man, a body pure and truly exempt from human intercourse. For being potent himself, and the universal Creator, he fashions the body in the virgin as a temple for himself and makes it as it were his peculiar instrument, being made known in it and dwelling within. And thus, having assumed the likeness of our condition, because all were under the chastisement of mortal corruption, he handed this body over to death in exchange for all and then conveyed it to the Father, doing this also from humane love, so that, all having died in him, the law imposing corruption on humans would be relaxed. (The point was that its authority had been fully exerted in the Lord's body, and it no longer had any grounds against human beings of his like.) And so that he could convert to incorruption the human beings who had reverted to corruption and restore them from death to life, he obliterated their death like a reed in the fire by making the body peculiarly his own and by the boon of the resurrection. ON THE INCARNATION 6.6–8.4.[1]

LOVE HAS ITS PRICE, FOR US AS FOR GOD. CLEMENT OF ALEXANDRIA: What remains to be said? Behold the mysteries of love, and then you will contemplate of the bosom of the Father, which the only-begotten Son alone has fathomed. Now God himself is love, and through love he was mingled with us. And that which is ineffable in him is the Father, and that which feels with us became mother. Having loved, the Father was made feminine, and the great token of this is the one whom he himself begot of himself, and the love engendered as the fruit of love. For this reason he himself also came down, for this reason he assumed humanity, for this reason he willingly underwent human sufferings, so that having been measured by the weakness of us his beloved, he might measure us in turn by his own power and leave to us a new testament when he had been poured out and had ransomed us as he proposed. I give you my love. But what is this and in what measure? He laid down his life for each of us, as the price of all, and this love he requires of us for one another. WHO IS THE RICH MAN WHO SHALL BE SAVED? 37.[2]

NO ONE WORD CAN TAKE THE FULL MEASURE OF THIS LOVE. PSEUDO-DIONYSIUS: Some religious teachers of our day, however, have held that the name of love is higher than that of charity. And the holy Ignatius writes, "My love has been crucified."[3] And in the introductions to the oracles, you will find one saying of the divine wisdom, I have become a lover of her beauty.[4] Let us not then be afraid of this term "love," and let us not be dismayed by some pusillanimous language about this. For it seems to me that the theologians consider the terms "love" and "charity" synonymous and that "love" in its true sense ought to be predicated of divine things all the more on account of these people's absurd apprehensions. DIVINE NAMES 4.12.[5]

IT WOULD NOT BE TRANSCENDENT LOVE WERE CHRIST NOT GOD. CYRIL OF ALEXANDRIA: "For God so loved the world that he gave his only-begotten Son."[6] If the great and superabundant love of God the Father is what the Lord has toward the world, it is recognized in the fact that his Son exposed himself to vicissitude for the sake of the world and on its account. It will therefore appear a small thing and of little worth if what was given for its sake is not the Son but a creature. And moreover the term "only-begotten" would be fictitious and untrue, for how could the Son, if he is one of the creatures, be thought of as the Only-begotten? But since the love of God the Father is great and incomparable, it follows that the one given for the sake of the world is his Son. For this it is that makes the deed so precious. And he is also the Only-begotten and is therefore not one of the creatures but the only one begotten of the Father. For that is what is signified by the

[1]SC 199:284-94. [2]GCS 17:183-84. [3]Ignatius *Epistle to the Romans* 7.2. The author purports to be a convert of Paul and hence an older contemporary of Ignatius. In this excerpt the translation "love" is reserved for the Greek term *eros*, and *agapē* is renderd by "charity"; elsewhere "love" is used for both. [4]Wis 8:2. [5]PDDN 157. [6]Jn 3:16.

name and the fact of being the Only-begotten. THESAURUS ON THE TRINITY 32.[7]

NOR WOULD IT BE LOVE IF IT WERE CO-ERCED. AUGUSTINE: Surely the Father would not have given up his Son for us, not sparing, unless he had already been placated. Does not this saying[8] seem contrary to the other—in that the Son dies for us and the Father is reconciled through his death? In this, however, as though it was the Father who first loved us, it is he himself who on our account does not spare the Son and he himself who gives him up to death for us. But I observe that the Father also loved us beforehand, not only before the Son died for us but also before the creation of the world, as the apostle testifies, saying, "As he chose us in him before the foundation of the world. Nor, when the Father did not spare the Son, was the latter given up against his will, for it is said of him, who loved me and gave himself for me."[9] All things then the Father, the Son and the Spirit of both do in concert. Nevertheless it is in the blood of Christ that we are justified and through the death of his Son that we are reconciled to God. ON THE TRINITY 13.11.15.[10]

Jesus' Suffering Predicted

THE CROSS IS FORESHADOWED IN THE PENTATEUCH. JUSTIN MARTYR: And indeed as to that which is said in the Law, "Cursed is he that hangs on a tree,"[11] it is not God's malediction on this crucified one that strengthens that hope of ours that depends on the crucified Christ but the fact that God predicted all the things that you and your like would do because of your failure to recognize that this man was the one before all things, the one who was to be the eternal priest of God, the king and Christ. DIALOGUE WITH TRYPHO 96.1.[12]

CHRIST IS THE SUFFERING SERVANT. JUSTIN MARTYR: And, when I had paused, Trypho said, "My dear fellow, these and similar Scrip-

tures require us to await a great and glorious one to assume the eternal kingdom as Son of man from the Ancient of Days. But this Christ that you speak of is so bereft of honor and glory as to succumb to the most extreme curse in the law of God, for he was crucified." And I said to him, "I must have spoken unclearly and to no purpose if I have not demonstrated, from the Scriptures that I have already rehearsed,[13] that his countenance would be inglorious[14] and his lineage obscure,[15] and that the rich would be made to die for his death,[16] and that by his stripes we have been healed,[17] and that it was foretold that he would be led as a sheep to the slaughter,[18] and that he was to have two advents, one in which he was to be pierced by you, the other in which you would know him whom you have pierced,[19] and your tribes will be cut down, tribe against tribe, your women-folk and your menfolk severally. But now I am advancing every possible proof through every argument from the writings that you deem holy and prophetic, hoping that some one among you may be of the number preserved for eternal salvation according to the grace of the Lord of hosts. In order, then, that the matter in question may become clearer to you, I shall recite to you the other words that were pronounced by the blessed David, from which you will perceive that Christ was also called Lord by the holy prophetic Spirit. . . . These then are the words that were spoken through David: "Sit at my right hand until I make your enemies your footstool. A rod of power the Lord shall send

---

[7]PG 75:544. [8]Rom 8:31-32. [9]Gal 2:20. [10]CCL 50A:402. [11]Deut 21:23, cited at Gal 3:13. [12]JMAA 210. [13]The unnamed servant of God in Is 53, whose death was to be an atonement for others, had been identified as the prophet himself, as king Hezekiah and as the people of Israel. At Mt 8:17 the verse "he has borne our infirmities" (Is 53:4) is cited as a prophecy of Christ's healings; at Lk 22:37 the saying "he was numbered with the transgressors" seems to be a loose allusion to Is 53:9-10. Only at Acts 8:31-35 is Isaiah's song expressly said to anticipate the work and death of Christ. [14]Is 53:2. [15]Is 53:8; cf. Acts 8:33. [16]Is 53:9. [17]Is 53:5; cf. 1 Pet 2:24. [18]Is 53:7; cf. Acts 8:32. [19]Zech 12:10; cf. Jn 19:37.

for you from Zion," and so on.[20] DIALOGUE
WITH TRYPHO 32.1-3, 6.[21]

HIS SUFFERING IS NOT TO BE DISPAR-
AGED. EUSEBIUS: Isaiah shows through these
words that Christ, unacquainted with all
delinquency on his own part, will take sins
on himself for the sake of humanity. On this
account he will also suffer as sinners do and
will be afflicted for our sake though not for his
own. And if he is to be wounded by the blas-
phemous words that strike him, this too will
be the work of our sins. And again when he is
beaten on account of our sins, as we also are,
because he has taken on himself our sinning
and the wounds of our evildoing, we are healed
by his stripes. PROOF OF THE GOSPEL 3.2.57.[22]

ISAIAH WAS BUT ONE OF HIS PRECUR-
SORS. CLEMENT OF ROME: You see, beloved,
what a pattern has been given to us.[23] For if
the Lord bore himself so humbly, what ought
we to do who, through him, have come under
the yoke of his grace? Let us become imitators
also of those who went about in goatskins and
sheepskins[24] proclaiming the coming of Christ.
I speak of the prophets Elijah and Elisha, Eze-
kiel also, and along with these the others who
bore witness: Abraham bore witness to him
mightily and was called the friend of God, and
humbling himself before the glory of God he
says vehemently, "I am dust and ashes."[25] And
again of Job it is written, Job was righteous and
blameless, true, God-fearing, abstaining from
all evil.[26] Yet he condemns himself, saying,
"None is free of foulness, not if his life is but a
day."[27] Moses was described as the faithful one
in the whole of his household,[28] and because
of his service God judged Egypt with plagues
and infamies. Yet he too, greatly as he was
honored, was not overweening but said before
the bush from which he received an oracle,
"Who am I, that you should send me? I am
poor in speech and slow of tongue."[29] . . . And
what shall we say of the testimony of David, to

whom the Lord said, "I have found a man after
my own heart, David the son of Jesse. I have
anointed him with everlasting oil."[30] Yet this
one too says to the Lord, "Have compassion on
me, Lord with your great compassion, and according to the multitude of your mercies wipe
away my iniquity."[31] . . . So many, then, there
are, and of such character, to witness that humility and submission through obedience have
been salutary not only for us but also for generations before us, when they also received his
oracles in truth and fear. 1 CLEMENT 16-19.[32]

THE SUFFERING SERVANT BECOMES THE
MARTYR LAMB. EUSEBIUS: Whatever might
seem in the foregoing discussion to be said of
him in a more lowly manner invites us to see
the lamb of God who takes away the sin of the
world and to think of his human tabernacle.[33]
For he was the lamb who takes away the sin of
the world according to John the Baptist, who
says, "Behold the lamb of God, who takes away
the sin of the world";[34] a lamb also was the
one who was led to the slaughter in Isaiah's
oracle, which says, "He was led as a sheep
to the slaughter and as a lamb that is dumb
before the shearer."[35] And it is of the same
one, as of a lamb, that it was said also, "For the
sins of my people he was led to death."[36] For it
behooved the lamb of God, the one assumed by
the great high priest[37] on behalf of the other
kindred lambs and of the entire human race,
to be led as a sacrifice to God. For "as by man
came death, by man came also the resurrection
from the dead,"[38] says the apostle, and "just as
by the offense of one all received condemna-

---

[20]Ps 110:1. [21]JMAA 126-27. [22]GCS 23:105. [23]In Is 53. [24]See
Heb 11:37. [25]Gen 18:27. [26]Job 1:1. [27]Job 14:4. [28]Num 12:7.
[29]Ex 4:10. [30]Ps 89:21. [31]Ps 51:3. [32]AF 46-50. [33]Jn 1:14.
[34]Jn 1:29. [35]Is 53:7. [36]Is 53:8. [37]Here Eusebius seems to con-
fine the title "priest" to the Word distinct from the flesh and the
title "lamb" for the manhood or "flesh." One would not guess
from the passage translated here that it is customary to assign
Eusebius to the Alexandrian tradition, which appears at times to
lose the duality of Christ's natures in the unity of his person.
[38]1 Cor 15:21.

tion, so by the righteousness of one all received justification of life."[39] Thus it was that he taught his disciples that he was life, light and truth, with the other titles that pertain to his sacred character, while to those uninitiated in his secrets he said, "Why do you seek to kill me, a man who has spoken the truth to you?"[40] PROOF OF THE GOSPEL 10, PROEM 4-7.[41]

JESUS' SUFFERING PREFIGURES NEW MYSTERIES. RUFINUS OF AQUILEIA: It is said that Jesus, having been struck in the side, poured forth water and blood at once. This indeed is a mystical sign, for he had said "that rivers of living water shall flow from his belly."[42] But he produced in addition the blood that the Jews had called down on themselves and their descendants.[43] Therefore he produced water to cleanse the believing, blood to condemn the incredulous. At the same time this can also be understood as a figure of the twofold grace of baptism: one that is given through the water of baptism, the other that is sought through martyrdom by the effusion of blood; for both of these are called baptism. . . . It is related also that he was made to drink vinegar, or wine mixed with myrrh, which is more bitter than gall. Hear what the prophet foretold of this: "And they gave me," says he, "gall for my drink, and they slaked my thirst with vinegar." Consonant with this is what Moses had said already about this people: "Their vine is from the vineyards of Sodom and their palms from Gomorrah. Their grape is the grape of gall, and theirs is the cluster of bitterness." And again in upbraiding them he says, "Foolish people and without wisdom, is this your repayment to the Lord?" The same things are announced beforehand in the Song, where even the garden in which he was crucified is indicated. What it says is, "I entered my garden, sister my spouse, and harvested my myrrh." Here he has clearly spoken of the wine mixed with myrrh that he was made to drink. COMMENTARY ON THE APOSTLES' CREED 23, 26.[44]

The Entry into Jerusalem

CHRIST'S APPROACH TO JERUSALEM IS BOTH HISTORY AND SYMBOL. PSEUDO-EPIPHANIUS: What is the descent from the Mount of Olives? Can it be anything but the descent to us of God the Word from heaven? What are the branches of the olive? The souls of the charitable. What is the road on which they rightly strew underfoot the practices of the virtues, having stripped the old person? What are the boughs of the palm trees? The pure hearts of the righteous, which flower like palms and abound like the cedars of Lebanon that are planted in the garden of the Lord and blossom. Rightly looking above to the true palm, they reveal in all ways both the victory over the tyrant and that over death, having delivered themselves from their tyranny by the power of Christ the victor. Who are those who lead? The righteous prophets. Who are those who follow? The apostles, and we of the nations who have believed with them. The city is Jerusalem above, and the temple the kingdom of heaven. HOMILY 2, ON PALM SUNDAY.[45]

THE CLEANSING OF THE TEMPLE IS HISTORICAL. AUGUSTINE: This account of the multitude of sellers who were cast out of the temple is given by all the Evangelists, but John introduces it in a remarkably different order.[46] For after recording the testimony given by John the Baptist to Jesus and mentioning that he went into Galilee at the time when he turned the water into wine, after he has also noticed the sojourn of a few days in Capharnaum, John proceeds to tell us that he went up to Jerusalem at the time of the Jews' Passover, and when he had made a scourge of

---

[39]Rom 5:18. [40]Jn 8:40. [41]GCS 23:445-46. [42]Jn 7:38. [43]Mt 27:25. [44]CCL 20:152, 159-60. [45]PG 43:505. [46]In the Fourth Gospel the cleansing of the temple is one of the earliest episodes in a three-year ministry; in the Synoptic accounts it follows his royal entry into Jerusalem and sets in train the events that lead to his death.

small cords, he drove out of the temple those who were selling in it. This makes it evident that this act was performed by the Lord not on a single occasion but twice over, but that only the first instance is put on record by John and the last by the other three. HARMONY OF THE GOSPELS 2.67.[47]

ALONG WITH THE LITERAL SENSE, IT CAN BE TAKEN FIGURATIVELY. ORIGEN: In the case of the four Evangelists, they handled many of the deeds and sayings resulting from the strange and miraculous power of Jesus, occasionally weaving into the Scripture, along with a literal account of things perceptible, that which was visible to them by the pure light of intellect. And indeed I venture to think that they even modified occurrences that had taken place rather differently in historical fact to further the mystical understanding of them, so that they assigned to one place a thing that occurred in another or to one time a thing that occurred at another time, and they reproduced what had been said in a certain way with a slight variation. For their business was, whenever possible, to say what was true both spiritually and bodily, but where it was not possible to do both, to rate spiritual above bodily truth, often preserving the spiritual truth in what one might describe as a bodily falsehood. COMMENTARY ON JOHN 10.5.[48]

IT SIGNIFIES THE EXPULSION OF VICE AND PASSION FROM THE SOUL. ORIGEN: The soul, naturally endowed with reason, can be a temple, being superior to the body by virtue of the reason implanted in it. It is to this that the Savior goes up from Capernaum, the lower and humbler region. There are found the earthly, foolish and pernicious motions that prevail before schooling is received from Jesus, and the things that are held to be goods but are not, and these the Savior drives out, plaiting a speech of instructive proofs and refutations,[49] so that his Father's house may be no longer a

place of merchandise but may embrace the cult of God that is celebrated, according to heavenly and spiritual laws, for its own salvation and that of many. And the ox is a symbol of earthly things, since it works the land, while the sheep is a symbol of the foolish and dull, as it is a servile beast beyond all other creatures. The dove is a symbol of light and credulous thoughts, and the coins of putative goods. COMMENTARY ON JOHN 10.24.[50]

CHRIST IS NOT ONLY THE SERVANT BUT ALSO THE SON OF GOD. CYRIL OF ALEXANDRIA: He commands as Master but guides them like a teacher to what is fitting, and he adds to the castigation an explanation of the offenses, not allowing the one who has been punished to fret with the shame of this. But it must be pointed out that at the same time he calls God peculiarly his Father, being himself the only one who comes of him by nature and has been truly begotten. For if it is not so, and the Word of God is among us as one of us, by adoption and insofar as the Father wills it, what reason has he for wresting to himself the common boast that is available to everyone, saying do not make my Father's house rather than our Father's house? COMMENTARY ON JOHN 2.1.[51]

JESUS ENTERED JERUSALEM WITH TWO MOUNTS. AUGUSTINE: Even had Matthew said nothing about the colt,[52] just as his fellow historians have taken no notice of the donkey, the fact should not have created any such perplexity as to produce the idea of an insuperable contradiction between the two statements, when the one writer speaks only of the donkey and the others only of the colt of the donkey. But how much less cause then for any disquietude ought there to be when we see that the one writer has mentioned the donkey to which

---

[47]NPNF 1 6:160. [48]SC 157:394. [49]Cf. the whip, unique to Jn 2:15. [50]SC 157:472. [51]PG 73:232. [52]Mt 21:1-9.

the others have omitted to refer, while at the same time not leaving unmentioned the donkey of which the others have spoken. Where it is possible to have supposed both objects to be included in the occurrence, there is no real antagonism, although the one writer may specify only the one thing and the other only the other. HARMONY OF THE GOSPELS 2.66.[53]

AN ALLEGORICAL MEANING CAN ALSO BE GIVEN TO THIS EPISODE. ORIGEN: How these men were sent out immediately after Jesus had resolved to go up to Jerusalem one cannot say in complete security, for there is some mystical intimation of the transformation of apostles into angels.[54] They were to be sent out in the present age, very much like the ministering spirits who are sent out for the sake of those who are going to inherit eternal life on account of this preaching. But if the donkey and the colt were to be the Old and New Testaments, on which the Word of God is mounted, it will not be at all difficult to explain how they are sent out, now that the Word had shone forth in them. They did not tarry, once the Word had entered Jerusalem[55] in those who had cast out all venal and mercenary thoughts. COMMENTARY ON JOHN 10.30.[56]

The Footwashing Before the Last Supper

PETER WAS WASHED ALREADY THROUGH THE BAPTISM OF JOHN. TERTULLIAN: "He who has washed once has no need of another."[57] Surely he would not have said this at all to one who had not been immersed? And this is the proof applied against those who deny the apostles even the baptism of John so that they may destroy the sacrament of the water. Could it even seem credible that for these persons the way for the Lord had not yet been prepared, and that by the baptism of John they were destined to open the way of the Lord throughout the whole world? The Lord,

though he owed no repentance, was immersed; was this not necessary for sinners? It follows that if others were not baptized, they were not yet companions of Christ but carpers at the faith, doctors of the law and Pharisees. From this one may also surmise that when the adversaries of the Lord declined immersion, those who followed the Lord accepted immersion and were not of the same mind as those who carped at them. This is all the more probable when the Lord to whom they adhered had extolled John, testifying that "among those born of women no one is greater than John the Baptist."[58] ON BAPTISM 12.3-5.[59]

THE NEW FOOTWASHING SIGNIFIES THE TENACITY AND THE EXPURGATION OF SIN. ORIGEN: On my *Homilies on Luke* I have compared the parables and investigated the meaning of breakfast in the sacred writings, and also what is signified in them by dinner. Here let it just be said that breakfast is the first meal that is fit for those who are making progress before the day of spiritual consummation, while supper is the final one, set in due course before those who are greatly advanced. Alternatively, one might say that breakfast is the sense intended in the ancient Scriptures, while supper is the mysteries hidden in the New Testament.

Now this has been said by way of preface to the examination of Jesus' reason for getting up from supper as supper was beginning, and for commencing to wash the feet of his disciples after pouring water into a bowl. For I surmise that those were supping with Jesus and were partaking of food with him on the day that marked the end of his life here were in need of some purgative, though not of what comes first in the body of the soul (as I might use this

---

[53]NPNF 1 6:159. [54]Origen held that humans would become angels in the resurrection, though it is not clear that (as is often alleged) he believed all human souls to have fallen from the angelic state. [55]That is, figuratively. [56]SC 157:494-96. [57]Jn 13:10. [58]Mt 11:11. [59]CCL 1:287.

term);[60] rather, as one might say, they needed to be cleansed of the final, the uttermost elements, those that cling to earth by necessity. And this purgative, in the first instance, can come from no one but Christ alone, but in the second it comes also from his disciples, to whom he said, "And you also ought to wash the feet of one another."[61] And for that matter, it seems to me that the Evangelist in this passage, as he is leading our minds from the place that we inhabit to the intellectual plane, has not observed continuity in his account of the physical washing. It is before the supper, before the reclining for supper, that those who need their feet to be washed are washed. But in the narrative, that point has been passed when Jesus, having begun to recline for supper, gets up from supper so that he, the teacher and Lord, may begin to wash the feet of his disciples when they have supped. For before the supper they were all cleansed and had become entirely clean, according to the verse: "Cleanse yourselves, become pure, expunge the iniquities from your souls before your eyes," and so on.[62]

But after that cleansing they were in need of a second application of water to their feet alone, that is, to the lowest part of the body. (For I believe that it is impossible for even the least and lowest parts of the soul to be soiled if one who is perfect appears among human beings.) Now the many, even after the cleansing of baptism, are full of the dust of sins, even in the head or in the part not far below that. But the genuine disciples of Jesus—so genuine as to reach the point of supping with him—require only that their feet should receive the washing from the Word. Now if you reflect on the varieties of sin and contemplate those that are sins by the robust and rigorous standard of the Word—by the many indeed not even regarded as sins—you see what those are on account of which their feet need to be washed by Jesus. And if such are the stains on the feet, what are we to do who are not even at the point of supping with Jesus and are not stained only on our feet?

After all, Jesus said to Peter, who did not know yet but was subsequently to apprehend the mystery of the washing of the feet that Jesus purified, "If I do not wash you, you will have no part with me."[63] You will ask what this means—that "you have no part in me at all unless I wash you clean," or that "you will have no part in me the teacher and Lord, but only in the things inferior to me, in which those participate who after having been cleansed have neither supped at the supper with me nor had their feet washed by me, or those who have supped but not been washed." It is said, "Behold, I stand at the door and knock. If anyone will open the door to me, I shall go in to him and shall sup with him and he with me."[64] By this I understand that perhaps on the one hand Jesus does not breakfast with anyone, since he has no need of instruction and the first rudiments; and on the other that no one breakfasts with him, but the one who eats with him can only be taking supper. . . . And I would venture to say that it follows from the saying, "If I do not wash you, you have no part with me," that he did not wash the feet of Judas. The devil had already put it into his heart that he should hand over his master and Lord, finding that he had not put on the whole armor of God[65] and did not have the buckler of faith by which one is able to quench all the flaming darts of the evil one. COMMENTARY ON JOHN 32.2.[66]

CLEANSING IMPLIES NO CHANGE IN THE RELATION OF CHRIST TO THE FATHER. ORIGEN: "Knowing," it says, "that the Father had put all things into his hand and that he came forth from God and was going to God, Jesus got up from the meal." Thus those things that had not hitherto been in Jesus' hands were put into his hands by the Father: it is not that

---

[60]Origen, who spoke in his treatise *On the Resurrection* of the translation of the *eidos* or "form" from the body to the soul, describes the attenuation of the body as the saint ascends in *On First Principles* 2.8, 11. [61]Jn 13:14. [62]Is 1:16. [63]Jn 13:8. [64]Rev 3:20. [65]Eph 6:13. [66]SC 385:188-94.

some were given and some withheld, but all, as David saw in the spirit when he said, "The Lord said to my Lord, 'Sit at my right hand, until I make your enemies your footstool.' "[67] For the enemies of Jesus were a portion of those whom Jesus knew, in the sense of fore-knowing, to have been given to him by the Father. And so that we may understand more clearly what it means to say "the Father put all things into his hands," let us consider also, "Just as all die in Adam, so in the Lord shall all be made alive."[68]

But if it is true both that the Father has given all things into his hands and that in Christ all shall be made alive, then there is no subversion of the justice of God and his handling of each thing according to its desert. This is clear because after "so in Christ shall all be made alive" comes the phrase "each in his proper order."[69]

Again you will perceive the different orders of those who have been made alive in Christ when the saying "the Father has given all things into his hands" is fulfilled, if you attend to the words "Christ the firstfruits, then those who are of Christ when he appears."[70] This end will come to pass with Christ at his appearing when "he shall hand the kingdom over to the God and the Father, having first done away with very rule and sway and power. . . . For he must reign until he has put all his enemies under his feet." Then, "the last enemy that shall be done away is death."[71] And this accords with the saying "the Father put all things into his hand." And the apostle says, to clarify the meaning of this, "When it says that all has been made subject, it is obvious that it excludes the one who has subjected all things to him."[72] . . . He knew that the Father had given all things to him and had given them into the hands that can hold the sum of things, in order that the sum of things might be under his hand; or else "the Father gave all things into his hand," that is, for his operations and bold undertakings. For, as he says, "My Father

is always working, and I work also."[73] And it was on account of the things that had gone forth from God that he came forth from God, for even that which at first did not wish to go forth from God had now come to be alien from God. The purpose was that the things that had gone forth might come in due course and order into the hands of Jesus and might be directed to go to God under his guidance, so that on account of his guidance they would be with God. COMMENTARY ON JOHN 32.3.[74]

THE PURGATIVE ACTION BECAME AN EC-CLESIASTICAL RITE.[75] AMBROSE: You came up from the font. What followed? You have heard the reading. The priest girded himself—it is indeed permitted to the presbyters to do it, but the ministry begins with the highest priest—the highest priest girded himself, I say, and washed your feet. What is this mystery? Surely you have heard that the Lord, having washed the feet of the other disciples, comes to Peter, and Peter says to him, "Will you wash my feet?" That is, "Do you, the Lord, wash the feet of a servant? Do you the spotless one wash my feet? Do you the maker of heaven wash my feet?" This you read elsewhere also: he comes to John, and John says to him, "I ought to be baptized by you; and will you be baptized by me?"[76] "I am a sinner, and have you come to a sinner as if to lay down your sins when you have committed no sin?" You see all righteousness,[77] you see the humility, you see the grace, you see the sanctification. "If I do not wash your feet," he says, "you will have no part with me."[78] ON THE SACRAMENTS 3.1.4.[79]

The Last Supper

---

[67]Ps 110:1. [68]1 Cor 15:2, but substituting "the Lord" for "Christ" and subsequently correcting the quotation. [69]1 Cor 15:22. [70]1 Cor 15:23. [71]1 Cor 15:23-25. [72]1 Cor 15:27. [73]Jn 5:17. [74]SC 385:198-202. [75]It has been a tradition in England that the sovereign should discharge this office on Maundy Thursday, the day before Good Friday. [76]Mt 3:14. [77]1 Pet 2:22. [78]Jn 13:8. [79]SAOS 24.

The Supper Was a Passover. Hippoly-tus:[80] This was the passover that Jesus desired to suffer on our behalf.[81] By suffering he delivered us from suffering, and by death he vanquished death, and through invisible food he made a gift of his immortal life. This was the salvific desire of Christ, this his spiritual love, to show that the types were but types and to give his holy body to his disciples in place of them: "Take, eat; this is my body. Take, drink; this is my blood, the new covenant, which was poured out for all for the remission of sins."[82] For this reason he does not desire to eat so much as he desires to die, that he might deliver us from the suffering caused by eating. And thus he plants tree against tree, and where long ago a hand was stretched out impiously for evil, he nailed his own untainted hand in piety to the cross, showing that in him that the whole of life is truly suspended. Paschal Homily 49-50.[83]

Christ's Eucharistic Actions Vindicate the Law. Chrysostom: And when they had eaten, he took bread and broke it. Why was it that this mystery was fulfilled at the season of the Passover? So that you may learn in all ways both that he is also the lawgiver of the old covenant and what things are foreshadowed in it through these acts. It was for this reason that he established the truth where the type had been. The evening was a sign that the times were fulfilled and that matters were approaching the very consummation at last. And he gives thanks, teaching us how this mystery is to be performed, showing that he does not go his death against his will, teaching us to bear with thanks whatever we may suffer and holding out good hopes to us from this also. For if the type was liberation from such great servitude, all the more will the Truth set free the inhabited world and will be handed over for the benefit of our nature. Homilies on Matthew 82.1.[84]

God Is Never Pleased by Carnal or Hypocritical Service. Origen: Compare

the Passover of the Lord and the Passover of the Jews, for the Passover of the Lord is the one according to the Law and the Passover of the Jews is that of the lawless. Therefore we must consider when the Passover and other days are said to be of the Lord and when they are said to be not of the Lord but of those convicted of sins. For example, in Exodus, after other matters, it is written in the first precept regarding the Passover, "And you must eat it with speed; it is the Passover of the Lord";[85] and in the second, "If your children say to you, 'What is this worship of ours?' you will say 'the sacrifice that is the Passover of the Lord, when he spared the houses of the children of Israel in Egypt.' " In Isaiah the Lord declares the new moons, the sabbath, the fasting and the festivals to be not his own but those of sinners. . . . It is written as follows: "Your new moons and your sabbaths and your great day I cannot endure; fasting and resting and your new moons and your festivals my soul hates."[86] And in one of the twelve prophets it is written, "I hate, I abhor your festivals."[87] And in the passage before us, the Passover was not that of the Lord but of the Jews.[88] And for this reason I believe that the Passover was prophetically declared to be theirs in the words "I hate, I abhor your festivals." For they performed not the work of God's festival but a defilement of that festival by killing Jesus.

And yet before that Passover of the Jews many went up to Jerusalem to sanctify themselves.[89] I would begin by saying that the many did not know how to sanctify themselves. Therefore, while they imagined that their own Passover was an offering of worship to God, they were so far from sanctifying themselves

---

[80]Both the authorship of this text and the reading of the final sentence are uncertain. [81]Wrongly deriving the Hebrew *pascha* ("Passover") from the same root as the Greek verb *paschō* ("I suffer"). [82]See Mt 26:26-28; 1 Cor 11:25. [83]SC 27:176-77. [84]PG 58:737-38. [85]Ex 12:11. [86]Is 1:13ff. [87]Amos 5:21. [88]Not that the Jews are more vicious than other people but that they, like other peoples are erring sinners who corrupt the gifts of God. [89]Jn 11:55.

that that they became more defiled than they had been before sanctifying themselves. For those who handed over Jesus said to Pilate, "It is not permitted to us to kill anyone."[90] And it was because of them that he said to the Savior, "Your own people and the high priests have handed you over to me." And indeed those who professed to be going up to sanctify themselves were the ones who cried out, saying to Pilate, "Do not release this man but Barabbas." And Barabbas was a robber.[91] And again, the Jews answered, "We have a law, and by the law he ought to die, because he made himself the Son of God."[92] . . . And this is what the Savior prophetically said to his disciple: "The hour is coming when everyone who kills you will think that he is offering worship to God."[93] What began at that point has been fulfilled. For those who saw fit to kill him thought that they were offering worship to God, and they went up to Jerusalem before their Passover so that they might sanctify themselves.[94] But the true sanctification took place not before the P:assover but during the Passover, when Jesus did for those who were being sanctified as the lamb of God and took away the sin of the world.[95] COMMENTARY ON JOHN 28.25.[96]

THE EUCHARIST MUST REPRESENT A REAL BODY. TERTULLIAN: Thus, having declared that he had desired with a great desire to eat the Passover,[97] as though it were his own (for it would have been unfitting for God to desire anything that belonged to another), he took bread and distributed it to his disciples, saying, "This is my body"[98]—by which he meant, a figure of my body. Yet there could have been no figure[99] had there been in truth no body; otherwise the imaginary thing, a mere phantom, could not have accommodated a figure. Or if his reason for representing the bread as his body was that he lacked a real body, then it was the bread that he should have given up for us. It would sort well with the fatuity of Marcion[100] that bread should be crucified. . . . He

did not understand that this was an ancient figure of the body of Christ, who had said through Jeremiah, "They have devised a device against me, saying, 'let us throw wood on his bread' "[101]—meaning plainly the cross on his body. AGAINST MARCION 4.40.[102]

A Foretaste of Betrayal

THE FORBEARANCE OF CHRIST NOT DUE TO IGNORANCE OR WEAKNESS. CHRYSOSTOM: Alas, what hardness of heart in the betrayer! Although he partook of the mysteries, he remained the same. And when he supped at the awful table, he was not changed. And this is what Luke means when he says that after this Satan entered into him—not so much despising the Lord's body[103] as toying with the shamelessness of the one who would betray him. The transgression indeed was greater for both reasons: first, that he came to the mystery with such thoughts, and second, that having approached, he became no better, either from fear or on account of benefits and honor. As for Christ, he did not restrain him, though he knew all; by this you may learn that he neglects none of those measures that conduce to correction. For this cause both before and after this event, he continuously reminded and admonished them, both through words and through deeds, through fear and threats, through honor and solicitude. And therefore afterwards, when he had let him go, he once again, through the mysteries, puts the disciples

---

[90]Jn 18:31. [91]Jn 18:40. [92]Jn 19:12. He then cites Jn 19:15; 11:55. [93]Jn 16:2. [94]Origen assumes that this sentence refers to the priests because it was they who (Jn 18:28) supposed themselves too pure to enter the house of the Roman governor before they had eaten the Passover. [95]Jn 1:29; 19:14. [96]SC 385:168-72. [97]Lk 22:15. [98]Lk 22:19. [99]Tertullian does not assert a real presence. [100]Marcion, a second-century heretic, accepted only Luke among the four Gospels but denied that the genuine text, correctly interpreted, bore witness to the humanity of Christ. [101]Jer 11:19 (LXX). [102]CCL 1:656. [103]As we might have guessed from the fact that Satan is not deterred by his previous discomfiture in the wilderness.

in mind of the sacrifice and in the midst of the meal speaks of the cross, making his passion bearable through the whole length of his discourse. For, if they were so confounded after all these great events and anticipatory sayings, what would they not have suffered if they had heard nothing of this? Homilies on Matthew 82.1.[104]

Christ's Fear Is No Contradiction, but an Index of His Divinity. Origen: Having said this, Jesus was troubled in spirit and said, "Truly, truly, I say to you, one of you will betray me."[105] Above he said, "Now is my soul troubled."[106] But now the words are "Having said this, Jesus was troubled in spirit." And the sort of thing that I wish to know in this place is, why is it not said, by analogy with "my soul is troubled," that the spirit of Jesus was troubled? And this I have ventured to investigate with due caution, having examined throughout the whole Scripture the difference between soul and spirit. Soul I observe to be a sort of medium, receptive alike to virtue and vice, whereas the human being's spirit that is within him is not receptive of the worse things. For the noblest things are said to be fruits of the spirit, not, as one might suppose, the Holy Spirit but the human. For in contradistinction to these the works of the flesh are said to be manifest, all being culpable, since no work of the flesh is worthy of praise.[107] Before this passage I have found it said that the spirit of a base person was hardened by the Lord God; for thus it is written in Deuteronomy, "And Sion the king of Eshbon did not wish us to pass through his realm, because the Lord God has hardened his spirit and made his heart stubborn, that he might be delivered into your hands on this day."[108] But this would be more appropriately examined in our comments on Deuteronomy; our present task is to say how it is that in the aforesaid passage Jesus is said to have suffered not a troubled soul or trouble in the soul or trouble of the spirit but trouble in the spirit. In order then that our examination

regarding the spirit may not fail of its purpose, it should be said that in the phrase my soul is troubled, the trouble is a passion, and of the soul; but in the phrase "Jesus was troubled in the spirit," the human phenomenon, the passion, is an effect of the overruling power of the spirit. For as the saint lives in spirit, which bears sway over the things in life—every activity, prayer and hymn to God—so whatever he does, he does in spirit, and whatever he suffers, he suffers in spirit. Now if that is true of the saint, all the more is it true of Jesus the chief of the saints, whose human spirit—inasmuch as he assumed a whole man—being within him shook the other human elements in him. And thus he was troubled in spirit, that he might bear witness and say with, as it were, his divine oath, the word *truly*: I say to you that one of you will betray me. For it seems to me that his spirit, having contemplated what the devil had already cast into the heart of Judas Simon Iscariot—the plan of betraying his teacher—was troubled because of his luminous perception of the future. And since the trouble originated from the knowledge in his spirit, which also fell into a troubled state, Jesus, it says, "was troubled in the spirit." Commentary on John 32.18.[109]

Judas Is Given the Opportunity of Repentance. Chrysostom: Ah, the shamelessness of Judas! For he too was present and came to share both the mysteries and the salt, and he was convicted at the very table when, even if one were a beast, one would have grown meeker. It is indeed for this reason that the Evangelist indicates that while they were eating Christ speaks of his betrayal, so that he may show that the wickedness of the betrayer is out of keeping both with the time and with the table. For, when evening had come, the disciples having done as Jesus instructed them, he was reclining with the Twelve. And as they

---

[104]PG 58:737. [105]Jn 13:21. [106]Jn 12:27. [107]Gal 5:19. [108]Deut 2:30. [109]SC 385:278-82.

were eating, he said, the text tells us, "Truly I say to you, one of you twelve will betray me." Now before the dinner he also washed their feet; and see how he spares the betrayer. For he did not say, "such and such a one will betray me," but "one of you," as though to give him a further opportunity of secretly repenting. And he chooses to cause fear in all of them that he might preserve this one. "One of you the twelve," he says, the ones who are with me everywhere, whose feet I have washed, to whom I have disclosed so much. Therefore unbearable sorrow now took hold of that holy band. And John says, "They were perplexed and looked at one another," and each asked, fearing for himself, even though they were conscious of no such motion in themselves. And this author says, "In their grief they each began to say earnestly to him, 'Is it I, Lord?'" And he answered, "The one to whom I give this sop when I have dipped it, that is he." See how he screened him when he desired to release the others from this trouble. For indeed they were dead with fear, and therefore they kept on asking. And he did this not only because he wished to free them from this agony but also because he desired to correct the betrayer. For Judas had often heard distractedly, remaining incorrigible and untouched by remorse; therefore, wishing to strike directly on him, he tears away his mask. Since in their grief they had begun to ask, "Is it I, Lord?" he answered, saying, "The one who has dipped his hand in the bowl with me is the one who will betray me." "The Son of man, therefore, goes as it is written of him; but woe to that man by whom the Son of man is betrayed. It would be good for him had that man never been born." There are some who infer that Judas was so brazen as not to honor his master but to dip his hand at the same time as he did. To me it seems, however, that Jesus did this rather by way of exhortation to him and drawing him into concord; for there is something nobler in this. HOMILIES ON MATTHEW 81.1.[110]

THE TREACHERY OF JUDAS WAS UNMASKED. EPHREM THE SYRIAN: For when Jesus distributed bread to the eleven without distinction, Judas came near to receive it as his companions came to do who had come near; but Jesus dropped the bread into the water, deprived it of consecration and by this means distinguished the morsel of Judas. Thenceforth it was known to the apostles that Judas was he who would betray Jesus. COMMENTARY ON THE DIATESSARON 19.3.[111]

THE FALL OF JUDAS RESEMBLES THAT OF ADAM. ORIGEN: By applying the expression "one of you" to Judas, he perhaps indicates that it is by reason of having a disposition not unlike that of the others that the apostolic order in which a high place had been allotted to him. For likewise I have read "See, Adam is become like one of us"—the expression here being not "like us" or "like me." But because it is one who has fallen from blessedness, the expression is "like one of us." Now this "like one" seems to me consonant with the expression, "You die like humans and fall like one of the princes."[112] For while there were many princes, one had fallen, and it is in close imitation of him that those who sin experience their own fall. For just as Adam fell when he was in a divine state, so it was with those to whom the Word says, "I have said you are gods and children of the most high":[113] they fell from blessedness not being primordially human beings;[114] they "die like humans and fall like one of the princes." And

---

[110]PG 58:731-32. [111]ELCEC 66. [112]Ps 82:7. [113]Citing Ps 82:6 in the manner of Jn 10:35. [114]This may imply that the words of the psalm were addressed to angels, but Origen does not say so, and, although he believed that humans could join the angels after death, it is not clear that he believed that angels had descended to the human condition, except in a handful of miraculous cases. He believes that the souls of Adam and Eve enjoyed an immediate consciousness of God and that their bodies were responsive to divine promptings. He also holds that the true self of a human is the rational nature, in which the body does not participate (*On First Principles* 1.7.1), and that the bodies of the redeemed will be much more tenuous than their fleshy domiciles in the present world.

I think that in the present saying he intimates, in a wonderful manner, that "the one who will betray me is not a stranger to my disciples—not even one of my many disciples but one of the apostles whom I distinguished by my own choice." There are many, therefore, who say, in condemnation of Jesus, "Crucify, crucify,"[115] and take this one from the earth;[116] but to betray him was the act of one who had seen and known him. COMMENTARY ON JOHN 32.18.[117]

GOD'S FOREKNOWLEDGE DOES NOT MAKE HIM RESPONSIBLE FOR THE SIN. ORIGEN: Suppose that a person learns, from one in no way responsible for the events, that such and such a thing has happened or will happen to such and such a one and fails to discern that that the one who teaches that something has happened or will happen is not at all responsible for the thing turning out as it does: he will imagine that the one who informed him that such and such a thing has occurred or will occur is the author of the things about which he teaches. Yet clearly he will err in imagining this. For example, someone might chance on a prophetic book that betrayed the facts about Judas the betrayer and suppose, because he has seen the fulfilment of this, that the book was the cause of this subsequent event—or again he might surmise that the book itself was not the cause, but the one who first wrote it or the one who inspired it—which is to say, God. In fact, however, the very words of the prophecies about Judas, when investigated, reveal that God was not the cause of Judas' treachery but only showed prescient knowledge of the deeds that would result, through this man's own fault, from his vicious character. And likewise if one reflects deeply on the doctrine that God knows all things beforehand and on the books in which he has, as it were, inscribed the account of his foreknowledge, he will conclude that the one who foreknows is in no way responsible for the things foreknown, nor are the books that have received the inscribed account of the foreknowledge of him who foreknows.

When God initially undertook the creation of the world, since nothing occurs without a cause, he traversed in his mind all things that were going to be, seeing that if *a* occurs *b* follows, and if *b* follows *c* ensues, and when *c* obtains *d* will occur. And thus having traversed the whole sequence of actions up to the end, he knows what will be, not being at all responsible for each thing that he knows turning out as it will. For it is just as though one were to see someone acting impetuously through ignorance and because of his impetuosity setting out foolishly on the road of stumbling: should he perceive that he is going to stumble and fall, he does not become responsible for that person's stumbling. This we must take to be the case with God: he foresees what sort of person each shall be, and sees clearly the reasons why he is going to be so and on what occasions he will sin or act rightly. And if it is proper to say that the foreknowledge is not the cause of the events (for God has no part with the one whose sin he foresees, whenever he sins), we shall say on the contrary—somewhat paradoxically, yet truly—that that which is to be is the cause of the foreknowledge of it. For it is not because it is foreknown that it happens but because it is to happen that it is foreknown. COMMENTARY ON GENESIS 3 AT PHILOKALIA 23.3, 8.[118]

PETER ALLOWED TO BOAST THAT HE MAY LEARN. CHRYSOSTOM: What are you saying, Peter? The prophet says, "The sheep shall be scattered," and Christ has confirmed the saying, yet you say, "Not so"? Was it not enough before, when you said, "God spare you,"[119] and your mouth was stopped? It is in fact for this reason that he permits him to fall, teaching him to obey Christ in all things and consider his declaration more authoritative than his own conscience. And the rest reaped

---

[115]Lk 23:21. [116]Acts 22:22. [117]SC 385:284-86. [118]SC 226:140-42, 154-56. [119]Mt 16:22.

not a little fruit from his denial, having contemplated the weakness of humanity and the veracity of God. For when he makes a statement, there is no more occasion for quibbling or secession from the mass. "For your boasting," it says, "you will see on your own head, not on another's."[120] For the right thing was to pray and say, "Assist us so that we do not fall away from you." He, however, confides in himself and says, "Even if all are offended in you, yet I never shall be." His meaning was "even if all suffer this, I shall not suffer it"; and little by little this led him to presumption. Now because Christ wished this, he acquiesced in his denial. For since he would not bear any words, either Christ's or the prophet's (though Christ's purpose in adducing the prophet had been to prevent his objecting), he is taught through deeds. That this was indeed his reason for acquiescing, so that he might correct him by this means, you can learn from his saying, "I have prayed for you, that your faith may not fail."[121] For this he said to make a strong impression on him and to show him that his fall would be more grave than that of the others and in more need of assistance. For there were two counts against him, first that he objected and then that he put himself above the others; or rather there was a third also, that he took everything on himself. Thus, in his remedy for this, Christ allowed the fall to take place, and for this reason, ignoring the others, he directs his words to him. "Simon, Simon," he says, "Satan has sought to sift you like wheat"—that is, to trouble them, agitate them and put them to the test—but I have prayed for you, that your faith may not fail. Now why, if Satan asked for them all, did he not say, "I have prayed for all of you"? Is it not obvious that it was for the reason that I have already stated, that he addresses his words to Peter to make an impression on him and to show that his fall is graver than that of the others? HOMILIES ON MATTHEW 82.3.[122]

Gethsemane

CHRIST'S WEEPING DOES NOT COMPROMISE HIS DIVINITY. AMBROSE: There are many who cling to this passage, turning the Savior's sorrow into an argument that his infirmity was implanted from the beginning, not taken on him for a season, with the aim of wresting the meaning away from the natural sense. For my part, not only do I not believe that it needs excuse but also there is no place where I wonder more at his piety and nobility. For he would have brought less good to me had he not taken my feelings on himself. Therefore he grieved on my account, when he had no cause for grief on his own, and having put aside the bliss of his eternal divinity, he labors under the heaviness of my infirmity. Yes, he took my sorrow on himself that he might bestow his bliss on me, and he came down to walk in our steps to the point of a miserable death so that he might recall us to walk in his steps to life. Therefore I speak with confidence of his sorrow because I proclaim the cross; for neither was it the appearance of incarnation that he assumed but the reality. Therefore he had also to take on grief, that he might vanquish and not merely repudiate sorrow. For the ones whom we praise for courage are not those who have felt not so much the grief as a numbing of their wounds, for it speaks of "a man in affliction and knowing how to bear infirmities."[123] He wished to teach us that, as we have learned from Joseph's story not to fear prison, so we should learn to vanquish death in Christ and (what is greater still) the means of vanquishing the pains of the death to come. For how could we imitate you, Lord Jesus, if we did not follow you as a man, if we did not believe you dead, if we had not seen your wounds? How could the disciples have believed that you were going to die, had they not discerned the sorrow of one about to die? Thus, up to this point, they sleep

[120]Gal 6:4. [121]Lk 22:32. [122]PG 58:741. [123]Is 53:3.

and know nothing of grief, while Christ grieves for them: for so we read that he bears our sins and grieves for us.[124] Therefore, Lord, it is not your wounds but mine that you grieve for, not your death but our infirmity; and we deemed that the grief was yours when you were grieving not for yourself but for me. EXPOSITIONS ON THE GOSPEL OF LUKE 10.56-57.[125]

EVEN THIS TRIAL WAS PROPHESIED. JUSTIN MARTYR: The words "All my bones have been poured out and scattered, my heart has become like melting wax in the midst of my belly" were a prophecy of what happened to him on that night when they came against him on the Mount of Olives. For in the recollections, which I say were put together by the apostles and their followers, it is written that sweat like drops of blood took hold of him,[126] as he prayed and said, "Let this cup pass, if it may be." Clearly his heart was trembling and his bones likewise, and that heart of his resembled wax melting into his belly, so that we might know that the Father has resolved that his own Son should be truly acquainted even with sufferings of this kind and may not say that this man, because he was the Son of God, did not partake of the things that pertain and happen to us. DIALOGUE WITH TRYPHO 103.7.[127]

HIS DEPARTURE AND RETURN WERE FOR THE INSTRUCTION OF THE DISCIPLES. CHRYSOSTOM: It was because they were clinging to him inseparably that he says, "Remain here while I go apart to pray."[128] For it was his custom to make his prayers apart from them. In doing this he taught us to cultivate silence and deep peace for ourselves in prayers. And he takes with him the three and says to them, "My soul is very sorrowful to death." For what reason does he not take all with him? So that they might not fall. Only these, the ones who had been witnesses of his glory. Yet these too, nonetheless, he lets go, and proceeding a little, he prays saying, "Father, if it is possible, let

this cup pass from me. Nevertheless, not as I will, but as you will." And when he returns to them, finding them asleep, he says to Peter, "Had you then not strength to stay awake with me one hour? Be wakeful and pray, that you may not enter into temptation. The spirit is eager, but the flesh is weak." He is not simply directing his words at Peter above the rest but also to the others who had been sleeping. But he strikes directly at him here too, for the reason that I have mentioned earlier. Then, since the others had said the same thing (for it says that when Peter had declared, "Even if I must die, I will not deny you," all the other disciples spoke likewise), he addresses himself to all, exposing their weakness. For those who elected to die with him had not strength even to stay awake and grieve with him when he was grieving, but sleep overcame them while he was praying strenuously. And so that the episode may not seem to be a sham, drops of sweat well forth for the reason already explained. And so that the heretics may not say that he counterfeits his agony, for this reason his drops of sweat were like gouts of blood, and an angel appeared to comfort him; countless indeed were the tokens of fear so that none could say that his words were a pretence.

This was also the reason for the prayer. In saying, then, "If it is possible, let it pass," he revealed his humanity. But in saying, "Nevertheless, not as I will but as you will," he revealed his virtuous and philosophic character, teaching us to follow God even when nature draws us the other way. For since it was not enough for the foolish merely to show his countenance, he adds words too. Again words alone were not enough. But there was also need of actions, and these he attaches to his words, so that even those who are straining to pick a

---

[124]Is 53:4. [125]CSEL 32.4:476-77. [126]Lk 22:44. Justin's recollections (*apomnēmneumata*) appear to have been a compendium of matter that is now dispersed among different gospels, not all of them canonical. [127]JMAA 220. [128]Mt 26:36.

quarrel may believe that he became a man and died. For if, when these things occurred, there are some who disbelieve this fact, it would have been far better had these things not occurred. Do you see through how many signs he reveals the truth of his condescension? Through his utterances and through his sufferings. Then it relates that when he returned he said to Peter, "Had you not strength to stay awake with me one hour?"[129] All slept, and he rebukes Peter, allusively reminding him what he had said. And the words with me do not mean simply that, but he says, as it were, "Had you not strength to stay awake with me, though you will lay down you life for me?" And the sequel conveys this very same thing by allusion, for he says, "Be wakeful and pray that you do not enter into temptation."[130] Do you see how once again he teaches them not to boast on their own account but to subdue their thoughts and maintain a lowly state of mind, referring all to God? And at one point he directs his words to Peter, at another to all of them. And to him he says, "Simon, Simon, Satan has sought to sift you like wheat, but I have prayed for you"; but to all in common, "Pray that you do not enter into temptation,"[131] everywhere curtailing their presumption and making them ready for combat. And so that he may not appear to be speaking with unqualified vehemence, he says, "The spirit is willing, but the flesh is weak."[132] And what he means is, "Even if you wish to look down on death, you will not be able to, until God extends his hand; for it is the state of mind that leads the flesh."

And again he conveys the same thing by allusion, saying, "Father, if it is not possible for this thing to pass from me, allowing me not to drink it, let your will be done."[133] Here he shows that he warmly assents to the will of God and that this is always to be followed and sought out. "And returning he found them asleep."[134] For apart from the lateness of the night, their eyes too had been made heavy by despondency. And up to the third time he

departed and uttered the same words, confirming that he was human. For in the Scriptures the second and the third are the index of truth. Thus Joseph also said to Pharaoh that "the dream has appeared to you a second time, for the sake of truth, and this has happened to persuade you that these things shall certainly come to pass."[135] And this same saying he uttered once, twice and a third time so as to give certain proof of his condescension. And what was the cause of his returning a second time? To convict them of being so steeped in despondency that they were not even sensible of his presence. Or rather he did not convict them but went a little distance, exposing their overwhelming weakness, in that even after being rebuked they were unable to show fortitude. But he did not keep watch while they slept and then rebuke them, so as not to add blows to the beaten, but having gone away and prayed and returned, he says, "Sleep again and take your rest." Now that was indeed the time to stay awake, but revealing that they will not easily bear even the sight of dangers but will flee and shrink from the combat—while anyway he does not need their assistance and it is absolutely necessary that he be handed over— he says, "Sleep on and take your rest. See, the hour is come, and the Son of man is given into the hands of sinners."[136] Again he shows that what is happening is an act of condescension. HOMILIES ON MATTHEW 83.1.[137]

HIS PRAYER REVEALS THE PRESENCE OF A HUMAN WILL. MAXIMUS THE CONFESSOR:[138] If you understand Jesus' prayer, "Father, if it is possible, let this cup pass from me," which gives the indication of resistance, as expressed by the man . . . just like us . . . what do you make of the rest of the prayer, "Let not what I

---

[129]Mt 26:40. [130]Mt 26:41. [131]Lk 22:31. [132]Mt 26:41. [133]Mt 26:42. [134]Mt 26:43. [135]A loose citation of Gen 41:32. [136]Mt 26:45. [137]PG 58:745-47. [138]Maximus opposed the monothelite view that Christ possessed only a single will at a time when it was almost the common teaching of the church.

will but what you will prevail"? Is it a matter of resistance or courage, of agreement or disagreement? Certainly no one of right mind will dispute that it is a matter neither of contention nor cowardice but of perfect harmony and concurrence.

And if it is a matter of perfect concurrence, whom do you understand as subject? The man who is just like us, or the man whom we consider in the role of Savior? If it is from the man who is just like us, then does our teacher Gregory[139] err when he declares "seeing as the human will does not always follow God but so often resists and contends with him"? For if it follows God, it is not resisting him; and if it is resisting him, it is not following him. These two assertions, being contrary, mutually nullify and exclude each other. If, however, you understand the subject of the phrase "Let not what I will but what you will prevail" to be not the man just like us but the man we consider as Savior, then you have confessed the ultimate concurrence of the human with the divine will, which is both his and his Father's; and you have demonstrated that with the duality of his natures there are two wills and two operations respective to the two natures and that he admits of no opposition between them, even though he maintains all the while the difference between the two natures from which, in which and which he is by nature.[140]

But if, constrained by these arguments, you proceed to say that the negation "Not as I will" comes not from the man who is just like us or from the man whom we consider in the role of Savior but rather refers, as a negation, to the eternal divinity of the Only-begotten— which excludes his willing something for himself separately from the Father—then you are compelled to refer what is willed, namely, the declining of the cup, to the very same eternal divinity. . . . Now if even the thought of such reasoning is repugnant, then clearly the negation here—"Not what I will"—absolutely precludes opposition and instead demon-

strates harmony between the human will of the Savior and the divine will shared by him and his Father, given that the Logos assumed our nature in its entirety and deified his human will in the assumption. It follows, then, that, having become like us for our sake, he was calling on his God and Father in a human manner when he said, "Let not what I will but what you will prevail," inasmuch as, being God by nature, he also has, as his human volition, the fulfillment of the will of the Father. Opusculum 6.[141]

It Is Not for Himself That He Sorrows. Hilary of Poitiers: He asks that the cup may pass with him, though without doubt it still remains with him, since at that time his mission to make a new covenant for the sins of many by pouring out his blood was being fulfilled. For he does not ask that the cup should not be with him but that it should pass away. Then he asks that his will should not be done, and what he himself desires to be done, he asks that this very thing should not be granted to him. For he says, "But nevertheless not what I want but what you want." The resolve to forgo the cup indicates that he shares in human anxiety, keeping in mind though that he was making no distinction between the will that he has in common with the Father and that which properly belongs to himself. In order, however, that he may not be understood to pray for himself and to be absolved both of the motive for the desire that he expresses and of the prayer not to obtain it, he begins this whole act of prayer with the overture, "My Father, if it is your will." So is there anything reserved for the Father of whose possibility he is uncertain? And if nothing is impossible for the Father, it is clear to whose condition this phrase "if it is

---

[139]Gregory of Nazianzus *Oration* 30.12. [140]Or "which he was, the same according to nature." Blowers and Wilken, from whom this translation is taken, speak of a "properly and perfectly irreducible relation between his person and natures." See *MCOCM* 75. [141]*MCOCM* 173-76.

possible" must appertain. For after this pleading in prayer follow the words "and he came to his disciples." . . . Can the cause of his sorrow and prayer that the cup should be passed on still be obscure? For he bids them watch and pray with him to this end, that they be not led into temptation, since, while the spirit indeed is ready, the flesh is weak. For those who were promising that, in the constancy of their faithful consciences, they would not be offended, were going to suffer offense because of the weakness of the flesh. Thus it is not for himself that he sorrows or for himself that he prays, for those whom he admonishes to pray with continual vigilance, lest the cup of his passion to fall to them. Clearly he prays that this should pass from him in order that it may not remain with them. ON THE TRINITY 10.37.[142]

PERHAPS HE WAS PRAYING FOR A DIFFERENT TRIAL. ORIGEN: Consider whether it is possible that the Savior, looking on the different types of cup, if I may put it thus, and on the consequences attached to each, and perceiving, with a particular depth of wisdom, how they differed, deprecated this particular type of death by martyrdom but was perhaps secretly praying for another that was harder to bear, so that he might produce some more universal benefit that would touch more people. But it was not yet the will of the Father that this should be, for he governed matters in due course and order by a wiser policy that did not accord with the counsel of the Son or with what the Savior had in view. EXHORTATION TO MARTYRDOM 29.[143]

CHRIST'S AGONY WAS COMMEMORATED IN PILGRIMAGE AND PAGEANT. EGERIA: And so when the cockcrow begins, the procession descends from Imbomon with hymns and arrives at that place where the Lord prayed, as it is written in the Gospel, "And he went on as far as the cast of a stone and prayed." For

in that place there is a well-appointed church, which the bishop enters with all the people. There a prayer is said that suits the place and the day, and a suitable hymn is also recited, while there is a reading from that very passage in the Gospel where he says to his disciples, "Watch and pray, lest you enter into temptation." After that whole passage has been read, prayer begins anew. And now from that point everyone, down to the smallest infant, descends on foot to Gethsemane. Because there is such a teeming multitude, wearied by vigils and weakened by daily fasting, they proceed very slowly with hymns toward Gethsemane. Over two hundred church candles are prepared in order to give light to the whole people. When they arrive in Gethsemane, a suitable prayer is first made, likewise a hymn is recited, and finally there is a reading from that passage in the Gospel where the Lord is put in bonds. While that passage is being read, the whole people cries out and moans with tears, so that it may be that all the groaning of the people is heard as far away as the city. And now from that hour that marks the arrest they go on foot with hymns to the city, arriving at the gate at that time when as it were one person begins to recognise another. From there they all, to the last one, proceed through the middle of the city, the great and the lesser, the rich, the poor, all arrayed there; it is the particular custom of that day that none puts an end to his vigil until the morning. In this way the bishop is led down from Gethsemane as far as the gate, and from there through the whole city as far as the cross. PILGRIMAGE.[144]

THE RESISTANCE OF THE DISCIPLES MAY BE EXCUSED BUT NOT CONDONED. CHRYSOSTOM: Who was this who cut off the ear? John says that it was Peter,[145] for this was a consequence of his ardor. But what we need to

---

[142]CCL 62A:490-91. [143]GCS 2, Origen 1:26. [144]ELS 534-35. [145]Jn 18:10.

investigate is, why were they carrying swords? For that they were carrying them is evident not only from this passage but also from what they said beforehand when questioned: "Here are two."[146] But for what reason did Jesus urge them to have them? For this is what Luke relates, that he said to them, "When I sent you out without purse or wallet or staff, did you lack for anything?" And when they said "Nothing," he said to them, "Well now, if one has a purse, let him take it, and likewise his wallet. And he who does not have one, let him sell his cloak and purchase a sword." And when they said, "Here are two swords," he said to them, "It is enough." For what reason, then, did he allow them to have them? To tell them that he would certainly be betrayed. Therefore he says to them purchase a sword, not meaning they should arm themselves—far from it—but to make the betrayal apparent through this saying. And for what reason, one may ask, did he tell them to have a wallet? He was teaching them henceforth to be sober and vigilant and to make great use of their own zeal. For in the beginning he inflamed them greatly by his own power, untried as they were, but after this he bids them use their own wings, like one leading fledglings out of the nest. Then, so that they would not imagine that it was through weakness that he let them go, he instructs them to take with them also their own resources, reminding them of former events with the words 'When I sent you out without a purse, did you lack for anything?'[147] His purpose was that they might learn his might from two things—from his earlier provision for them and from the manner in which he now left them to themselves.

But from where came the swords that they had there? They had just come outside from the dining table. It is probable therefore that there were swords there because of the lamb, and that these men, having heard that some would be coming out against him and expecting to fight for their master, took them up for assistance, though this was merely their own notion. Consequently, when Peter uses his sword, he is rebuked and with a heavy admonition. For he resisted the oncoming servant ardently, yet resisting not on his own behalf but doing this on behalf of his master. Christ, however, did not allow any injury to occur, for he both healed him and performed a great miracle, sufficient to demonstrate both his benevolence and his power and at the same time both the devotion and the meekness of his disciple. For he acted first with devotion, then with obedience, since when he heard the words "Put the sword in its sheath,"[148] he obeyed at once and after this did nothing of the kind. Another witness says that they asked, "Shall we strike?"[149] but he forbade them and healed the man. And he rebuked his disciple and with an admonition, to persuade him, "for all those who take the sword," he says, "shall perish by the sword." And he adds a reason, saying, "Do you suppose that I am not able to call on my Father, who will furnish me more than twelve legions of angels? But how shall the Scriptures be fulfilled?"[150] By these words he quenched their violent spirit, showing that this was also what the Scriptures required. For this cause he also prayed here that they would meekly bear what befell, having learned that in this way too it happens according to the will of God. And he pacified them in these two ways, first by reproaching their evil counsels—"for all who take the sword," he says, "shall die by the sword"—and second by showing that he did not endure this against his will: "for I am able," he says, "to call on my Father." Now why did he not say, "Do you suppose that I am not able to destroy them all?" Because it was more persuasive for him to put it in this way, since they did not yet have the proper opinion of him. And a little before he had said, "My soul is very sorrowful to death," and "Father, let this

---

[146]Lk 22:38.   [147]Lk 22:35.   [148]Mt 26:52; Jn 18:11.   [149]Lk 22:49. [150]Mt 26:53.

cup pass from me," visibly agitated and sweating and being comforted by angels. Since then he displayed many human traits, it would not have seemed persuasive for him to say, "Do you suppose that I cannot destroy them all?" For this reason he says, "Do you suppose that I am not able presently to call on my Father?" And this thing again he expresses modestly, saying, "He will furnish me twelve legions of angels." For if one angel destroyed 185,000 fully armed men,[151] was there need of twelve legions against a thousand men? Not at all. But he tempers the remark to their fear and weakness, since they were dead with fear. For this reason he also builds in the Scriptures, saying, "How then will the Scriptures be fulfilled?" stirring fear in them from this quarter also: "For if this is what they require," he says, "will you take up arms to oppose them?" HOMILIES ON MATTHEW 84.1.[152]

Trial Before the Jews

THE PRESENCE OF TWO HIGH PRIESTS BETRAYS THE DECADENCE OF JERUSALEM. EUSEBIUS: The high priest according to the divine law was required to celebrate the liturgy for the whole period of his life and to hand it on to his true-born son. But at the times appointed, the oil had been spilled in accordance with the prophecy.[153] But then Herod, and the Romans after him, set up high priests as seemed good to them without judgment or respect for the Law, according the honor to men of common rank and no distinction. They made merchandise and traffic of the name, presenting the title year by year, now to one and now to another. It was for this reason, as it seems to me, that when the holy Evangelist Luke recorded the time of our Savior's proclamation, the words that he used to mark it were in the fifteenth year of the reign of Tiberius Caesar, when Pontius Pilate was governor of Judea, while Herod, Philip and Lysanias were tetrarchs and Annas and Caiaphas high

priests.[154] For how could these two have been high priests at the same time if the legislation concerning the high priests had not been set at nought?[155] And in any case Josephus attests this by writing, "Valerius Gratus, the general of the Romans, having dismissed the high priest Ananus, declared Ishmael son of Phebas high priest, then having deposed this person after a short time, announced that the high priest was Eleazar the son of the high priest Ananus. But when a year had elapsed, he dismissed this man also and handed over the high priesthood to Simon the son of Kathimus. Yet, the time during which this man had held the honor was no more than a year, and his successor was Joseph, otherwise Caiaphas."[156] This I have been obliged to set down by reason of the words "The oil shall be spilled, and there is no crime in it,"[157] the import of which I take to be indisputable. PROOF OF THE GOSPEL 8.2.98-101.[158]

CAIAPHAS'S HOUSE WAS JUDGED IN A.D. 70. PRUDENTIUS: Fallen is the lofty house of Caiaphas the blasphemer, where the holy face of Christ was beaten. This is the end that awaits sinners, whose life will be buried forever in ruinous tombs. In these halls the Lord stood bound and, lashed to a column, offered his back, like that of a slave, to the blows of the whip. Still that venerable column stands, and it upholds a mighty temple, teaching us to live innocent of all misdeeds. DITTOCHAEUM.[159]

HEROD'S DOOM WAS ALSO FORETOLD.[160] JUSTIN MARTYR: And the words "They opened their mouth against me like a roaring lion" signify the then king of the Jews, also bearing the name of Herod, as the successor of that Herod who, when Christ had been born, killed all the infants born in Bethlehem at that

---

[151]2 Sam 19:35. [152]PG 58:751-53. [153]Dan 9:26-27 (LXX).
[154]Lk 3:1. [155]Jn 18:13-14 [156]Josephus *Antiquities* 18.2.2.
[157]Dan 9:26-27 (LXX). [158]GCS 23:385-86. [159]PL 60:107.
[160]See Lk 13:32; 23:11.

time. . . . The other Herod, succeeding Arche-laus, received the dominion that was allotted to him, and Pilate sent Jesus in bonds to him as a favor. And God, foreknowing that this was going to happen, spoke as follows: "And having bound him they sent him as a gift to the king of Assyria."[161] Or else he used the expression "roaring lion" of the accuser himself,[162] whom Moses in fact calls the serpent, though in Job and Zechariah he is called the accuser while by Jesus he is styled Satan. DIALOGUE WITH TRYPHO 103.3.[163]

CHRIST'S SILENCE WAS A FULFILLMENT OF PROPHECY. JUSTIN MARTYR: The power of his mighty Word, through which he never failed to expose the Pharisees and the scribes as they set their traps for him, restrained itself like a mighty and superabundant spring from which the water has gone when he kept silence before Pilate, choosing not to say anything to anyone (as has been shown in the recollections of the apostles[164]) so that he might possess also the lively fruit of which Isaiah speaks when he says, "The Lord gives me a tongue to know when I ought to speak a word."[165] DIALOGUE WITH TRYPHO 102.5.[166]

CHRIST TURNS THE HIGH PRIEST'S QUESTION AGAINST HIMSELF. ORIGEN: "And the high priest said to him, 'I adjure you by the living God that you tell us if you are the Christ, the Son of God.' "[167] And we do in fact find that adjuration is occasion-ally a custom in the Law. For in Numbers the Law says that "the priest shall adjure her (that is, the woman in whose husband a spirit of jealousy has arisen) and he (that is, the priest) shall say to the woman, 'If no one has slept with you, and if you have not transgressed so as to be defiled by a man who is not your own, you shall be unharmed by the accursed water of this ordeal.' "[168] . . . However, it was not proper for our Lord to reply to the adjuration of the chief priest, as

if he had suffered coercion against his own will through his adjuration. For this reason he did not deny that he was the Christ, the Son of God, nor did he openly declare it, but as if he himself was accepting another's sworn testimony (he being the very same who was pronounced to be Christ the Son of God in the priest's question) he said, "You have said" it.[169] And since everyone who acts sinfully is born of the devil, and the chief priest was acting sinfully when he laid an ambush for Jesus, he was therefore a child of the devil and as one born of the devil was imitating his own father. Twice the latter had doubtingly asked the Savior "if you are the Son of God," as is rewritten in the account of his tempta-tion. For to say "if you are the Son of God" is much as though one should say "if you are the Christ, the Son of the living God." Rightly indeed one can say in this passage that to make a doubt whether Christ is the Son of God is a work of the devil and the chief priest laying an ambush for our Lord. But Peter was not found to be such a one, for without the slightest hesitation he declared, "You are the Christ, the Son of the living God,"[170] and he did not add here the word *if*. On this account he is called blessed, because "it was not flesh and blood that had revealed this to him but God the Father who is in heaven." Those, however, who say with hesitation "if you are the Son of God" are strangers to all blessed-ness. For it was because the chief priest was not worthy of the doctrine of Christ that Christ does not instruct him and does not say "I am" but takes the word from his mouth and turns it back on him to his discomfiture, say-ing, "You have said it," so that in this way he

[161]Hos 10:6 with additions; Justin may be blending this with Hos 11:10, where an agent (probably God) is compared with a roaring lion. [162]See 1 Pet 5:8. The Greek appellation *diabolos*, from which we derive the word *devil*, means "a slanderer." [163]JMAA 219. [164]See Jn 19:10; 1 Pet 2:23. [165]Is 50:4. [166]JMAA 217. [167]Mt 26:63. [168]Num 5:19. [169]Mt 26:64; Lk 22:70. The answer can be either a weak affirmation or a denial; it is the latter at Mt 27:11. [170]Mt 16:16.

might be seen to have been discomfited rather than instructed. COMMENTARY ON MATTHEW 110.[171]

THE HUMILIATION OF CHRIST IS A FULFILLMENT OF PROPHECY. ORIGEN: In my view those men behaved vilely, when, hearing Jesus say, "However, I say to you, that henceforth you shall see the Son of man sitting at the right hand of power and coming in the clouds," they presumed to spit in his face. For their notion of him was that they could shame him as a liar and that he would not be able to bear the ignominy of being spat on, though he was sitting at the right hand of power and was to come in the clouds. This was because they did not know the speeches of Isaiah the prophet, who foretold this very thing of him—speaking, moreover, in the person of the Lord our Savior: "What of it that I came, and there was no man? I called, and there was none to obey? Is not my hand strong enough to rescue them, or can I not snatch them out? Behold, with my curse I shall make the sea desert, and the streams too I shall make desert, and the fish will be dried up in them for this cause, that they have no water, and in their thirst they shall expire. And I shall clothe the heaven with darkness, and as sackcloth shall be its covering. The Lord gives me a tongue for teaching, that I may know how I ought to speak the word. In the morning he set me down, and in me he has set an ear for hearing, and the teaching of the Lord shall open my ears, yet I am no unbeliever, nor do I gainsay him. My back, for all that, I have offered to the lash and my cheeks to buffeting, yet my face I have not turned from the shame of spitting, and the Lord God has become my helper."[172] For all who are of the church confess that it is Christ who says, "The Lord, the Lord has given me a tongue for teaching"[173] with the rest that I have set forth. . . .

For whom, though, was it proper to say "I came," if not for Christ who came into the world? Or whose part was it to say "I have called, and there was none to obey," if not his who came to call the Jewish people but was not heard and therefore did not rescue the people or snatch them out but gave them up? Yet it is Christ who says, "Behold, with my curse I shall make the sea desert, and the streams too I shall make desert," he being the one who is to effect the consummation of the world. For he it is who will "clothe the heaven with darkness" and clothe it as though "with sackcloth," and who, receiving a "tongue for teaching" from the Father, knew how "he ought to speak the word" that God had confided to him. And he "set in him an ear" that he might hear in the hearing of all, and the "teaching" of the Father "opened the ear" for him because he was "no unbeliever" when the Father sent him, nor did he "gainsay him," and by this very work he taught meekness and laudable humility to those who desired to learn. His goal, however, in teaching us this by his deeds, baring "his back to the lash and his cheeks to buffeting" and not turning his face from "the shame of spitting," was (in my opinion) that when we deserved to suffer these enormities, he rescued us by suffering them on our account. For he was not "dead for us"[174] in order that we should not die but that we should not die for ourselves. He was bruised by blows and spat on for us, in order that we should not suffer all these things, as we deserved, on account of our sins, but should suffer them and embrace them gratefully for the sake of righteousness. . . .

That the insult of spitting is in fact regarded as a grave insult is manifest also in the Law, where it is written that the widow of a dead man, if the brother of her husband will not take her, is to go up to the man who has refused to take her to wife and in the presence of elders remove "one of his shoes from his feet,

---

[171]GCS 38 (11):229-31. [172]Is 50:2-7. [173]Neither citation of Is 50:4 (LXX) is exact: the Greek reads "The Lord, the Lord, gives me a tongue for teaching." [174]Rom 5:8.

spitting into his face and saying, 'So shall they do to a man who has not raised up the house of his brother.' "[175] Therefore Christ did not turn his face away from the shame of spitting, so that his visage might be glorified more than the visage of Moses was glorified[176]—with glory so great and of such a kind that compared with his glorification the glorification of Moses' visage might be abolished, just as in sight of the sun the light of the moon is abolished and just as knowledge that is partial is abolished "when that which is perfect is come."[177] Yet they bruise the holy head of the church with blows, on account of which they themselves suffer the blows of Satan, not to prevent them from being puffed up and thus perfect their virtue[178] but so that they might be delivered to the avenging enemy to be repaid for their sinful act in beating Jesus. And not content merely to spit on his face and bruise him with blows, they bruised him also with their open hands and made sport of him, saying, "Prophesy to us, who has struck you?" For this reason they have received an eternal blow and have been deprived of all prophecy, struck and chastised, and even then they would not submit to discipline, the very thing that Jeremiah prophesied of them: "You have lashed them, and they grieved not, and they would not submit to discipline."[179] And now those who injure a single member of the church and do these things to him are spitting in the face of Christ, bruising Christ with blows and chastising him with open hands. COMMENTARY ON MATTHEW 111-13.[180]

YET HIS FOES PAY TRIBUTE TO HIS MAJESTY.
JEROME: When Jesus is beaten and spat on and ridiculed, he is wearing not his own garments but those that he had assumed on account of our sins. When, however, he is crucified and the pageant of horseplay and mockery goes before him, then he receives his former garments[181] and assumes his proper insignia, whereon the elements quake and the creation

witnesses to its Creator. COMMENTARY ON MATTHEW 4.1647-54.[182]

Jesus Tried and Crucified as King of the Jews

THE INSCRIBED RUBRIC HAS A TRUE SENSE.
AMBROSE: A rubric is also written on the cross.[183] It is customary for a procession to go before the victor; the triumphal chariot of the Lord, however, was preceded by a noble procession of the resurgent dead. Usually also the rubric indicates the number of subjugated peoples. In those triumphs the captivity of nations, wretched in defeat and perishing ignominiously, would be listed in some order or other. This procession blooms with the celebration of peoples redeemed. Worthily are they yoked in such a grand triumph, that heaven, earth, the sea and the regions below may be transformed from corruption to celebration.

Now the rubric is written and is placed above the cross, not beneath the cross, because "primacy shall be on his shoulders."[184] Now what is primacy but his everlasting virtue and divinity? . . . Let us read this rubric. "Jesus of Nazareth," it says, "king of the Jews." Rightly the rubric is above the cross because the kingdom that Christ possesses is not of the human body but of the divine power. Rightly the rubric was written above the cross, because even though the lord Jesus was on the cross, he nonetheless shone forth above the cross in royal majesty. . . . The rubric, then was no mean thing. As for the place of the cross, it was either in the open where it would be manifest to all or would be above the place of Adam's burial, as the Hebrews[185] allege. It was

---

[175]Deut 25:7. [176]2 Cor 3:7. [177]1 Cor 13:9. [178]An allusion to the edifying "thorn in the flesh" (1 Cor 12:7-9). [179]Jer 5:3. [180]GCS 38 (11):231-36. [181]Mt 27:28. [182]CCL 77:269. [183]"Jesus of Nazareth, the King of the Jews": Jn 19:19; cf. Mt 27:37; Mk 15:26; Lk 23:38. [184]Is 9:6. [185]I take this to mean Jews converted to Christianity, since "Hebrew," unlike "Jew," is a term of honor in the patristic vocabulary.

certainly fitting that the firstfruits of our life should be in the same locality where our death originated. EXPOSITIONS ON THE GOSPEL OF LUKE 10.111-14.[186]

THE KINGLY GARMENTS REPRESENT THE CHURCH. AUGUSTINE: Matthew by saying "they divided his garments, casting lots,"[187] wishes us to understand that the tunic, for which they cast lots, is also included in the division of his whole raiment, inasmuch as while all the clothes, of which this formed part, were divided, this was the one for which they cast lots. Luke too speaks in the same manner: dividing his garments, they cast lots; for in their division they came to the tunic, for which they cast lots so that there might be a complete division of his garments among them. But what difference does it make whether the words are "dividing," "they cast lots" (which is what Luke says) or "they divided, casting the lot" (which is what Matthew says), except that Luke, in saying "lots," put the plural for the singular? This expression is not unusual in the Scriptures, though a number of codices are found to have the word *lot*. And it is Mark alone who seems to have introduced a sort of question; for by saying "they cast the lot for them, as to who should take which," he seems to have spoken as though the lot were cast for all the garments, not for the tunic alone. But even here brevity makes for obscurity, for his saying they cast lots for them is equivalent to saying that they cast lots while they were being divided, which was in fact the case. For the division of his whole raiment would not have been completed had it not been made clear by lot who was also to take that tunic, so that in this way the strife of those who were dividing might be ended, or perhaps rather that none should arise. Therefore his words "who should take what," seeing that this is entrusted to the lot, should not be referred to all the garments that were divided. For the lot was cast to see who would take that tunic. He omitted to say in his narrative what

it was, and how, when equal shares had been made, this alone remained and was put to the lot so that it would not be torn apart. It was for this reason that he used the words that he wrote, who should take what, meaning who should take that tunic. The whole of his meaning would be something like this: they divided his garments casting the lot for them to see who should take the tunic that was left over after sharing them equally.

Now it may be that someone will ask what is signified by the division of his garments into so many shares and that casting of lots for the tunic. The fourfold raiment of the Lord Jesus Christ is a figure of his fourfold church, which consists of four parts, spread as it is across the whole earth and distributed equally, that is, harmoniously, in all those parts. For this reason he says elsewhere that he will send his angels who will gather his elect from all four winds, which can surely mean only from the four parts of the world, the east, the west, the north and the south. That tunic put to the lot, however, signifies the union of all the parts that is enclosed in the bond of peace. Now the apostle, when about to speak of charity, says, "I shall show you a more excellent way,"[188] and in another place says "to know also the love of Christ which excels knowledge"[189] and again elsewhere "above all these charity, which is the bond of perfection."[190] If therefore charity has a more excellent way and excels knowledge and is above all precepts, then it is with justice that the garment by which it is signified is said to have been woven from the top down. And it was seamless, so that it could not be unstitched at any time and made up a single piece because it brings all together in one. Likewise among the apostles, when their number was actually twelve, that is, three lots of four, and a question was put to all, Peter alone replied, "You are Christ," and it is said to him, "I shall

[186]CSEL 32.4:497-98. [187]Mt 27:35; cf. Mk 15:24; Lk 23:34. [188]1 Cor 12:31. [189]1 Cor 3:19. [190]1 Cor 3:14.

give to you the keys of the kingdom of heaven," as though he alone had received the power of binding and loosing.[191] One man spoke these words on behalf of all and received this commission as though he were a personification of unity itself; so it is that one acts on behalf of all, because there is unity in all. Thus it is that here when it said "woven from the top down," it added "throughout the whole."[192] If we refer this to what it signifies, no one is excluded from this if he is found to belong to the whole. It is by virtue of being a whole, as the Greek language indicates, that the church is called catholic. As for the lot, what is commended in it but the grace of God? For when the lot is agreed on, there is one thing in which all have an interest, just as in unity all have an interest also in the grace of God. And when the lot is cast, it falls out according to God's secret judgment, not according to the merits of any one person. TRACTATES ON THE GOSPEL OF JOHN 118.3-4.[193]

Words from the Cross

THE PARDONING OF THE THIEF IS A PLEDGE TO US. AMBROSE: A very fine example to induce conversion, in which indulgence is shown so quickly to the thief and the pardon is fuller than the prayer; for the Lord has always granted more than is asked. For he asked that the Lord should be mindful of him when he came into his kingdom, while the Lord said, "Truly, truly I say to you, this day you shall be with me in paradise."[194] For it is life to be with Christ, because where Christ is there is the kingdom. Quickly, therefore, the Lord forgives, because he was quickly converted. And that seems to account for the fact that the others speak of two thieves reviling him, whereas Luke speaks of one reviling and one petitioning. Perhaps the latter too reviled him at first but was suddenly converted. And it is no wonder if he forgave the convert when he showed indulgence to those who were dishon-

oring him. EXPOSITIONS ON THE GOSPEL OF LUKE 10.121-22.[195]

THE SALVATION OF THE ONE THIEF FORESHADOWS THE JUDGMENT OF ALL. LEO THE GREAT: When everything that the divinity allowed to be done in the limiting veil of the flesh had been carried out, Jesus the Son of God was nailed to a cross that he himself had carried—along with the two thieves, one on his right, the other on his left, crucified in the same way. Even in the very appearance of the gallows was shown that criterion that would be applied when he comes to judge human beings. Faith on the part of the believing thief prefigured those who were to be saved, while wickedness on the part of the blasphemer foreshadowed those who were to be condemned. SERMON 55.1.[196]

THE BELOVED DISCIPLE GIVES TESTIMONY. AMBROSE: Now women were standing to watch this, and his mother too was standing there, as devoted loyalty overcame her sense of danger. But the Lord as he hung in the cross, making light of his own danger, commended his mother with loyal affection. It was not beside the purpose for John to recount this at greater length, for others had already described the earthquake, the darkness obscuring the sky and the withdrawal of the sun. Matthew and Mark, who gave a richer account of human and moral matters, had added "God, my God, look on me! Why have you forsaken me?"[197] so that we might see that Christ's assumption of the human state continued up to the cross. Luke for his part has declared that the pardon granted to the thief by priestly

---

[191]While Augustine held the Roman see in high esteem, he does not maintain in his mature works that submission to Rome is the test of catholicity or that the gift of the keys to Peter (Mt 16:15-19) invests his successors in Rome with a monarchical authority over the church. [192]Jn 20:23. [193]CCL 36:655-56. [194]Lk 23:43. [195]CSEL 32.4:500. [196]CCL 138A:323. [197]Mt 27:46; Mk 15:34.

intercession coincided with his petition, in the same role, for the forgiveness of the Jews who were persecuting him. John, therefore, who entered more deeply into the divine mysteries, made it his task, rightly enough, to proclaim that she who had given birth to God remained a virgin.[198] Thus it is he alone who tells me what the others did not tell me, how he called to his mother from his place on the cross. John thought it a matter of greater moment that the one who had vanquished torments and punishments—vanquished the devil—should apportion the duties of family affection than that he was bestowing the heavenly kingdom. For if it is a godly act for the Lord to grant pardon to a thief, it is even more godly for the mother to be honored by the son. And let it not be thought incongruous that I have mentioned his absolution of the thief before his calling to his mother; for it is not absurd that in my writing the one who came to save sinners should first fulfill that office by the redemptive salvation of the sinner. And after all he says, "Who is my mother and who are my brothers?"[199] because he had not come to call the righteous but sinners. But those words had their own context. Even here on the cross he is not unmindful of his mother but calls to her, saying, "Behold your son," and to John, "Behold your mother."[200] Christ gave his testament from the cross, and John put his signature to the testament,[201] his own testimony being worthy of the testator. A great testament, not of money but of life, which was written not in black ink but in the spirit of the living God. "My tongue is the pen of a scribe with a rapid hand."[202] EXPOSITIONS ON THE GOSPEL OF LUKE 10.129-31.[203]

The Manner of His Death

THE DEATH IS ABOVE ALL A STUDY IN FORBEARANCE. CHRYSOSTOM: If you see your heart boiling, press the cross to your breast and seal it. Forget something of what befell you, and cast off like dust all anger at the memory of past occurrences. Consider his words, his deeds. Consider that he is the master, you a slave. He felt on your behalf, you on your own—he on behalf of those who had received his benefits yet crucified him, you on your own behalf. He had cause for anger at those who contemned him; you frequently take offense at those you have wronged. He in the sight of the whole city, or rather the whole Jewish people, both foreigners and natives, on whose behalf he uttered his charitable words, whereas in your case few are present. And what rendered him all the more contemptible was the defection of his disciples. For those who had hitherto been his attendants had fled, while his enemies and opponents, having had him crucified openly, contemned and reviled him, lampooning, taunting and mocking him—Jews and soldiers from below, the thieves from on high and on either side. Yes, the thieves too contemned him, both covered him with reproach. How then does Luke say that one rebuked this? The fact is that both things happened, for at first they both reproached him, but later that was no longer so. For so that you might not think that the episode was preconcerted or that the thief was not really a thief, the text shows you from his contemptuous behavior that up on his cross he was a thief and an enemy but repented all of a sudden. Now bearing all these things in mind, take thought. For what are your sufferings to compare with those of your Master? Have you been publicly contemned? No such thing. Are you mocked? Yet not your whole body, not whipped and naked. And even if you have suffered blows, it was not in this wise.

Fix your mind with me on the culprits, the motive and the occasion. And what was hardest of all to bear, while this was happening, no

---

[198]See Origen *Homilies on Leviticus* 8.3; Jerome *Against Jovinian*. [199]Mk 2:17; Lk 5:32. [200]Jn 19:26-27. [201]See Heb 9:15-17; Gal 3:17-18. [202]Ps 45:1. [203]CSEL 32.4:504-5.

one protested, no one denounced the events. But on the contrary, all spurned him, all joined in the mockery and jeering and reviled him as a buffoon, an impostor, a liar, who was unable to make good his words by deeds. But he is silent under all this, preparing the most potent medicine for us by his longsuffering. Yet we, hearing of this, do not show forbearance even to our servants, but, worse than wild creatures, we set about them and beat them, cruel and inhuman in our own affairs while making small account of God's affairs. Even toward our friends we show the same disposition. If someone grieves us, we cannot bear it, and if we are treated with contempt we grow wilder than beasts, although we read these passages every day. The disciple betrayed him; the others forsook him and fled. His beneficiaries spat on him, the servant of the high priest struck him, the soldiers rained blows on him. Those who were present jeered at him and reviled him, and the thieves condemned him. And he uttered no word against any but overcame them all by his silence, teaching you through his deeds that the more meekly you bear it, the more you will overcome those who abuse you, and you will be a wonder to all. Homilies on Matthew 87.2-3.[204]

The Darkness and the Cry of Dereliction Go Together. Chrysostom: This is the sign that he promised to give when they asked for one before, saying a wicked and adulterous generation seeks a sign, and there shall be no sign given to it but the sign of Jonah the prophet.[205] He was referring to the cross and his death, the tomb and his resurrection. And again, revealing the strength of the cross in another way, he said, "When you have lifted up the Son of man, you shall know that I am."[206] His meaning is this: "When you have crucified me and appear to have the better of me, then you will know my strength." For after he was crucified, the city was destroyed, Jewish practices ceased, they were deprived of both

their way of life and their liberty, while the proclamation flourished and the word spread to the ends of the inhabited world. And everywhere the land and the sea, the inhabited and the uninhabitable alike, tell forth his power. This then is what it tells us, and the other things that took place at the time of the cross. And indeed it was much more wonderful that these things should occur when he was nailed to the cross than when he was still walking on the earth. And the miracle lay not only in this, but because the sign that they were seeking did in fact come from heaven. And it affected the whole inhabited world, which had never happened before. It happened in Egypt alone at the time when the Passover was about to be accomplished. For that event was also a type of this. And look what time it happens: at midday, so that all who inhabit the world might learn, since everywhere in the inhabited world it was day. And this was sufficient to convert, not because of the magnitude of the miracle but because it occurred so opportunely. For this happened after the carousing and the farce of lawlessness, when they had relaxed their anger and ceased to jeer, when they had had their fill of mockery and had had their say in everything as they wished. Then he reveals the darkness, so that, having thus set aside their wrath, they might profit from the wonder. For this was more wonderful than a descent from the cross, that he effected this while still on the cross. If they regarded it as his doing, they should have believed with a sense of awe; or even if not as his doing but the Father's, they should even so to be pricked at heart, for then the darkness was a sign of his wrath at their brazenness.

For that it was indeed no eclipse but a sign of wrath and indignation was clear not only from these factors but also from the time. For there hours remained, but the eclipse came in one moment of time. And those who beheld

[204]PG 58:771-72. [205]Mt 12:39. [206]Jn 8:28.

it were aware of this, as we know because this has happened also in our own generation. Then how was it, you may say, that not all felt wonder and did not regard this as God's work? Because the human race at that time was in bondage to sloth and wickedness. And this was but one wonder, which passed quickly, and no one cared to examine the cause of it. Impiety was, moreover, a prepossession and a habit with them. Nor did they know what the cause of the occurrence was but thought that perhaps it had taken place because of an eclipse or some other natural chain of causes. And why do you wonder at those outsiders devoid of knowledge, who did not try to learn by inquiry on account of their extreme slothfulness, when even those in Judea, after so many wonders, did not cease to dishonor him, although he plainly showed them that he was the author of this event? It was therefore on this account and after this that he uttered this saying, that they might know that he still lived and that he had effected this and thereby become more amenable.

And what he says is, "Eli, Eli, lama sabachthani,"[207] so that they might see that he honors the Father up to his final breath and is no enemy of God. For this reason he also uttered a prophetic verse, bearing witness to the Old Testament up to his final hour. And not only prophetic, but also in Hebrew, so that it might be familiar and wholly evident to them. Thus in everything he reveals his unanimity with the Father. But see even from this point their unholiness, their incontinence, their irrationality. They thought, the text says, that Elijah was the one whom he invoked, and forthwith they gave him gall to drink. And another came to him and opened his side with a lance. What could have been more lawless, more brutal than these men who pressed their madness so far as even at the end to dishonor his dead body? Examine with me how he used their lawless actions for our salvation. For after the blow the streams of our salvation poured down

from it. "And Jesus, crying with a loud voice, gave up the ghost."[208] This is what he meant by "I have power to lay down my soul, and I have power to take it up again. And I lay it down of myself."[209] For this was his reason for crying aloud, that he might show the event to be an exertion of power. HOMILIES ON MATTHEW 88.1.[210]

CHRIST PERCEIVED HIS DEATH AS A CONSUMMATION. AMBROSE: At last, after he had drunk the vinegar, "all things," he says, "were accomplished,"[211] inasmuch as the entire mystery of his assumption of mortality had been fulfilled, so that all frailties had been consumed and only the joy of immortality remained. And thus he says, "Into your hands, Lord, I commend my spirit." And rightly is the spirit commended, for what is commended is certainly not lost. The spirit is therefore a good pledge, a good deposit. Hence it is that Paul too says, "Timothy, guard the good deposit."[212] For it is to the Father that he commends the spirit, and thus he says, "because you will not leave my soul in hell."[213] Now behold the great mystery: now he commends his spirit to the Father, now he sits in the bosom of the Father, for there is no other who can contain the whole Christ. Thus he says, "I am in the Father and the Father in me."[214] But when he is in the higher sphere, he illuminates the lower, that redemption may be universal. For "Christ is all, and all are in Christ,"[215] even if Christ acts in particulars. The flesh dies that it may rise again; the spirit is commended to the Father, that heavenly things also may be released from the bond of wickedness and there may be peace in heaven, as a mark for things on earth to pursue. "And having said this he gave up his spirit."[216] And well he is said to have given up, as he did not lose it un-

---

[207]Mt 27:46. [208]Mt 27:50. [209]Jn 10:18. [210]PG 58:775-76. [211]Jn 19:30. [212]2 Tim 1:14. [213]Ps 16:10. [214]Jn 14:10. [215]Col 3:11. [216]Conflating Lk 23:46 with Jn 19:30.

willingly. Thus Matthew says, "He loosed his spirit,"[217] because we, unlike him, loose a thing not voluntarily but lose it by necessity. For this cause he added "in a loud voice,"[218] in which there is either a glorious declaration that he descended even to death for our sins—therefore I shall not blush to confess what Christ did not blush to declare in a loud voice—or an evident manifestation of God as he testifies successively to his divine and bodily nature. For what you read is, "Jesus cried out in a loud voice, saying, 'God, my God, look on me. Why have you forsaken me?' "[219] It was the man who cried out, on the point of death through separation from the Godhead. For since the Godhead is exempt from death, death could certainly not be present unless life departed, for the Godhead is life. EXPOSITIONS ON THE GOSPEL OF LUKE 10.125-27.[220]

THE WORDS *IT IS FINISHED* EXPRESS A CALM SUBMISSION TO HIS DESTINY.

CHRYSOSTOM: Do you see how he does everything calmly, yet with power? And this the sequel proves, for when all was accomplished, "he bowed his head"—this had not been nailed—"and gave up the ghost."[221] This means "died." Now bowing the head does not usually cause one to expire, but here it does. For it was not that, having expired, he bowed his head, as it is for us, but that when he had bent his head he expired. From all this the Evangelist has demonstrated that he is Lord of all. HOMILIES ON JOHN 85.2.[222]

---

[217]Mt 27:50; the contrast in Latin is between the verbs *emittit* ("lets forth") and *amittit* ("loses"). [218]Lk 23:46; cf. Mt 27:46. [219]Mt 27:46. [220]CSEL 32.4:502-3. [221]Jn 19:30. [222]PG 59:462-63.

AND WAS BURIED

σταυρωθέντα τε ὑπὲρ ἡμῶν	crucifixus etiam pro nobis	For our sake he was crucified
ἐπὶ Ποντίου Πιλάτου,	sub Pontio Pilato,	under Pontius Pilate;
καὶ παθόντα **καὶ ταφέντα,**	passus **et sepultus est;**	he suffered death **and was buried.**
καὶ ἀναστάντα τῇ τρίτῃ ἡμέρᾳ	et resurrexit tertia die,	On the third day he rose again
κατὰ τὰς γραφάς,	secundum Scripturas;	in accordance with the Scriptures;
καὶ ἀνελθόντα εἰς τοὺς οὐρανούς,	et ascendit in coelum,	he ascended into heaven
καὶ καθεζόμενον	sedet	and is seated
ἐκ δεξιῶν τοῦ πατρός,	ad dexteram Patris;	at the right hand of the Father.
καὶ πάλιν ἐρχόμενον μετὰ δόξης	et iterum venturus est, cum gloria,	He will come again in glory
κρῖναι ζῶντας καὶ νεκρούς·	judicare vivos et mortuos;	to judge the living and the dead,
οὗ τῆς βασιλείας οὐκ ἔσται τέλος.	cujus regni non erit finis.	and his kingdom will have no end.

HISTORICAL CONTEXT: Had Christ not been buried or had the place of his burial been unknown, the resurrection could not have been verified. Had the tomb not been guarded, it would have been possible to surmise that the body was stolen. Christians who had seen the resurrected Christ with the eye of faith did not require such evidence, and for this reason the discovery of the empty tomb, so memorably recounted in all four Gospels, is omitted from Paul's catalogue of witnesses (1 Cor 15:1-8). It is sometimes overlooked in earlier creeds, and the insertion of this clause in the developed Nicene Creed perhaps betokens an apologetic purpose. It also attests the importance that the Holy Sepulcher had acquired as a place of pilgrimage.

OVERVIEW: The flow of blood and water portends the death of the saints, both sacramental and physical (GREGORY OF ELVIRA). It is foreshadowed in the histories of Moses and Adam (CYRIL OF JERUSALEM). Christ died to deliver us from death (IGNATIUS) and thereby teaches us to accept it with courage (IGNATIUS). Obedience to death is a token of his real humanity (TERTULLIAN) and the means of life for us (IRENAEUS).

Those who deny the manhood are as much in error as those who deny the Godhead (MARIUS VICTORINUS), and in doubting one we are forced to doubt the other (PRUDENTIUS). Paradox is the hallmark of divine action whether in the Lord's birth, death or resurrection. We expect nothing less of God (TERTULLIAN).

The site of the tomb was prophesied (CYRIL OF JERUSALEM), and the garden is a mirror of paradise (CYRIL OF JERUSALEM), as Solomon foresaw (AMBROSE). In attempting to forestall the resurrection, the authorities gave us the means to verify it (CHRYSOSTOM). If the incarnation was not the only way open to God, it was the most fitting (AUGUSTINE), and Christ accepted it for our sake without loss of dignity (AUGUSTINE). Adam's whole race was accursed before the death of Christ (EPIPHANIUS), which he suffered to expiate our guilt, not his own (CHRYSOSTOM), demonstrating

his universal love by his outstretched hands (ATHANASIUS).

Through Christ we acquire a knowledge that exceeds that of Adam and Eve (GOSPEL OF TRUTH). Moses' elevation of the brazen serpent gave both Jews and Greeks a dim presentiment of the truth (JUSTIN). As the Jews fail to understand this (JUSTIN), so the cross is a sign of judgment on all unbelievers (MELITO), though at the same time a pledge of victory to the faithful (IGNATIUS). As Christ restores Adam (ROMANUS), so his cross reproduces the human figure (JUSTIN). As a tree was the cause of the fall, so it is now a means of deliverance (EPHREM). The good thief steals what Adam snatched in vain (ROMANUS), and the power of wood to save or condemn can be recognized throughout history (ROMANUS).

Christ's death renews the creation (ANDREW), and the entire creation depends on it (VALENTINUS). It is God who died on the cross (MELITO), and death for that reason could not hold him (APOLLINARIS). Yet God is by nature incapable of suffering (TERTULLIAN), so that the suffering properly takes place in the flesh (LEO). Were Christ not a perfect man, it would not be humanity that is saved (ORIGEN). God suffers, then, but only in his flesh (CYRIL OF ALEXANDRIA). In Christ there are two natures (THEODORET), which must not be confused (TERTULLIAN). We do not say that the flesh suffers (CYRIL OF JERUSALEM) but that the Word incarnate suffers (CYRIL OF JERUSALEM), much as the soul is conscious of bodily suffering (CYRIL OF JERUSALEM). The analogy is imperfect, since the lower soul is passable by nature (THEODORET), and it would be heresy to substitute the Word for the human soul in Christ (THEODORET). The Godhead participates impassably in the body's afflictions (THEODORET).

Many have died for another's sake, only Christ for the redemption of the world (ORIGEN). In his passion he is one with all humanity (MARIUS VICTORINUS). His death makes endurance possible and baptism efficacious (IGNATIUS); thus we may rest securely in his finished work (IGNATIUS), though this does not preclude growth in faith and understanding (GREGORY OF NAZIANZUS). Christ's perfect divinity entailed an act of perfect condescension (CYRIL OF ALEXANDRIA). Paul and John bear testimony to his sacrifice (THEODORET), which was voluntary (GAUDENTIUS) and experienced by both natures (CYRIL OF ALEXANDRIA), though it did not deprive the Word of his divine attributes (CYRIL OF ALEXANDRIA).

Christ's abasement and restoration are foretold in the story of Joseph (CHRYSOSTOM). The raised hands of Moses prefigure the cross (JUSTIN), while the victories of the first Joshua anticipate those of the resurrected Christ (APHRAHAT). He consummates the marriage extolled by Solomon (AMBROSE) and surpasses the patience of Job (EPHREM, AUGUSTINE). We see types of redemption in the deliverance of Daniel (APHRAHAT) and in the sufferings of Mordecai (APHRAHAT), while in his cry from the cross the redeemer makes common cause with the prophets of Israel (CHRYSOSTOM).

No other sufferer has borne such humiliation (CHRYSOSTOM). Those who think themselves wise scoff at his sacrifice (METHODIUS), while philosophers deny it (AUGUSTINE). The pains that he voluntarily endured (ORIGEN) comprehend ours (EUSEBIUS) and serve as an exhortation to us throughout life (AUGUSTINE). He was at once priest and victim (GREGORY OF NAZIANZUS), offering up his own body (BARNABAS), superseding the ancient Passover (LEO), though only by the will of God the Father (ORIGEN). Christ, like Noah, performs a sacrifice on behalf of all (EPHREM). His ministry ennobles that of the Israelite priesthood (IRENAEUS) and at the same time puts an end to carnal offerings (AUGUSTINE).

The ransom discharges a debt that human beings could not have paid (LETTER TO DIOGNETUS). It was a form of persuasion (IRENAEUS), perhaps a bargain with the devil (ORIGEN), though it may be said that such traffic is unworthy of God (ADAMANTIUS) or that God is the true recipient of the fee (GREGORY OF NAZIANZUS). The devil was certainly overreached (ORIGEN), and the ransom may also be conceived as a bait (GREGORY OF NYSSA). Christ the ransom cannot be neatly distinguished from Christ the victor (PELAGIUS). At the same time, we are not dispensed from obedience (ORIGEN), and the price reveals the enormity of our sin (PROSPER). Christ shed his blood, not to appease an implacable Father (IRENAEUS, AUGUSTINE) but to honor the claims of justice (AUGUSTINE).

Christ is the lamb who redeemed Isaac (EPHREM). Isaac is also a type of Christ (AMBROSE), so the allegory is twofold (GREGORY OF NYSSA). Christ is also prefigured in the Passover lamb (MELITO), even in the very details of the sacrifice (JUSTIN). We should not forget the scapegoat (JUSTIN) or the wrath of the lamb (ON RIDDLES IN THE APOCALYPSE). It was his suffering that abolished the charge (THEODORET). This was prefigured in the acts of Joshua (EUSEBIUS) and in a psalm (EUSEBIUS). For Christ, the atonement was the destined climax of the incarnation (GREGORY OF NAZIANZUS); for us, it is an expiation of sin (AUGUSTINE).

The cross unites Jew and Greek (MARIUS VICTORINUS), and its conciliatory work is foreshadowed in Scripture (IRENAEUS). The law is no longer a barrier (CHRYSOSTOM), and faith is now the condition of reconciliation to God (GAUDENTIUS). All can be saved (IRENAEUS), but only because all are sinners (PROSPER). Noah's ark is God's promise of universal deliverance (PROSPER), and reconciliation by faith is followed by inward renewal (HERMAS). Christ defeats the devil by adopting his serpentine form (TERTULLIAN). The devil is justly vanquished (AMBROSIASTER), both in the air (ATHANASIUS) and on Calvary (MAXIMUS). The cross, where the demons thought themselves victorious (ORIGEN), is in fact the scene of victory for Christ (AUGUSTINE). His cross was a trophy even before he mounted it (AMBROSE); his death on it was an exhibition of courage (ATHANASIUS) and an instrument of justice (AUGUSTINE). Hence we celebrate the day of his passion (CONSTANTINE), and the church goes forth as an army (VENANTIUS FORTUNATUS).

These rich spoils have been won with pain (VENANTIUS FORTUNATUS), and we in turn must take pains to preserve them (GAUDEN-TIUS). Since Christ died, he must have tarried in hades (POLYCARP), as texts can be cited to show (IRENAEUS). Had he not descended, he could not have ascended (AMBROSIASTER) or redeemed the patriarchs (CYRIL OF JERUSALEM). The possession of a soul made this descent possible (ORIGEN). Whether or not some Gentiles were among the redeemed (CLEMENT OF ALEXANDRIA), their abode was set apart from that of the lost (TERTULLIAN). The descent is anticipated by Jonah's captivity in the whale (GREGORY OF NYSSA), which was an earnest of mercy as well as of judgment (DRACONTIUS).

The sabbath was consecrated in honor of Easter Saturday (GREGORY OF NYSSA). The interval, which embraces three nights and days in all (GREGORY OF NYSSA), is no long time for the cleansing of our accumulated sin (GREGORY OF NYSSA). It was the soul that performed this, while the body remained in the tomb (GREGORY OF NYSSA).

The Certainty of His Death

THE WOUND OF THE LANCE PREFIGURES BAPTISM AND MARTYRDOM. GREGORY OF ELVIRA: Furthermore those waters that were drawn forth from the rock[1] were a typological prefiguration of the streams that flow from Christ's belly in the sacrament of baptism[2] and that would flow from the side of Christ to be a cup of salvation for those who thirst.[3] For who is unaware that our Lord, who is a fount of living water leaping up into everlasting life, when

he was suspended on the wood of the cross, poured out from the wound in his side not only blood but waters flowing in a broad stream? By this he showed that his spouse, that is, the church, derives her being from his side, in the manner exemplified by the first humans, just as Eve derived her being from a rib of Adam's. Thus the church clearly has two baptisms, of water and of blood, from which come the faithful in the church and the martyrs. ORIGENIST TREATISE 15.12-13.[4]

A NUMBER OF INTERPRETATIONS. CYRIL OF JERUSALEM: The signs of Moses commenced with blood and water, and the signs of Jesus ended with the same elements. First Moses changed the river to blood, and Jesus at the end produced water from his side with blood. It was equally on account of the two voices, that of the judge and that of the clamoring mob, or on account of those who believed and those who did not. For Pilate said, "I am innocent," and washed his hands with water, while the clamoring mob kept saying, "His blood be upon us."[5] Thus of the two effluences from his side, the water was for Pilate as much as the blood was for the clamoring mob.

Again, it may be conceived differently: the blood for Jews, the water for Christians. For to them as conspirators belongs the judgment of blood, but to you the believer comes now salvation by water. For nothing happened by chance. Our fathers in exegesis have also handed down another reason for the event. For since in the Gospels baptism has a sort of double power—first the one vouchsafed through water to those who are being illumined, and second the one that the holy martyrs receive through their own blood in persecutions—blood and water issued from the Savior's side to confirm the grace of the confession of

---

[1]Ex 17:6. [2]Jn 7:38. [3]Not only alluding to the eucharistic chalice but glancing at Jn 18:11, Lk 22:42, and other references, where the cup is a symbol of martyrdom. [4]CCL 69:115. [5]Mt 27:24-25.

Christ that takes place both in illumination and in the epochs of martyrdom. And there is yet another reason for the wound in the side. The woman who was fashioned from the side became the instigator of sin, but Christ, who had come to bring pardon equally to men and women, was pierced in his side for the sake of women, so that he might loose the power of sin. CATECHETICAL LECTURE 13.20-21.[6]

The Necessity of His Death

IF CHRIST DID NOT DIE, WE ARE NOT SAVED. IGNATIUS OF ANTIOCH: All these things he suffered on our behalf, that we might be saved. And he truly suffered, as he truly raised himself again, not as some infidels say, in semblance only[7]—it is they who are only a semblance. . . . For my part, I know and believe that he was in the flesh after his resurrection also. And when he came to those about Peter, he said to them, "Take, touch me, and see that I am no incorporeal demon."[8] And straightway they touched him and believed, united to him in flesh and in spirit. On this account, they despised death, were found indeed superior to death. And after his resurrection he supped with them and drank as one in the flesh, although he was spiritually one with the Father. TO THE SMYRNEANS 2-3.[9]

BELIEVERS CAN ADD THE TESTIMONY OF OBEDIENCE. IGNATIUS OF ANTIOCH: If these deeds of our Lord were only a semblance, then I am bound but in semblance. And why have I given myself as a present to death? To fire, to the sword, to wild beasts? Why, because to be near the sword is to be near God, to be in the company of beasts is to be in God's company. But only in the name of Jesus Christ. I undergo all things to suffer with him, strengthened by him who became the perfect man. TO THE SMYRNEANS 4.2.[10]

PAUL BEARS WITNESS TO HIS TRUE HU-

MANITY. TERTULLIAN: The apostle would not have declared him[11] to have become obedient to death if he had not been constituted of a mortal substance. Still more plainly does this appear when he adds the heavily-laden words "even unto the death of the cross." For he would not exaggerate the atrocity by extolling his power in a conflict that he knew to have been imaginary or a mere fantasy. In that case Christ would rather have eluded the cross than experienced it. There would then have been no virtue in his suffering but only an illusion. AGAINST MARCION 5.20.4-5.[12]

ONLY TRUE DEATH COULD YIELD TRUE LIFE. IRENAEUS: If then, the Lord obeyed the law of death that he might become "firstborn from the dead,"[13] and having lingered up to the third day in the depths of the earth, rose after that in the flesh, so that, having displayed the wounds of the nails to his disciples, he ascended in this form to the Father: how can they escape confusion who say that the depths are this world itself, and that their own inner man, forsaking the body, ascends to the supercelestial place? AGAINST HERESIES 5.31.2.[14]

AS MUCH A SIN TO DENY HIS MANHOOD AS TO DENY HIS GODHEAD. MARIUS VICTORINUS: There are two types of misunderstanding of Christ, or rather one class of two descriptions, who are enemies of Christ.[15] For some in their carnal thoughts deride the cross, thinking of Christ as merely a man raised on a cross. . . . On the other hand, there are those who think of Christ only as a spirit. They do not think

---

[6]CHOO 2:78-80. [7]Noting that the risen Christ appeared only to the faithful, that he could pass through solid obstacles and that even his intimates sometimes failed to recognize him, certain Christians (generally described today as Gnostics) held that the resurrection body, if not phantasmal, was at least free of material properties. [8]See Lk 24:39. This quotation, however, is from the apocryphal *Gospel of Peter* and appears also (with a caveat) in Origen *On First Principles* proem 9. [9]AF 184-86. [10]AF 186. [11]Phil 2:8. [12]CCL 1:724-25. [13]Col 1:18. [14]SC 153:392. [15]Phil 3:18.

of him as incarnate or crucified. They too are enemies of Christ, having death as their end. COMMENTARY ON PHILIPPIANS 3.19.[16]

IF HE IS NOT TRUE MAN, HE IS NOT TRUE GOD. PRUDENTIUS: Human beings alone had the honor to receive an aspect malleable to the right hand of God and to be born by the smith-like fashioning of the deity. Why then was such indulgence shown to our clay that, having been worked by the hands of God, it should become holy through divine art when it had already been ennobled by his touch? Since God had resolved to mingle Christ with the untainted earth, he had matter that he could fashion in his divine grasp and deposit as a dear pledge. Now ruined nature had indeed deserted the creature formed from the compacted earth and had given way to the death now due to it. But the indissoluble nature of God willed that our unbalanced earth, defiled from the beginning by our own conduct, should become his, and thus no longer be subject to defilement. Christ is our flesh, for me he is dissolved, for me he rises. I am dissolved by my own death, but I rise by the power of Christ. When Christ dies, when he is put in the tomb with mourning, I see myself; when he stands up from the tomb to return, I see God. If his having my members is a fantasy, so is his being God. Christ must be a liar in both, if Christ knows how to put on a false appearance. If he is not true man, when death itself proves him a man, nor is he true God when the glory of his achievement proves him God. APOTHEOSIS 1033-55.[17]

PARADOX IS THE HALLMARK OF DIVINE ACTION. TERTULLIAN: If then you[18] do not deny the incarnation as being impossible or dangerous to God, it remains that you must reject and traduce it as being unworthy. . . . Yet certainly the human being that Christ loved was compacted in the uncleanness of the womb, was brought forth through the

shameful regions, was nurtured in childish recreations. It was for this one's sake that he descended, that he submitted himself to every humiliation, even to death, the death of a cross.[19] Certainly he loved the one whom he purchased at great cost. If Christ is his creator, it was right for him to love his own; if he is from another God, Christ's love was all the greater,[20] as he was willing to redeem what belonged to another. And thus with humankind he loved its mode of birth, its flesh. Nothing can be loved without that whereby it is what it is. Now take away the birth, and show me the human being. Take away the flesh, and present the one whom God redeemed. If these are what compose the human whom God redeemed, it is you who make shameful to him what he redeemed and make unworthy what he would not have redeemed had he not loved it. . . . What is more unworthy of God, or more shameful? To be born or to die? To bear flesh or the cross? To be circumcised or to be nailed? To be educated or to be buried? To be put in a pen or to be buried in a vault? . . . Answer this now, you murderer of truth. Was God not truly crucified? Not truly dead and truly crucified? Not truly restored to life? As much, I suppose, as he was truly dead. So Paul made a false resolution to know nothing among us but "him crucified";[21] falsely he maintained that he was buried, falsely he taught his restoration to life. False then too is our faith, and all that we hope from Christ a phantom. Basest of men, you defend the killers of God, for Christ suffered nothing from them if he did not suffer truly. Spare the one hope of the world! Why will you undo the indignity that is necessary to faith? Whatever is unworthy of God is profitable to me. I am saved, so long as I am not abashed on account of my

---

[16]*MVCEP* 108. [17]LCL, Prudentius 1:196. [18]The Marcionites, who denied the reality of Christ's body. [19]Phil 2:8. [20]*Adamavit*, perhaps a pun on the name of Adam. This sentence rebuts the Marcionite position that the God who redeems the spirit is not the creator of the material world. [21]1 Cor 2:2.

Lord. "He who is abashed on my account," he says, "I shall be abashed on his." I shall find no other matter to abash me, so as to prove me, when I scorn to blush, duly shameless, happily befooled. The Son of God was born; it causes no shame, because it is shameful. And the Son of God died; it is absolutely credible because it is incongruous. And having been buried, he rose again. It is certain, because it is impossible.[22] Yet how will all this be true of him, if he himself was not true, if he did not truly possess in himself what could be nailed, what could die, what could be buried and restored to life? On the Flesh of Christ 4-5.[23]

The Burial

The Burial Place Was Foreseen as a Testimony (Martyrion). Cyril of Jerusalem: Let us seek to know precisely where he was buried. Was his a hand-wrought tomb? Did it overshadow the earth like the tombs of kings? Was the monument built of assembled stones? And what was set above it? Tell us, prophets, the exact truth about the tomb— where was he laid, and shall we seek him? And they say, Look in the hard rock that you have hewn out: look and see. In the Gospels you have, in a hewn tomb, which was hewn from rock. Again it says in the Song, "I went down into the garden of nuts";[24] for it was a garden where he was crucified. Yes, even if it has now been greatly embellished by royal gifts, it was still a garden before, and there remain now both the signs and the relics. Do you see that the prophet foresaw that the place of the resurrection would be called the Martyrium? For with what reason is this site of Golgotha and the resurrection not called a church like the other churches but the Martyrium? Perhaps on account of the prophet who said, "For a testimony [martyrion] to the day of my resurrection."[25] And from where did the Savior arise? It says in the Song of Songs, "Rise, come, my companion,"[26] and in what follows, "in a recess

of the rock."[27] By "recess of the rock" it means perhaps the cave before the door of the Savior's sepulcher, hewn out of the very rock, which it was the custom there to have before monuments. Now indeed it is no longer visible, since what the recess at the front has been worn away since by the largesse of our times. For before the construction of this monument by royal munificence, there was a recess at the front of the rock. But where is the rock that holds the recess? Does it lie in the middle of the city or by the walls and on the outskirts? And is it by the old walls or the outworks that came later? Well, it says in the Song, "in a recess of the rock, close by the outwork."[28] Many are the testimonies to our Savior's resurrection. . . . The rock of the monument, which received him, and the stone shall stand up face to face against the Jews. For it saw the Lord: it is this stone, which was rolled away at that time, that will bear testimony to the resurrection, lying there to this day. Now our present kings in their piety have clad in silver and decked with gold this holy church in which we are present, the church of the Resurrection of God the Savior; and they have embellished it with the finery of silver and gold and precious stones. This house of the holy church was built and embellished, as you see, by the Christ-loving will of the emperor Constantine, of blessed memory. Catechetical Lecture 13.35; 14.5; 14.6; 14.9; 14.22; 14.14.[29]

This Garden Is the Antitype of Paradise. Cyril of Jerusalem: Adam suffered a condemnation: "Cursed is the ground in your toil; thorns and darnel it shall bear for you."[30]

---

[22]This dictum is often inaccurately quoted as credo *quia absurdum,* "I believe because it is absurd." Tertullian is not commending faith in the teeth of evidence; he is arguing that, because God has the power to do what is impossible for humans, the resurrection is a work of the kind that we trust him to perform. [23]CCL 2:878-81. [24]Song 6:10. [25]Zeph 3:8 (LXX). [26]Song 2:13. [27]Song 2:14. [28]Song 2:14. [29]As collated in *ELS* 625-27. [30]See Gen 3:17-18.

For this reason Jesus accepts the crown of thorns, that he may remit the punishment. And for this reason he was buried in the ground, that the accursed ground might receive a benediction instead of a curse. On the occasion of the sin, fig leaves were used as clothes. For this reason Jesus made the fig the last of his parabolic signs. For as he is getting ready to go to his passion he curses the fig tree—not every fig, but this one alone on account of the typology, saying, "No one is to eat fruit from you again."[31] Let the condemnation be remitted. And, this being the time when the fig was clothed in leaves, he came at a season when nothing is found to eat. Who does not know that in the season of winter figs do not bear fruit but are merely clothed in leaves? This being what everyone knew, did Jesus then not know it? But he made as if to seek them in full knowledge, not failing to find them unawares but making a figure of the curse that affected only the leaves. And now that we have touched on matters in paradise, I am truly amazed by the truth in the type. In paradise the fall, in the garden salvation. From wood came the sin, and sin went as far as the wood. In the afternoon they were concealed from the Lord as he walked about, and in the afternoon the thief is led into paradise by the Lord. Catechetical Lecture 13.18-19.[32]

Solomon's Garden Is Another Type of It. Ambrose: Do not spurn the diet of which Christ says, "I have entered into my garden, sister-spouse of mine. You will harvest myrrh with my perfumes; I have eaten bread with my own honey and drunk wine with my own milk."[33] In the garden, that is, in paradise, is the banquet of the church, where Adam was before he committed sin. There Eve reclined before she created and bore transgression. There you will harvest myrrh, that is, the burial of Christ, so that, buried with him in baptism,[34] you too may rise again to life with him as he rose again from the dead. Cain and Abel 1.5.19.[35]

The Subterfuge of the Authorities Worked Against Them. Chrysostom: Everywhere error causes itself to stumble and blends its voice unwillingly with truth. Now consider: it was necessary that he should be believed to have died and been buried and to have risen again. See then how their words bear witness to all these events. We are mindful, they say, that that impostor while still alive—which means he had died—said, "I shall rise after three days." Command then that the tomb should be secured—which means he was buried—lest perhaps his disciples should come and steal him. Does it not follow that if the tomb has been sealed, there will be no wrongdoing? Thus it was through your precautions that the proof of the resurrection became irrefutable. . . . Do you see how they strive unwillingly in the cause of truth? For they were the ones who went forth, it was they who made the request and they who sealed it with a guard, so that it was they who accused and convicted one another. How, pray, would they ever have performed a theft on the sabbath, and how? It was not even permitted to appear in public. And even if they transgressed the Law, how would men so craven have dared to appear in public? How would they have been able to convince the mob? What would they have said, what would they have done? What would have given them courage to stand up on behalf of the corpse? What return would they have looked for, what recompense? When he was alive and had merely been bound, they fled at the sight; and would they have dared to speak freely after his death if he had not risen? What sense would there be in these actions? From this it is evident that they would not have conspired or been able to fabricate a resurrection if none had occurred. . . . Consider, I beg you, the laughable mischief of these people. For it says, "We are mindful that this impostor

---

[31]Mk 11:14. [32]CHOO 2:74. [33]Song 5:1. [34]Rom 6:4. [35]CSEL 32.1:356.

when still alive said 'after three days I shall rise again.' "[36] Now if he was an impostor, a forger of lies, what were you afraid of, running here and there with all this zeal? We were afraid, it is said, that the disciples would steal the body and deceive the multitude. But it has been shown already that this is completely devoid of sense. Yet it is true that vice, bellicose and shameless as it is, will undertake the most senseless projects. And they command that the tomb be secured for three days: fighting on behalf of their own prepossessions and wishing to prove that before this he had been an impostor, they carry their wickedness even to the tomb. But it was on that account that he rose more quickly, so that they might not say that he lied or that he was stolen. For there was no offense in this, to rise more quickly, whereas to do it more slowly was highly suspect. For if he had not risen then, when they were ensconced there and keeping guard, but after the third day when they had departed, they would have something to say and say in return, however absurd. For this reason then, he pre-empted them and rose, so that they would have not even the most transparent of excuses. HOMILIES ON MATTHEW 89.1-2.[37]

The Divine Economy

THERE WAS NO MORE SUITABLE WAY.
AUGUSTINE: Now there are some who say, "Was there then no other means for God to liberate humankind from the wretchedness of this mortality, so that he chose that his only-begotten Son, co-eternal with him as God, should become a man, assuming a human soul and flesh, and having been made mortal should suffer death?" It is not enough to rebut this by asserting that the means by which God deigned to liberate us through the man Jesus Christ, the mediator of God and humankind, was good and consonant with God's dignity. No, we must also show not that God lacked any other possible means (for all things lie equally in his power) but that there was no more fitting means of healing our wretchedness, nor should there have been one. For what was so necessary to raise our hope and to liberate the minds of mortals as they groveled, in despair of immortality, under the terms of this mortality,[38] than to demonstrate to us how much we mattered to God and how much he loved us? And what could be a more manifest and signal proof of this than that the Son of God, immutably good in himself and remaining what he was while taking from us on our account what he was not, deigning to enter into fellowship with our nature without any detriment to his own, should of his own accord take our ills on him with no ill desert on his part? And that thus, without any good desert on our part, he should confer his gifts on us who now believe how much God loves us and hope for the things of which we despaired, even though no such largess was owed to our bad deserts which went before? ON THE TRINITY 13.10.13.[39]

CHRIST SUFFERED AND DIED ONLY FOR
US. VENANTIUS FORTUNATUS: "For as a rational soul and flesh constitute one human being, thus Christ, God and man, is one."[40] Although God, the Son of God, assumed our filthy and mortal flesh, the precondition of our redemption, he nonetheless in no way defiled himself, nor did he exchange the nature of the Godhead. The reason is that, just as when the sun or fire have touched anything, it cleanses what it touches and in no way defiles itself thereby, so too God assumed the carnal condition of our humanity, yet in no way defiled himself thereby but cleansed that fleshly nature of ours that he has assumed, and purified it from the blots and stains of sins and vices. That was

---

[36]Mt 27:63. [37]PG 58:781-83. [38]Death being the determined reward of sin at Rom 5:12; 6:23, and other references. [39]CCL 50A:399-400. [40]Quotation from the Athanasian Creed, which, despite its name, exists only in Latin and is unlikely to have been composed before the sixth century.

what Isaiah said: "He himself has borne our infirmities and carried away our ills."[41] This was the purpose of his being born according to his humanity, that he might bear our infirmities and carry away our ills, not because he himself had the infirmities and ills within—for he is the salvation of the world—but so that he might take them away from us, when, by the grace and sacrament of his holy passion, having taken away the proscription,[42] he has bestowed on our souls redemption and salvation equally. Exposition of the Catholic Faith.[43]

Removing a Curse

Until Christ Delivered Us, We Were Under a Curse. Epiphanius: In the law there was a curse against Adam's transgression until the advent of the one who was from above and who, clothing himself with a body from the mass of Adamic humanity,[44] turned the curse into blessing. Panarion 42.12.3.[45]

He Submits to the Curse of Another. Chrysostom: The people were liable to punishment since they had not fulfilled the whole Law. Christ satisfied a different curse, the one that says, "Cursed is everyone that is hanged on a tree."[46] Both the one who is hanged and the one who transgresses the Law are accursed. Christ, who was going to lift that curse, could not properly be made liable to it, yet he had to receive a curse. He received the curse instead of being liable to it, and through this he lifted the curse. Just as, when someone is condemned to death, another innocent person who chooses to die[47] for him releases him from that punishment, so Christ also did. Homily on Galatians 3.13.[48]

His Desire to Embrace the World. Athanasius: Should one of our own— for the sake of instruction, rather than argument— want to know why he did not do it otherwise but endured the cross, let him learn that no

profit would come of doing it otherwise than in this way. For if he came to bear the curse that had come on us, how else could he have become a curse had he not accepted the death that resulted from the curse? For that is how it is written: "Cursed is he that is hanged on a tree."[49] Furthermore, if the death of the Lord is the ransom for all, and by this death "the midwall of the partition was dissolved"[50] and the calling of the nations began in consequence, how could he have called us to him had he not been crucified? For it is only on the cross that one dies with hands outstretched. For this reason it also behooved the Lord to endure this and to stretch out his hands, so that with one he might draw the ancient people, and with the other those from the nations and join both in himself. That is what he declared, saying by what death he was going to ransom everyone: "When I am lifted up, I shall draw all people to me."[51] On the Incarnation 25.1-3.[52]

The Plan of God Made Manifest

Through Vision Comes Knowledge. Gospel of Truth: He was nailed to a tree, and he became a fruit of the knowledge of the Father. It did not, however, cause destruction because it was eaten, but to those who ate it, it gave cause to become glad in the discovery, and he discovered them in himself and they discovered him in themselves. Gospel of Truth 18.23-32.[53]

The Cross Was Revealed Beforehand to Hebrew and Greek. Justin Martyr: And in accordance with the working and inspiration that came from God, Moses took bronze

---

[41]Is 53:4. [42]Col 2:13-14. [43]PL 88:590-91. [44]This image does not, as is commonly thought, originate with Augustine. [45]GCS 31, Epiphanius 2:156. [46]Deut 21:23, quoted at Gal 3:13. [47]Though not a reliable gloss on the Roman law of Chrysostom's time, this is a rare and early instance of the doctrine of vicarious atonement in the Greek East. [48]IOEP 4:59. [49]Deut 21:23; Gal 3:13. [50]Eph 2:14. [51]Jn 12:31. [52]SC 199:354-56. [53]GT 41.

and fashioned the type of a cross, and he set it on the holy tabernacle, saying to the people, "If you gaze on this type and have faith, you will be saved."[54] And he wrote that when this happened the serpents died, but he testified that the people escaped death. Plato,[55] having read this and not rightly understanding it, and conceiving it not as a type of a cross but rather as a letter X, declared that the power next after God had been formed into an X pervading the cosmos. FIRST APOLOGY 60.3-5.[56]

THE BRAZEN SERPENT PORTENDS THE DEFEAT OF SATAN. JUSTIN MARTYR: Tell me, then, was it not God who enjoined you through Moses not to make any image or likeness at all of things in heaven above or of things on earth, and the same who in the wilderness through Moses caused the brazen serpent to be made and set it up for a sign, a sign through which those bitten by serpents were saved; and is he not innocent of unrighteousness?[57] Yes, for as I have said, through this he proclaimed the mystery by which he proclaimed the undoing of the serpent's power, which had caused the transgression of Adam to come about, and salvation to those who believe in the one who under this sign, namely, that of the cross, was going to die from the bites of the serpent, these being evil practices, idolatry and other unrighteous works. DIALOGUE WITH TRYPHO 94.1-2.[58]

THE CROSS IS A CONSPICUOUS JUDGMENT ON THE UNBELIEVER. MELITO OF SARDIS: Look on Abel, who was likewise murdered; on Isaac, who was likewise bound; on Joseph, who was likewise sold; on Moses, who was likewise abandoned; on David, who was likewise persecuted; on the prophets, who suffered likewise for the sake of Christ. Look too on the sheep that was sacrificed in Egypt, the one who has trampled Egypt and has saved Israel through his blood. And indeed the mystery of the Lord is proclaimed by the voice of prophecy, for

Moses says to the people, "You shall see your life hung up before your eyes night and day, and you shall not believe in your life."[59] ON PASCHA 59-61.[60]

YET THE BELIEVER CAN FIND ASSURANCE IN THE SAME SPECTACLE. IGNATIUS OF ANTIOCH: He was truly nailed in the flesh on our account by Pontius Pilate and Herod the tetrarch, and we come from the fruit of this, from his passion for which we bless God. It was so that by his resurrection he might raise a signal[61] to all ages for the saints who are faithful to him, whether among the Jews or among the nations, in the one body of his church. To THE SMYRNEANS 1.2.[62]

Restoring Creation

THE HUMAN FORM PREFIGURES THE CROSS. JUSTIN MARTYR: The human shape differs in nothing from the irrational animals except that it is upright[63] and can stretch out its arms, and in the face it carries what we call the nose projecting from the forehead, being also that through which an animal breathes; and this displays nothing so much as the form of the cross. FIRST APOLOGY 55.4.[64]

OUR OWN SIN PROVIDES THE WEAPONS OF DELIVERANCE. EPHREM THE SYRIAN: With the weapon of the deceiver the Firstborn clad himself, in order that with the weapon that killed he might restore to life again. With the tree wherewith Satan killed us, Christ delivered us. With the rib that was drawn out of Adam [i.e., Eve], the wicked one drew out the heart of Adam. There rose from the rib [i.e.,

---

[54]Deut 32:22, quoted at Jn 3:19, though Justin may not have known this. [55]See Plato *Timaeus* 36b-c on the world-soul. The letter X (representing in Plato the interweaving of the same and the other) is also the first letter of Christ in Greek. [56]JMAA 69. [57]Deut 32:22. [58]JMAA 208-9. [59]Deut 28:66. [60]MOPF 32. [61]Is 5:26. [62]AF 184. [63]Classical authors cited the erect posture of human beings (but not the extension of the arms) as a proof of innate divinity. [64]JMAA 66.

Mary] a hidden power that cut off Satan as Dagon;[65] for in that ark a book was hidden that cried aloud and proclaimed the conqueror! There was then a mystery revealed, in that Dagon was brought low in his own place of refuge! The accomplishment came after the type, in that the wicked one was brought low in the place in which he trusted. Hymns on the Nativity 3.[66]

The Cross Reaches Down to Hades.
Romanus the Melodist: Pilate set up three crosses on Golgotha, two for the robbers and one for the Giver of life. Seeing this, Hades said to those of the underworld: "Oh, acolytes and officers of mine, who has driven the nail into my heart? He has pierced me suddenly with a wooden lance, and I shall be broken asunder. I am in torment within, I am sick in my belly, my senses throw my spirit into turmoil, and I am forced to belch up Adam and those who were given to me by the wood of Adam. Wood is leading these folk back to paradise." When the serpent of wily counsel heard this, he came swiftly hissing and crying, "Hades, what is wrong with you. Why do you complain for nothing? Why do you send forth groans? This wood that you tremble at, I gave birth to it above for the son of Mary. I revealed this to the Jews for our profit. For this is the cross, to which I have nailed Christ, purposing to destroy the second Adam with wood. Let it not trouble you; it will not tear you to pieces. Remain in charge of those whom you possess, for not one of those whom we hold in tyranny is escaping again to paradise." "Come back to your senses, Belial," cried Hades. "Come quickly, open your eyes, and see the root of the cross within my soul. It has gone down into the depths of me, that it may draw up Adam like iron.[67] Elisha once foreshadowed this symbolically when he drew back the axe from the river. The prophet dragged up the heavy with the light, foretelling to you and teaching you that Adam will be led up by wood from

wretchedness to paradise." Canticle 22 [38], Strophe 1-3.[68]

The Good Thief Is the Antitype of Adam. Romanus the Melodist: For he was placed as a seal on the cross, as a treasure chest holding a flawless pearl in a perishable case. On the cross the thief of good character snatched this away. Nailed for his theft, he committed robbery[69] and was summoned back to paradise. Canticle 22 [38], Strophe 17.7-12.[70]

Wood the Instrument of Election and of Damnation. Romanus the Melodist: Oh, how did we fail to remember the types of this wood? For of old they were displayed in many forms, in many ways, among those who were being saved and those who were perishing. Noah was saved by wood, while the whole world perished in its disobedience. Moses was glorified by it, wielding his rod like a scepter; Egypt, however, was crushed by the plagues that he caused, as though it had fallen into deep torrents. Yes, what he has now performed the cross showed forth of old in a figure; for Adam is on his way back to paradise. Canticle 22 [38], Strophe 13.[71]

Through the Redemption of Adam, All Creation Is Renewed. Andrew of Crete: He who of old hid the tyrant persecutor in the waves of the sea has been hidden under the earth by the children of those whom he saved. Let us, however, like the ten wise maidens, sing to him, for he has been glorified in a glorious way. They who dwell above the heavens and they who dwell below the earth, seeing you on your throne above and in the tomb below,

---

[65]1 Sam 5:4, Dagon was a wooden idol of the Philistines. [66]NPNF 2 13:232. [67]Iron resembles adamant, a substance supposed to be named after Adam. [68]SC 128:286-90. [69]See Phil 2:6, where Christ declines to imitate Adam's theft. Romanus may also be offering a gloss on Mt 11:14; he is alluding to the parable of the pearl (Mt 13:46). [70]SC 128:308. [71]SC 128:302.

were shaken by your death; for you were seen in death to be the absolute master of life. That you might fill all places with your glory, you came down to the lowest places of the earth. Thanks to you my being is no longer hidden in Adam; corrupt as I was, you have renewed me in your burial, lover of humankind. The creation, when it saw you suspended on the cross—you who suspended the whole earth on the waters with no trouble—was seized with wonder and cried out, "There is none holy but you, O Lord." EASTER SATURDAY CANON.[72]

ALL HISTORY DEPENDS ON THE CROSS.

VALENTINUS (VIA HIPPOLYTUS): All things I see suspended on the spirit and all things riding on the spirit; the flesh suspended from the soul, the soul depending from air, and the air suspended from the aether; and from the abyss fruits being brought forth, and a youngling brought forth from the womb. REFUTATION OF ALL HERESIES 6.37.7.[73]

God's Own Sacrifice

THE PASSION IS THE DEATH OF GOD. ME-

LITO OF SARDIS: Indeed the law became word and the old became new, proceeding together from Zion, yes, from Jerusalem. And the command became grace, and the type became truth. The lamb became son and the sheep man, and the man God—for, begotten as son and revealed as a lamb, offered as a sheep and buried as man, he rose up from the dead as God, being by nature God and man. He is all things: law in judging, word in teaching, grace in saving, father in begetting, son in being begotten, sheep in suffering, man in his burial, God in his rising again. ON PASCHA 7-9.[74]

CONSEQUENTLY, THE DEATH COULD NOT

BE FINAL. APOLLINARIS OF LAODICEA: The death of a man does not abolish death, nor does one who has not died rise again. From this it is manifest to all that it was God himself who

died; therefore it was not possible for Christ to be mastered by death. FRAGMENT 95.[75]

THE DIVINE NATURE IS, HOWEVER, IMPER-

TURBABLE. TERTULLIAN: You blaspheme by saying not only that the Father died but also that he was crucified. For the curse of the crucified, which through the Law applies to the Son, seeing that Christ was "made a curse for us," you turn into a blasphemy on the Father when you convert Christ into the Father. But when we say that Christ was crucified, we do not curse him but allude to the curse of the Law. After all, when the apostle said this, he was not blaspheming. But just as what admits of being said may be said without blasphemy, so what does not admit of this is blasphemy if it is said. Thus the Father did not share in the Son's suffering—that is the way in which they hope to mitigate the blasphemy that they fear to inflict directly on the Father, conceding now that the Father and Son are two. On this view the Son suffers while the Father shares his suffering. Yet in this too they are fools. For what does it mean to share in suffering but to suffer with another?[76] But if the Father cannot suffer, then he cannot share in suffering. You attribute nothing to him as if to a mortal and are afraid to make him liable to suffer though you think him liable to share in suffering. But in fact the Father is no more able to share in suffering than the Son is able to suffer insofar as he is God. . . . The text has him exclaim in his suffering, "My God, my God, why have you forsaken me?"[77] Thus either the Son was suffering, abandoned by the Father, and the Father, having abandoned the Son, did not

---

[72]*PGV* 431-32. [73]*HROH* 253. [74]*MOPF* 4-6. [75]*ALSS* 229.
[76]The Monarchians, as Tertullian represents them, upheld the impassibility of the Godhead by contrasting the *compassio* or sympathy of the Father with the *passio* or true suffering of the Son. Tertullian retorts that the implied distinction between the Father and the Son contravenes the premise of the Monarchians and as the *com* of *compassio* is the preposition meaning "with," the Monarchian Godhead suffers as much in the Father as in the Son. [77]Mt 27:46.

suffer; or if the Father was suffering, to what God did he cry out? But this was the voice of flesh and blood—that is of a man—and not of the Word or the Spirit[78]—that is, of God. It was uttered for this reason, to reveal that God is impassable, having abandoned the Son insofar as he gave up the man in him to death. AGAINST PRAXEAS 29-30.[79]

WITHOUT THE FLESH, THERE WOULD BE NO PASSION. LEO THE GREAT: What does it mean to dissolve Jesus[80] but to separate his human nature from him and with presumptuous conceits to empty the sacrament, by which alone we have been saved? If one darkens counsel with regard to the nature of Christ's body, he will necessarily also be afflicted by the same blindness with regard to his passion. For if he does not think the cross of the Lord a deception and does not doubt that a true punishment was borne for the sake of the world, he must acknowledge the flesh of the one whose death he confesses. Nor should he doubt that the one whom he perceives to have been passable was a man with our kind of body, since the denial of the true flesh is a denial of a corporeal passion also. If then he has adopted the Christian faith and has not turned his ear from the preaching of the Evangelist, let him see what nature it was that hung transfixed by nails on the wood of the cross. Let him understand whence the blood and the water flowed when the flank of the crucified one was pierced by the soldier's lance,[81] so that the church of God might be washed both by baptism and by the eucharistic chalice. LETTER 128 (TO FLAVIAN) 5.[82]

ONLY BY THE DEATH OF A DIVINELY PERFECT MAN CAN WE BE SAVED. ORIGEN: Therefore he himself also says, "Now you seek to kill me, a man who has spoken the truth."[83] Now it was a man who died, and a man was not the truth, the wisdom, the peace and the righteousness, of which it was written, "And the

Word was God."[84] It was not the Word who died[85]—the truth, the wisdom and the righteousness. For the "image of the invisible God, the firstborn of all creation,"[86] is not liable to death. But it was for the people that this man died, the purest of all living creatures, who took on himself our sins and failings,[87] as one who was able to loose, to destroy and to annihilate the sin of the whole world by taking it on himself, because he had done no sin, nor was there found any guile in his mouth,[88] nor had he known sin.[89] COMMENTARY ON JOHN 28.18.[90]

GOD DOES INDEED SUFFER, BUT ONLY AS MAN. CYRIL OF ALEXANDRIA: What we mean when we say that he suffered and rose again is not that God the Word suffered in his own nature either blows or piercing with nails or the rest of the wounds (for the Godhead is impassable, as it is also incorporeal); but that since the body that he made his own suffered these things, he himself is said to have suffered these things for our sake. For the impassable one was in the passable body. Our belief with regard to his dying is of the same kind, for in his nature the Word of God is immortal and indestructible, is life and giver of life. But again since his own body "by the grace of God," as Paul says, "tasted death on behalf of all,"[91] he himself is said to have suffered death on our behalf, not that he went so far as to experience death insofar as concerns his own nature (for it would be insanity to assert this or to think it) but that, as I have just declared, the flesh that was his

---

[78]In Tertullian's work *Against Praxeas*, *spiritus* often denotes the whole divine nature, as at Jn 4:24. The next sentence implies that the Godhead of the Son, being one with the Father's, is equally impassible. [79]ECC 1-2. [80]The Latin reading of 1 Jn 4:3, where the true text denounces those who deny that Christ is come in flesh. [81]Cf. 1 Jn 5:6; Jn 19:34. [82]DFS 213. [83]Jn 8:40. [84]Jn 1:1. [85]Such language was exact enough for its time, but later generations saw that if we exempt the Word, or God, from the sufferings of his flesh, we deny the unity of Christ. [86]Col 1:15, here applied strictly to the Word without reference to the incarnation. [87]Is 53:8. [88]1 Pet 2:22. [89]2 Cor 5:21. [90]SC 385:138-40. [91]Heb 2:9.

tasted death. And so too when his flesh was raised up, again one speaks of his resurrection, not as if he had fallen into corruption—God forbid!—but because, once again, it was this body of his that rose. SECOND LETTER TO NESTORIUS 5.[92]

THERE ARE TWO DISTINCT NATURES IN THE INCARNATE CHRIST. THEODORET OF CYR: The divine Peter in his catholic epistle stated that Christ suffered in the flesh.[93] Now when one hears the name Christ here, one understands not the incorporeal Word but the Word enfleshed. But in fact the name Christ denotes each of the natures, but the addition of "in the flesh," juxtaposed with suffering, signifies not each nature but the one that suffered. For when one hears that Christ suffered, one again understands him to be impassable as God, and one attaches the suffering only to the flesh. For likewise when we hear Peter saying again that God swore to David that Christ would be raised up from the fruit of his loins,[94] we do not say that God the Word took his origin from the seed of David;[95] rather, we say that his flesh is of one kind with David, which God the Word assumed. Just so one who hears that Christ suffered in the flesh ought to acknowledge the suffering of the flesh while confessing the impassibility of the Godhead. ON THE CHANGELESSNESS OF GOD THE WORD 11.[96]

THE TWO NATURES ARE NOT TO BE CONFUSED. TERTULLIAN: Had he been a third something, an amalgam of both like electrum, there would not have been such distinct tokens of each nature. Rather, the spirit would have performed carnal works and the flesh spiritual works by transference, but under some third species, through amalgamation. Thus either the Word would have been dead or the flesh would not have been dead, if the Word had been converted into flesh. Either the flesh would have been immortal or the Word mortal. But because

the two substances acted discretely, each according to its inherent character, each was responsible for its own works and the outcome of them. AGAINST PRAXEAS 27.[97]

THE FLESH IS THE MEDIUM, NOT THE TRUE SUBJECT OF SUFFERING. CYRIL OF ALEXANDRIA: If indeed in the providential scheme[98] there were no mention of something passable by nature, my critics would have been right to say that, in the absence of anything passable by nature, it would be absolutely necessary somehow for the suffering to fall on the nature of the Word. In fact, however, everything that includes the flesh in the providential scheme is contained in the statement that he was actually enfleshed (for in no other way was he enfleshed than by partaking of Abraham's seed and being made like his brothers in all things and having assumed the form of a slave). Consequently, people are babbling aimlessly when they deduce, as an inevitable consequence, that he must endure in his own nature, for he has the flesh as a substrate and it would be reasonable to posit this as the subject of the suffering, since the Word is impassable. Yet we do not for this reason exclude him from the predication of suffering; for just as his body came into existence as his own, so too all that pertains to the body, excepting sin, could be no less properly said to belong to him, since he providentially took it to himself. SECOND LETTER TO SUCCENSUS 2.[99]

THE ENFLESHED WORD IS THE TRUE SUBJECT OF THE PASSION. CYRIL OF ALEXANDRIA: We confess that the very Word who was born from God the Father, even though he was impassable in his own nature, suffered in flesh for us according to the Scriptures and was in

---

[92]CASL 6-8. [93]1 Pet 4:1. [94]Acts 2:30. [95]Here as elsewhere Theodoret comes close to exempting God, and not merely the Godhead, from the infirmities of the flesh. [96]TCE 263. [97]CCL 2:1200. [98]The noun *oikonomia*, "providential design," is often a synonym for the incarnation in the Greek fathers. [99]CASL 86.

the crucified body, taking to himself the sufferings of his own flesh, although without suffering. "By the grace of God" and "on behalf of all he tasted death,"[100] having yielded to it his own body, even though he was by nature life and was himself the resurrection. His goal was, after trampling death by his ineffable power, to become, in that first flesh of his own,[101] the firstborn from the dead and firstfruits of those who sleep, leading human nature on the upward path to incorruption. To this end, as I have just said, by the grace of God he tasted death on behalf of all and revived on the third day after spoiling hades. Thus, even if it is said that the resurrection from the dead took place "through a man,"[102] we understand that the man is the Word begotten of God and that it is through him that the might of death has been undone. THIRD LETTER TO NESTORIUS 6.[103]

THE UNION RESEMBLES THAT BETWEEN SOUL AND BODY. CYRIL OF ALEXANDRIA: Let a human being of our own kind serve us as a model again. For we are aware of his possessing two natures, one of the soul and the other of the body. But we divide them in conception alone and make the distinction as it were in bare speculation or the reveries of the mind, without parceling out the natures or crediting them with any absolute power of dissociation. In fact, we know that they belong to one, so that the two are no longer two, but the whole living creature is constituted from both. Just so then, even if we predicate humanity and divinity of Emmanuel, the humanity is none the less proper to the Word, and one Son is involved in the conception. At any rate, when the inspired Scripture says that he suffered in the flesh,[104] it is better that we also should say this than that he suffered in the nature of his humanity—though certainly this too is an expression that, if some had not used it perversely, would have done no wrong to the mystery of the Word. SECOND LETTER TO SUCCENSUS 5.[105]

THE ANALOGY IS NECESSARILY IMPERFECT. THEODORET OF CYR: Those who urge that God the Word suffers ought to examine the meaning of this statement. And if they would venture to say that when the body was nailed the divine nature bore its anguish, let them learn that the divine nature did not perform the functions of the soul. For God the Word assumed a soul along with the body. ON THE CHANGELESSNESS OF GOD THE WORD 10.[106]

THE WORD DID NOT REPLACE THE SOUL. THEODORET OF CYR: But even if one accepts the statement in an Arian sense, this will serve no less to demonstrate the immortality of the divine nature. For he gave this up to the Father, he did not consign it to death.[107] Yet even those who deny that he assumed a soul, calling God the Word a creature and asserting that he himself took the place of a soul in the body, declare that he was not given up to death but entrusted to the Father. [108] What pardon then can there be for those who confess that there is one nature in the Godhead and concede to the soul its proper immortality, yet have the brazen hardihood to maintain that God the Word, who is consubstantial with the Father, tasted death? ON THE CHANGELESSNESS OF GOD THE WORD 12.[109]

THE GODHEAD PARTICIPATES, WITHOUT SUFFERING, IN THE SUFFERING OF HIS BODY. THEODORET OF CYR: When we say that the body or the flesh or the humanity suffered, we do not separate the divine nature. For it was united to the humanity that hungered, thirsted and labored—even indeed when it was sleeping and when it underwent the ordeal of

---

[100]Heb 2:9. [101]Translating word for word: in the same flesh that he had assumed for the first time through the incarnation. [102]1 Cor 15:21. [103]CASL 20-22. [104]1 Pet 4:1. [105]CASL 92. [106]TCE 263. [107]Equating spirit with soul (Lk 23:46). [108]Whatever Theodoret may suspect, this was not the position of Cyril, who knew well enough that Apollinaris and the Arians had been condemned for holding it. [109]TCE 264.

the passion—enduring none of these things but allowing the humanity to experience the sufferings proper to its nature.[110] In the same way, it was united to it during its crucifixion, so that by the passion it might undo death, not experiencing anguish from the passion but taking the passion to itself, as being proper to its own temple and the flesh united to it. Through this flesh believers function as members of Christ, and he is called the head of those who have believed. ON THE CHANGE-LESSNESS OF GOD THE WORD 16.[111]

The Appropriation of the Finished Work

ONLY ONE HAS DIED FOR THE SINS OF ALL. ORIGEN: Tales are rife among Greeks and barbarians of the numerous occasions when some specific danger prevailed—a plague, for example, a sickly atmosphere or a famine—and release came when some individual gave himself up for the common weal and thus appeased the evil spirit who was at work; and they do not spurn or slight the contemplation of such feats. To take up the question whether such tales are true or not is beside our present purpose, except to remark that there has been no story, nor could there be a story, of anyone who, in order that the whole world might be purified, was able to undergo death on behalf of the whole world for its purification, when it was bound to perish if he did not do so. Jesus alone was able to take to himself the whole load of sins on the cross that was for all things other than God; he alone was able to bear it by his great might. For he alone was able to bear subjection, as the prophet Isaiah has it, saying, "A man under blows and knowing what it is to bear subjection."[112] And he it was who bore our sins and suffered ignominy for our sakes, and the punishment that was necessary for our instruction and reconciliation fell on him. COMMENTARY ON JOHN 28.19.[113]

CHRIST'S SUFFERING UNITES HIM TO THE WORLD. MARIUS VICTORINUS: When in that mystery his body hung from the cross and in it crushed the power of the world, the whole world was crucified through him. In the cross he identified with every person in the world. In doing so, he made everything that he suffered universal, that is, he caused all flesh to be crucified in his death. Therefore I too am fixed to the cross and to the world.[114] COMMENTARY ON GALATIANS 6.14.[115]

OUR SALVATION IS NOT OUR OWN DOING. IGNATIUS OF ANTIOCH: My spirit is the refuse of the cross, which is a stumbling block to those without belief but to us salvation and everlasting life. "Where is the wise? Where is the scoffer?"[116] Where are the boasts of those who are credited with understanding? For, by God's dispensation, our God Jesus Christ was conceived by Mary from the seed of David[117] but also of the Holy Spirit. And having been born he was also baptized, that by his passion he might purify the waters. TO THE EPHE-SIANS 18.[118]

BECAUSE IT COMES FROM GOD, IT IS SE-CURE. IGNATIUS OF ANTIOCH: I praise Jesus Christ, the God who has thus made you wise. For I have perceived that you are established in immovable faith, as though nailed to the cross of the Lord Jesus Christ in flesh and blood and cemented by love in the blood of Christ, abounding in our Lord, who is truly of David's line according to the flesh, Son of God accord-ing to the power and will of God, having truly been born of the virgin and baptized by John, that all righteousness might be fulfilled in him. TO THE SMYRNEANS 1.1.[119]

THE BLESSINGS OF SALVATION. GREGORY OF NAZIANZUS: He vouchsafed to mortals a twofold purification through the ever-flowing

---

[110]Note that in Antiochene Christology, as in Alexandrian, the flesh suffers only so far as the Godhead wills it. [111]TCE 264-65. [112]Is 53:3. [113]SC 385:140-42. [114]Gal 6:14. [115]CSEL 83.2:171. [116]1 Cor 1:20; Rom 3:27. [117]Rom 1:3. [118]AF 148. [119]AF 184.

spirit, which purged the sinfulness that I inherited through the flesh, and through our own blood.[120] For mine it was, which Christ my God spilled out, a deliverance from primordial woes and a ransom for the world. Had I not been a changeable mortal but a being of adamant, I should have required from the mighty God only the sort of command that would nurse me, save me and exalt me to great glory. But as it is, God did not form me as a god but made me a creature of double inclination, leaning for support on many things, of which one is the grace of baptism for mortals. The children of the Hebrews escaped destruction through the anointing of blood that purified their doors, while the firstborn race of the Egyptians was destroyed in a single night. Similarly, to me also this is the seal of God who deflects all evils, a seal for the young indeed, but for those growing older a balm and a perfect seal, divinely flowing from Christ the giver of light, so that, having escaped the abyss of woe and raised my neck a little from its burden, I may advance toward life again with returning steps. PERSONAL POEMS 8.77-95.[121]

The Self-Emptying of Christ

THE SAYING HE EMPTIED HIMSELF PRESERVES HIS DIVINITY. CYRIL OF ALEXANDRIA: Now he is said to have been emptied[122] because before the emptying he possessed in his own nature the fullness implied in conceiving him as God. For it is not that one has ascended to the fullness from a state of emptiness, but rather that he has lowered himself from divine exaltation and ineffable glory. It is not that he was a lowly man who has been glorified and exalted, but rather that in his freedom he assumed the form of a slave. It is not that, being a slave, he leaped up into the glory of freedom: the one who was in the form of the Father, and his equal,[123] came to be in human likeness, rather than being a man who

has been enriched by participation in the likeness of God. ON THE CREED 15.[124]

THE TESTIMONIES OF PAUL AND JOHN CONCUR. THEODORET OF CYR: Look what the proclamations have in common. The Evangelist said, "The Word became flesh";[125] the apostle said, "having come to be in human likeness." The Evangelist said, "and tabernacled among us"; the apostle, "having assumed the form of a slave." Again the Evangelist said, "And we beheld his glory, glory as of the unique one from the Father"; the apostle, "who being in the form of God, thought it not robbery to be equal with God." And, in a word, they both teach that, being God and Son of God and clad in the glory of the Father, and having both the same nature and the same power as the one who begot him, the one "who was in the beginning and with God and was God,"[126] and was the author of the creation, assumed the form of a slave. ERANISTES 1.72-73.[127]

THE HUMILIATION WAS NOT FORCED ON CHRIST. GAUDENTIUS: Paul says, "having assumed the form of a servant"—not altogether made into a servant—and "made in human likeness."[128] For what was done in him was life; therefore what was done in him according to the flesh was life for us. As he himself testifies, "I came that they might have life and have it in abundance."[129] Then he added, "and found in fashion as a man," for what the fashion of God is in its full greatness—that which is properly God himself, in other words—no one has ever seen.[130] Then, he says, "He humbled himself,

---

[120]See 1 Jn 5:7, and note that Gregory joins with the Western tradition in maintaining that we inherit a sinful tendency that can be purged only by the Spirit through the mediation of water. [121]GNPA 46. [122]Phil 2:7. The kenotic theory, which holds that certain attributes of divinity were laid aside by the Word at his incarnation, was unknown to the church fathers. [123]Cyril substitutes "Father" for "God" (Phil 2:6) and puts his own construction on "thought it not robbery to be equal with God." [124]CASL 112. [125]Jn 1:14. [126]Jn 1:1-3. [127]TCE 89-90. [128]Phil 2:7. [129]Jn 10:10. [130]Jn 1:18.

being made obedient to the point of death, even death on a cross."[131] This means that his spontaneous humility was coupled with the Father's will as he voluntarily bore the cross, so that his death might become the life of those who believe. TRACTATES 19.27-28, WHETHER THE FATHER IS GREATER THAN THE SON.[132]

THE HUMILIATION INVOLVES BOTH NATURES. CYRIL OF ALEXANDRIA: If someone wishes to labor the question how he was enfleshed and made man, let him contemplate God the Word from God when he has assumed the form of a slave and come to be in human likeness, as it is written.[133] In this one thing alone, indeed, the distinction of the two natures—indeed, of the two hypostases[134]—may be observed. For Godhead and humanity are not the same thing in natural quality. If they were, then how was the Word, being God, made empty, lowering himself among his inferiors, that is, to this state of ours? The fact is that when the mode of the incarnation is canvassed, the human mind cannot but perceive the ineffable and unconfused collation of the two with one another to form a unity, and once they are united it in no way disjoins them, but believes and steadfastly admits that the issue of both is one God, Son, Christ and Lord. LETTER TO ACACIUS 14.[135]

THE WORD DID NOT SURRENDER HIS OMNIPRESENCE. CYRIL OF ALEXANDRIA: If the Son, being consubstantial with the Father, emptied the heavens of his presence when he became man,[136] it follows surely that the earth too was empty of the Father's substance, seeing that he did not become man or frequent the company of human beings, but rather—if I may speak for a while in their inane manner—remained in heaven. How then did the Savior say, "The Father who remains in me performs the works himself"?[137] How does he say through the prophet, "Do I not fill heaven and earth, says the Lord"[138] and again, "I am a

God who is near, says the Lord, and not a God afar off."[139] For Christ, born of the Father according to nature, has all things near him and fills all things together with the Father. . . . He shone forth from his substance indeed and blazed like light, yet he did not become external to him but is at once from him and in him. Among us it is true that parents are older than their children; but nothing could be less true of God. For the Son has always co-existed with the Father, possessing an unoriginated nature in common with his own progenitor, so that the eternity of the Father too may be always manifest. For there never was[140] when this was not so. ANSWER TO TIBERIUS 2.[141]

The Endurance of the Saints

CHRIST'S SUFFERINGS MAY BE COMPARED WITH THOSE OF JOSEPH. CHRYSOSTOM: Thus it is that the blessed Joseph has become a byword everywhere, because by his evil sufferings he got the better of those who wrought them. For his brothers and the Egyptian women were among those who conspired against him; yet he it was who subdued them all. No indeed, do not tell me of the prison in which he abode or of the palace where she spent her days. Tell me instead which was defeated, which was worsted, who despaired and who was elated. For as to her, she failed to subdue not only the just one but even her own passion. He on his side got the better both of her and of his perilous affliction. . . . He is silent and thus is condemned, for all those events were types of this. And he was in his chain, she in her palace. And what of this? It was he after all who became more illustrious than every crowned

---

[131]Phil 2:8. [132]PL 20:987-88. [133]Phil 2:7. [134]Cyril elsewhere differentiates *hypostasis* from "nature," denouncing those who speak of "two *hypostases*" in anathema 4 of his third letter to Nestorius. [135]CASL 50. [136]Phil 2:7. [137]Jn 14:10. [138]Jer 23:24. [139]Jer 23:23. [140]"There was when he [i.e., the Son] was not" is a phrase anathematized and implicitly attributed to Arius at the Council of Nicaea in 325. [141]CASL 142-46.

head, while she spent her days in her royal chambers in a worse state than any prisoner. HOMILIES ON MATTHEW 84.4.[142]

THE HANDS OF MOSES PRESAGE THE CROSS. JUSTIN MARTYR: When the people were at war with Amalek and the leader in battle was the son of Nun who was called by the name of Jesus [Joshua], Moses for his part prayed to God, stretching forth his arms on both sides. Hor and Aaron supported his arms, so that they would not relax because of his growing weary. For if there were any yielding in this shape that resembled that of the cross, the people lost ground. DIALOGUE WITH TRYPHO 90.4.[143]

THE CAPTAIN OF SALVATION FOR THE FIRST PEOPLE OF GOD WAS ALSO A JESUS. APHRAHAT: Also Joshua the son of Nun was persecuted, as Jesus our redeemer was persecuted. Joshua the son of Nun was persecuted by the unclean nations, and Jesus our redeemer was persecuted by the foolish people. Joshua the son of Nun took away the inheritance from his persecutors and gave it to his people; and Jesus our redeemer took away the inheritance from his persecutors and gave it to strange nations. DEMONSTRATION 21.11.[144]

SOLOMON SET AN EXAMPLE OF AUSTERITY. AMBROSE: When the bride has been led to the bridegroom, they sing a nuptial anthem, proclaiming love to the daughters of Jerusalem: "Come forth and behold in King Solomon, in the crown with which his mother has crowned him in the day of his espousal."[145] They sing a marriage song and invoke the other powers of the heavens or souls to behold the love that Christ has to the daughters of Jerusalem. For this reason he also deserved to be crowned by his mother like a son of love, as Paul shows by saying that "God has rescued us from the power of shadows and translated us into the kingdom of the

son of his love."[146] Thus he is the son of love and is himself love, not having love among his accidental qualities but having it always in his own essence like the kingdom of which he says, "I was born in this."[147] And so they say, "Come forth," that is, come out from the cares and broodings of the world, come out from chafing over the body, come out from the vanities of the world and see what love the king of peace[148] has in the day of his espousal. See how glorious he is because he has given resurrection to bodies and joined souls to himself. This is the crown of the great contest, this is the illustrious wedding gift of Christ: his blood and his passion. What more could he give, who did not spare himself[149] but offered his own death on our behalf? ISAAC, OR THE SOUL 5.46.[150]

THE FORTITUDE OF JOB WAS PROVERBIAL.[151] EPHREM THE SYRIAN: Let Job praise him with us, who bore sufferings for himself, and our Lord bore for us the spitting and the spear and the crown of thorns, and scourges, contempt and reproach, yes, mocking. Blessed be his mercy! HYMNS ON THE NATIVITY 13.34.[152]

CHRIST EXPRESSED THE SAME PATIENCE EVEN IN HIS DYING WORDS. AUGUSTINE: You have heard of the patience of Job, and you have seen the end of the Lord.[153] Why "the patience of Job," and not "you have seen the end of the same Job"? You would then be craving double; you would say, "If I keep on giving thanks to God, I receive double like Job." We know the patience of Job, and we know the end of the Lord. What end of the Lord? "My

---

[142]PG 58:756-57. [143]JMAA 204. [144]NPNF 2 13:397. The last sentence couples Mt 21:43 with Heb 3:11 (cf. Ps 95:5). The neat reversal of fortunes in this passage ought to serve as an admonition to Christians, not as a charter for anti-Semitism. [145]Song 3:11. [146]Col 1:13. [147]Jn 18:37. [148]The meaning of the name Solomon. [149]Adapting Rom 8:32, "who spared not his own Son." [150]CSEL 32.1:670-71. [151]See Jas 5:11. [152]NPNF 2 13:250. [153]Jas 5:11.

God, my God, why have you forsaken me?" The words are those of the Lord as he hung on the cross; as if he abandoned him with respect to present happiness but did not abandon him with respect to everlasting immortality. Such is the end of the Lord. SERMON TO CATECHU-MENS, ON THE CREED 10.[154]

DANIEL TOO WAS DELIVERED FROM THE UNGODLY. APHRAHAT: Daniel also was persecuted as Jesus was persecuted. Daniel was persecuted by the Chaldeans, the congregation of heathens; Jesus also the Jews,[155] the congregation of wicked people, persecuted. Daniel the Chaldeans accused, and Jesus the Jews accused before the governor. Daniel they cast into the pit of lions, and he was delivered and came up out of its midst uninjured. Jesus they cast down into the pit of the dead, and he ascended and death had no dominion over him. DEMONSTRATION 21.18.[156]

JESUS SAVES THE WORLD AS MORDECAI SAVED HIS PEOPLE. APHRAHAT: Mordecai also was persecuted as Jesus was persecuted. Mordecai was persecuted by the wicked Haman, and Jesus was persecuted by the rebellious people. Mordecai by his prayer delivered the people from the hands of Haman. Jesus by his prayer delivered his people from the hands of Satan.[157] Mordecai was delivered from the hands of his persecutors, and Jesus was rescued from the hands of his persecutors. Because Mordecai sat and clothed himself with sackcloth, he saved Esther and his people from the sword. Because Jesus clothed himself with a body and was illuminated, he saved the church and its children from death. DEMONSTRATION 21.20.[158]

CHRIST HONORS THE PROPHETS OF ISRAEL TO THE END. CHRYSOSTOM: Why be amazed concerning those without the covenant, who knew nothing and on account of their extreme dissoluteness had not even sought to learn,

when even those in Judea, after so many wonders, continued to insult him, although he had clearly shown them that it was he himself who had done these things foretold by the prophets. For this reason even after this he speaks out, that they may learn that he lives and that he himself has done this and that they may therefore grow more tractable. And he says "Eli, Eli, lama sabachthani,"[159] so that up to his last breath they may see that he honors the Father and is no enemy of God. For this cause he gave out a prophetic utterance, testifying up to his final hour to the old covenant. And not simply a prophetic utterance, but a Hebraic one, so that it might be intelligible and evident to them. And through all things he proves that he is of one mind with the one who begot him. HOMILIES ON MATTHEW 88.1.[160]

The Passive Obedience of the Son

CHRIST EXCEEDS ALL OTHER SUFFERERS IN HUMILITY. CHRYSOSTOM: Some say, "Look, he became obedient willingly; he is not equal to the one whom he obeyed."[161] Witless fools, this does not at all diminish him, for we obey our friends, and no such consequence follows. He obeyed as a son obeys a father, not descending to the rank of a slave but vindicating his wonderful paternity most of all by this very fact of paying honor to the Father. Just as he is greater than all and no one is equal to him, so also he vanquished all by his honoring of the Father, not under constraint or unwillingly, but in this too he proved his

---

[154]CCL 46:192. [155]The use of this name, though not the implied incrimination of all living Jews, is authorized by such texts as Jn 19:7. [156]NPNF 13:399. [157]Mt 6:13; Jn 17:15; Lk 22:31-32. The illustration is all the more piquant because in the book of Esther it is Haman, not Mordecai, who goes to the scaffold—a fact that did not escape Christian spectators when the hanging of Haman was celebrated in the Jewish feast of Purim. [158]NPNF 13:400. [159]Mt 27:46. [160]PG 58:776. [161]Medieval piety forgot, and some modern theologians seem not to know, that the Greek and Latin words that we render as "suffering" denote not so much pain as passivity.

excellence. I know not what to say! Indeed it was a great thing to become a slave, and quite beyond words, but to undergo death was so much greater again. Yet there is another thing greater and stranger than this. What is that? That not every death is alike. For this man appeared to be the most reprobate of all, this man full of ignominy, this man accursed. For, as it says, "Cursed is everyone that hangs on a tree."[162] For this reason also the Jews were eager to destroy him in this manner, so that they might render him utterly reprobate and so that even if no one shunned him on account of his execution, they would do so because it was such an execution. For this reason again, two thieves were crucified with him in the midst, so that he might share his glory with them and fulfill the saying, "and he was numbered with the transgressors."[163] Yet all the more the truth shines forth, and with all the more brilliance. For since so many stratagems had been devised against his glory by his enemies, and yet he shone forth, the revelation was all the greater. For it was not by killing him but by killing him in this way that they thought to render him abhorrent and to make him seem abhorrent beyond all others; yet they failed completely. And likewise both the thieves were of the vilest class, yet one of them repented. HOMILIES ON PHILIPPIANS 7.3.[164]

To the Worldly-Wise His Passion Seems Ignoble. METHODIUS: That, truly, is to be accounted as in reality the most beautiful, even though it is condemned and despised by all else—not that which people fancy to be beautiful. Thus it is that, although by this figure he has willed to deliver the soul from corrupt affections, to the signal putting to shame of the demons, we ought to receive it and not to speak evil of it, as being that which was given to deliver us and set us free from the chains that for our disobedience we had incurred. For the Word suffered, being in the flesh affixed to the cross, that he might bring

humankind, who had been deceived by error, to it supreme and god-like majesty, restoring to it that divine life from which it had been alienated. By this figure, indeed, the passions are blunted; passion of passions having taken place by the passions, and the death of death by the death of Christ. FRAGMENT 2, ON THE CROSS AND PASSION OF CHRIST.[165]

This Is the Truth That Philosophers Cannot Swallow. AUGUSTINE: I read [in the writings of Platonists] that God the Word was born not of flesh or "of blood, not of a human will or the will of the flesh,"[166] but of God. That "the Word was made flesh and dwelled among us,"[167] however, I did not find there. In those books I discovered copious and manifold testimonies that the Son was "in the form of the Father, not thinking it robbery to be equal with God,"[168] since that was exactly what he was already. But that "he emptied himself, assuming the form of a servant, made in the likeness of humanity and found in fashion as a man," that he "humbled himself, being made obedient to the point of death, even the death on the cross," and "that God therefore exalted him from the dead, bestowing on him the name above every name so that every knee should bow at the name of Jesus, of beings in heaven or on earth, and every tongue confess that Jesus the Lord is in the glory of the Father"[169]—all this these books do not contain. CONFESSIONS 7.9.14.[170]

His Pains Were Not Less Because They Were Voluntary. ORIGEN: After this Celsus says, "If this was what he chose, and if he underwent chastisement in obedience to the Father, it is clear that since he was

---

[162]Deut 21:23, cited at Gal 3:13. [163]Is 53:12. [164]*IOEP* 5:78. [165]ANF 6:400. [166]Jn 1:13. [167]Jn 1:14. [168]Phil 2:6. [169]Augustine's Latin does not correspond exactly to the Greek of Phil 2:7-11. He resembles Paul, however, and differs from some modern commentators, in declining to dwell exclusively on the suffering of Christ. [170]ACO 1:80.

God and this was his will, the things that he accepted voluntarily were neither painful nor grievous." And he has not observed that he has said things that are flatly contradictory. For if he grants that he underwent chastisement, since this was what he chose, and he yielded himself to the Father in obedience, it is evident that he did indeed undergo chastisement, and the afflictions laid on him by those who chastised him could not fail to be painful. If the afflictions were nether painful nor onerous because that was his will, why does he grant that he underwent chastisement? He has not perceived that once he had assumed the generated body, this body that he assumed was itself a receptacle of troubles and the pains that befall those who are embodied, if by pains we understand that which is not voluntary. Therefore, just as he willingly assumed a body that differed in nature from human flesh, in the same way he assumed along with the body both its pains and its griefs, and he had no power to prevent this from making him suffer, since it was in the power of those who applied them to cause him painful and grievous afflictions. AGAINST CELSUS 2.23.[171]

HIS SUFFERING COMPREHENDS OURS. EUSEBIUS: How does he make our sins his own, and how is he said to bear our iniquities, if not insofar as we are said to be his body, in the words of the apostle: "You are the body of Christ and members severally."[172] And just as when one member suffers, all the other members suffer with it, so when all the members suffer and ail, he too by the principle of sympathy takes on himself the labors of the suffering members and makes our maladies his own, suffering and laboring on our behalf by the law of philanthropy. This is what it meant for him, being the Word of God, to assume the form of a slave[173] and be conjoined to the common tabernacle of us all.[174] PROOF OF THE GOSPEL 10.1.21-22.[175]

THIS IS NOT MERELY A CREED, BUT A PATTERN FOR LIFE. AUGUSTINE: He humbled himself, "being made obedient even to death on a cross,"[176] so that none of us, while being able to face death without fear, might shrink from any kind of death that human beings regard as a great disgrace. ON FAITH AND THE CREED 11.[177]

Jesus as Priestly Victim

THE PRIEST AND THE UNIVERSAL SACRIFICE. GREGORY OF NAZIANZUS: He prayed; but who was it who heard the prayer of the supplicant? He was a sacrifice, yet a high priest; a supplicant, yet God. He dedicated his blood to God and cleansed the whole world. A cross raised him aloft, yet it was sin that was fixed by the nails. PERSONAL POEMS 2.74-77.[178]

HE OFFERS UP HIS OWN BODY. EPISTLE OF BARNABAS: For the Savior's purpose, in suffering his body to be given up to corruption, was that we might be sanctified by the remission of sins; this is effected by the sprinkling of his blood. EPISTLE OF BARNABAS 5.1.[179]

IT WAS A NEW SACRIFICE. LEO THE GREAT: "Christ our Passover has been sacrificed,"[180] as the apostle says. Offering himself to the Father as a new and real sacrifice of reconciliation, he was crucified—not in the temple, where the worship is now completed, or within the enclosure of the city, which was to be destroyed because of its crime, but outside and beyond the camp.[181] That way, as the mystery of the ancient sacrifices was ceasing, a new victim would be put on the altar, and the cross of Christ would be the altar not of the temple but of the world. SERMON 59.5.[182]

---

[171]SC 132:346-48. [172]1 Cor 12:27. [173]Phil 2:7. [174]Jn 1:14. [175]GCS 23:450. The vocabulary is strikingly Antiochene for one who is often regarded as a champion of the Alexandrian school. [176]Phil 2:8. [177]CSEL 41:14. [178]GNPA 8. [179]AF 282. [180]1 Cor 5:7. [181]Heb 13:11-12. [182]CCL 138A:355-56.

THE SACRIFICE IS EFFICACIOUS. ORIGEN: How could he be a comforter and a means or seat of propitiation but for the power of God, which dispels our infirmity, flowing into the souls of believers by the dispensation of Jesus, he being himself its principal, the very power of God? COMMENTARY ON JOHN 1.33.[183]

Fulfilling the Type

AS NOAH PRESERVED, SO CHRIST RE-DEEMED THE WORLD. EPHREM THE SYRIAN: In revelation, Lord, it has been proclaimed that that lowly blood that Noah sprinkled[184] wholly restrained your wrath for all generations. How much mightier, then, shall be the blood of your Only-begotten, that the sprinkling of it should retrain our flood! For it was but as mysteries of him that those lowly sacrifices gained virtue, which Noah offered and stayed by them your wrath. Be propitiated by the gift on my altar, and stay from me the deadly flood. So shall both your signs bring deliverance, to me your cross and to Noah your bow![185] Your cross shall divide the sea of waters, your bow shall stay the flood of rain. NISIBENE HYMNS 1.2.[186]

CHRIST'S OBLATION CONSUMMATES AND SUPERSEDES THE OLD PRIESTHOOD. IRE-NAEUS: As for offerings and oblations and sacrifices, the populace received all these as a type, in the same way as it was shown to Moses on the mountain,[187] by the one God, the very same whose name is now glorified in the church among all peoples. Now it is proper that earthly things that are dispensed to us should be types of those that are celestial—bearing in mind that they are creatures of the same God. For there was no other way of imitating the likeness of things spiritual. But to say of things supercelestial and spiritual—things that to us are invisible and ineffable—that they are types of other celestial things and of another pleroma,[188] and that God is the likeness of another Father—this is the opinion

of people who have strayed far from the truth, people thoroughly stupid and dull-witted. For such people, as I have already shown, will be forced to go forever contriving types of types and likenesses of likenesses, never fixing their minds on the one true God. AGAINST HER-ESIES 4.19.1.[189]

THE CARNAL RITES ARE ABROGATED. AU-GUSTINE: As the one who was to do away with the sacrifices that took place under the levitical priesthood in succession from Aaron, it was necessary that he should not be of the tribe of Levi, lest it should appear that the cleansing of sins belonged to that same tribe and that same priesthood that had been temporally a shadow of things to come. This cleansing the Lord accomplished presenting himself as the burnt offering prefigured in the old priesthood. And he enjoined the celebration of a rite analogous to that burnt offering as a memorial of his own passion in the church, in order that he might be a priest for eternity, not in succession from Aaron but in succession from Melchizedek. ON EIGHTY-THREE VARIED QUESTIONS 61.2.[190]

Christ the Ransom

THE RANSOM WAS NECESSARY BECAUSE WE WERE POWERLESS. LETTER TO DIOG-NETUS: But when our unrighteousness was complete, and it had become fully manifest that the wage to be expected from it was pun-ishment and death, the time came that God had appointed for the manifestation of his goodness and power. O the exceeding benevo-lence and love of God! He did not abhor us,

---

[183]SC 120:178. [184]Gen 8:20-22. [185]Gen 9:16. [186]NPNF 2 13:167. [187]Ex 25:40. [188]Allusion to the Valentinian myth, in which a spiritual fullness or *plērōma* emerges from the ineffable Godhead before the creation of the world. The fullness of the ages (Gal 4:4) and the fullness of God in Christ (Col 2:9) were regarded by the Valentinians merely as types of the heavenly *plērōma*. See *Against Heresies* 1.1 and other references. [189]SC 100:614-16 [190]CCL 44A:125.

nor did he spurn us, nor did he bear a grudge, but he was longsuffering in forbearance, and in his pity he himself took on him our sins; he himself gave his own son as a ransom[191] for us, the holy for the lawless, the unoffending for the offender, the righteous for the unrighteous,[192] the incorruptible for the corruptible, the immortal for the mortal. For what else was able to cover[193] our sins but his righteousness? In whom was it possible for us lawless and impious ones to be justified but in the Son of God alone? O for the sweet exchange, the imponderable working, the unforeseen bounties, that the lawlessness of many should be hidden in the one righteous man and the righteousness of one should justify many who were lawless![194] Having, therefore, in the foregone time proved our own nature incapable of attaining life, he has now revealed the Savior who is capable of saving even the incapable. He has willed that on both accounts we should trust in his goodness, regarding him as our nurse, father, teacher, counselor, physician, mind, light, honor, glory, strength and life. LETTER TO DIOGNETUS 9.2-6.[195]

PERSUASION BEFITS THE LORD. IRENAEUS: There was no other way that we could learn but by seeing our own teacher and hearing his voice with our own ears, so that, having become imitators of his deeds and doers of his word, we might enjoy communion with him. We received increase from the one who is perfect and prior to every state, and having been made anew by him who alone is good and better than all, the one who possesses the gift of immortality, we have been created according to his likeness[196]—predestined as we were, by the Father's foresight, to be what we were not yet—created indeed as the beginning of creation.[197] In times foreknown we received this through the ministry of the Word, who is perfect in all, because the potent Word, who is also true man, has duly redeemed us by his blood, giving himself as a ransom for those

who have been led into captivity. Apostasy[198] held sway over us unrighteously and had estranged us against nature, making us its own disciples, when by nature we belonged to God Almighty. But the Word of God, potent in all and not falling short of his own righteousness, strove righteously also against apostasy, ransoming from it that which was his, not by force, as it initially gained sway over us, but by persuasion, since it befits God to obtain what he wills by persuasion, not by force. AGAINST HERESIES 5.1.1.[199]

IF GOD PAID THE PRICE, IT WAS SATAN WHO RECEIVED IT. ORIGEN: If then we have been "bought with a price,"[200] as Paul too states, we were undoubtedly bought from someone, whose thralls we were, who also demanded the price that he wanted for relinquishing power over those whom he was detaining. But the one who detained us was the devil, to whom we had been forcibly translated by our sins. He, then, demanded as his price the blood of Christ. Until, however, the blood of Jesus was given—blood so precious that it sufficed alone for the redemption of all—it was necessary that those who were being reared in the Law should each give blood on his behalf, in imitation (as it were) of the future redemption. For the same reason we, for whom the payment in the blood of Christ has been discharged, are under no necessity of giving a price for ourselves, that is, of offering the blood of circumcision. COMMENTARY ON ROMANS 2.13.[201]

---

[191]Our word *redemption* means in origin a "buying back," and so does the Greek word *lytron*, as at Mk 10:45: to give his life as a ransom for many. But who demands the ransom? If we are bought with a price (1 Cor 6:20), to whom is it paid? [192]See 1 Pet 3:18. [193]See 1 Pet 4:8 but also Rom 3:25, where the Hebrew equivalent of the Greek *hilastērion* ("mercy seat," hence "propitiation") has the sense of "covering." [194]See Rom 5:18-19. [195]*AF* 546-48. [196]Gen 1:27. [197]Jas 1:18; Col 1:15. [198]I take this term to denote not the devil, who is said to be vanquished at *Against Heresies* 5.20, but the rebellious temper of those whom he seduces. [199]SC 153:16-20. [200]1 Cor 7:23. [201]*AGLB* 16:172.

BUT PERHAPS WE NEED NOT IDENTIFY THE RECIPIENT. ADAMANTIUS: You say that Christ was the purchaser? Who then was the vendor? Has the simple adage that the buyer and seller are brothers not reached your ears? If the devil, evil as he was, sold to the good one, he is not evil but good. For the one who envied humans at the beginning was no longer moved by envy, as he has given his portion to the good one. Thus, now that he has desisted from envy and from all evil, he will be righteous. More probably, it was God who made the sale; more probably still, the people who sinned, having pawned themselves through their sins, have been redeemed again through his longsuffering. DIALOGUE.[202]

THE IMAGE CONTAINS AN INSOLUBLE MYSTERY. GREGORY OF NAZIANZUS: I ask, to whom was the blood of God poured out? If to the evil one, alas that what is Christ's should go to the wicked. If to God, how so, when we were in the power of another? The ransom always belongs to the one who has power. Or is this true, that he made an offering to God, so that God might snatch us from the one who had power and receive Christ as an equivalent for the fallen one? For the one who anointed[203] is not to be taken captive. That is our belief, but we revere the mysteries. DOGMATIC POEMS 1.1.10.[204]

THE DEVIL UNDERSTOOD NOTHING OF THE TRANSACTION. ORIGEN: According to the Father's will he assumed the form of a slave and offered a victim for the entire world, giving up his blood to the prince of this world in accordance with the wisdom of God, whom none of the princes of this world has known; for if they had known, they would not have crucified the Lord of glory. Nor did they know that that blood for which they thirsted would quench not their thirst so much as their powers and bring destruction on their kingdom or that they were suffering what the Lord spoke of in

the Gospel: "Behold now, the prince of this world is judged"; and again, "I saw Satan fall like lightning from heaven."[205] COMMENTARY ON ROMANS 4.11.[206]

THE VICTIM MAY BE REGARDED AS A BAIT. GREGORY OF NYSSA: In order that the one who was demanding payment for us might be readier to take him, his divinity was hidden under the veil of our nature, so that, as in the catching of fish with lines, the hook of his divinity was swallowed up along with the bait of his flesh. The purpose was that, as life made its home with death and the light shone in the darkness, light and life might cause their opposite concept to vanish. For it is not in the order of nature that darkness should endure in the presence of light or death remain when life is at work. ADDRESS ON RELIGIOUS INSTRUCTION 24.[207]

CHRIST OUR RANSOM IS ALSO CHRISTUS VICTOR. PELAGIUS: Through sin we had been sold to death—as Isaiah says, "You were sold by your sins"[208]—but Christ, who did not sin, conquered death. For we were all condemned to death, to which he handed himself over, though it was not his due, so that he might redeem us with his blood. This is why the prophet prophesied, "You were sold for nothing, and without money you will be redeemed."[209] That is, because you received nothing for yourselves and had to be redeemed with Christ's blood. COMMENTARY ON ROMANS.[210]

TO BE RANSOMED IS NOT MERELY TO BE FORGIVEN. ORIGEN: Let us consider more closely what is meant by the ransom that is in Christ Jesus. What is called a ransom is that which is given to enemies for those whom they

---

[202]GCS 4:52-54. [203]Perhaps the most obscure phrase in a very elliptical passage. I take it to denote the Word, as the one who anoints the manhood. [204]PG 37:470. [205]Lk 10:18. [206]AGLB 33:351-52. [207]COGN 92-93. [208]Is 50:1. [209]Is 52:3. [210]PCER 82.

hold in captivity, so that they may restore them to their original freedom. The human race, then, was being held in captivity by sin, as though vanquished in war. Then came the Son of God, who was made for us, not only wisdom from God and righteousness and sanctification, but also a ransom. He gave himself as the ransom—that is, he gave himself up to the enemies, pouring out his own blood to slake their thirst. And this is the ransom paid for those who believe, just as Peter writes in his letter, saying, "because you were not ransomed with corruptible silver or gold but with the precious blood of the only-begotten Son of God." Perhaps it was also this that Solomon represented in a mystery, saying "the ransom of a man's soul is its proper wealth." For if you inquire what the proper wealth of a soul is, you will find that its wealth consists in wisdom and righteousness and sanctification. Now all these terms the apostle applies to Christ. Thus Christ is the wealth of the soul; hence he is also its ransom. COMMENTARY ON ROMANS 3.7.[211]

THE QUALITY OF THE RANSOM. PROSPER OF AQUITAINE: When, therefore the captives are redeemed at this price, let them perceive what a prison it was that trapped them, what a disease it was that had gripped them, from which they could not be delivered by any aid but the death of the physician. And because nothing remains from Adam's great riches to adorn the naked and console the needy, the former should not be so pleased by this exchange of the great as to be puffed up by the victory and perversely to take pride in the very cause of their wretchedness. SONG OF INGRATITUDE 2.901-9.[212]

The Shedding of Blood

THE FATHER IS NO TYRANT. IRENAEUS: He it is who is the Creator, our Father in love, our Lord in power, our maker and fashioner in wisdom, and it is by transgressing his command that we have been made his enemies. And on account of this, in these last days he has restored us to friendship by his own incarnation, having been made "a mediator between God and humankind."[213] On our behalf in fact he has propitiated the Father, against whom we had sinned, and has healed our disobedience through his obedience, imparting to us the intimacy that comes of subjection to our maker. AGAINST HERESIES 5.17.1.[214]

IT WAS NOT THE BLOOD THAT INDUCED THE FATHER TO LOVE HIS CREATION. AUGUSTINE: But what is meant by "justified in his blood"?[215] What, pray, is there in this blood that the faithful should be justified by it? And what is meant by "reconciled through the death of his Son"?[216] Does it mean, say, that when God the Father was angry with us, he saw the death of his Son on our behalf and was thus at peace with us? Is it conceivable that the Son of God was already so much at peace with us that he even deigned to die for us, yet the Father up to this time was so angry with us that he would not be at peace unless his Son died for us? And what of another place in which the teacher of the Gentiles says, "What shall we say to this? If God is for us, who is against us? He who spared not his own Son, but gave him up for the sake of us all, how will he not give all things to us with him?"[217] Is it possible that the Father would have "spared not his own Son" and "given him up for us" if he had not already been at peace? Does it not appear that the one position is at variance with the other? According to the first, the Son dies for us and the Father "is reconciled to us through his death." In the second, by contrast, as though the Father had loved us first, he himself on our behalf "spared not his own Son"; he gives him up to death for our sake. But I observe that even before this the

[211]*AGLB* 16:234-35. [212]*PS* 95:96. [213]1 Tim 2:5. [214]SC 153:220-22. [215]Rom 5:9. [216]Rom 5:10. [217]Rom 8:32.

Father loved us, not only before his Son died on our behalf but before he created the world, as the apostle himself bears witness, saying "as he chose us before the foundation of the world."[218] Nor was the Son given up, as it were, unwillingly when the Father "spared him not", since of him it is said, "who died for me and gave himself up for me." All things, then, are jointly performed by the Father and the Son and the Spirit of both.[219] Nevertheless, we are justified in the blood of Christ and reconciled to God through the death of his Son. How this came to pass I shall explain to the best of my ability here so far as may seem needful. ON THE TRINITY 13.11.15.[220]

JUSTICE DEMANDED THE PAYMENT OF THE DEBT. AUGUSTINE: By a sort of divine justice, the human race had been given up into the power of the devil, for the sin of the first man passed at conception[221] into all those who were born from mingling of the two sexes, and the debt of the first parents was binding on all their posterity. . . . Yet it was not by the power of God but by justice that the devil was to be overcome. For what is more powerful than the Almighty, or what creature's power can be likened to the power of its Creator? But when the devil through his own base perversity became a lover of power, a defaulter from justice and an opponent of it (and likewise human beings imitate him all the more, the more they neglect or even repudiate justice, striving for power and either rejoicing when they acquire it or burning with lust for it), it pleased God that, in order to extricate us from the devil's power, the devil should be overcome by justice, not by power. And therefore human beings too, in imitation of Christ, would seek to overcome the devil by justice, not by power. . . . What, then, is this justice by which the devil was overcome? What but the justice of Jesus Christ? And how was he overcome? Because when he found in him nothing worthy of death, he put him to death notwithstanding.[222] And thus it is just that the debtors

whom he was detaining should be released scot-free through believing in him whom he had put to death where no debt was owed. This is what it means to say that we are justified in the blood of Christ. Thus indeed it was for the remission of our sins that his innocent blood was shed. ON THE TRINITY 13.12.16–14.18.[223]

Christ the Lamb

THE LAMB WAS NOT MERELY A TYPE. EPHREM THE SYRIAN: Let Isaac praise the Son, for by his goodness he was rescued on the mount from the knife, and in his stead there was the victim, the lamb for the slaughter. The mortal escaped, and he that quickens all died. HYMNS ON THE NATIVITY 13.29.[224]

ISAAC ENACTS THE TYPE. AMBROSE: There is a fitting type in the donkey, as there is truth[225] in the colt of the donkey. But this animal signifies the folk of the nations, who were previously under the yoke but now subject to Christ. Isaac therefore is a type of Christ, who was to suffer. He came on a donkey, in order to prefigure the future belief of the folk of the nations. Likewise the Lord, when he came to undergo his passion on our behalf, loosed the colt of a donkey. As he sat on it, it was meek and docile, entrusting its back to Christ. . . . Isaac carried wood for himself; Christ carried the beam of his own cross. Isaac was accompanied by Abraham, Christ by the Father; neither Isaac nor Jesus was alone. ON ABRAHAM 1.8.71-72.[226]

---

[218]Eph 1:4. [219]Augustine insists throughout *On the Trinity* that the Spirit proceeds from both the Father and the Son, though the creeds of the day said only (at most) "from the Father." [220]CCL 50A:401-2. [221]Translating *originaliter*. Augustine held that the penalty of Adam's sin was that lust became the inevitable concomitant of procreation, Adam's descendants thereby inheriting both his guilt and a disposition to sin. [222]Augustine here allows the devil to coalesce with Pilate, in keeping with his principle that our sin is our own, whatever may be suggested to us by demons. [223]CCL 50A:402, 404, 406. [224]NPNF 2 13:249. [225]That is, fulfillment of the type.

**A TWOFOLD ALLEGORY CAN BE PRO-
POUNDED.** GREGORY OF NYSSA: In the story
one can see the whole mystery of holiness. The
lamb was dangling, caught in the wood by the
horns, while the Only-begotten carries on his
own person the cross of fruitfulness. You see
how the one who upholds all by the power of
his word is the same one who carries the load
of all our crosses, at the same time he is taken
up by the cross, bearing it as God and being
borne by it as the lamb. Thus the Holy Spirit
has symbolically distributed the whole mystery
between the beloved Son and the emblematic
sheep, so that in the sheep the mystery of
death is revealed and in the Only-begotten
the life that was not cut off by death. ON THE
THREE DAYS' INTERVAL.[227]

CHRIST IS THE LAMB OF THE PASSOVER.[228]
MELITO OF SARDIS: You will marvel on hearing of this new visitation. For this it was that
engulfed the Egyptians: long night and darkness palpable, the touch of death, angelic tribulation and hell swallowing up their firstborn.
But what is more marvelous and more fearful
you have yet to hear. In the palpable darkness
impalpable death was lurking, and while the
wretched Egyptians touched the darkness,
death sought them out and, at the angel's command, touched the firstborn of the Egyptians.
. . . Such was the visitation that engulfed
Egypt and rendered it suddenly childless.
Israel, for its part, was protected by the sacrifice of the sheep and was therewith illumined
by the outpoured blood, and the death of the
sheep was found to be a wall for the people.
ON PASCHA 22-23, 30.[229]

**THERE IS PROPHECY IN THE DETAILS
OF THE SACRIFICE.** JUSTIN MARTYR: The
mystery of the sheep, which God has commanded to be sacrificed as a Passover, was a
type of the anointed One, with whose blood,
in accord with the word of faith in him, those
who have faith in him anoint their houses—

that is to say, their own persons.[230] For all Jews
are aware that the form that God fashioned
as Adam became the house of the insufflation
that was from God. That this ordinance was in
fact temporary I demonstrate as follows. God
does not permit the sheep of the Passover to be
sacrificed anywhere except in the place where
his name is invoked. For he knew that after the
passing[231] of Christ, when the place of Jerusalem was to be handed over to your enemies,
all offerings would come to an absolute stop.
And the command that this sheep was to be
cooked whole was a symbol of the passion that
Christ was to suffer on the cross. For the sheep
when cooked is cooked in a shape resembling
the shape of the cross. One skewer pierces it
lengthways from the nethermost limbs to the
head, while another again pierces it through
the diaphragm, from which the limbs of the
sheep depend. DIALOGUE WITH TRYPHO
40.1-3.[232]

**THE LAMB WAS NOT THE ONLY SIGNIFI-
CANT VICTIM.** JUSTIN MARTYR: And the two
goats of similar kind that were required in the
fast, one of which became an outcast, while
the other served as an offering,[233] were an
annunciation of the two advents of Christ. In
the first the elders and priests of your nation
sent him away as an outcast, laying hands
on him and putting him to death.[234] In that
second advent of his you will know him in
the same place of Jerusalem as the one who,
dishonored by you, became an offering for all
sinners who wish to repent and who fast as
Isaiah directed.[235] DIALOGUE WITH TRYPHO
40.4.[236]

---

[226]CSEL 32.1:548-50. [227]GNO 9:275. [228]See Jn 1:29; 19:36.
[229]MOPF 12, 16. [230]That is, Christians do privately what
Ex 12 required the Jews to do communally. [231]Playing on the
words *pascha* ("Passover") and *paschō* ("I suffer"), which were
often, though wrongly, supposed to be etymologically related.
[232]JMAA 137. [233]Lev 16:15-22. [234]The Baptist seems to
conflate this goat and the Passover lamb (Jn 1:29). [235]See Is 59.
[236]JMAA 137.

THE LAMB ALSO JUDGES. RIDDLES IN THE APOCALYPSE: "Who are not written in the Lamb's book of life"[237] means that before the lamb, that is, the church, existed, it was marked out for eternal life in the knowledge of God; or else the lamb means Christ, insofar as Christ's assumption of flesh was already marked out in the providential scheme of God. "Who was slain from the foundation of the world" means that it was prophesied and prefigured from the foundation of the world that Christ would be slain; or else "the lamb slain from the foundation of the world" means the church, as Cain killed Abel. RIDDLES IN THE APOCALYPSE OF JOHN 69.[238]

Christ Made Sin

CHRIST BLOTTED OUT THE INDICTMENT BY HIS SUFFERING. THEODORET OF CYR: If our Savior and Lord "nailed to the cross the indictment against us," as the apostle declares, that means that he nailed the body. For it is in the body that everyone nails down the enticements of sin, like so many bills. For this reason he gave up his own body, which was free of all sin, on behalf of those who had sinned. ON THE CHANGELESSNESS OF GOD THE WORD 15.[239]

THE ASSUMPTION OF SIN IS FORESHADOWED BY ANOTHER JESUS. EUSEBIUS: In a very similar manner[240] Paul writes about him, saying, "Him who knew no sin he made sin for us,"[241] so that we might become in him the righteousness of God; and Christ redeemed us from the curse of the Law, having become a curse for us.[242] All these things were foreshown by inspiration in the prophecy in the words, Joshua put on filthy clothes.[243] But he put these away in his ascent to heaven, his return to his own from our captivity, and was crowned with the diadem of his Father's Godhead, and clad himself in the brilliant robe of the paternal light and was invested with

the godly miter and the other vestments of the high priesthood. And it is not difficult to give the sense of what is said of the devil, who is even now an opponent of Christ's teaching and of the church that has been established by him throughout the inhabited world, withstanding our Savior against whom he waged his first campaign when the Savior appeared to rescue us from our captivity to him. Laying an ambush against him through suffering, he tempted him a first time and a second; but on all these occasions, he overthrew the devil and his invisible foes and enemies in his host and made us captives his own, constructing from us, as from living stones,[244] the house of God and the regimen of piety, so that one may properly apply to him the scriptural saying, "Behold a man whose name is the dawn."[245] PROOF OF THE GOSPEL 4.17.18-21.[246]

THE VICARIOUS ASSUMPTION OF SIN WAS PROPHESIED. EUSEBIUS: Punished on our account, and bearing the retribution that was not his own due but ours on account of the multitude of our transgressions, he became to us the cause of the remission of sins inasmuch as on our behalf he accepted death, transferring to himself the blows, the insults and the ignominy that were due to us, after wresting to himself the curse that we had merited and becoming a curse for us.[247] . . . Next he adds, "Uphold me on account of my sinlessness."[248] Now see how, in addressing a prayer to his God and Father,[249] he ventured to employ such frankness of speech as to bear testimony to his own sinlessness, for all that he said above, "Heal my soul, because I have sinned against

---

[237]Rev 13:8. [238]CCL 107:274. [239]TCE 264. [240]This passage follows citations of Is 53:4 and Jn 1:29 and now resumes an exposition of Zech 3, in which the high priest Joshua (Jesus) is defended against the reproaches of the devil. [241]2 Cor 5:21. [242]Gal 3:13. [243]Zech 3:3. [244]Linking 1 Pet 2:5 to Zech 3:9. [245]Zech 6:12, though the Hebrew is generally taken to mean "the branch." The subject is the high priest Joshua, whose name is the Hebrew prototype of Jesus. [246]GCS 23:198-99. [247]Gal 3:13. [248]Ps 41:4. [249]See Jn 20:17.

you."[250] We have in fact already explained[251] the sense of "I have sinned," and Symmachus[252] has expressed it more clearly by writing, "Heal my soul, even if I have sinned against you." This is what could be said with regard to our sins, which our Lord took on himself. The words "uphold me on account of my sinlessness" express the absolute purity of his own nature. To teach us that this is the immovable foundation of life and the salvation that follows his resurrection, he adds, "And you have established me before you forever." PROOF OF THE GOSPEL 10.1.23.37-40.[253]

THE OUTWORKING OF THE INCARNATION. GREGORY OF NAZIANZUS: And so the passage "the word became flesh"[254] seems to me to be equivalent to that in which it is said that he was made sin or a curse for us; not that the Lord was transformed into either of these—how could he be?—but because by taking them on himself, he took away our sins and bore our iniquities. LETTERS ON THE APOLLINARIAN CONTROVERSY 101.[255]

FOR US, THE PENALTY PROVES OUR SIN. AUGUSTINE: How can the Pelagians say that only death was transmitted to us through Adam? For if the cause of our dying is that he died, yet he died on account of his sins, they are saying that the punishment passes on without the sin and that innocent little ones are punished by an unjust penalty, since they incur death without deserving death. The catholic faith acknowledges this only of the one mediator of God and humanity,[256] who deigned for our sake to undergo death, that is, the punishment of sin without the sin. AGAINST TWO LETTERS OF THE PELAGIANS 4.4.6.[257]

The Reconciliation of the World

JEW AND GREEK ARE RECONCILED. MARIUS VICTORINUS: Souls born of God's fountain of goodness were being detained in the world.

There was a wall in their midst:[258] a sort of fence, a partition made by the deceits of the flesh and worldly lusts. Christ by his own mystery, his passion and his way of life destroyed this wall. He overcame sin and taught that it could be overcome. He destroyed the lusts of the world and taught that they ought to be destroyed. He took away the wall in the midst. It was in his own flesh that he overcame the enmity. The work is not ours; we are not called to set ourselves free. Faith in Christ is our only salvation. COMMENTARY ON EPHESIANS 2:14-15.[259]

ELISHA'S AXE PRESAGES THE CROSS. IRENAEUS: By this the prophet revealed that, having carelessly lost the sound word of God through wood, we were to recover it again through the economy of wood. Now it is because the Word of God resembles an axe that John the Baptist says of it, "Already the axe is laid to the root of the tree,"[260] while Jeremiah says likewise, "The word of God is like a double axe splitting the rock."[261] This word, therefore, hidden as it was from us, was revealed to us, as I have just said, by the economy of wood. For as we lost it by wood, so again it has been made manifest to all through wood, displaying the height and length and breadth in itself, and (as one of our elders said), gathering both peoples to the one God. AGAINST HERESIES 5.17.4.[262]

THE FENCE OF THE LAW IS REMOVED. CHRYSOSTOM: I think that the wall between Greek and Jew is common within both. It is the hostility proceeding within the flesh. This was the midwall cutting them off, as the prophet says:[263] Do not your sins stand in the

[250]Ps 41:12. [251]At *Demonstration* 10.1.23, where the words are said to be spoken "in our person" by one who has "made our sins his own." [252]Translator of the Hebrew Scriptures into Greek, often held to be more faithful than the Septuagint (though not, in the eyes of all Christians, more authoritative). [253]GCS 23:450, 453. [254]Jn 1:14. [255]LCC 3:222. [256]1 Tim 2:5. [257]CSEL 60:526. [258]Eph 2:14. [259]*MVCEP* 155. [260]Mt 3:10. [261]Jer 23:29. [262]SC 153:232-34. [263]Is 59:2.

midst between you and me? But when the Law came, this enmity was not dissolved; rather, it increased. . . . The law was a fence, but this was made for our security. This is why it was called a fence, that it might fence us in. . . . O what love of humanity. He gave us a law that we might keep it, but when we failed to keep it and deserved punishment, he dissolved the Law. HOMILIES ON EPHESIANS 5.[264]

THERE IS NO DELIVERANCE WITHOUT FAITH. GAUDENTIUS: The Lord Jesus recalled to himself all creatures that the rebellious spirits, iniquitously usurping his divinity, had taken in charge, so that all things would be subject to the dominion of the one through whom the whole world order came into being, the one who has protected and will protect those who believe in him from the lash of repentance through the sign of the cross, according to these words: "And the blood will be a sign to you in your homes, in which you will abide, and I shall see the blood and shall spare you."[265] TRACTATES 6.11, ON THE EXODUS, READING 6.[266]

FORGIVENESS IS OFFERED TO ALL. IRENAEUS: Now by the words that the Lord spoke on the cross, "Father, forgive them, for they know not what they do,"[267] the long-suffering and forbearance and compassion and goodness of Christ are manifested, in that he was suffering and he pardoned those who had used him ill. For the Word of God who said to us, "Love your enemies, and pray for those who use you hardly,"[268] did this himself on the cross. So great was his love of the human race that he interceded even for those who were putting him to death. AGAINST HERESIES 3.18.5.[269]

SALVATION IS FOR ALL BECAUSE ALL ARE SINNERS. PROSPER OF AQUITAINE: There is thus no reason for doubting that Jesus Christ our Lord died for the impious and sinful, for if anyone is found to be exempt from that

number, Christ did not die for all. Yet certainly Christ did die for all, and therefore of all human beings there was none, before the reconciliation effected through the blood of Christ, who was not either sinful or impious. THE CALL OF ALL NATIONS 2.16.[270]

NOAH'S ARK IS A SYMBOL OF THIS UNIVERSAL DELIVERANCE. PROSPER OF AQUITAINE: But holy Scripture shows us how many works of divine grace were revealed in the preservation of Noah, with his sons and his daughters-in-law, in whom resided the seed of all nations: in that ark of miraculous capacity, which was able to hold every species of animal, so far as was necessary to restore it, the church that is to gather to itself every race of humans was prefigured. Through the wood and water the redemption by the cross of Christ is disclosed; in those who were saved from the devastation of that world the sum of all nations receives a blessing; the gift of fertility is renewed, and except for the ban on eating blood and strangled beasts, the freedom to eat what one wishes is extended, and the assurance of salvation is cemented in the testimony of the multicolored rainbow, which is a sign of manifold grace. THE CALL OF ALL NATIONS 2.14.[271]

PARDONED AND RENEWED. HERMAS: And he himself purged our sins, having toiled much and endured many hardships; for no one can dig without hardship or labor. He himself, then, having purged the sins of the people, showed them the ways of life, having given to them the law[272] that he received from his Father. SHEPHERD, SIMILITUDE 5.6.2.3.[273]

---

[264]*IOEP* 5:149-50. [265]Ex 12:13. [266]PL 20:879. [267]Lk 22:34. [268]Mt 5:44. [269]SC 34:322. [270]PL 51:702-3. [271]PL 51:698-99. [272]Either because his commandments came from the Father (Jn 14:31) or because he was thought to have restored the first tables given to Moses on Sinai but destroyed when he discovered the golden calf. [273]*AF* 436.

Christus Victor

By Adopting the Form of the Tempter, Christ Destroys Him. Tertullian: That image in the form of a suspended brazen serpent contained the figure of the Lord's cross, which was to liberate us from serpents, that is, from the angels of the devil;[274] simultaneously through that same image he put the devil, that is, the serpent, to death by hanging. On Idolatry 5.[275]

No Less Than the Devil Deserved. Ambrosiaster: For they had become criminals in that, whereas their authority for detaining souls lay in the fact that they had sinned, they themselves were found to be far more heinous sinners when they killed the one who had vanquished them by his sinlessness. And thus, as he said, they were justly despoiled in public, that is, on the cross.[276] Commentary on Colossians 2.15.6.[277]

Christ Cleanses the Air of Demons. Athanasius: The devil, the enemy of our race, having fallen from heaven, roams through this lower air of ours, and holding sway there over the other demons who were with him as his fellows in disobedience, produces vain imaginings by means of them in those whom he deceived while striving to hinder those who are ascending. And this is what the apostle says: "according to the prince of the power of the air, who now works in the sons of disobedience."[278] Now the Lord came to cast down the devil, to cleanse the air and to prepare for us the upward path to the heavens, through the veil, as the apostle says, that is, his flesh. Now this has to come about through death, but through what other death could this have come to pass, if not the one that takes place in the air, I mean on the cross? For the only one who dies in the air is the one who expires on the cross. For it was by being lifted up in this way that he cleansed the air of all diabolic

activity and all the intrigue of the demons, saying, "I saw Satan fall as lightning,"[279] and preparing the path to heaven restored it, saying, "Let your rulers raise the gates; be lifted up, you everlasting gates."[280] For it is not the Word who is begging for entrance at the gates, being the Lord of all, nor was there anything in creation closed to the Creator. Rather, it was we who were begging for entrance, whom he himself bore up through his own body. On the Incarnation 25.5-6.[281]

Triumph on the Cross. Maximus the Confessor: This, then, is how, in his initial experience of temptation,[282] he put off the principalities and powers, removing them from human nature and healing the liability to hedonistic passions, and in himself cancelled the bond of Adam's deliberate acquiescence in those hedonistic passions. For it is by this bond that human will inclines toward wicked pleasure against its own best interest and that humankind declares in the very silence of its works its enslavement, being unable, in its fear of death, to free itself from slavery to pleasure.

Then, after having overcome and frustrated the forces of evil, "the principalities and powers," through his first experience of being tempted with pleasure, the Lord allowed them to attack him a second time and to provoke him, through pain and toil, with the further experience of temptation so that, by completely depleting them, within himself, of the deadly poison of their wickedness, he might utterly consume it, as though in a fire. For he put off the principalities and powers at the moment of his death on the cross, when he remained impervious to his sufferings and, what is more, manifested the natural human

---

[274]It was widely held that the false gods of the nations were fallen angels. [275]TDI 30. [276]Col 2:14. [277]CSEL 81.3:187. [278]Eph 2:2. [279]Lk 10:18. [280]Ps 24:1. [281]SC 199:356-58. [282]See Irenaeus *Against Heresies* 5.20 above, where the wilderness is the scene of the only victory over Satan which this author ascribes to Christ.

fear of death, thereby driving from our nature the passion associated with pain. Human will, out of cowardice, tends away from suffering, and humankind, against its own will, remains utterly dominated by the fear of death, and in the desire to live, clings to its slavery to pleasure. So the Lord put off the principalities and powers at the time of his first experience of temptation in the desert, thereby healing the whole of human nature of the passion connected with pleasure. Yet he despoiled them again at the time of his death, in that he likewise eliminated from our human nature the passion connected with pain. QUESTIONS TO THALASSIUM 21.[283]

DEFEATED IN THE HOUR OF THEIR IMAGINED VICTORY. ORIGEN: The hostile powers, having handed over the Savior into the hands of people, did not perceive that they had handed him over for the salvation of anyone. So far as they were concerned, since none of them knew the wisdom of God that was hidden in a mystery, they had handed him over to be killed, so that his enemy death might take him into subjection, like those who die in Adam. COMMENTARY ON MATTHEW 13.8.[284]

THE VICTORY IS ALREADY SECURE ON THE CROSS. AUGUSTINE: Now it is not hard to perceive the defeat of the devil when the one whom he had put to death rose again. What requires a deeper understanding is to see the defeat of the devil at the point when it seemed to him that he was the victor, that is, when Christ was put to death.[285] For then it was that that blood, being that of one who had no sin whatsoever, was shed for the remission of our sins. The reason was that, just as the devil had a right to detain those whom he had bound by the death appointed[286] for those who are guilty of sin, it was right for him to release these on account of the one who had suffered the penalty of death without being guilty of any sin. The strong man was overcome by this

justice and bound by this bond, so that he was deprived of the vessels[287] that in his possession had been vessels of wrath with him and his angels but were now turned into vessels of mercy. ON THE TRINITY 13.15.19.[288]

THE CROSS WAS HIS TROPHY BEFORE IT WAS ELEVATED. AMBROSE: But now the victor takes up his trophy. The cross is imposed on his shoulders like a trophy, because, whether it was Simon of Cyrene or he who carried it, Christ carried it in humanity and humanity in Christ. Nor are the pronouncements of the Evangelists at variance, when the mystery is at one, and our own path was set in good order by the fact that he first raised his own cross as a trophy and then handed it to the martyrs to raise. It is not a Jew who carries the cross but a stranger and pilgrim, nor does he lead but follows, in accordance with what is written: "Take up your cross and follow me."[289] For it is not his own cross that Christ mounts but ours. Nor was that the death of his Godhead but the kind that a man dies. Thus he says, "God, my God, look on me! Why have you forsaken me?"[290] It was a fine act to put off his regal garments as he was about to mount the cross, so that you may know that he suffered as a man, not as God the king, and that even if Christ is both, it was nonetheless as a man, not as God, that he was nailed to the cross. But it is the soldiers, not the Jews, who know what sort of garments are fit for Christ at a given time. At the bar of judgment he stands like the victor, but to his passion he goes like a lowly criminal.

Now, since we see the trophy already, he mounts his chariot in triumph, and he does not hang from the trunks of trees or four-horse wagons the booty that he has brought back from a mortal enemy, but he hangs the

[283]MCOCM 112-13.   [284]GCS 40 (10):202.   [285]See Col 2:13-14.
[286]Taking *conditio mortis* to imply that death is the wages of sin (Rom 6:23; 5:12).   [287]Alluding to Mk 3:27; Rom 9:22-23.
[288]CCL 50A:407.   [289]Lk 9:23.   [290]Mt 27:46.

captive spoils of the ages on his triumphal scaffold. We do not see here whole peoples with their arms bound behind their backs or the statues from leveled cities and the idols of captured towns, nor do we wonder at the bowed necks of captive kings, which is the usual spectacle in a human triumph; nor are the bounds of his victory marked out by the frontier of a territory. Instead we see the cheering populace of nations, brought back not for torment but for reward, kings worshiping with unforced affection, cities dedicated with willing zeal and the statues from the towns molded into a better shape, their dyed features giving way to the color of devout faith. Arms we see, and the laws of the victor traversing the whole earth, the prince of this world a captive and the spirits of wickedness that are in high places[291] obeying the command of a human voice. The powers are subdued, and the various forms of virtue shine forth in our conduct, not in silken robes. Chastity blazes, faith is resplendent, and devout courage, though it puts on the weeds of death, rises again. A single triumph of God, the cross of the Lord, has caused almost all human beings to triumph. It is therefore opportune to consider in what guise he mounts it. I see him naked; that then is the way that one mounts if one is preparing to overcome the world, so as to dispense with worldly aids. Adam, who sought out garments, was conquered; the conqueror is the one who put off his costume. And when he mounted he was such as nature made us at God's behest; such was the first man when he lived in paradise, such was the second man when he entered into paradise. And so that he would not conquer for himself only but for all, he extended his hands so as to draw all to him,[292] so that he might release things that had hitherto been earthly from the knot of death and, suspending them from the yoke of faith, reconcile them with things in heaven. EXPOSITIONS ON THE GOSPEL OF LUKE 10.109-10.[293]

THIS DEATH WAS AN EXHIBITION OF HIS COURAGE. ATHANASIUS: A doughty wrestler, great in understanding as in courage, would not select his antagonists for himself, lest he should arouse the suspicion of shirking particular men. Instead he would leave that prerogative to the spectators, and especially if they chanced to be his enemies, so that, having overthrown whomsoever they caused him to fight, he might be agreed to be stronger than all. In the same way Christ the Lord, the life of all and our savior, did not devise his own death for his body, lest he should seem to be shirking another. ON THE INCARNATION 24.3.[294]

EQUALLY AN INSTRUMENT OF JUSTICE. AUGUSTINE: What then is the righteousness by which the devil was defeated? What, but the righteousness of Jesus Christ? And how was he defeated? Because he found in him nothing worthy of death, yet killed him nonetheless. And thus it is right that the debtors whom he detained should be set free when they believe in him whom he killed without any debt. This is what it means for us to be justified in the blood of Christ. ON THE TRINITY 13.14.18.[295]

THE DAY OF THE PASSION IS GLORIOUS. CONSTANTINE: The splendor that outshines day and the sun, the prelude to the resurrection, the new composition of bodies that have travailed in times past, the sanction of the promise and the road that leads to eternal life, the day of the passion[296] is here. ORATION TO THE SAINTS 1.[297]

THE CHURCH CAN BE SEEN AS AN ARMY. VENANTIUS FORTUNATUS: The banners of the

---

[291]Eph 6:12. [292]Jn 12:31. [293]CSEL 32.4:496-97. [294]SC 199:352. [295]CCL 50A:406. [296]What this can mean but Good Friday I do not know, although there is no indisputable evidence that this day was observed in the church before the death of Constantine. Similar prologues can be found in paschal homilies designed for Easter Sunday, but they do not describe it as the day of the passion. [297]CSEL 47:286-87.

king appear; the mystery of the cross shines forth, that scaffold on which the creator of the flesh was hung in flesh. His inward parts transfixed by nails, his hands and feet outspread, the victim is sacrificed here for the sake of redemption. There it was that, wounded further by the fell point of the lance, he poured out water and blood that he might cleanse us of our wrongdoing. Now is fulfilled the prophecy of David, when he said to the nations in his trusty song, "God has reigned from the tree."[298] Stately and radiant tree, robed in the purple of kings, whose worthy trunk was chosen to touch such holy members; on its arms the ransom of the ages hung; a balance was made of his body, and he bore off the spoils of hell. You spread a perfume around the bark; in your sweetness you excel nectar. Yours is the joy of fertile fruit, the acclamation of noble triumph. Hail to the altar; hail to the victim for the glory of the passion, whereby he carried off death by life and restored life by death. HYMN TO THE HOLY CROSS (2).[299]

THE AGONY IS PAST, BUT HIS WORK CONTINUES. VENANTIUS FORTUNATUS: The blessed cross shines forth, where the Lord hung in flesh and cleansed our wounds with his own blood. There the holy lamb tore the sheep away from the mouth of the wolf, having meekly become a victim for us in his sacred love. It was there, his hands impaled, that he redeemed the world from calamity and by his own funeral sealed up death's road. There that hand that snatched Paul from sin and Peter from death was held fast with bloody nails. O sweet and noble wood, abounding mightily, when you bear such novel fruits on your branches! Your novel scent causes the corpses of the dead to rise and those who had lost the light of day return to life. Beneath the leaves of this tree none is burned by the heat, not by the moon at night or the sun at midday. Planted, as it were, by running waters, you sparkle and scatter fresh blossoms over your gorgeous

crown. Amid your arms there is a clinging vine, from which well sweet wines, crimson as blood. THE BLESSED CROSS SHINES FORTH.[300]

WE MUST TAKE CARE NOT TO SQUANDER THE VICTORY. GAUDENTIUS: We must take care, beloved brethren, that by our own turpitude we should destroy the effect of Christ's victory, in which he triumphed over the devil, redeeming us from his captivity with his precious blood and depriving him of his sway over the human race. Through the deceits of the flesh we may subject ourselves once again to the cruel sovereignty of that tyrant, insulting our Redeemer, who therefore rightly censures and rebukes us with the complaint, "What profit is there in my blood?"[301] "Without purpose," he might say, "my blood has been shed for you if your conduct and conversation are such that the devil, the author of vain desires, once again holds sway in you." TRACTATES 12.13, THE JUDGMENT OF THIS WORLD.[302]

The Descent to the Dead[303]

THE DEATH OF CHRIST ENTAILED A SO-JOURN IN HADES. POLYCARP OF SMYRNA: Jesus Christ, who endured for the sake of our sins even to the point of meeting death, and whom God raised, having dissolved the pains of hades. LETTER TO THE PHILADELPHIANS 1.2.[304]

---

[298]An apocryphal verse, the authenticity of which was zealously defended by Justin Martyr. [299]OBMLV 75-76. [300]OBMLV 76-77; Latin title, *Crux Benedicta Nitet.* [301]Ps 29:10. [302]PL 20:931-32. [303]The statement in the Apostles' Creed, "he descended to the dead (or into hell)," is no doubt regarded by most Christians today as an amplification of the previous clause, which declares that Christ died and was buried. Early Christians, however, envisaged a literal descent to the nether regions, which resulted in the deliverance of the patriarchs and other faithful members of the Old Covenant. The chief prooftext (1 Pet 3:19-21) seems to hint at the redemption of fallen angels. Modern commentators, while rejecting the subterranean geography and its picturesque concomitant, the "harrowing of hell," may still be glad of this assurance that Christ died for at least some of those who predeceased him, and not only for those of his own and later times. [304]*AF* 206. It is possible that hades here is nothing more than a picturesque synonym for death.

SCRIPTURE ABOUNDS IN PROOFTEXTS.

IRENAEUS: He spent three days where the dead were, as the prophet says of him. It is recorded that the Lord of his dead saints, of those who had already gone to sleep in the soil of burial, descended to them to draw them forth and deliver them. And the Lord also says, "Just as Jonah remained three nights and three days in the belly of the whale, so shall the Son of man be three days in the heart of the earth."[305] The apostle says, moreover, "What does it mean, he ascended, but that he descended into the depths of the earth?"[306] This too David said in prophesying of him: "And you have snatched my soul forth from the underworld below."[307] And when he rose again on the third day, he said to Mary, who saw him first and was worshiping him, "Touch me not, for I have not yet ascended to the Father."[308] AGAINST HERESIES 5.31.1.[309]

THE DESCENT WAS NECESSARY.

AMBROSIASTER: He is said to have descended in order to ascend, unlike humans who have descended in order to remain there. For by decree they were held in the nether world. But this decree could not hold the Savior. He has conquered sin; therefore, after his triumph over the devil, he descended to the heart of the world, so that he might preach to the dead, that all who desired him might be set free. It was necessary for him to ascend.[310] He had descended to trample death underfoot with his own power, then only to rise with the captives. COMMENTARY ON EPHESIANS 4.9[311]

RELEASE FOR THE SAINTS OF THE ELDER COVENANT.

CYRIL OF JERUSALEM: Tell me, would you have the living enjoy his grace, and that when the greater part of them are not holy, while those who have been shut up through all the ages following Adam should not receive this liberty? . . . David was there, and Samuel, and all the prophets, including even John the Baptist, the one who said

through his emissaries, "Are you he who comes, or should we wait for another?" Would you not have him descend to release such as these? CATECHETICAL LECTURE 4.11.[312]

IT IS THE SOUL OF CHRIST THAT DESCENDS.

ORIGEN: These three elements were separated at the time of the passion; they were reunited at the time of the resurrection. How? The body in the tomb, the soul in hades, the spirit committed to the Father. The soul in hades: You do not give up my soul to hades.[313] If he committed his spirit to the Father. it was as a [temporary] deposit.[314] DIALOGUE WITH HERACLIDES 7.16-25.[315]

PERHAPS THIS MISSION WAS ALSO DIRECTED TO THE GENTILES.

CLEMENT OF ALEXANDRIA: Just as the proclamation has come now in due season, so in due season the Law and the prophets were given to the barbarians and philosophy to the Greeks to attune their ears to the proclamation.[316] So it is that the Lord who delivered Israel says, "At an acceptable season have I heard you, and in the day of salvation I have succored you. I have given you, as a testament to the nations, to tabernacle on earth and to be heirs to the inheritance of the wilderness, saying to those in chains 'Come forth' and to those in darkness 'Be revealed.' "[317] For if the Jews are the ones in chains, of whom the Lord also said, "Come forth from chains," those who will, voluntarily chained as they are, and he says of them that they have heaped up "burdens hard to bear" on themselves by their human officiousness: it is clear that those in darkness will be those whose ruling faculty is buried in idol worship.

---

[305]Mt 12:40. [306]Eph 4:9. [307]Ps 86:13. [308]Jn 20:17. [309]SC 153:390-92. [310]See Eph 4:9. [311]CSEL 81.3:97-98. [312]CHOO 1:102. [313]See Ps 16:10; Acts 2:27. [314]Lk 23:46. [315]OTP 63. [316]Philosophy, like the other arts of life, is regarded by Clement as a dispensation from God to those in waiting for the gospel (Stromateis 1.30; 6.156-61). The philosophers are not, however, among those who have received a true notion of God by immediate inspiration at 6.42-43. [317]Jer 49:8-10.

For those who were righteous according to the Law were lacking in faith, and therefore the Lord used to say as he cured them, "Your faith has made you whole."[318] But for those who were righteous according to philosophy it was not only faith that was needed but also renunciation of idolatry. As soon as the truth was revealed, they repented of their conduct, and on this account the Lord preached the good news to those in hades.

What the Scripture declares is, "Hades says to perdition, 'We have not seen his form, but we have heard his voice.' "[319] It was not of course the place itself that acquired a voice and spoke the foregoing words; but those who had been relegated to hades and had given themselves to perdition as though they had voluntarily cast themselves from some ship into the sea—these it is who heard the mighty voice of God. For who in his right mind, imputing injustice to providence, would suppose that even the souls of sinners are under one condemnation? What do they say that the Lord did not preach to those who perished or rather to those who had been fast bound, in the flood, and to those held under guard and watch?[320] It has been shown, in fact, in the second book of the *Stromateis* that the apostles, in imitation of the Lord, preached the good news to those in hades. For it was necessary there as here, in my view, that the best of the disciples should become imitators of the teacher, so that while he made conversions among the Hebrews,[321] they should convert the nations—that is, those who had lived in righteousness according to the Law and philosophy, yet not perfectly, but had committed sin in the course of their lives. For it was fitting to the divine economy that those who lived for the most part righteously, attaining the highest merit and repenting of their delinquencies, even if they should be in another place, should each be saved according to his own knowledge, being confessedly among the people of God Almighty.

The Savior performs the work, I believe, since his own work is to save. And this therefore is what he did for those who decided to believe in him through the proclamation, rescuing them to salvation wherever they chanced to be. If indeed the Lord descended to hades for no other purpose than to preach the good news in his descent, then he preached either to all or to the Hebrews alone. If, then, it was to all, then all who have believed will be saved, even if they are from the nations and happen to have made their confession already there, since the chastisements of God are salvific and pedagogic, leading to conversion and preferring the repentance of the sinner to his death. They can see these things more purely once their souls are rid of their bodies, even if they are darkened by passions, because they are no longer wedded to the flesh. And if it was only to Jews that he preached, who were lacking only in knowledge through the Savior and in faith, it should still be clear that, since God is no respecter of persons, the apostles, there as here, preached the good news to those among the Gentiles who were ripe for conversion. STROMATEIS 6.6.44-46.[322]

THOSE WHO AWAITED SALVATION LIVED APART FROM THE DAMNED. TERTULLIAN: This previous discussion of mine[323] will also be of value with regard to the subsequent narrative of the rich man in pain in hell and the pauper resting in Abraham's bosom. For this story too, so far as the surface of Scripture goes, is introduced abruptly; in what it intends to teach, this also is of a piece with the reference to the evil treatment of John and the stigmatization of Herod's evil marriage. It represents the outcome for both—Herod's tor-

---

[318]Mt 9:22. [319]Job 28:22. [320]1 Pet 3:19-20, with some elaboration from the apocryphal but popular *Book of Enoch*. [321]Clement, like other Christians, tends to use "Hebrew" as a term for deserving members of the twelve tribes of Israel, "Jew" for the opponents of Christ and their latter-day descendants. (His usage is not, however, consistent in the present passage.) [322]GCS 15:453-55. [323]On Lk 16:18-31.

ments and John's respite—so that Herod may now hear the words "they have Moses and the prophets; let them hear them." But Marcion wrests it to another purpose, namely, to argue that both the Creator's wages, the torment and the respite alike, are laid up in hell to those who have obeyed the Law and the prophets. By contrast he identifies a heavenly breast and heaven belonging to Christ and his own god.[324] Our response to this Scripture itself will correct his vision, since it distinguishes hell from the bosom of Abraham, where the pauper is. For hell, in my view, is one place, and Abraham's bosom is another. For it also says that a great gulf divides those regions and forbids a crossing from either side. Indeed, the rich man would never have raised his eyes, and from afar, except to look up from a level far below through the towering depths of that unmeasured interval. From this it is apparent to anyone who has ever heard of the Elysian fields that a certain place is set apart that is known as the bosom of Abraham, to receive the souls of his children, even from the nations, since he is the father of many nations who will be enrolled in the stock of Abraham, and by virtue of the same faith with which Abraham believed in God, under no yoke of the Law and without the sign of circumcision. And so it is that region that I affirm to be the bosom of Abraham, higher than hell even if it is not heavenly, to offer a temporary respite to souls of the righteous, until the consummation of things effects the resurrection of all with full payment of their wages. Then the heavenly promise will be made good that Marcion claims for his own god as though it had not been proclaimed by the Creator. This is a stage in Christ's preparation of his ascent to heaven, as Amos says,[325] clearly for his own people, where there is also an everlasting place, of which Isaiah says, "Who will announce to you the everlasting place, unless of course it is Christ walking in righteousness, declaring the right way, holding unrighteousness and

iniquity in detestation?"[326] But if an everlasting place is promised and an ascent into heaven is being prepared by the Creator, who promises also that the seed of Abraham shall be as the stars of heaven (because of the heavenly promise, of course): why is it not admissible, while keeping the promise intact, to say that the bosom of Abraham is a temporary lodging for the souls of the faithful, in which an image of what is to be is already drawn and a certain candidature for each judgment is in prospect? It also admonishes you heretics while you are alive that Moses and the prophets proclaimed one God, the Creator, proclaiming also one Christ who is his, and that both the judgment to everlasting punishment and that to everlasting salvation are laid up with the one God, who kills and makes alive.

Nonetheless, says Marcion, the behest of our God from heaven requires not that Moses and the prophets be heard, but Christ: "Hear him."[327] Rightly so. For by that time the apostles had already paid sufficient heed to Moses and the prophets, having followed Christ by believing in Moses and the prophets. For Peter would not have consented to say "You are the Christ"[328] before he had heard Moses and the prophets and believed them, for it was by them alone hitherto that Christ had been proclaimed. Their faith had therefore deserved that this should actually be confirmed by a heavenly voice requiring that he should be heard whom they knew to be spreading the gospel of peace, the gospel of good news, announcing the everlasting place and preparing for their sake his own ascent to heaven. In hell, however, the words "they have Moses and the prophets; let them hear them"[329] are spoken of those who have no belief whatever in the torments that Moses and the prophets announce for the riches of

---

[324] The Father of Christ in Marcion being good in contradistinction to the just god who created the world and subjected it to law. [325] Amos 9:6 (LXX). [326] Is 33:14-15 (LXX). [327] Lk 9:35. [328] Lk 9:20. [329] Lk 16:29.

pride and the pleasures of glory after death. And these are ordained by the same God who casts dynasties from their thrones and lifts the beggar from the dung. Since therefore the Creator is equally competent to pronounce either of these antithetical judgments, there is no need to posit a difference in gods but only in the things decreed. Against Marcion 4.34.[330]

The Descent Is Anticipated in the Story of Jonah. Gregory of Nyssa: We may understand most economically and plainly from the prophecy in which the mystery is clearly prefigured. I am speaking of Jonah, who went down into the whale without suffering, and without suffering came back up again from the whale; his three days and as many nights in the innards of the whale prefigured the Lord's sojourn in hades. On the Three Days' Interval.[331]

The Mercy and Power of Christ. Dracontius: Jonah, that guileless offender, uttered lying words and earned his pardon after being in the belly of the whale; we hear of the thief who hung on the cross earning pardon and of the Lord Christ entering hell. On the Praises of God 3.639-42.[332]

The First Sabbath. Gregory of Nyssa: You marvel at the sublime Moses, who rehearsed by the power of his knowledge the entire creation of God. Consider then the blessed sabbath of that first creation, and through that sabbath recognize in this sabbath the day of rest that God commended above all other days. For it was on this day that the Only-begotten truly rested from all his labors, having kept the sabbath in his flesh through the economy of death. And, when he had returned anew to what he was through the resurrection, he raised with him all that was linked to him, having become life and resurrection and rising and dawn and day to those in darkness and

the shadow of death. On the Three Days' Interval.[333]

The Interval Was Three Days and Three Nights.[334] Gregory of Nyssa: It was evening when that sacred and holy body was consumed, and then the night before the Friday succeeded that evening. Then the Friday was cut in two by the insertion of night and is reckoned as two nights and one day. For if "God called the darkness night"[335] and at the third hour "darkness fell on the whole earth,"[336] this is the night that made a new incision in the middle of the day, marking out two segments of the day, one from the morning to the sixth hour, one from the ninth to the evening. Thus up to this point there are two nights and two days. Then with the night before the sabbath and after this the day of the sabbath, you have the three days and the three nights. On the Three Days' Interval.[337]

In This Interval the Stains of Sin Were Erased. Gregory of Nyssa: Is the grace tardy? Did it take a long time to effect so great a good? Do you care to consider the exceeding power of the things accomplished in so short a time? Count up, I pray, all the generations of humanity that intervened between the first emergence of evil up to the deliverance, and how many human beings are numbered in their myriads in each generation. Is it possible to comprehend in a number the mass of those who in age after age were brought low by evil, so that the evil wealth of turpitude, distributed to each severally, increased through each? And thus evil always went on proliferating with each successive generation, poured out on the mass without limit, until, having arrived at the ultimate degree of evil, it had mastered the whole of the human race. Thus the prophet says compendiously

---

[330]CCL 1:637-39. [331]GNO 9:277. [332]PLM 5:90. [333]GNO 9:274. [334]See Mt 12:40 on Jonah. [335]Gen 1:5. [336]Mt 27:45. [337]GNO 9:289.

that all have strayed, all have done iniquity, and there is not one among them that is not a tool of evil. This immense accumulation of evil from the foundation of the world up to the providential action of the Lord in his passion—does the one who in three days dissolved the whole sum seem to have given a small proof of his exceeding power? Is it not in fact mightier than all that wonder workers have done in story? ON THE THREE DAYS' INTERVAL.[338]

HOW COULD HE BE IN HADES WHEN HIS BODY WAS IN THE TOMB? GREGORY OF NYSSA: One solution of this question is that no place is inaccessible to God, in which all things subsist. Another, which is the subject of our present argument, is that God had refash-

ioned the whole man into the divine nature by commingling with himself, but at the time when his providential scheme was realized in the passion, he did not indeed part either from that which had once been mixed with it (for God cannot repent of his gifts), but the Godhead voluntarily unyoked the soul from the body, while showing that he himself remained in both. For through the body, in which he did not experience the corruption of death, he overcame the one who wielded the might of death, while through his soul he guided the thief on the road that leads to paradise. ON THE THREE DAYS' INTERVAL.[339]

---

[338]GNO 9:284. [339]GNO 9:293.

ON THE THIRD DAY HE ROSE AGAIN

σταυρωθέντα τε ὑπὲρ ἡμῶν	crucifixus etiam pro nobis	For our sake he was crucified
ἐπὶ Ποντίου Πιλάτου,	sub Pontio Pilato,	under Pontius Pilate;
καὶ παθόντα καὶ ταφέντα,	passus et sepultus est;	he suffered death and was buried.
καὶ ἀναστάντα τῇ τρίτῃ ἡμέρᾳ	**et resurrexit tertia die,**	**On the third day he rose again**
κατὰ τὰς γραφάς,	secundum Scripturas;	in accordance with the Scriptures;
καὶ ἀνελθόντα εἰς τοὺς οὐρανούς,	et ascendit in coelum,	he ascended into heaven
καὶ καθεζόμενον	sedet	and is seated
ἐκ δεξιῶν τοῦ πατρός,	ad dexteram Patris;	at the right hand of the Father.
καὶ πάλιν ἐρχόμενον μετὰ δόξης	et iterum venturus est, cum gloria,	He will come again in glory
κρῖναι ζῶντας καὶ νεκρούς·	judicare vivos et mortuos;	to judge the living and the dead,
οὗ τῆς βασιλείας οὐκ ἔσται τέλος.	cujus regni non erit finis.	and his kingdom will have no end.

HISTORICAL CONTEXT: No creed could dispense with this clause, as Paul had averred that if Christ were not risen, faith would be vain and believers still in their sins. He even states that Christ was "raised on account of our justification"[1] and includes the phrase "on the third day" in the short creed that prefaces his list of witnesses.[2] This clause was affirmed

---

[1]Rom 4:25. [2]1 Cor 15:4.

here, not to counteract any recent heresy but to cement the condemnation of those who, from Paul's time on, had argued that the resurrected Christ was only a phantom or not the same man who had died.[3] The addition of "on the third day" not only hints that the event had been discreetly foretold at Hosea 6:2 but also renders it impossible for the pagan critic to argue that the passage of time had clouded the memories of the original witnesses.

OVERVIEW: The resurrection was not without witnesses (GOSPEL OF PETER). It is implicit in the incarnation (EPHREM), as death cannot hold the Lord of life (ROMANUS). Thus the conquest of death is complete (DRACONTIUS), redeeming the universal fall of the species in Adam (ROMANUS). In the resurrection we see the harvest of the cross (GOSPEL OF PHILIP), and in every natural harvest we see an earnest of the resurrection (CLEMENT OF ROME). Every miracle therefore points to this (PSEUDO-EPIPHANIUS).

The first day of the week is now the Lord's day (GREGORY OF TOURS), commemorating a new creation (GREGORY OF NYSSA). Hence is it not the sabbath (SEDULIUS SCOTUS), or rather it is a spiritual sabbath (GREGORY OF NYSSA) and the birthday of an everlasting king (GREGORY OF NYSSA).

Both manhood and Godhead are visible in the resurrection (AMBROSE). Thomas bore witness to his divinity (SECOND COUNCIL OF CONSTANTINOPLE), while, if his body differs in quality from that of fallen humans (CLEMENT OF ALEXANDRIA), it anticipates the condition of the saints in heaven (MARIUS VICTORINUS).

The Certainty of the Resurrection

THE GUARDS WITNESSED CHRIST'S RETURN. GOSPEL OF PETER:[4] When the first light was breaking on the sabbath, the crowd came from Jerusalem and the surrounding area so that they might see the sealed tomb. But on the night when the Lord's day began to grow light, as the soldiers were keeping their watch at their post in pairs, a great voice rose in heaven, and they saw the heavens opened and two men[5] coming down from there, full of radiance and standing by the tomb. And that stone that had been set across the door, rolling by itself, gave way little by little. The tomb was opened, and both the young men entered. When they saw this, the soldiers roused the centurion and the elders, for they too were present keeping watch. And as they were recounting what they had seen, they saw three men emerging again from the tomb, the two supporting the third and the cross in their wake. The heads of the two reached heaven, while that of the one whom they were leading rose above the heavens. They heard a voice from the heavens saying, "You have preached to them that were asleep"; and from the cross came the answer, "Even so." GOSPEL OF PETER 9-10.[6]

THE RESURRECTION MIRRORS THE INCARNATION. EPHREM THE SYRIAN: In December, when the seed is hidden in the earth, there sprouted forth from the Womb the Ear of life. In March, when the seed was sprouting in the air, a Sheaf sowed itself in the earth. The harvest thereof, Death, devoured it in hell; which the Medicine of life that is hidden therein did yet burst open! In March, when the lambs bleat in the wilderness, into the Womb the Paschal Lamb entered! Out of the stream from which the fishers came up, he was baptized and came up who encloses all things in his net; out of the stream whereof Simon took, out of it the Fisher of people came up and took him. . . . The sea when it bore him was still and calmed, and how came the lap of Joseph to bear him?

---

[3]Cf. Lk 24:37. [4]A fanciful amplification of Mt 28:4, dating from the late first or early second century. [5]Moses and Elijah perhaps, as at Mk 9:3ff. and parallels. The *Ascension of Moses* was a popular document among Christians; for the ascent of Elijah to heaven, see 2 Kings 2:11. [6]*GAP* 86.

The womb of hell conceived him and was burst open, and how did the womb of Mary contain him? The stone that was over the grave he broke open by his might, and how could Mary's arm contain him? You came to a low estate, that you might raise all to life. HYMNS ON THE NATIVITY 3.[7]

DEATH COULD NOT SUBDUE THE LORD OF LIFE. ROMANUS THE MELODIST: When after his crucifixion the King went down all the way to hades, his light shone in the darkness and illumined the nether regions. But the darkness cannot encompass Christ;[8] he prevailed over the darkness. For like Jonah, he too was in the maw of the vault, having gone where he would while in the tomb, and sleepless even on his funeral bed. For his divinity was not sundered from his body. Therefore, on seeing this fearful miracle of his, Hades cried,[9] "Come hither, Death: let us now see what sort of light has been kindled by the life and resurrection." CANTICLE 27 [45], STROPHE 5.[10]

HIS VICTORY WAS COMPLETE. DRACONTIUS: Wretched hell, insatiably hungry for ghosts and wont to exult in death, quakes in agony and repines groveling at the newcomer, for this newcomer brought future losses. Hell groans that souls whom it held fast in an eternal dungeon will now return to enjoy the light; it mourns this breach of the infernal law. Unable to bear the light, it wishes that the Lord, the king of heaven, would return to the ethereal vapors, lest Christ the invincible radiance should bear down the whole of chaos or deprive the black fiends of the entire host by calling back souls to the upper world through his Father's might. ON THE PRAISES OF GOD 2.541-51.[11]

IN RESCUING ADAM, CHRIST REVERSED THE FALL. ROMANUS THE MELODIST: Savior, you came unsown from the belly, leaving to the Virgin that which belongs to virginity,[12] just as now by the tomb you have undone what belongs

to the tomb. As you have left the garment of Joseph behind in the tomb, you have taken from the tomb the father of Joseph.[13] Adam has come in your train; Eve has followed you; Eve does service to Mary. But you the whole earth adores, singing the victory hymn, "the Lord is risen." CANTICLE 24 [41], STROPHE 20.[14]

THE RESURRECTION IS THE FLOWERING OF THE CROSS. GOSPEL OF PHILIP: Philip the apostle said, "Joseph the carpenter planted a garden because he needed wood for his trade. It was he who made the cross from the trees that he planted. His own offspring hung on that which he planted. His offspring was Jesus, and his planting was the cross." But the tree of life is in the middle of the garden. However, it is from the olive tree that we get the chrism, and from the chrism the resurrection. GOSPEL OF PHILIP 73.[15]

NATURE ITSELF IS BIG WITH PORTENTS OF THE RESURRECTION. CLEMENT OF ROME: Let us consider, beloved, how the Lord is constantly showing us that there will be a resurrection. Let us see, beloved, how resurrection takes place in season. Day and night display the resurrection to us: day dawns after the sleep of night; the day departs and the night returns. Let us take the harvest: how and in what way does the sowing occur? The sower has gone out and cast each of the seeds in the ground, and when they fall, dry and naked into the ground, they disintegrate. Then from this disintegration the mighty providence of the Lord makes them rise again, and from the one arise many bearing fruit. 1 CLEMENT 24.[16]

[7]NPNF 2 13:230. [8]Jn 1:5. [9]Allusion to Jn 11:25 (overture to resurrection of Lazarus). [10]SC 128:582. [11]PLM 5:86. [12]From the fourth century onwards, it was the common belief of Christians that Mary had no other children after Jesus and that her body retained no tokens of her pregnancy or labor. [13]See Gen 39:12-16; 50:7-13. [14]SC 128:450. [15]NHS 20:189 (translated by W. Isenberg). [16]AF 56. Clement is blending Jn 12:24 with the parable of the sower (Mk 4:1ff.).

THIS IS THE COMPLETION AND KEY OF EVERY MIRACLE.

PSEUDO-EPIPHANIUS: We ought to be constantly mindful of your love for our brethren in adversity and in that very hour, most dread, when we take in our hands the pearl beyond price, the body of Christ. Then let us pray constantly on behalf of our brethren: "You, God, who are alone good,[17] now as of old, you, Master, who in your love for humanity did deliver Israel from slavery in Egypt through the Passover and did vouchsafe grace to them through the blood of the lamb, grant to your world now freedom from harsh slavery, through your unsullied body and precious blood. You who did accept the tears of the harlot, accept today your church with its groaning under slavery. You who did accept the appeal of the believing thief, accept the petition of your believing people. You who did accept the repentance of Peter and his groaning, accept also the weeping of us beggars. You who did not turn away the tears of the Syrophoenician woman, receive the suit of your puny church on account of its great captivity, as it cried to you, God, today, saying, 'O God, who did rise from the dead after three days, raise your believing people from amid their foes. You who did lift up Adam from death, lift up the horn of the Christians. You who are God now and of old, who did take the form of a servant, ransom your lowly people from slavery. You who did become a child for us, save the multitude of our children from the sword.'" HOMILY 3, ON THE RESURRECTION OF CHRIST.[18]

The Third Day

THE FIRST DAY OF A NEW WEEK MARKED A NEW BEGINNING.

GREGORY OF TOURS: We believe that the Lord's resurrection took place on the first day, not (as some claim) on the seventh. This is the day of our Lord's resurrection, which we call properly the Lord's day[19] on account of that holy resurrection of his. This day first saw the light in the beginning, and this was the first that was worthy to behold the Lord rising from his tomb. HISTORY OF THE FRANKS 1.24.[20]

THE RESURRECTION IS A NEW CREATION.

GREGORY OF NYSSA: "This is the day that the Lord has made,"[21] another apart from those days that came to be in the beginning of the creation, by which time is measured. It is the beginning of another creation. For in this day God makes "a new heaven and a new earth,"[22] as the prophet says. What kind of heaven? The firmament of faith in Christ. What kind of earth? I mean the good heart, as the Lord says, the earth that drinks the rain that comes on it and burgeons with a manifold crop. ON THE THREE DAYS' INTERVAL.[23]

SUNDAY IS TO BE DIFFERENTIATED FROM THE SABBATH.

SEDULIUS SCOTUS: After that melancholy sabbath, the festal day began to shed its luster, the day that, being most pleasing to the Lord in his lordship, receives its name from his majesty, being known as the Lord's day in commemoration of its having received the great honor of being the first to behold the origin of the world when it was born and the power of Christ when he rose again. For so the book of Genesis, a perspicuous record of facts, declares that on sabbath of the seventh day God rested from all his labors. And thus it is plainly apparent that the head of the world is that day which, being the first, is the one from which the sabbath is reckoned in due order as the seventh. The glory of the eternal king, illuminating it with the further trophy of his resurrection, ordained that this day should retain the primacy over all days

---

[17]Mk 10:18. [18]PG 43:473. [19]Because Christ was the sun of righteousness, Christians could continue to use the name *Sunday* (*dies solis*) with a good conscience. The French name *dimanche*, however, derives from *dies dominica* (Lord's day), a Christian neologism. [20]GTO 44. [21]Ps 118:24. [22]Is 65:17. [23]GNO 9:279.

that had been granted to it by a holy sanction. Paschal Treatise 5.26.[24]

God's Sabbath Succeeds That of the Flesh. Gregory of Nyssa: You marvel at the lofty Moses who, by the power of his understanding, handled the entire creation of God. There you see the blessed sabbath of the first making of the world; through that sabbath recognize the present sabbath, the day of rest that God blessed above the other days. For in this day it was that the Only-begotten truly rested from his labors, when through the providential scheme fulfilled in his death he made sabbath in his flesh[25] and, having returned again to what he had been through the resurrection, he raised also everything else that pertained to him, becoming life and resurrection and dawn and morning and day to those in darkness and the shadow of death. On the Three Days' Interval.[26]

It Is a Day of Rejoicing.[27] Gregory of Nyssa: If the natal day of a human king,[28] or a feast of triumph, opens his prison, will Christ, in his rising, not bring release to those in tribulation? Beggars, receive your food; you who are palsied and maimed in the body, receive the medicine for your ills. For through the hope of the resurrection, virtue is sought out and vice is hated, whereas if the resurrection is taken away, one saying will be found to prevail in all: Let us eat and drink, for tomorrow we die.[29] Paschal Sermon.[30]

The Risen Lord of Glory

The Resurrection Manifests Both Humanity and Divinity. Ambrose: The reason for his displaying the marks of the nails and the wound of the lance, and for his eating before his disciples, was to assure them by all means of the resurrection of our nature through its renewal in him. While, through the blessed nature of his Godhead, he re-

mained changeless, unalterable, impassible, immortal, lacking nothing, he nonetheless by his indulgence permitted all sufferings to befall the temple that was his own. Likewise he raised this by his own power, and through his own temple he effected the perfect renewal of our nature. But if any say that Christ was a mere man, or that God the Word was passible, or that he was converted into flesh, or that he had a body united to him in essence,[31] or that this has come down from heaven,[32] or that it was a phantom,[33] or that God the Word, being mortal, had need of a resurrection from the Father,[34] or that he assumed a body without a soul or a man without mind[35] or that the two natures of Christ, confused in one mixture, became one nature;[36] and if they do not confess that our Lord Jesus Christ consists of two natures unconfused but a single person, insofar as there is one Christ and one Son:[37] these the catholic and apostolic church anathematizes. On the Christian Faith.[38]

Thomas Acknowledged His Lordship After the Resurrection. Second Council of Constantinople (553): To his other blasphemies [Theodore[39]] added the assertion that after the resurrection, when the Savior breathed on his disciples and said, "Receive the Holy Spirit,"[40] he did not impart the Holy Spirit but breathed on them in a figure. And the same man said that Thomas's confession, "My Lord and my God,"[41] after he had

---

[24]CSEL 10:295. [25]The flesh rests in the tomb while the soul performs its task among the dead. [26]GNO 9:274. [27]See Gen 40:20-21. [28]In Scripture, only the wicked celebrate their birthdays: Origen *Homilies on Leviticus* 8.3. [29]1 Cor 15:32. [30]GNO 9:251. [31]Forms of Gnostic heresy. [32]The heresy of Apelles, also imputed to Apollinaris. [33]The heresy of Marcion. [34]A caricature of Arian teaching. [35]The heresy of Apollinaris. [36]Another form of Apollinarianism, proleptically refuted by Tertullian and others. [37]In content and diction this is a Chalcedonian definition before Chalcedon. [38]PL 16:849. [39]Theodore of Mopsuestia (d. 428) was so opposed to Apollinaris's teaching that he declined to accept the communication of idioms, which allows us to credit Jesus the man with the attributes of God. [40]Jn 20:22.

touched the hands and side of the resurrected Lord, was not said of Christ by Thomas, but rather that Thomas, stupefied by the miracle of the resurrection, sang a hymn to God who had raised up Christ. . . . If anyone does not anathematize him . . . let him be anathema. ANATHEMA.[42]

His Body May Not Have Been as Ours in All Respects. CLEMENT OF ALEXANDRIA: At 1 John 1 he is not speaking only of the flesh but of the virtues of the same Son. Like a ray of the sun penetrating right to these nethermost regions, this ray when it came in the flesh became palpable to his disciples. It is said in traditions that when John was touching the body that was there from without, he put his hand deep within, and the solidity of the flesh in no way resisted him but gave way to the hand of the disciple. This is his reason for declaring, And our hands have handled the word of life; he who came in the flesh was made tangible, just as was the life that was manifested.[43] HYPOTYPOSES.[44]

As Christ Is a Spirit, So Shall We Be. MARIUS VICTORINUS: What was fulfilled in Christ in the flesh was this: that he should save souls and also cause immortality to be given to the flesh through resurrection. This he accomplished by the power of his cross. . . . When we rise and are changed and are made spiritual in body, soul and spirit[45] (for all these there make up one person and are one spirit), the body in which we have been humbled will be raised. It will be of the same and an equal form to the body of Christ's own glory.[46] So too we shall be spirits as he himself is a spirit. COMMENTARY ON EPHESIANS 3:21.[47]

---

[41]Jn 20:28 [42]DEC 118-20. [43]1 Jn 1:1-2. [44]CAO 3:485. This story is apocryphal, but if Jn 20:19 implies that the body of Christ could pass through doors, it was evidently of a rarer stuff than ours. [45]See 1 Thess 5:23; for Christ as spirit, see 1 Cor 15:45. [46]Phil 3:21. [47]MVCEP 109-10.

IN ACCORDANCE WITH THE SCRIPTURES

σταυρωθέντα τε ὑπὲρ ἡμῶν	*crucifixus etiam pro nobis*	*For our sake he was crucified*
ἐπὶ Ποντίου Πιλάτου,	*sub Pontio Pilato,*	*under Pontius Pilate;*
καὶ παθόντα καὶ ταφέντα,	*passus et sepultus est;*	*he suffered death and was buried.*
καὶ ἀναστάντα τῇ τρίτῃ ἡμέρᾳ	*et resurrexit tertia die,*	*On the third day he rose again*
κατὰ τὰς γραφάς,	**secundum Scripturas;**	**in accordance with the Scriptures;**
καὶ ἀνελθόντα εἰς τοὺς οὐρανούς,	*et ascendit in coelum,*	*he ascended into heaven*
καὶ καθεζόμενον	*sedet*	*and is seated*
ἐκ δεξιῶν τοῦ πατρός,	*ad dexteram Patris;*	*at the right hand of the Father.*
καὶ πάλιν ἐρχόμενον μετὰ δόξης	*et iterum venturus est, cum gloria,*	*He will come again in glory*
κρῖναι ζῶντας καὶ νεκρούς·	*judicare vivos et mortuos;*	*to judge the living and the dead,*
οὗ τῆς βασιλείας οὐκ ἔσται τέλος.	*cujus regni non erit finis.*	*and his kingdom will have no end.*

HISTORICAL CONTEXT: During the controversies of the second century, catholic Christianity had defined a body of Scripture that afforded the only ground of proof for doctrine. The systematic harmonization of the canonical writings and the continuous exegesis of individual books remained, however, the province of lay theologians and the presbyters; the duty of a bishop was to proclaim the received tradition of the church, and he turned to commentary only when some adversary had cited the text in support of a position that could not be squared with ecclesiastical teaching. As their writings demonstrate, however, the bishops who swayed the great councils were more than equal to their antagonists in the management of scriptural evidences; the present clause is at once an interpretation of Hosea 6, an echo of 1 Corinthians 15:4 and an acknowledgment that the church is founded on the Word of God.

OVERVIEW: Christ predicted his resurrection (TERTULLIAN), which was ordained from the beginning (GREGORY OF NYSSA), prophesied in Hosea (TERTULLIAN) and anticipated in the return of Jonah (ATHANASIUS). The resurrec-

tion frees us from death (ATHANASIUS). Our deliverance is commemorated in every cock-crow (PRUDENTIUS), every new day (HYMN FOR COMPLINE), every spring (VENANTIUS FORTUNATUS). For all that, it was not foreseen before it was accomplished (NEMESIUS OF EMESA).

Christ saves all (GREGORY OF NYSSA), reversing the effects of Adam's sin (GREGORY OF NYSSA). While the body remains (CYRIL OF ALEXANDRIA), all resurrection is spiritual (TREATISE ON THE RESURRECTION), and thus we should not repine at suffering in the present body (ATHANASIUS).

Christ commends belief without ocular proof (GAUDENTIUS); this is his guarantee of salvation to the Gentiles (AUGUSTINE). As the women approached him through love and humility (CHRYSOSTOM), we too can discover him through love of neighbor (CHRYSOSTOM). For a testimony we have the Lord's day itself (IGNATIUS).

The Jews prepared their own witnesses (SEDULIUS SCOTUS); the faithful guard could not choose but see (EPHREM). The body lay long enough in the tomb to prove that it was

dead (ATHANASIUS); it is trifling to suppose
that the corpse was stolen without the wrappings (CHRYSOSTOM) or that it was taken by
the gardener (TERTULLIAN). The appearances
of the resurrected Jesus can be harmonized
(JOSEPH'S BIBLE NOTES). They were designed
for the edification of believers (ATHANASIUS),
and we need not cavil because none were
vouchsafed to the incredulous (ORIGEN).

According to the Scriptures

**THE RESURRECTION ELUCIDATES CHRIST'S
TESTIMONY TO HIMSELF.** TERTULLIAN: We
imagined, said the disciples at Emmaus, that
this one was the Redeemer of Israel—clearly
meaning their own Christ, that is, the Christ
of the Creator. So little had he said to them
of his being any other. Otherwise they would
not have supposed that he was the Christ of
the Creator, nor, being supposed the Christ
of the Creator, would he have tolerated this
supposition had he not been the one whom he
was supposed to be. . . . He did indeed repri-
mand them: "O senseless and slow of heart in
not believing all that he said to you!" In saying
this he proved himself to be not of another
God but of the Creator. For the angels said the
same things to the women: "Remember what
he said to you in Galilee, that it was necessary for the Son of man to be handed over and
crucified and raised on the third day." And
why was it necessary, if not because it had been
so written by God the creator? Therefore he
rebuked them because the passion was sufficient to cause them scandal and because they
shrank from putting faith in the resurrection
proclaimed to them by the women. Thus it was
that they had not believed him to be the one
whom they had supposed him to be. Therefore, wishing that he should be believed to be
the one whom they supposed, he confirmed
that he was the one that they had supposed,
namely, the Christ of the Creator, the Redeemer of Israel.

And as to the reality of his body, what could
be clearer? As they were uncertain whether he
was a phantom—indeed, were believing him to
be a phantom—he said, "Why are you per-
turbed? And why do thoughts slip into your
hearts? See my hands and feet, that I am the
very man; for a spirit does not have bones, such
as you perceive to be mine."[1] Now Marcion,
that industrious man, did not wish to purge
his gospel of certain expressions that contra-
dicted him, so that, on the plea of not having
erased what he might have erased, he could
either deny that what he had erased had been
erased or affirm that they had been erased
with justice. The only ones that he spares,
however, are those that he misrepresents as
profoundly by interpretation as by deletion.
He would rather have the words say "A spirit
has not bones, such as you perceive to be my
case," as if "such as you perceive to be my case"
were to be referred to the spirit and meant
that, like a spirit, he did not have bones. But
what would be the purpose of this convolution
when he could have asserted simply, "Because
a spirit has not bones, just as you see that I do
not have them"? AGAINST MARCION 4.43.[2]

**TO CHRIST THIS WAS THE RIPENING OF AN
ETERNAL PLAN.** GREGORY OF NYSSA: Now it
was Christ who arose on this day, God impassible and immortal (pause a while, heathen, be
not so prompt in laughter, until you have heard
the whole). He had not suffered by necessity,
nor was he forced to take the road down from
heaven, nor did he find in the resurrection a
boon unforeseen and beyond his hopes. No,
he knew the end of all things, and he had
made the beginning accordingly. In the eyes

---

[1]The Latin word *habeo*, and its Greek original, meant not only "to
possess" but also "to be in a certain condition." Tertullian accepts
the former sense here, Marcion the latter, with some violence
to the syntax. In the form ascribed to Marcion, a participle
(*habentem*) is substituted for the infinitive *habere*. It is not clear
whether this is an intrigue on his part or an unimportant lapse,
either of his own pen or Tertullian's. [2]CCL 1:661-62.

of his divinity he had knowledge of all that lay before him, and before his descent from heaven he saw the commotion of the nations,[3] the hardheartedness of Israel, Pilate sitting in judgment, Caiaphas rending his clothes, the factious people chafing, Judas betraying and Peter fighting for him; and he saw himself transformed after a while by his resurrection into incorruptible glory. Having all this inscribed in his knowledge, he did not withhold his grace from humanity or delay the scheme of providence. . . . Our Savior in his benevolence voluntarily suffered contumely and dishonor, since he foresaw his glorious return and volunteered to die for humanity, since he also foresaw his rising. Paschal Sermon.[4]

Hosea Had Prophesied Resurrection on the Third Day. Tertullian: It was necessary also that the one who buried the Lord should be told of beforehand and at the same time justly blessed, seeing that the prophecy does not overlook the service of the women who met before dawn at the tomb with a preparation of spices. For the Word spoke of this through Hosea: "That they may seek my face, he says, they will keep watch before dawn, saying, 'Let us go and turn to the Lord, for he it is who has snatched us out and will cure us, has stricken us and will have mercy on us: he will heal us after two days, and on the third day we shall rise again.' "[5] For who would not believe that these words were turned over again and again in the thoughts of those women amid the sorrow of their present loss, which seemed to them to have been inflicted on them by the Lord, and also the hope of the resurrection which they rightly saw as the means of their restoration? When, however, the corpse was not found, "his burial was taken from the midst," as Isaiah says.[6] Yet in that place there also appeared two angels.[7] That was the number of attendants that the Word of God, who stands by the evidence of two witnesses,[8] was accustomed to have. Against Marcion 4.43.[9]

Jonah Prefigured the Harrowing of Hell. Athanasius: What he says is "just as you, Father, are in me, and I in you, that they all may be one."[10] But in saying again "just as," he shows that those who come to be in the Father are far away—far away, that is, not in place but by nature. For God is not remote in place, but in nature alone all things are remote from him.[11] And, as I said before, the one who employs the locution "just as" is not conveying sameness or equality but giving an example of what he is saying under one particular conception. This again we can learn from the Savior himself when he says, "Just as Jonah was in the belly of the whale three days and three nights, so too shall the Son of man be in the heart of the earth."[12] Yet Jonah was not such as the Savior, nor did he descend to hades like the Savior. Nor indeed was the whale hades. Moreover, when he was spewed forth, Jonah did not bring forth those who had been previously swallowed by the whale. The words "just as," then, do not indicate the slightest likeness or equality, but that the former event is one thing, the latter another. And so, therefore, we also do not come to be in the Father as the Son does or come to be in the Son in the same way as the Father does, even though the Son says "just as." Against the Arians 3.23.[13]

The Gift of Life

The Resurrection Is the Defeat of Death. Athanasius: When after night the sun rises, and the whole of the neighboring land is illumined by it, not the slightest doubt remains that the sun who sheds his light everywhere is also the one who drove away the darkness and illumined everything. In just the same

[3]Ps 2:1. [4]*GNO* 9:248. [5]Hos 5:15–6:2. [6]Is 57:2 (LXX). [7]Jn 20:12. [8]Ingeniously conflating the two senses of "Word of God." Cf. Gen 18:2; Mk 9:3 and parallels; Jn 8:17; Rev 11:3. [9]CCL 1:661. [10]Jn 17:23. [11]God is not remote in the sense of location, but in respect to his very nature all created things are entirely different from him. [12]Mt 12:40. [13]PG 26:369-72.

way, death was trampled and brought into contempt from the time when the Savior made his appearance in the body for our salvation, and the end of the Cross became manifest; this was enough to make plain that he himself was the Savior, the one who had also appeared in the body, the one who had trampled death, and was displaying the trophies of victory over it every day in his disciples. ON THE INCARNATION 29.3.[14]

THE COCK-CROW HERALDS CHRIST'S RESURRECTION AND OURS. PRUDENTIUS: Then it was that the one who had denied him bewailed the wickedness that had slipped from his mouth while his mind remained blameless and his spirit preserved its faith. Never after that did he speak with such a loose tongue, and, as soon as he was conscious of the cock's crowing, the righteous man ceased to sin. Thus it is that all of us believe in this hour of quiet when the cock crows in exultation, Christ rose from the underworld. Then the strength of death was bowed, then the law of hell was suppressed, then the superior force of day compelled the night to retire. DAILY ROUND 1.57-72.[15]

A CONFIRMING SIGN OF OUR REDEMPTION. HYMN FOR COMPLINE: Christ, who are light and day, you lift the shades of night. Morning star[16] bearing light before you, foretelling the radiance of the blessed, defend us, we pray, in this night, holy Lord. Let there be rest in you, and grant us a night of peace. Let not heavy sleep invade us or the enemy[17] surprise us, lest the flesh, consenting to him, should render us guilty in your sight. Let our eyes receive sleep, while our heart is always awake for you. May your right hand protect the servants who love you. Watch over us, defender, restrain the plotters, direct your servants whom you have purchased with your blood. Remember us, Lord, in this encumbering body; Lord and defender of souls, be with us. HYMN FOR COMPLINE.[18]

EACH SPRING IS A NEW TROPHY OF THIS MIRACLE. VENANTIUS FORTUNATUS: The verdant wood, whose mane of leaves was torn away in the season of winter, renews its leafy canopy; myrtle willow, fir, hazel, brook willow, maple—each tree applauds in the loveliness of its own locks. The bee, quitting its hive in order to build honeycombs, purloins sweet liquor from flowers, humming as it crouches. The bird, which in winter's cold was sluggish, dumb and bereft of song, returns to its caroling; henceforth the nightingale employs her windpipe as a well-tempered instrument, and the air grows sweeter with the echoing melody. See, the beauty of the regenerate earth declares that all blessings have returned with their Lord. For now on all sides the woods hail Christ with their foliage and the meadows with their flowers as he proceeds in triumph after the woes of hell. The laws of the netherworld have been overthrown, and as God makes his journey above the stars he is duly praised by the light, the pole, the land, the sea. See, God who was crucified reigns in all things, and all created beings make their prayer to the creator. Hail, festal day, to be held in honor for all time—day on which God overwhelmed the netherworld and makes the stars his seat. VERSES ON THE RESURRECTION.[19]

THIS IS NOT THE RESURRECTION ENVISAGED BY PAGANS. NEMESIUS OF EMESA: The Stoics affirm that at stipulated periods, when the planets have been restored to the same coordinates that they occupied at the beginning when the universe came together, all that exists is consumed by fire and annihilated, and after this the universe is restored to its original state exactly, the stars returning likewise, and each pursuing its previous course without change. . . . Nothing will occur that differs from what

---

[14]SC 199:368-70. [15]LCL, Prudentius 1:8-10. [16]Lucifer, the light bearer; cf. 2 Pet 1:19. [17]Satan: 1 Pet 5:8. [18]OBMLV 51-52. [19]OBMLV 77-78.

was done before, but all things down to the least will act in the same way without any change. It is because of this restoration, they say, that Christians fondly imagine a resurrection; but in this they are greatly deceived. For the sayings of Christ envisage a single, not a periodic, resurrection. ON HUMAN NATURE 38.309-11.[20]

Pardon and Glory

ALL ARE SAVED BY ONE. GREGORY OF NYSSA: He was led back to the true and living God, and those who through the adoption followed the Son were not cast out or banished from their paternal inheritance. Thus the one who had made himself the firstborn of the good creation among many brothers[21] drew to him the whole nature in which he partook through the flesh that was mingled with him. ON THE THREE DAYS' INTERVAL.[22]

THE RESURRECTION OVERTURNS THE EF-FECTS OF ADAM'S SIN. GREGORY OF NYSSA: He has wiped out summarily every memorial of our condemnation. Then children were born in sorrow; now there is birth without pangs. Then we were born as flesh from flesh; now what is born is spirit from spirit. Then we were born as sons of humankind; now as children of God. Then we were dissolved into earth from the heavens;[23] now the heavenly one has also made us heavenly. Then sin held sway through death; now righteousness through life receives might in turn. One man then unlocked the approach to death; now by contrast life is brought in through one. ON THE SACRED AND SAVING PASCH.[24]

THE GLORIFIED BODY DOES NOT CEASE TO BE HUMAN. CYRIL OF ALEXANDRIA: It would be incongruous to assert that the body was changed into the nature of the Godhead and equally so to assert that the Word was changed into the nature of the flesh. For just as the latter is impossible (as he is unchangeable and unalterable[25]), so is the former. For it simply cannot come to pass that anything in the created order should be capable of translation into the essence or nature of the Godhead. And the flesh is a creature. Consequently, when we say that the body of Christ is divine, it is because it is also the body of God and irradiated by ineffable glory, incorruptible, holy, life-giving. But as for its being changed into the nature of the Godhead, not one of the holy fathers has imagined or asserted this, and I am not disposed to assert it either. FIRST LETTER TO SUCCENSUS 10.[26]

THE TRUE RESURRECTION IS SPIRITUAL. VALENTINIAN TREATISE: The Savior swallowed up death—of this you are not reckoned as being ignorant—for he put aside the world, which is perishing. He transformed himself into an imperishable Aeon and raised himself up, having swallowed the visible by the invisible,[27] and he gave us the way of our immortality. Then indeed, as the apostle said,[28] we suffered with him, and we arose with him, and we went to heaven with him. Now if we are manifest in this world wearing him, we are that one's beams, and we are embraced by him until our setting, that is to say, our death in this life. We are drawn to heaven by him, like beams by the sun, not being retrained by anything. This is the spiritual resurrection, which swallows up the psychic in the same way as the fleshly. GNOSTIC TREATISE ON RESURRECTION 45.14–46.2.[29]

HOPE FOR THE FUTURE BRINGS JOY IN TRIBULATION. ATHANASIUS: Of old, before the Savior made his divine sojourn on earth,

---

[20]*NENH* 111. [21]See Col 1:15. [22]*GNO* 9:305. [23]That is, from living below the skies. [24]*GNO* 9:310. [25]These words are borrowed from the anathemas to the Nicene Creed of 325, which upheld the full divinity of Christ, both on earth and in heaven. [26]*CASL* 80. [27]See 1 Cor 15:53-54; 2 Cor 4:18. [28]See Rom 6:4-6; 2 Cor 4:9-10; Phil 2:5-12. [29]*GTRNH* 14-16.

all lamented the dead as though destruction awaited them, but now that in these latter days the Savior has raised his body, death is no longer fearful—rather, those who are in Christ trample it as a thing of no account and choose to die rather than deny their faith in Christ. For they know that when they die they are not undone but live and become incorruptible through the resurrection. But as for the devil, he who of old exulted basely in death, his labor is now undone, and he is left as the only one who is truly dead. On the Incarnation 27.2-3.[30]

The Grounds of Faith

We Can Believe Without the Visible Presence of the Savior. Gaudentius: When the Savior said to Thomas, "You believe because you have seen; blessed are those who have not seen and believe,"[31] he willed that all future believers should find instruction in him, that our own people, resembling Thomas in being absent when Christ appeared to the apostles, should give undoubting credence to their reports and not demand to see him in the flesh when they have learned from the testimony of the apostles that he rose again and was seen after his passion on the cross. For now that he has returned to heaven and is present only by his virtues in this world, there is no necessity for him to appear every day to believers, individually and collectively, in bodily form at everyone's behest. Let it be enough for us that Thomas's curiosity has answered the doubts of the scrupulous thereafter. Tractates 17.8, On the Communion of Saints.[32]

Otherwise Gentiles Could Not Be Saved. Augustine: He saw and touched a man and confessed him to be God, whom he had neither seen nor touched.[33] But through the one thing he had seen and touched, he believed the other, putting away all doubt. Jesus

said to him, "Because you have seen, you have believed." He does not say, "you have touched me," but "you have seen," because vision is in a way the universal sense. For it is apt to be named by way of the other four senses also, as when we say: hear and see how well it sounds, smell and see how good its scent is, taste and see how good its flavor is, touch and see how nice and warm it is. Everywhere the term "see" is heard, while it is not denied that vision is strictly the property of the eyes. Thus it is that here too the Lord says, "Put your finger in here, and see," meaning what else but "touch and see"? Therefore whether it was by looking or by touching also, he says, "Because you have seen me, you have believed."[34] Admittedly it could be said that the disciple did not venture to touch when he offered himself to be touched, as it is not written, "and Thomas touched him." Yet whether it was only by observation or also by touching that he saw and believed, what follows is rather a proclamation and commendation of faith among the Gentiles: "Blessed are those who have not seen and have believed." He expresses himself in the past tense, as one who in his determinate counsel knows that which is yet to be as a thing accomplished. Tractates on the Gospel of John 121.5.[35]

We Can Also Know Him as the Women Did. Chrysostom: Consider how Jesus also through these women sends the good news to his disciples. As I have often said, he is bringing honor and good hope to that class of people who for the most part are without honor. He is healing that which has been put to hardship. Would one of you perhaps wish to do what secured their fame and grasp the feet of Jesus? If any of you wishes, you are able now to grasp not only the hands and feet but also

---

[30]SC 199:362-64. [31]Jn 20:29; cf. Jn 20:8, where the beloved disciple believes after seeing not Christ but the folded graveclothes. [32]PL 20:962. [33]Jn 20:27-28. [34]Jn 20:29; cf. Jn 1:50. [35]CCL 36:667-68.

that sacred head itself, tasting of those mysteries that inspire awe in a pure conscience. And not here only, but also in that day you shall behold him, coming with his ineffable glory and with the host of angels, so long as you have chosen to be lovers of humankind. And you shall hear not only the words of greeting spoken in this case but "Come here, you blessed of my Father; receive the kingdom prepared for you before the foundation of the world."[36] Let us then become devout lovers of God and the brethren, exhibiting love to all, in order that we may hear these words and entertain Christ himself. And as for you women who go about in gold trappings, consider the race that these women ran, and late though it is, put away this morbid craving for gold. Accordingly, if you would emulate these women, take up the giving of alms in exchange for these ornaments that you put around you. Tell me, what is the profit of these precious stones and these robes inlaid with gold? It is said, the soul takes joy and pleasure in them. I have asked you what profit, and you have told me the harm instead. Homilies on Matthew 89.3.[37]

We See the Resurrected Christ in Our Indigent Neighbor. Chrysostom: Do you see the manly courage of the women? Do you see their compassion? Do you see how nobly they use their possessions, even to death?[38] Let us imitate the women; let us not leave Jesus in his tribulations. For they poured out all these expenses on the one who had died and hazarded their own lives; we, however— yes, I am always saying the same thing—do not even feed the pauper or clothe the naked, but when we see him begging we pass by. . . . Stay, then, believing the one who said, "You gave to me."[39] For had you not given to him, he would not have deemed you worthy of the kingdom. Had you not turned him away—if it were some nobody that you had neglected—he would not have sent you to Gehenna. But since it is he who has been despised, the accusation is all

the more heinous. Thus it was that Paul persecuted him, and so he said accordingly, "Why do you persecute me?"[40] Let us take the attitude that we are giving to Christ when we give. For his words are more trustworthy than our vision. When, therefore, you see the pauper, remember the words through which he showed that he is the one being fed. For even if it is not Christ in appearance, it is nonetheless in this guise that he receives and begs. Be abashed, therefore, when you do not give to the one who begs. Homilies on Matthew 88.3.[41]

Sunday Is a Pledge and an Exhortation for Believers. Ignatius of Antioch: No longer keeping the sabbath, but living according to the Lord's day, in which also our life has dawned through him and through his death— though some deny this,[42] through this mystery we received faith. On account of this we abide, so that we may be found disciples of Jesus Christ our only teacher. How shall we be able to live without him? To the Magnesians 9.1-2.[43]

Resurrection Evidences

Unbelievers See Their Own Discomfiture. Sedulius Scotus: If, after the cruel tortures of the cross, after the wounding blows of iron, after the burial of the body in death, you butchers have not yet completed your bloody work, have not yet slaked your iniquitous thirst with the death of the innocent and prefer to think that this Lord of unequalled power, who has so often led souls out of the underworld, was not going to recall yours: well then, go on pursuing evil plans that suit your own character, cherish your sensual

---

[36]Mt 25:34. [37]PG 58:784-85. [38]Meaning either "even when Christ is dead," or (as I think) "even at the risk of death to themselves." [39]Mt 25:35, 41. What follows here is addressed to those who have heard the last judgment. [40]Acts 9:4. [41]PG 58:778-79. [42]Perhaps alluding to Judaizers, who shunned persecution by aping the outward forms of Judaism, pleading that Christ had come as an angel, not a man, and thus would not require his people to be martyrs. [43]AF 154.

intrigues, arm them with pretexts on which treason feeds, seal the fastenings of the tomb, put soldiers on guard, close the sepulcher with a stone and order everything with your accustomed malignity. Who will be able to keep God in custody, when all things are open to him and nothing stands in his way? He reigns in heaven, he commands the straits, he is sovereign even in hell. Why then, you shapeless mob, do you waste your efforts on laborious vigils? Why strive to investigate a faith that, even when you have proved it, you do not wish to own? PASCHAL TREATISE 5.25.[44]

THE GUARDS WERE RELUCTANT WITNESSES. EPHREM THE SYRIAN: That your resurrection might be believed among the gainsayers, they sealed you up within the sepulcher and set guards; for it was for you that they sealed the sepulcher and set guards, O Son of the living One! When they had buried you, if they had neglected you and left you and gone, there would have been room to lie and say that they did steal, O quickener of all! When they craftily sealed your sepulcher, they made your glory greater! A type of you therefore was Daniel, and also Lazarus; one in the den, which the Gentiles sealed up, and one in the sepulcher that the people opened. Their signs and their seals reproved them. Their mouth had been open if they had left your sepulcher open. But they went away because they had sealed it, and they closed up their own mouths. Yes they closed it, and when they had senselessly covered your sepulcher, all the slanderers covered their own heads. But in the resurrection you persuaded them concerning your birth; since the womb was sealed and the sepulcher closed up, being alike pure in the womb and living in the sepulcher. The womb and the sepulcher being sealed were witnesses to you. HYMNS ON THE NATIVITY 8.1-5.[45]

THE DELAY SUFFICES TO PROVE HIS DEATH. ATHANASIUS: Having made the cre-

ation aware at some length of the presence of its maker, he did not allow that temple of his, the body, to stay for long, but having simply let it be seen to be slain by the machinations of death, he rose suddenly on the third day, bearing as trophies and spoils of victory over death the incorruptibility and impassibility that had now accrued to his body. He could indeed have raised up his body as soon as he died, but the Savior, with good foresight, did not do this, for then someone might have said that he had not truly died, or that death had not truly taken hold of him, had he made his resurrection apparent at once. ON THE INCARNATION 26.1-2.[46]

THE ABANDONED GRAVECLOTHES PROVE THAT THE CORPSE WAS NOT STOLEN. CHRYSOSTOM: What is the significance of the headcloth, with myrrh clinging to it? For that is what Peter saw lying there.[47] Well, if they had wanted to steal it, they would not have stolen the body naked. Not only would they have wished to avoid sacrilege, they would not have wanted to linger and delay, retarding and arresting their own enterprise. All the more so when there was myrrh, such a viscous preparation that clings to the body and the garments. Thus it would not have been easy to part the garments from the body, but those who were doing this would have required a great deal of time. HOMILIES ON MATTHEW 90.2.[48]

IT IS ABSURD TO SUPPOSE THAT THE GARDENER STOLE THE BODY. TERTULLIAN: This is he, let me say, the son of a carpenter or a whore,[49] the destroyer of sabbaths, the Samaritan who has a demon,[50] this is he whom he bought from Judas, this is he who

---

[44]CSEL 10:294. [45]NPNF 2 13:241. [46]SC 199:360. [47]Jn 20:6-7. [48]PG 58:788-89. [49]Juxtaposing Mt 13:55 with the Jewish or pagan allegation that Christ was born of Mary's adultery with a centurion. Tertullian is ironically endorsing a series of calumnies against Jesus that will recoil on his accusers at the last judgment. [50]Jn 4:48.

was beaten with rods and buffets, fouled with spittle, made to drink gall and vinegar; this is he, whom his pupils covertly bore away, that he might be said to have risen, or whom perhaps the gardener dragged away, lest his lettuces should be damaged by the frequent traffic of visitors. [51] On the Spectacles 30.5-6.[52]

Accounts of His Appearances to the Disciples Can Be Harmonized. Joseph's Bible Notes:

The ten epiphanies of the Lord to his own, which took place after he rose from the dead: First, to the women who accompanied Mary at the tomb.[53]

Second, to Peter alone, as Paul also says: "Next he appeared to Peter."[54]

Third, the doors being closed, to the disciples on the first day of the sabbath, when Thomas was absent.[55]

Fourth, in the breaking of bread, to the companions of Cleopas on their departure for Emmaus.[56]

Fifth, in the presence of Thomas and the rest of the disciples, when he called Thomas also, after[57] the latter had felt his hands and side.[58]

Sixth, in Galilee by the sea of Tiberias, at the catch of the 153 fish.[59]

Seventh, once to the five hundred, as Paul relates.[60]

Eighth, to James, as Paul relates.[61]

Ninth, on the mountain in Galilee, where the Lord gave them their commission, according to Matthew.[62]

Tenth, on the Mount of Olives, rising up into heaven.[63]

Joseph's Bible Notes.[64]

The Miracle Is a Sign to Believers, No Less Than to Unbelievers. Athanasius: How could this man's disciples have had the boldness to preach his resurrection, if they had not been able to see that he had previously died? Or how would they have been believed when they claimed that he had first died then risen again, if they had not had as witnesses of his death the very people to whom they now preached with boldness? After all, even when his death and resurrection happened in the sight of all, the Pharisees were not willing to believe it but compelled those who had seen the resurrection to deny this. Had all this happened in secret, what pretexts for unbelief would they not have devised? On the Incarnation 23.3.[65]

He Was Visible Only to the Eye of Faith. Origen: Do not wonder if not all the crowds who believed in Jesus see his resurrection, when Paul, writing to the Corinthians, says as though they could not receive more, "I for my part have resolved not to know more among you than Christ Jesus and him crucified."[66] And to the same effect is, "For you are not yet able; no even now you are not able, for you are still carnal."[67] Thus it is, you see, that the word, divinely judicious in all that it does, wrote about Jesus, who before the passion appeared to multitudes without distinction, though not at all times, but after the passion no longer made his appearances in this manner but with a certain discrimination, to each in due measure. But just as it is written that "he was seen" by Abraham or by one of the saints, and this seeing does not occur continuously but at intervals, and he did not appear to all: so I would have you understand that much the same discretion was exercised in permitting the Son of God to be seen as in permitting it to those men that they should see God.

To the best of our ability in a treatise of this kind, then, we have made our defense against

---

[51]There is evidence in later sources that this was a claim advanced by certain Jews; it was no doubt a tendentious inference from Jn 20:15. [52]CCL 1:253. [53]Mt 28:1. [54]1 Cor 15:5. [55]Jn 20:19. [56]See Lk 24:35. [57]The Greek text implies that the touch preceded the calling but may require emendation. [58]Jn 20:27. [59]Jn 21:11. [60]1 Cor 15:6. [61]1 Cor 15:7. [62]Mt 28:16. [63]Acts 1:12. [64]*JBN* 334. This material dates from the fifth century. [65]SC 199:348-50. [66]1 Cor 2:2. [67]1 Cor 3:2-3.

the objection of Celsus that "if he really wished to manifest his divine power, he would have been seen by his abusers, by the one who had condemned him, and in sum by all." It was not, after all, necessary that he should be seen by the one who had condemned him or by his abusers. In fact, Jesus was sparing the one who condemned him and his abusers, so that they might not be struck by blindness of the kind that struck those in Sodom, when they had designs on the beauty of the angels whom Lot had as guests. And this is revealed through these words: "Stretching out their hands, the men drew Lot into the house with them and closed the door. But the men by the door of the house they struck with blindness, from the lesser to the great, and they sought the door without success."[68] The power of Jesus was divine, and he wished to manifest it to everyone who was able to see it—to see it, that is, according to the measure of his capacity. And indeed there was no other reason for his refusing to be seen except the powers of those who lacked the capacity to see him. And it is pointless for Celsus to strike up in this vein: "For having died he was not afraid of any person, and being God, as you say, he was not sent out in the first place only so that he could remain hidden." Yes, in fact, he was sent out not only so that he could be known but also so that he could remain hidden. For even to those who knew him not all of him was known, but something of him remained hidden from them. And to some he was not known at all but opened the gates of light to those who had been children of darkness and night, but as they made progress became children of day and light. And the Lord our Savior came to us rather as a good physician for those full of sin than for the righteous.[69] AGAINST CELSUS 2.66-67.[70]

---

[68]Gen 19:10-11. [69]Mt 9:12-13. [70]SC 132:442-44.

HE ASCENDED INTO HEAVEN

σταυρωθέντα τε ὑπὲρ ἡμῶν	*crucifixus etiam pro nobis*	*For our sake he was crucified*
ἐπὶ Ποντίου Πιλάτου,	*sub Pontio Pilato,*	*under Pontius Pilate;*
καὶ παθόντα καὶ ταφέντα,	*passus et sepultus est;*	*he suffered death and was buried.*
καὶ ἀναστάντα τῇ τρίτῃ ἡμέρᾳ	*et resurrexit tertia die,*	*On the third day he rose again*
κατὰ τὰς γραφάς,	*secundum Scripturas;*	*in accordance with the Scriptures;*
καὶ ἀνελθόντα εἰς τοὺς οὐρανούς,	**et ascendit in coelum,**	**he ascended into heaven**
καὶ καθεζόμενον	*sedet*	*and is seated*
ἐκ δεξιῶν τοῦ πατρός,	*ad dexteram Patris;*	*at the right hand of the Father.*
καὶ πάλιν ἐρχόμενον μετὰ δόξης	*et iterum venturus est, cum gloria,*	*He will come again in glory*
κρῖναι ζῶντας καὶ νεκρούς·	*judicare vivos et mortuos;*	*to judge the living and the dead,*
οὗ τῆς βασιλείας οὐκ ἔσται τέλος.	*cujus regni non erit finis.*	*and his kingdom will have no end.*

HISTORICAL CONTEXT: The ascension of Jesus after his resurrection is predicted at John 20:17, described at Luke 24:51 and Acts 1:1-9 and presupposed at Ephesians 4:8. His exaltation as Lord is commemorated at Philippians 2:9-11. One cogent rebuttal of those who held that Christ was not in all respects divine was the fact that the church not only acknowledged him as Lord but also offered prayers to him in its liturgy. The word translated "ascended" can also mean "returned," and the framers of the creed will have been conscious that the Son of man is said at John 6:51 and John 6:62 to have his proper seat in heaven. In retaining this clause from the earlier creeds, however, they have allotted it to a postion that clearly indicates that the ascension did not bestow a new dignity on the eternal Son but revealed him for what he had always been; and that he did not bring his human element down from heaven but assumed it on earth, so that this, unlike the Godhead, is now exalted for the first time.

OVERVIEW: Christ, having vanquished Satan by his righteousness, perfected his triumph through power (AUGUSTINE). He rebuked the suppliant Magdalen because she still conceived him as a man (AUGUSTINE); elsewhere she is the paradigm of a more judicious faith (AMBROSE). It is by faith, not carnal vision, that we know the ascended Christ (AUGUSTINE). While Christ did not shun the eyes of the faithful after the ascension (JOSEPH'S BIBLE NOTES), this consummation is a clear proof of his divinity (AMBROSE). The hymn in Philippians does not show that this divinity was acquired rather than eternal (ATHANASIUS); nor can such a meaning be elicited from Acts 2:36 (GREGORY OF NYSSA). He is exalted in both natures (THEODORE), bearing the flesh that did not appertain to him before the incarnation (CYRIL OF ALEXANDRIA).

Jesus' Departure

THE ASCENSION PERFECTS THE WORK OF RIGHTEOUSNESS. AUGUSTINE: What then is this righteousness by which the devil was vanquished? What but the righteousness of Jesus Christ? And how was he vanquished? Because when he had found noting worthy of death, he killed him nonetheless. And certainly it was right that he should release the debtors who were in his power when they believed in the one whom he had killed without any debt. . . . What is more righteous than to persevere to the point of death on the cross for righteousness, and what more potent than to rise from the dead and ascend to heaven in the very flesh in which he had been killed? His vanquished the devil first by righteousness, then by power. ON THE TRINITY 13.14.18.[1]

MARY MAGDALEN HAD TOO LOW A NOTION OF THE SAVIOR. AUGUSTINE: When the woman responded to him by recognizing him and calling him master, Jesus taught her the faith; and that gardener in her heart, as it were, sowed the grain of mustard seed in his own garden. What then is meant by "Do not touch me"? And as if a reason for this prohibition were being sought, he added, "for I am not yet ascended to my Father." What is this? If when he stands on earth he is not touched, how will he be touched by humans when he takes his seat in the heavens? Certainly before he ascended he offered himself to be touched by his disciples, saying, as the Evangelist Luke informs us, touch and see, for "a spirit has not flesh and bones, as you see me to have"; and when he said to his disciple Thomas, "Place your hand within here, and see my hands, and put forth your hand and put it in my side." Yet who would be so foolish as to suppose that while he wished himself to be touched by his disciples before he had ascended to the Father, he nonetheless did not wish to be touched by women until he had ascended to the Father? No, one cannot allow anyone to think so unwisely, even if he wishes. For we read that even women after the resurrection touched Jesus before he had ascended to the Father, among them Mary Magdalen. For Matthew relates that Jesus encountered them, saying, " 'Greetings.' They went up to him," he says, "and took hold of his feet and worshiped him."[2] This is omitted by John, but it is a true report of Matthew's.

It can only be then that some mystery hides in these words; whether we discover it or fail to discover it, we cannot doubt that it is there. He may, then, have said "do not touch me, for I am not yet ascended to my Father" because in that woman was prefigured the church of the Gentiles, which did not believe in Christ except when he had ascended to the Father. Or it may be that this is the way that Jesus wished us to believe in him, that is, to touch him in a spiritual sense, because he and the Father are one. In a certain sense he ascends to the Father in the deepest understanding of one who has advanced so far in knowledge of him that he perceives him to be equal to the Father. It was possible for Mary to believe in him in such a way as to think him unequal to the Father, and this is absolutely forbidden when it is said to her, "Do not touch me," that is, "Do not believe in me in the way that suits your present understanding: do not let your perception reach so far as to know what I have been made for your sake, without penetrating to that on account of which the flesh was made." How indeed can she not have been still believing in him carnally, when she was weeping for him as for a man? "For I have not yet ascended," he says, "to my Father." "There you will touch me, when you believe me to be God, not unequal to the Father." "But go to my brethren and say to them, 'I ascend to my Father and your Father.' " He does not say, "our Father," and therefore he is "mine" in one way, "yours" in another: "mine" by nature, "yours" by grace. And my God and your God. Nor did he say here "our God," and therefore here too he is mine in one sense, yours in another: my God because I too as a man am his subject, your God because I am a mediator between him and you. TRACTATES ON THE GOSPEL OF JOHN 121.3.[3]

---

[1]CCL 50A:406-7. [2]Mt 28:9. [3]CCL 36:667-68.

THE MORE DISCERNING FAITH IS MORE HIGHLY HONORED. AMBROSE: One Mary Magdalen was ignorant, according to John; the other Mary Magdalen has knowledge, according to Matthew; for the same one cannot both have knowledge at first and then be ignorant after. Therefore if there were many Maries, perhaps there were also many Mary Magdalens, since Mary is a personal name, Magdalen the name of a place. Therefore you should understand her to be another. The former is permitted to touch the feet of the Lord;[4] the latter is forbidden to touch the Lord.[5] The former was worthy to see an angel; the latter when she first came saw no one. The former announced to the disciples that the Lord was risen; the latter informs them that he has been stolen. The former rejoices; the latter weeps. To the one Christ came already in his glory, while the other seeks a Christ who is still dead. The former saw the Lord and believed, while the latter could not recognize him when she saw him. The former adored him with a faithful spirit; the latter grieved in loving uncertainty. . . .

Thus Scripture makes a plain distinction between one Mary and the other. The one runs forward that she may see Jesus, the other turns back; the former greets him, the latter is disabused. Therefore what you read is, "Jesus says to her, 'woman.'"[6] The one who does not believe is a woman and is still marked out by the name of her physical gender; for the one who believes attains the state of a perfect man, in the measure of the stature of the fullness of Christ,[7] no longer bearing the name of a period of life, a bodily gender, the fickleness of youth, the garrulity of an old man. Therefore Jesus says, "Woman, why do you weep?" as though to say, "God demands not bare tears but faith." Tears are good, if you recognize Christ. "Whom do you seek?" he asks, for the Lord condemns tardy labors. But he did well to add the word *whom*, not because he is in doubt as to whom she is seeking but because she does not recognize the one whom she is seeking. For the one who is sought is not known if he is not recognized when seen. And thus she saw Christ and thought him a gardener, for this is what you read: "She, thinking that he is the gardener, said to him, 'Sir,[8] if you have taken him, tell me where you have laid him, and I will take him up.'"[9] Uncertain as she was in faith, she was not fickle in speech: although she thought him a gardener, she nonetheless used the name of the Son of God. Although she does not yet believe, she has the air of a believer, for it was he himself who had taken up the body in raising it. Thus the woman's error was pardonable, since even though she ought not to have doubted that the body of Christ had been assumed by the glory of the resurrection, she was at least desirous of being taught by Christ. And in her devotion she gave earnest of faith sufficient to enable her to take that corpse up from the ground and seek him at the right hand of God.

And therefore after these words she is now called not woman but Mary; for her generic name as one of a crowd is one thing, while her special name as a person who follows Christ is another. . . . Without doubt she was rightly forbidden to touch the Lord, for we touch Christ not by the bodily sense of touch but by faith. "For I have not yet," he says, "ascended to my Father," meaning "I have not yet ascended for you, since you seek me among the dead." And so she is sent to those of stronger understanding, that they might preach the resurrection and she might learn by their example. For just as in the beginning a woman was the cause of sin for the man, while it was the man who carried out the sin, so now the woman who had first experienced his death was the first to see the resurrection, first with the remedy as in the order of sin. And so that

---

[4]Mt 28:9. [5]Jn 20:17. [6]Jn 20:15. [7]Eph 4:13. [8]In Latin this is *Domine* ("Lord"), so that she inadvertently calls Christ by his true title. [9]Jn 20:16.

she should not bear the stigma of perpetual guilt among men, as the one who had communicated sin to the man, she also communicates grace, and by her testimony to the resurrection she redresses the sorrow of the ancient fall. In ancient times, death had issued forth through the mouth of a woman; here through the mouth of a woman life is restored. But because she had not so much steadfastness in preaching and her sex did not have so much strength to discharge the office of spreading the gospel, it was entrusted to men.[10] Through Jesus the woman was not only absolved from sin, but grace was also given abundantly to her, so that the one who had previously deceived one man might now persuade many; and in the same way it was proper that the man, who of old had been rash in belief, should redeem his deposit with interest, so that he who on his own behalf had been facile in belief should now be equipped for preaching to others. But let us look at the actual words of his injunction: "Do not touch me, for I am not yet ascended to my Father. Go instead to my brethren and say to them, 'I ascend to my Father and to your Father, to my God and to your God.' " How had you not ascended, Lord Jesus? In what way were you not there, when you had commended your spirit into the hands of the Father?[11] Or when could you possibly not be there, you who are always in the Father, always with the Father? You yourself, after all, have said, "If I descend to the underworld, you are there; if I take my wings before the dawn and dwell at the end of the sea, there nonetheless your hand will guide me."[12] . . .

It was not, then, that the Lord was too proud to be touched by a woman, for Mary had also anointed his feet with an ointment; nor did he disdain her touch; but he is teaching us how to advance, since not everyone is able to touch in his second rising the Christ whom they touched when he sojourned in this life and this body. Let the one who would touch Christ mortify his members and put on bowels of compassion like

one who is to rise again, and let him not hesitate to proclaim the tidings to those on earth. What then is meant by "touch me not"? Do not apply your hand to things too great for it, but go to my brethren, that is, to the more perfect—for "whoever has done the will of my Father who is in heaven, the same is my brother and sister and mother"[13]—because the resurrection is rather beyond the capacity of all except the more perfect, and this faith is a privilege reserved for the more instructed. EXPOSITIONS ON THE GOSPEL OF LUKE 10.153-65.[14]

AFTER THE ASCENSION, VISION YIELDS TO FAITH. AUGUSTINE: Although the Lord had performed many visible miracles, from which faith itself, as if from drawing its first milk, had sprung up and from that tenuous beginning had attained its proper strength (for it is all the stronger when it does not require such things): nevertheless, his desire was that the promised good that we hope for should be anticipated without sight, so that the just should live by faith.[15] So much was this the case that he, when resurrected on the third day, did not wish to linger in human company, but having given them a demonstration of the resurrection in his own flesh, he ascended to heaven, taking his presence also from their eyes, and he did not bestow on any of them in their flesh a good of the kind that he had exhibited in his own flesh. His aim was that they should live in faith and that, while the reward of that righteousness by which one lives in faith will be visible hereafter, it should in the meantime

---

[10] The argument may seem needlessly hostile to women but is almost certainly truer to the mind of the Fourth Evangelist than the co-option of Mary as the first apostle in some modern writing. It is regrettable that we have heard Ambrose quoted so few times as saying that women participate in the remedy of sin, being the first to experience the Lord's death and the first to see the resurrection; they redressed the sorrow of the ancient fall and now no longer need to bear the stigma of perpetual guilt among men, and that through a woman life is restored—rather than their negative correlates when considered only under the fallen condition of humanity. [11] See Lk 23:46. [12] Ps 139:8-10. [13] Mt 12:50 [14] CSEL 32.4:513-15, 517-19. [15] Hab 2:7.

be awaited without sight. ON THE MERITS AND FORGIVENESS OF SINS AND ON INFANT BAPTISM 2.32.52.[16]

The Ascended Christ

HE CONSENTED TO BE SEEN AFTER THE ASCENSION. JOSEPH'S BIBLE NOTES: How many times, after his ascent to heaven, did the Lord appear to his own disciples?

First, to Stephen the protomartyr, when the heavens opened as he was being killed by the Jews.[17]

Second to Paul as he was traveling toward Damascus with the purpose of putting the saints in chains.[18]

Third, to Paul in Jerusalem, when he appeared to him and said, "Be not afraid, Paul, for as you have borne witness to me in Jerusalem, so you must bear witness in Rome."[19]

Fourth, to James the Just, as Hegesippus and Clement record, when he had been dragged up by the Jews to the wing of the temple so that he might say what is the gate of Jesus. JOSEPH'S BIBLE NOTES.[20]

CHRIST IS REVEALED AS THE TRUE SON OF GOD. AMBROSE: "I ascend to your Father, my God and your God." He made a good distinction, as he was speaking to a woman; for our nature has nothing in common with that of Christ, except as regards the human state. To him he was Father by an essential act of procreation, to us by voluntary adoption; to him by nature, to us through grace; God to him in the unity of the mystery, to us in celestial power. But how was it, then, that Thomas touched Christ when he had not yet believed? The fact is that he had doubted not the resurrection but the character of the resurrection, and it was necessary for him to teach me by his touch, as Paul too has taught us: "For this corruptible must put on incorruption, and this mortal must put on immortality."[21] Thus the unbeliever will believe and the procrastinator

will not be able to doubt; for we believe more readily what we see. Yet Thomas had cause for wonder when he saw the body passing through ways that were closed to bodies when all was locked and the bolts were not disturbed. Thus it was a wonder how bodily nature had passed smoothly through an impenetrable body, invisible in its approach yet visible to the gaze, easy to touch but hard to comprehend. EXPOSITIONS ON THE GOSPEL OF LUKE 10.167-68.[22]

THE EXALTATION IS NOT THE CAUSE BUT A TOKEN OF CHRIST'S DIVINITY. ATHANASIUS: Now since they find a pretext in God's own words and labor to impose their own sense on it by distorting exegesis, it is necessary to give them as much of an answer as is necessary to vindicate the words and to show that while the meaning of these is sound, they understand them wrongly. Now they argue that it is said by the apostle, "Therefore God has highly exalted him and favored him with the name above all names, so that at the name of Jesus every knee shall bow in heaven, as on earth and below the earth."[23] And in David: "For this reason God, your God, has anointed you with the oil of gladness beyond your fellows."[24] Then they infer, as though they were saying something wise, "If he was exalted for this reason, receiving favor, and if for this reason he was anointed, he received the wages of his free choice. But if he was free to choose in his actions, he cannot but be of a changeable nature." This Eusebius of Nicomedia[25] and Arius have dared not only to say but also to write, and their followers do not shrink from babbling it in the middle of the public square, not perceiving what follies their reasoning entails. For if he has received what he possessed as the wages of free choice, he would not have possessed them had he not

---

[16]CSEL 60:122. [17]Acts 7:55. [18]Acts 9:4. [19]Acts 23:11. [20]*JBN* 336 [21]1 Cor 15:53. [22]CSEL 32.4:519-20. [23]Phil 2:9-10. [24]Ps 45:8. [25]A protector of Arius, who disliked the Nicene tenet that the Son is from the substance of the Father.

been seen to perform the work required of him. It seems to follow, therefore, that, possessing them through virtue as he was made perfect, he was called the Son and God for this reason and is not the true Son.[26] For that which comes from something according to nature is a true offspring, as Isaac was to Abraham and Joseph to Jacob and the ray to the sun.[27] But there are some who are so called only through virtue and favor, having the favor that they have received rather than natural affinity and being of a different kind apart from what has been given to them. Such are those people who have received the Spirit by participation, of whom he also said, "I have begotten sons and exalted them, but they have set me at nought."[28] It was doubtless because they were not sons by nature that they changed and the Spirit was taken from them and they were disinherited. And if they repent, the God who at the beginning bestowed grace on them in this wise will receive them again and, having given them light, will call them children again.

If, however, they speak of this way about the Savior, he will be shown to be neither true, nor God, nor Son nor like the Father, and to have God as the Father not of his essential being but only of the favor bestowed on him; thus he will resemble all the rest in having God as the creator[29] of his essential being. And being such as these men say, he will manifestly not possess the name Son from the beginning, granting this to be the prize of his toil and progress, which could not have occurred except when he became man and assumed the form of a slave.[30] For then it is that, "having been obedient to death," he is said to have been exalted and to have received the name as an act of grace, "that at the name of Jesus every knee shall bow." What then was he before this, if it is now, on becoming man, that he has been exalted, has begun to be worshiped and been called Son? For—granting their false opinion that he was exalted and called Son when he became man— he seems not to have perfected the flesh but

rather himself to have been perfected through it. What therefore was he before this? For if the Lord is God, Son, Word, but was not these things before he became man, then either he was something else before this and subsequently partook of these things through virtue, as we have said, or otherwise (and let this fall on their own heads), that he did not even exist before this but was wholly man by nature and nothing more. This, however, is not the mind of the church, but that of Paul of Samosata[31] and the Jews. Why, then, if they are of the same mind as those men, do they not undergo circumcision as Jews, but simulate Christianity while waging war against it? For if he did not exist, or existed but was later perfected, how did all things come into being through him, or how did the Father rejoice in him beforehand if he was not perfect?[32] And how did he, if he has only now been perfected, rejoice before this in the Father's sight?[33] . . . Thus he was not a man who subsequently became God, but being God, he subsequently became man, the better to divinize us? Suppose that it was at the time when he became man that he was called Son and God: before he became man, God called the ancient people his sons,[34] and he made Moses god to Pharaoh,[35] and the Scripture says with regard to many that God stands in the assembly of gods,[36] and thus it is clear that

---

[26]It is uncertain whether the words "true God" (1 Jn 5:20) apply to the Father or to the Son, but the Nicene symbol of 325 appears to refer this verse to the Son and Jn 17:3 to the Father. [27]See Heb 1:3. [28]Is 1:2. [29]Athanasius strongly distinguishes begetting and creating. The Nicene Creed, however, condemns only the term "made," and the appended anathema on the word "created" does not appear in versions of the creed that are independent of Athanasius. Even after the Nicene Council, Eusebius of Caesarea continued to hold that begetting and creating (though not making) are synonymous in the Bible. [30]Phil 2:8. [31]Bishop of Antioch, condemned in 268 for his overweening conduct and for maintaining that Christ was a "bare man" temporarily inhabited by the Spirit. [32]Identifying Christ with the Wisdom of Prov 8:30 and thus anticipating the objection that the Word or Logos of Jn 1:3, through whom the world was created, may not have been a personal agent before he took flesh. [33]Prov 8:30. [34]Gen 18:2. [35]Ex 7:1. [36]Ps 82:1.

he was called both Son and God after them. How then were "all things through him" and "he himself before all"?[37] Or how was he "firstborn of all creation,"[38] when before him there were some called sons and gods? How did the first partakers not partake of the Word? This is no true doctrine but a mirage of latter-day Judaizers. How is it possible for people to know God the Father at all? For there could be no adoption as children without the true Son who said, "No one knows the Father except the Son and the one to whom the Son has revealed him." How could divinization occur without the Word and before him when he nonetheless says to his brethren the Jews, "if he called those gods to whom the Word of God came"?[39] But if all who have been called children and gods, whether on earth or in heaven, have been adopted as children and divinized through the Word, and if the Son himself is the Word, it is clear that all are so through him and that he himself is before all, or rather that he alone is the true Son, that he alone is the true God from the true God,[40] not having received this as the wages of virtue or being anything else apart from this but being this by nature and in essence. For he is the offspring of the Father's essence,[41] so that none may doubt that, in the likeness of the unchangeable Father, the Son too is unchangeable.

Let us, therefore, having knowledge of the Son, confront their irrational notions[42] with the means that God provides. And next it will be good to adduce God's own words, the better to demonstrate the unchangeableness of the Son, the immutable nature that he derives from his Father and the unsoundness of their opinions. Now writing to the Philippians the apostle says, "Let that mind be in you that was also in Christ Jesus, who, being in the form of God, thought it not robbery to be equal with God but emptied himself, assuming the form of a slave, coming to be in the likeness of a man and being found in fashion as a man he humbled himself."[43] . . . What could be more

transparent or more conclusive than this? For he was not perfected from an inferior state but rather, being God, assumed the form of a slave, and in assuming it was not perfected but humbled himself. . . . That which was humbled will be that which was exalted. And if the word *humbled* refers to the assumption of the flesh, then it is clear that the word *exalted* refers to it also. For it was the man who was in need of this on account of the humiliation that flesh and death entail. Since, then, the Word was an image of God and was immortal, he assumed the form of a slave and underwent death on our behalf as a man as in his own flesh, so that through this death he might, on our account, bring himself home to the Father. For this reason he is also said as a man to have been exalted on our account and for our sake, so that, just as by his death we have all died in Christ, so conversely in Christ we may be exalted, roused from the dead and going up to the heavens, "where Christ entered as our forerunner."[44] . . . And just as he himself, who sanctifies all, says conversely to the Father that he is sanctifying himself on our behalf,[45] not so that the Word may himself be made holy but that he in himself may sanctify all of us: so therefore our present text too says "exalted him,"[46] not that he might be exalted (for he is the most exalted) but that he himself might become righteousness for our sake and that we might be exalted in him and enter in though the gates of heaven, which he has already opened on our behalf. . . .

Moreover, the words "favored him" are not written with reference to the Word himself; for he was already worshiped, even before he became man, as we have said, by the angels and by the whole creation, because of his peculiar

---

[37]Jn 1:3. [38]Col 1:15. [39]Jn 10:35. [40]A direct quotation from the Nicene Symbol of 325. Arius admitted that the Son was God but not that he was true God. [41]Another citation from the Nicene Symbol, in the appendix to which the notion that the Son is subject to change is anathematized. [42]Athanasius here distinguishes *ennoiai* ("true conceptions") from *epinoiai* ("willfully false conceptions"). [43]Phil 2:6-8. [44]Heb 6:20. [45]Jn 17:19. [46]Phil 2:9.

relation to the Father. For just as Christ, as man, dies and was exalted, so as man he is said to receive what he always possessed as God, so that such a favor might also come as a gift to us. For the Word was not diminished by taking a body, so as to seek to obtain a favor, but rather imparted divinity to that which he put on and made this all the more a favor to the human race. For just as he is always worshiped, being the Word and "being in the form of God," just so, being the same one and having become man, he nonetheless has the whole creation under his feet, bending the knee to him at that name, confessing that when the Word became flesh and underwent death in the flesh this did not detract from the glory of his Godhead but was "for the glory of God the Father."[47] . . . See then, that folly of God, as humans deemed it, surpassed all things in glory through the cross.[48] For our resurrection is stored up in him,[49] and it is no longer Israel alone but all the rest of the nations, as the prophet foretold, who leave their own idols and acknowledge the true God, who is the Father of Jesus Christ.[50] And as the illusory play of the demons is suppressed, the only one who is truly God is worshiped in the name of our Lord Jesus Christ. That it is also the Lord who came to be in a body and was called Jesus who is worshiped, and that he is surely the Son of God should be apparent, as has been said, from the fact that it was not the Word, insofar as he is the Word, who received such a favor, but we ourselves. For it is through our affinity with his body that we have become the temple of God[51] and have been made the children of God henceforth, so that in us the Lord is worshiped already, and those who see us "declare," as the apostle says, "that God is truly in them."[52] AGAINST THE ARIANS 1.37-43.[53]

THE EXALTATION IS NEWS TO US, BUT NO NEW THING TO CHRIST. GREGORY OF NYSSA: Yet there are some who pour contumely on the simple-mindedness of our proclamation, exploring the essence of God through syllogisms and desiring to show that the one who brought all things into existence through creation is himself part of the creation. As an ally in this endeavor, they drag on, as though they gave substance to their blasphemy, the words of Peter when he said to the Jews, "Let it be known to all the household of Israel that God has made the same one Lord and Christ, this Jesus whom you have crucified."[54] This is the premise of their demonstration that the essence of the only-begotten God is created. What then, tell me, were the Jews to whom the word came really there before the ages? Did the cross antedate the world? Was Pilate before the whole creation? Was Jesus first and after this the Word? Was the flesh senior to the divinity? Was it before the world that Gabriel announced the news to Mary? Is it not rather that the man in Christ received his beginning through birth under Caesar Augustus, while the Word who was in the beginning, our God and King, is before the ages, as prophecy testifies? Do you not see what confusion you bring on the Word, stirring the top into the bottom, as the proverb says? It was the fiftieth day after the passion when Peter proclaimed this to the Jews, saying, "This man whom you crucified, God has made Christ and Lord." Will you not attend to the order of his speech, to what is said first and what second? For he did not say "the one whom God made Lord you have crucified," but he says, "The same whom you have crucified, this one God has made Christ and Lord." For this it is clear that Peter is speaking not of that which was before the ages but of that which was after the economy. How can you not see through this explanation that the content of your argument has been completely inverted? Why instead do you play the clown with a meretricious twist of the sophism, say-

---

[47]Phil 2:10-12. [48]See 1 Cor 1:18-31. [49]See Col 3:3. [50]Jn 17:3. [51]Eph 2:21. [52]1 Cor 14:25. [53]PG 26:88-101. [54]Acts 2:36.

ing that if we believe that the visible man was made Christ and Lord, it will be necessary for the Lord to empty himself into the human condition once more[55] and to undergo a second birth? What extra force does this give to your opinion? How does what has been said prove that the essence of the King of creation is created? For my part indeed, I say that on the contrary our position has been corroborated by those who fight against us, and that while the orator forces the argument to an absurd conclusion in his efforts to overturn it, his excessive zeal has blinded him to the fact that he is really fighting alongside his adversaries? For if it is right to believe that the Son's transition was from the superior state to the lowly, and if the nature superior to the creation is the divine and uncreated one, while humans are created, then a little reflection will lead him to the truth by his own way of reasoning, and he will agree that the uncreated came to exist in the creation through love of humanity. . . .

Eunomius,[56] in the very text before us, offers the following exegesis of the words: "Peter is speaking of the one who was in the beginning and is God,[57] and it is this one whom he declares to have become Christ and Lord." Thus, whatever he once was, it is this one who became Christ and Lord according to Eunomius. In the same way the history says of David that, being the son of Jesse and set over the flocks he was anointed as king—not that the anointing made him a man but that it transformed him, being according to his nature whatever he was, from a private person to a king. So how through these words of Peter is it established that the essence of the Son was made if, as Eunomius affirms, the one whom God made Christ and Lord was in the beginning and was God? For the term "lordship" denotes not essence but authority, and the title Christ indicates kingship, but the definitions of essence and of kingship are distinct. But in any case this is what Scripture declares to have happened in the case of the Son of God, and

so let us see what is the most reverent and consistent interpretation. Of which is it seemly to say that they became partakers of some more exalted thing by progression, God or a human being? Who is such a child in understanding as to think that the divine arrives by increments at perfection? On the other hand, to surmise this of human nature is not unreasonable, since the voice of the gospel clearly attributes growth in a human manner to the Lord: for "Jesus," it says, "grew in age and wisdom and grace."[58] So then, what is it more logical to suppose from the discourse of the apostle, that the God who was in the beginning became Lord by progression or that the lowliness of human nature was taken up from fellowship with the divine to the most exalted dignity? For the prophet David also, as from the mouth of the Lord, says, "I have been set up as king by him"[59] all but saying, I have become the anointed.[60] And as then, as though from the Father to the Son, he says, "Exercise lordship in the midst of your enemies,"[61] meaning the same as "become Lord of your enemies." Just as the designation "king" does not signify what the essence consists in, but only advancement to dignity, and the one who urges the exercise of lordship is not at that time commanding what is not to come into being but is really giving him power over unbelievers, so the blessed Peter, saying that he has become Christ—that is, king of all—added the same one, so that he might separate the essence from the description of its perceived concomitants. AGAINST EUNOMIUS 3.4.[62]

THE EXALTED CHRIST IS ONE PERSON IN TWO NATURES. THEODORE OF MOPSUESTIA: To make clear the perfect union that had occurred, he speaks of one person only, saying,

---

[55]Phil 2:7. [56]So-called Neo-Arian, who maintained that, as the Son was generated and the Father ingenerate, they were of different essences and hence that only the Father was properly God. [57]Jn 1:1. [58]Lk 2:52. [59]Ps 2:6. [60]In Gk, *Christos*. [61]Ps 109:2. [62]*GNO* 2:153-54, 157-58.

"When you see the Son of man ascend to the place where he was before."[63] If it were not as I have explained it, he ought to have said, "When you see the Son of Man ascend to the place where that which was in him was before." His meaning is that you will comprehend the grandeur of the divine nature that resides in me, and you will marvel at the wonders that are accomplished in me and in you on my account. Such too is the sense of this saying: "None had ascended to the heavens save him who descended from the heavens, the Son of man who is in the heavens."[64] His meaning is not that no one has ever ascended but that "I for my part have ascended to the heavens by virtue of the divine nature that resides in me and is still above the heavens." . . . It was not his purpose to make a distinction, asserting that none has ascended into the heavens save for the Son of man, in whom resides the one who was in the heavens and who came down from them. He did not approve this fashion of speaking and made use of a joint expression, as if to say that it is a question of one person only, in order to demonstrate and confirm the miracles accomplished in the one who was visible. CATECHETICAL HOMILY 8.11-12.[65]

Now the Word Has Flesh in Heaven.[66] CYRIL OF ALEXANDRIA: When we affirm that our Lord Jesus Christ is from heaven and from above, we do not mean in affirming this that his holy flesh was brought down from above or from heaven, but we rather follow the inspired Paul, who declared very clearly, "The first man was of the earth, earthy; the second man is from heaven."[67] And we are mindful that the Savior says, "None has gone up into heaven, if not the one who has come down from heaven, the Son of man,"[68] even though he was born, as I said but lately, of the holy virgin. The fact is that God the Word, in his descent from above and from heaven, "emptied himself,"[69] taking the form of a servant and playing his part as Son of man while remaining God as he was, since he is by nature unchangeable and immutable. But being considered as one with his own flesh, he is said to have come down from heaven and is called the man from heaven, being perfect in divinity and perfect as the same one in humanity and being considered as in a single person.[70] For there is one Lord Jesus Christ,[71] even if we do not overlook the difference of the natures, from which we affirm that the ineffable union has been forged. LETTER 39.5-6, TO JOHN OF ANTIOCH.[72]

---

[63]Jn 6:62. [64]Jn 3:13. [65]HCTM 203. [66]The tenet falsely ascribed to Apollinaris, who adduced Jn 3:13 and Jn 6:33 to show that the man could be said to have descended because he was also God. [67]1 Cor 15:45. [68]Jn 3:13. [69]Phil 2:7. [70]Rendering the Greek literally. The term *prosōpon* ("person") is not so characteristic of Cyril as of the Antiochene school whose representative Nestorius he had deposed in 431 at the Council of Ephesus. When he does employ the term, he insists that Christ is (or is in) a single *prosōpon*, whereas Nestorius seems to envisage a coalescence of two *prosōpa* into one. [71]1 Cor 8:6. [72]DFS 202-3.

AND IS SEATED AT THE
RIGHT HAND OF THE FATHER

σταυρωθέντα τε ὑπὲρ ἡμῶν	crucifixus etiam pro nobis	For our sake he was crucified
ἐπὶ Ποντίου Πιλάτου,	sub Pontio Pilato,	under Pontius Pilate;
καὶ παθόντα καὶ ταφέντα,	passus et sepultus est;	he suffered death and was buried.
καὶ ἀναστάντα τῇ τρίτῃ ἡμέρᾳ	et resurrexit tertia die,	On the third day he rose again
κατὰ τὰς γραφάς,	secundum Scripturas;	in accordance with the Scriptures;
καὶ ἀνελθόντα εἰς τοὺς οὐρανούς,	et ascendit in coelum,	he ascended into heaven
καὶ καθεζόμενον	**sedet**	**and is seated**
ἐκ δεξιῶν τοῦ πατρός,	**ad dexteram Patris;**	**at the right hand of the Father.**
καὶ πάλιν ἐρχόμενον μετὰ δόξης	et iterum venturus est, cum gloria,	He will come again in glory
κρῖναι ζῶντας καὶ νεκρούς·	judicare vivos et mortuos;	to judge the living and the dead,
οὗ τῆς βασιλείας οὐκ ἔσται τέλος.	cujus regni non erit finis.	and his kingdom will have no end.

HISTORICAL CONTEXT: This clause announces the fulfillment of Christ's prophecy in Matthew 26:4, Mark 14:62 and Luke 22:69. It also ratifies the vision of Stephen the protomartyr (Acts 7:56) and sustains the harmony between the two Testaments, since the same words are applied at Psalm 110:1 and Daniel 7:13 to an anonymous personification of the chosen people. While the locution "right hand of the Father" must be understood metaphorically, the reference to Christ's sitting can be reasonably construed to imply that even when ascended he retains his human attributes. This does not appear to have been contested in the fourth century, though some writers professing orthodoxy had spoken as though the worship of God the Son and Jesus the man could be divided. When the Constantinopolitan Creed of 381 was promulgated anew at the Fourth Ecumenical Council in 451, the extinction of the manhood by the Godhead of the risen Christ had been openly proclaimed, and the significance of the present clause will therefore have been all the more apparent.

OVERVIEW: As God is incorporeal, the right hand is metaphorical (AUGUSTINE). Likewise Psalm 24 must be applied figuratively to Christ (JUSTIN), as a dramatic account of his descent and return (GREGORY OF NYSSA). Isaiah foretells the enthronement of the risen Son (EUSEBIUS), and he is the one saluted in Psalm 110 and Psalm 72 (TERTULLIAN).

Christ's Enthronement

THE SESSION AT GOD'S RIGHT HAND.
AUGUSTINE: Sitting you must understand to mean dwelling, just as we say of a person that he kept his seat in that land for those years. Scripture says in the same way that one kept his seat in a city for such and such a time. Does this mean that he sat and never got up? It is clear, then, that people's dwellings are called their seats. . . . What you are to believe, then, is that Christ dwells at the right hand of the Father. That is where he is. And do not let your heart say to you, "What is he doing?" Do not inquire into what it is not given you to know. That is where he is, and that is sufficient for you. He is blessed, enjoying the blessedness that is called the right hand of

the Father; the right hand of the Father is the name of that same blessedness. For if we understand carnally his sitting at the right hand of the Father, the Father will be at his left. SERMON TO CATECHUMENS 11.[1]

PSALM 24 WILL NOT BEAR A TEMPORAL APPLICATION. JUSTIN MARTYR: "Lift up your heads, you gates, and be lifted up, you everlasting doors, and the king of glory shall enter in. Who is this king of glory? The Lord powerful and mighty in battle. Lift up the gates, you rulers, and be lifted up, you everlasting doors, and the king of glory shall enter in. Who is this king of glory? The Lord of hosts, this is the king of glory."[2] Thus it is made plain that this lord of hosts is not Solomon.[3] But when our Lord Christ has risen from the dead and ascended to heaven, then those who are appointed in heaven as rulers under God are bidden to open the gates of the heavens so that this one who is the king of glory may enter in and, having ascended, sit down at the right hand of the Father, until he makes his enemies a stool to put under his feet, as has been revealed through the other psalm. For when those who rule in heaven saw him deformed and dishonored in aspect and without glory, they did not recognize him and asked, "Who is this king of glory?" And the Holy Spirit answers, either in the person of the Father or in his own, "The Lord of hosts, this is the king of glory." For everyone will agree that no one would have dared to say "Who is this king of glory?" concerning Solomon—glorious king as this man was—or with regard to the spectacle of the testimony of those who stood by the gates of the temple in Jerusalem. DIALOGUE WITH TRYPHO 36.4-6.[4]

THE PSALM DRAMATIZES CHRIST'S DESCENT AND RETURN. GREGORY OF NYSSA: This sublime prophet, having caused himself to go forth from himself[5] in order that he might not be weighed down by the load of the body, and having mingled himself with the supramundane powers, relates their songs to us when, leading the pageant of the Lord on his downward path, they command the mundane angels to whom human life has been entrusted to raise the portals, saying, "Lift up the gates, you rulers, and you everlasting gates, be lifted up, and the king of glory shall enter in." Whatever state he is in, the one who compasses all in himself accommodates himself to the measure of the one who receives him (for not only does he become a human among humans, but by the same principle he cannot fail, when he comes among angels, to contract himself to their nature). For this reason the warders ask, "Who is this king of glory?" And because of this the supramundane angels reveal to them "the mighty one, potent in war," who is to grapple with the one who has taken human nature captive and to overthrow the one who has the power of death, so that—the last enemy having been done away—humanity may be called to freedom and peace. Then he reports the same utterances for a second time (for now the mystery of death has been fulfilled, and victory over the enemies has been secured, and the cross has been raised as a trophy, and in his "turn he who has taken captivity captive has gone up to the height, the one who has given the good gifts of life and lordship to humanity"[6]), and again it is necessary that the supernal gates should be opened to him. Our guardians are the counterparts to the pageant and are commanded to open to him the supernal gates, so that he may once again be glorified among them. But, clad as he is in the soiled robe of our life, his garments bearing a red stain from the winepress of evil people, he is not recognized. For this reason their voices address this inquiry to those who lead the pageant: "Who is this king of glory?"

---

[1]CCL 46:195. [2]Ps 24:7-10. [3]The view ascribed by Justin to his Jewish interlocutors. [4]JMAA 132-33. [5]That is, falling into an ecstasy, though without suspension of the rational faculty (see 2 Cor 12:1-3). [6]Ps 68:18; cf. Eph 4:8.

Then their answer is no longer "the mighty one, potent in war," but "the Lord of hosts": the one who surpasses all in might, the one who has recapitulated all things in himself,[7] the one who holds first place among all, the one who has restored all things to the first creation. This is king of glory. See how much sweeter for us is the banquet that David prepared, having mingled his own grace with the luster of the church. Let us too, therefore, imitate the prophet, as it is possible for us to perfect the imitation, in love toward God, in meekness of life, in forbearance toward those who hate us, so that the prophet's teaching of the divinely ordered polity may become for us an education in Christ our Lord. Glory is his to ages of ages. Amen. On the Ascension.[8]

This Enthronement Is the One Foreseen by Isaiah. Eusebius: Ought we to say that the prophet[9] saw only the one who, as we have already shown, associated visibly with the patriarchs in Abraham's time? For we have learned already that this one was at once God and Lord and even angel, and the captain of the Lord's forces. The present text, however,[10] as it prepares to prophesy his approach to humanity,[11] looks forward to his divine kingship, in the exercise of which it speaks of seeing him seated on a throne "high and lifted up." This throne of his would be the one discussed above, in the psalm about the beloved.[12] . . . And our interpretation of the passages here is confirmed by the Evangelist John, who, having adduced the present passage of Isaiah, in which it is said, "For the heart of this people is waxed fat, and their ears are heavy to hear, and their eyes they have sealed,"[13] he applies them to Christ, saying, "These things Isaiah said, when he beheld his glory and bore witness of him."[14] The prophet, therefore, having seen him take his seat on the paternal throne of divine glory and kingship, and having been inspired by the Holy Spirit and preparing in due course to adumbrate his approach to human-

ity and his birth from the virgin, he witnesses beforehand to the knowledge and the celebration of glory that is going to spread through all the world, bringing in the seraphim who form a ring and say, "Holy, holy, holy, Lord of hosts, the whole earth is full of his glory."[15] Now who would the seraphim be who attend the Christ of God, if not either the chorus of angels and divine powers or else that of the prophets? For the name seraphim means the beginning of their mouths. The prophets and apostles were such, since through their mouths came the firstfruits of the saving proclamation, and on this account they have received this title. So too the winged powers of the Holy Spirit, as they are called, conceal what is first and last in the knowledge of the Word of God, as being ineffable and inscrutable by nature, but what is midmost in his economy they reveal, because this alone is by nature intelligible to human beings, while loftier matters and those that come after are numbered in silence among the ineffable. Proof of the Gospel 7.1.5-10.[16]

The Prophecies Cannot Be Applied to Mortal Kings of Israel. Tertullian: But it is necessary to justify the application to my case of those Scriptures that the Jews also try to argue away from us. They say that Psalm 110 is addressed to Hezekiah, because he sat at the right of the temple, and God turned his enemies from him and took them away. For this reason, then, they say that the other words, "before the morning star I begot you from the womb," pertain to Hezekiah and to the birth of Hezekiah. We produce the Gospels (of whose veracity we must certainly have convinced them a little in such a long work as this): they declare that the Lord was born in the night, that this may be before the morning star, as we understand even better

---

[7]Eph 1:10. [8]GNO 9:325-26. [9]Is 6:1-13. [10]Is 6:1-13. [11]Is 7:14-25. [12]Ps 110. [13]Is 6:10 (lxx). [14]Jn 12:41. [15]Is 6:3. [16]GCS 23:298-99.

from the star[17] and from the angel's testimony when he announced to the shepherds at night that Christ had been born at that very point, and from the place of his birth, since it is at night that people gather in an inn. Perhaps it was also a symbolic event that Christ should be born at night, as he was to be the light of truth to the darkness of ignorance. But neither would God have said "I have begotten you," except to a true son; for even if he says to the entire people, "I have begotten sons," he did not, however, add "from the womb." Now why would he have added such a redundant phrase as "from the womb," as if there were doubt as to any person's being born from the womb, unless because he wished it to be understood more subtly of Christ: I have begotten you from the womb, that is, from the womb alone, without the seed of a man, attributing to the flesh what is from the womb and to the spirit what is from himself. On this follows, "You are a priest forever." Yet Hezekiah was not a priest, and not forever, even if he had been one. "After the order," he says, "of Melchizedek." What had Hezekiah to do with Melchizedek, a priest of the Most High, and furthermore not circumcised, though he pronounced a blessing on the circumcised Abraham after receiving his offering of a tithe? But the order of Melchizedek sorts well with Christ, seeing that Christ, the peculiar and lawful vicar of God, the pontifex of the uncircumcised priesthood, was at that time established among the nations whom it fell to his lot to be received by (for the most part), while he will deign to be known at last by the seed of Abraham when he comes to embrace and bless them at the end.

There is also another psalm beginning, "God, grant your judgment to the king"—that is, to Christ in his future reign—"and your righteousness to the son of the king"[18]—that is, to the people of Christ. For his children are those who are reborn in him. Yet this psalm too is said to be addressed to Solomon. But can we not learn, from the words that are applicable

only to Christ, that the others also pertain not to Solomon but to Christ? He descends, it says, like rain on a fleece and like dewdrops dripping on the earth. This is a description of his peaceable and invisible descent from heaven to earth. Solomon, however, though he drew his descent from somewhere, did not descend like rain, as it was not from heaven. But I shall bring forward some easier texts. "He shall reign," it says, "from sea to sea and from the river to the ends of the earth."[19] This was granted to Christ alone. Solomon ruled Judea only, and that was no great territory. "All kings shall adore him." Whom do all adore, if not Christ? "And all nations shall serve him." Whom do all serve, if not Christ? "Let his name be for everlasting." Whose name is everlasting, if not Christ's? "Before the sun his name shall abide."[20] For before the sun was the Word of God, that is, Christ. And in him shall all nations be blessed. In Solomon no nation is blessed, but in Christ all are. What then, if this psalm also proves him to be God? "And they shall call him blessed," because "Blessed is the Lord God of Israel, who alone does miracles; blessed is the name of his glory, and the whole world shall be filled with his glory."[21] Solomon, by contrast, I venture to say, lost even that glory that he possessed in God, having been seduced into idolatry by a woman.[22] And so when in the middle of the psalm this also is written, "His enemies shall lick the dust"[23]—clearly meaning, to be put under his feet[24]—this will also be pertinent to the purpose for which I have both introduced this psalm and justified my interpretation of it: to confirm that both the glory of the kingdom and the subjection of the enemies are in accordance with the plan of the Creator. AGAINST MARCION 5.9.[25]

---

[17]See Mt 2:19. [18]Ps 72:1. [19]Ps 72:8. [20]Ps 72:17; but the Hebrew reads "as long as the sun." [21]Ps 72:18-19. [22]Alluding to Jewish traditions that represent the Queen of Sheba as a demon or servant of demons. [23]Ps 72:9. [24]See Heb 2:8; 1 Cor 15:27. [25]CCL 1:690-91.

HE WILL COME AGAIN IN GLORY TO JUDGE THE LIVING AND THE DEAD

σταυρωθέντα τε ὑπὲρ ἡμῶν	crucifixus etiam pro nobis	For our sake he was crucified
ἐπὶ Ποντίου Πιλάτου,	sub Pontio Pilato,	under Pontius Pilate;
καὶ παθόντα καὶ ταφέντα,	passus et sepultus est;	he suffered death and was buried.
καὶ ἀναστάντα τῇ τρίτῃ ἡμέρᾳ	et resurrexit tertia die,	On the third day he rose again
κατὰ τὰς γραφάς,	secundum Scripturas;	in accordance with the Scriptures;
καὶ ἀνελθόντα εἰς τοὺς οὐρανούς,	et ascendit in coelum,	he ascended into heaven
καὶ καθεζόμενον	sedet	and is seated
ἐκ δεξιῶν τοῦ πατρός,	ad dexteram Patris;	at the right hand of the Father.
καὶ πάλιν ἐρχόμενον μετὰ δόξης	**et iterum venturus est, cum gloria,**	**He will come again in glory**
κρῖναι ζῶντας καὶ νεκρούς·	**judicare vivos et mortuos;**	**to judge the living and the dead,**
οὗ τῆς βασιλείας οὐκ ἔσται τέλος.	cujus regni non erit finis.	and his kingdom will have no end.

HISTORICAL CONTEXT: The return of Christ in judgment, predicted (for example) in Mark 8:38 and 1 Thesssalonians 4:16, is an article of previous creeds and inseparable from the preaching of the gospel. It is because Christ rose as the firstfruits of the elect that the believer is confident of his own resurrection (1 Cor 15:12-20). This clause reminds the faithful that the resurrection and exaltation of Christ are not remote historical facts or truths for Sundays; and because it implies that those whom Christ commends will be those who acknowledge him as Lord, it also tells us why the church thought it imperative to define the nature and origin of this lordship. The words "in glory," authorized though they are by Mark 8:38 and a host of other passages, were omitted in the earlier Nicene Creed of 325, perhaps because it was feared that they would be taken to mean that he would acquire this glory for the first time at the second coming. This inference is refuted by John 17:5.

OVERVIEW: Christ is judge in heaven as on earth (AUGUSTINE); prophecy makes him inseparable from the judgment (SIBYLLINE ORACLES).

The Judge of All

CHRIST IS THE FINAL JUDGE BECAUSE HE WAS THE FIRST. AUGUSTINE: This dispensation is not merely temporal, like his birth according to God's will, but also was and will be. For our Lord was on earth and is now in heaven, and he will be in manifest glory[1] the judge of the living and the dead. For he will come just as he ascended, in accordance with the authoritative statement of the Acts of the Apostles.[2] ON FAITH AND THE CREED 15.[3]

JUDGMENT IS INSEPARABLE FROM THE PERSON OF THE JUDGE. SIBYLLINE ORACLES:[4]

---

[1]Augustine adds these words from the Nicene Creed, though he is commenting on the so-called Apostles' Creed, which continued to serve in his time as the Latin touchstone of orthodoxy. [2]Acts 7:56; 13:40. [3]CSEL 41:17. [4]In these verses, falsely attributed to the Sibyl, a pagan seer, the first letters of consecutive lines spell out the formula *Iēsous Chreistos Theou Huios Sōtēr Stauros* ("Jesus Christ, God's Son, Savior, Cross"). The first five words

In sign of coming judgment earth shall sweat;
Eternal monarchy shall come from heaven
Straightway to judge the flesh and all the
world.
Outcasts and the elect shall look on God,
Uplifted at time's end with all the saints,
Set on his throne to judge all flesh ensouled.

Chaff now and earth shall all the world
become;
Riches and all their idols people shall break;
Earth, sky and sea shall be consumed in
flames;
Invading fire shall breach the gates of hell.
Sinner and saint shall rise to day's free light;
Their flesh the fire shall test eternally.
Of secret deeds none shall remain unknown,
Since God's torch shall unlock the heart's
recess.

Then shall all people wail and gnash their
teeth;
Eclipse shall hide the sun and dancing stars,
Oblivion wrap the heavens and the moon's
light,
Uplifting hollows, casting down high peaks.

Huge sorrow then shall fall on humankind.
In peak and plain there shall be no distinction.
Ocean shall bear no ships, as thunderbolts
Strip the burned land of springs and sounding
rivers.

Sounds of lament shall trumpet forth from
heaven,
Omen of squalor, grief and cosmic pain.
Then yawning earth shall open Tartarus;
Emperors all shall come before God's throne;
Rivers of holy flame shall pour from heaven.

Signs manifest to all people there shall be;
True people shall crave the branches of the
cross.
As people grow pious Christ will shock the
world,
Unveiling the elect with his twelve springs.
Rod shall be shepherd, ruling as with iron.
Our God is this, set forth now in acrostics,
Savior immortal, king who died for us.
SIBYLLINE ORACLES 8.217-50.[5]

---

yield the acronym *ichthus* ("fish") a common symbol of Christ among the first believers. [5]ECC 43.

AND HIS KINGDOM WILL HAVE NO END

σταυρωθέντα τε ὑπὲρ ἡμῶν	*crucifixus etiam pro nobis*	*For our sake he was crucified*
ἐπὶ Ποντίου Πιλάτου,	*sub Pontio Pilato,*	*under Pontius Pilate;*
καὶ παθόντα καὶ ταφέντα,	*passus et sepultus est;*	*he suffered death and was buried.*
καὶ ἀναστάντα τῇ τρίτῃ ἡμέρᾳ	*et resurrexit tertia die,*	*On the third day he rose again*
κατὰ τὰς γραφάς,	*secundum Scripturas;*	*in accordance with the Scriptures;*
καὶ ἀνελθόντα εἰς τοὺς οὐρανούς,	*et ascendit in coelum,*	*he ascended into heaven*
καὶ καθεζόμενον	*sedet*	*and is seated*
ἐκ δεξιῶν τοῦ πατρός,	*ad dexteram Patris;*	*at the right hand of the Father.*
καὶ πάλιν ἐρχόμενον μετὰ δόξης	*et iterum venturus est, cum gloria,*	*He will come again in glory*
κρῖναι ζῶντας καὶ νεκρούς·	*judicare vivos et mortuos;*	*to judge the living and the dead,*
οὗ τῆς βασιλείας οὐκ ἔσται τέλος.	**cujus regni non erit finis.**	**and his kingdom will have no end.**

HISTORICAL CONTEXT: Of the clauses from the creed of 381 encompassed by the present volume, this is the most substantial addition to the Nicene Creed of 325. A heresy based on 1 Corinthians 15:28 had declared that in the last days Christ and all that belonged to him would be taken into the Father, so that God, in being all in all, would cease to be a Trinity. (The heretic who was alleged to have maintained this was Marcellus of Ancyra, a friend of Athanasnius, though he incurred no ecumenical condemnation in his lifetime and would probably have considered the charge unjust.) The purpose of this clause, then, is to make it clear that just as the second person (or hypostasis) of the Trinity has existed from eternity, so he will continue to exist for all eternity after the end of the created order—in willing submission to God the Father but without surrendering either his own identity or the individuality of the saints.

OVERVIEW: While the Son has already established a kingdom in the present world (AUGUSTINE), his glory will not be diminished when the kingdom of the Father supervenes (AUGUS-

TINE). It is the elect, not the Savior, who will be made subject (GREGORY OF NYSSA, AUGUSTINE), and through this mediatorial action (GREGORY OF NYSSA), death will be banished together with sin (AUGUSTINE).

Christ is the one priest of the new covenant (EUSEBIUS). A sacrificial priesthood remains (ORIGEN), but the levitical cult has been superseded (CHRYSOSTOM).

The Eucharist may be regarded as our oblation on earth (HIPPOLYTUS). It unites the congregation (IGNATIUS) and witnesses to the incarnation of Christ (IRENAEUS). While it may be regarded as a new Passover (PASCHAL HOMILY), it is one in which the worshipers offer themselves (LITURGY OF ST. MARK). The Passover lamb is an adumbration of Christ (ORIGEN).

Christ's Eternal Kingdom

CHRIST HAS ESTABLISHED A KINGDOM IN THIS WORLD. AUGUSTINE: First it was necessary to demonstrate to us the vanity of the human notion of his kingdom, among Gentiles as among Jews; what Pilate had heard from the latter implied that he ought to be punished by death because he had pretended to an unlawful sovereignty. Perhaps too it is customary for those in power to envy those who aspire to power, and clearly precautions had to be taken in case his kingdom was hostile either to the Romans or to the Jews. Now what the Lord said—"My kingdom is not from[1] this world"[2]—could in fact have been said in response to the magistrate's first question, when he said to him, "Are you the king of the Jews?" But instead he asked him in his turn whether he was saying this of himself or had heard it from others, and by Pilate's response he wished to show that it was the Jews who were laying this as a criminal charge against him. Thus he made plain to us that human counsels, which he knew well[3] are futile, and his reply to these after Pilate's response was more aptly fitted both to Jews and to Gentiles: "My kingdom is not of this world." If he had made this response as soon as Pilate put a question to him, he would have seemed to be replying only to Gentiles who held this opinion of him, and not to Jews as well. But now, because Pilate answered, "A Jew? Your own people and the high priests have handed you over to me,"[4] he deflected any suspicion that might have caused it to be though that he had spoken of himself in calling Jesus the king of the Jews, by demonstrating that it was from the Jews that he heard it. Then by saying, "What have you done?" he makes it sufficiently plain that this was the charge laid against him, as though he were saying, "If you deny that you are a king, what have you done to cause you to be handed over to me?" This implies that it would not have been remarkable that one who styled himself a king should be handed over to the judge for punishment, whereas if he were not saying this, it was necessary to ask of him what he might have done so as to deserve to be handed over to a judge.

Listen, Jews and Gentiles; listen, circumcised and uncircumcised; listen, all kingdoms of earth: I lay no curb on your dominion in this world. "My kingdom is not of this world." Do not be afraid with that baseless fear that dismayed the elder Herod when he heard that Christ had been born, so that he slaughtered so many children in order to bring about his death, made more cruel by timidity rather than anger. "My kingdom," he says, "is not of this world." What more would you have? Come to the kingdom that is not from this world; come by believing, and do not wax savage through fear. It is indeed said of God the Father in prophecy, "I am established as king by him on Zion the holy mountain,"[5] but that Zion and that mountain are not of this world. For what is his kingdom if not those who believe in him, to whom he says, "You are not of the world, just as I am not of the world"?[6] And this although he wished them to be in the world, for which reason he said of them to the Father, "I ask not that you take them from this world but that you preserve them from evil."[7] Thus it is that he says not, "My kingdom is not in this world," but "My kingdom is not of this world." And when he was proving this with the words, "If my kingdom were from this world, my servants would fight on behalf of it and I would not be delivered to the Jews," he says not, "my kingdom is not here," but "it is not from here." For his kingdom is here up to the end of the age, having tares mingled in it until the reaping; for the reaping is the end of the age when the reapers, that is, the angels, will come and will collect from his kingdom all that causes offense.[8] And this would not happen if his kingdom were not here. But at the same time, it is not from here, because we are pilgrims in the world, and thus he says to his kingdom, "You are not of the world, but I have chosen you from the world."[9] They were therefore of the world when they were not his kingdom

---

[1]"From," not "of," is the proper sense of the Greek. [2]Jn 18:36. [3]Jn 2:25. [4]Jn 18:35. [5]Ps 2:6. [6]Jn 17:16. [7]Jn 17:15. [8]Mt 13:38-41. [9]Jn 15:19.

but belonged to the prince of the world. Of the world therefore is every human being who, while having indeed been created by the true God, is nonetheless born of the stock that has been corrupted and sentenced to condemnation since Adam. But whatever is reborn in Christ from that source is made a kingdom that is no longer of the world. For so it was that God snatched us from the powers of darkness and translated us into the kingdom of the Son of his own love. It is of this kingdom that he says, "My kingdom is not of this world," and "My kingdom is not from here." Tractates on the Gospel of John 115.1-2.[10]

He Will Also Rule in the Kingdom of the Father.[11] Augustine: Those who deny the equality of the Son of God with the Father are apt to impose their own sense on this text, in which the apostle says, "Now when all things have been subjected to him, then also the Son himself will be made subject to him who has made all things subject, that God may be all in all."[12] This error, mitigated by the name of Christianity, would not have arisen among them were it not for their failure to understand the Scriptures. For what they say is, "If he is equal, how will he be made subject?" Which is very much like that question concerning the Gospel: if he is equal, how is the Father greater?[13] But the principle of the catholic faith is that when in some passage of Scripture the Son is said to be less than the Father, it should be construed with respect to his assumption of humanity. When there are sayings that demonstrate his equality, they are to be taken according to his divinity. . . . Since, however, many things proper to his person—without reference to what concerns his assumption of humanity—are also said of him in such a way that one does not understand the Father as anything but the Father, or the Son as anything but the Son, the heretics imagine that in passages thus expressed and understood, there can be no equality. It is written,

for example, "All things were made through him,"[14] meaning clearly through the Son, that is, through the Word of God; by whom, then, but the Father? Yet nowhere is it written that the Son effected any creation through the Father. Again it is written that the Son is the image of the Father,[15] yet nowhere is it written that the Father is the image of the Son. Then it is written that one is the begetter and one the begotten, with others that pertain not to the inequality of substance but only to the proper character of the persons. When the heretics say in these cases that there cannot be equality, because they apply gross minds to the investigation of these sayings, they are to be subdued by the weight of authority. For if these passages could not be understood to mean that the one through whom all things were created is equal to the one by whom they were created, image to the one whose image he is, the begotten to the begetter, the apostle would not conceivably have stopped the mouths of factious persons by using this very term[16] when he says, "not thinking it robbery to be equal with God."[17]

Thus those things that are written with an eye to the distinction between the Father and the Son are partly written thus with respect to the proper characters of the persons and partly with respect to the assumption of humankind; but at the same time, the deity, the unity and the equality of the divine substance of the Father and the Son remain. And therefore it is rightly asked in this place whether it is with regard to the proper characters of the persons or with regard to the assumption of humanity that the apostle said, "Then also the Son himself will be made subject to him who has made all things subject." It is usual in Scripture for

---

[10]CCL 36:643-45. [11]The contrary view was generally attributed to Marcellus of Ancyra and was excluded by the words "and his kingdom will have no end" in the Creed of Constantinople (381). This formulation may not have been known to Latin authors of Augustine's time. [12]1 Cor 15:28. [13]Jn 14:28. [14]Jn 1:3. [15]Col 1:15. [16]That is, equality. [17]Phil 2:6.

the context to shed light on a proposition, when those things written nearby that have bearing on the present question are examined in discussion. And thus we find that Paul arrived at this place after saying above, "Now, however, Christ has risen from the dead as the firstfruits of them that slept"; for the resurrection of the dead was his subject. This was done in the Lord by virtue of the assumption of humanity. . . . Now there are other things in this passage,[18] the whole text of which I have just quoted, First, that it says, "when he has handed over the kingdom to God and the Father,"[19] as though the Father does not already possess the kingdom. Then that it is said, "until he has put all his enemies under his feet,"[20] as though after this he will not go on reigning and this is the import of the words "the end" above.[21] On this the heretics put their own impious construction, as though by "end" he meant the termination of his kingdom, whereas in the Gospel[22] it is said that "his kingdom will have no end." And finally, where it is said that "When all things have been made subject to him, then also the Son himself will be made subject to him who has made all things subject," they choose to understand this as though at present either there was something not yet subject to the Son or the Son was not subject to the Father.

The solution of the question, therefore, lies in the manner of speaking. For it is a frequent device in Scripture to speak of that which is always the case as becoming so for someone when he begins to be conscious of it. Thus we are wont to say in our prayer, "Hallowed be your name,"[23] as though it has not been hallowed at some time. "Hallowed be," then, means "let it be known to be hallowed," and likewise also the meaning of "when he has handed over the kingdom to the Father" is "when he has proved that the Father reigns and that which is now believed by the faithful and denied by the infidel becomes evident through visible manifestation." . . . As for "he must

reign until he has put all his enemies under his feet," this means his kingdom must be made manifest up to the point where all his enemies confess that he is reigning; for that is what it means to say that all his enemies will be under his feet. If we understand this of the righteous, the meaning of enemies is that they will be made righteous from a state of unrighteousness and will be subjected to him by believing. Of the unrighteous, who have no share in the future beatitude of the righteous, it may be taken to mean that when that manifestation of his kingdom occurs, they for their part will confess in their consternation that he reigns. On Eighty-Three Varied Questions 69.1-5.[24]

It Is We Who Experience the Consummation. Gregory of Nyssa: When then the good comes to permeate all things, then that body of his will be subjected to his life-giving power, and thus the subjection of this body is described as the subjection of the Son who is mingled with his own body, which is the church. This is what the apostle means when he writes the following words to the Colossians: "Now I rejoice in my sufferings and do my part in filling up in my flesh what is wanting in the afflictions of Christ, for the sake of his body, which is the church."[25] And to the Corinthian church he says, "You are a body of Christ and members severally."[26] And his teaching on this matter he sets out more clearly to the Ephesians when he says, "Speaking truth in love, we shall in all respects grow into him, Christ, from whom the whole body, jointed and compacted by every link that sustains it, effects the increase of the body in the measure of each part, that he may build up himself in love."[27] He implies that Christ builds himself up as each new person is added

---

[18]He had just quoted 1 Cor 15:21-28. [19]1 Cor 15:24. [20]1 Cor 15:25. [21]1 Cor 15:24. [22]Lk 1:33. [23]Mt 6:9. [24]CCL 44A:184-89. [25]Col 1:24-25. [26]1 Cor 12:27. [27]Eph 4:15-16.

to the faith. And the time when he stops building himself up will be the time when the increase and perfection of his body has reached its due measure, and there is nothing left to be added by building, because all have been built in on the foundation of the prophets and apostles[28] and added to the faith. This is the time when, according to the apostle, we shall all come into the oneness of faith and the knowledge of the Son of God, to a perfect man, to the measure of the stature of the fullness of Christ.[29] On the Subjection of the Son.[30]

It Is the Saints, Not the Word, Who Are Made Subject. Augustine: Now although the saying, "Then also the Son himself will be made subject to the one who has made all things subject" is said with regard to the assumption of humanity (this being how the question arose, when he was speaking of the resurrection of the dead), it is nonetheless rightly asked whether it is said of him only insofar as he is the head of the church[31] or with regard to Christ as his whole, counting his members along with his body. For when he says to the Galatians, "He did not say 'seeds' as if it were in many but as if it were in that one seed of yours,"[32] he did not wish us to understand in this place only the Christ who was born of Mary, as he shows by saying subsequently, "For all of you are one in Christ Jesus."[33] . . . And in many places of Scripture[34] we find that the manner of naming Christ requires all his members to be understood along with him, it being said to them, "You are the body of Christ and his members."[35] Thus our understanding of the verse, "Then also the Son himself will be made subject to him who has made all things subject," is not absurd if we understand by Son not only the head of the church, but also all the saints with him, as they are one in Christ, one seed of Abraham—subject, that is, with regard to their contemplation of eternal truth with the aim of obtaining

beatitude, resisting by no motion of the mind and in no part of the body, so that in that life, in which none clings to his status as an individual, God may be all in all.[36] On Eighty-three Varied Questions 69.10.[37]

This Is the Meaning of Mediation. Gregory of Nyssa: It is in this very same sense that the Lord is described as mediator between God and humanity by Paul. For he who abides in the Father and has come to be among humans accomplishes his mediation in this, that he makes all one in him and one through himself with the Father. This is what the Lord says in the Gospel, making his prayer to the Father, "That all may be one—that as you, Father, are in me and I in you, so they too may be in us."[38] For by this he plainly declares that the one who abides in the Father, having united us with himself, achieves through himself a conjunction between us and the Father. On the Subjection of the Son.[39]

The Conquest of Death Entails the Conquest of Sin. Augustine: It is commonly asked what is meant by "Then will come to pass that which is written, 'Death is swallowed up in victory.' Where, death, is your contention; where, death, is your sting? Now the sting of death is sin, but the power of sin is the law."[40] Death in this passage I suppose to signify the carnal disposition that resists the good will because of its pleasure in tasting temporal goods. For it would not be said, "Where, death, is your contention?" had it not resisted and fought back. How it contends the following passage explains: "The flesh lusts against the spirit and the spirit against the flesh. For these

---

[28]See Lk 2:52; Eph 2:20. [29]Eph 4:13. [30]GNO 3.2:18-19. [31]Col 2:19. [32]Gal 3:16. [33]Gal 3:28. Augustine does not believe, as many modern critics of Paul do, that he made the mistake of referring a collective noun in Hebrew to an individual subject. [34]He had also quoted 1 Cor 12:12. [35]1 Cor 12:27. [36]1 Cor 15:28. [37]CCL 44A:195-96. [38]Jn 17:22. [39]GNO 3.2:21. [40]1 Cor 15:54-56.

are opposed in turn one to the other, so that you cannot perform what you will."[41] Therefore through perfect sanctification it comes to pass that very carnal appetite is made subject to our spirit, that is, to the good will, as it receives illumination and increase of life. And just as now we see that we do without many childish pleasures that it would have pained us harshly to be deprived of when we were children, so we may believe that it will be with every carnal pleasure when perfect sainthood has restored the whole person. At present, however, so long as there is that in us which resists the good will, we have need of God's help through good people and good angels, so that before our wound is healed it may not be so noxious as to destroy even the good will.

Now it was by sin that we merited this death, the sin that before this lay wholly within the freedom of the will, when in paradise no grief on account of a pleasure denied resisted the good will of human beings, as it does now. To take an example: if there is someone who has never taken pleasure in hunting, he is absolutely free to chose or not to choose to hunt, nor does he suffer pain when anyone prohibits this. But if he uses this freedom wrongly and goes hunting in defiance of the prohibiting order, gradually the pleasure creeps up on his soul and kills it, so that if he should wish to refrain, he cannot do so without trouble and anguish; before, by contrast, when he did not act thus, he was in perfect health. Thus "the sting of death is sin" because through sin a pleasure comes into being that is able to resist the good will and make common cause with grief. This pleasure, because it lies in the weakness of a mind made worse, we rightly call death. "But the power of sin is the Law," because those deeds that the law prohibits are much more culpable and heinous when committed than they would be if prohibited by no law. And so it is that "death will be swallowed up in victory," when every part of the human person is sanctified, so that the pleasure of the flesh is overwhelmed by perfect pleasure in spiritual goods. ON EIGHTY-THREE VARIED QUESTIONS 70.[42]

The Eternal Priesthood

THERE IS ONE TRUE PRIEST. EUSEBIUS: It is proper that he alone should bear the authentic likeness of the Father, having been shown to be the sole companion of the Father's throne. Thus it is obvious that it was not right for any generated thing to be allotted to the right hand of the almighty rule and sovereignty, excepting only the one who, through the texts that we have at hand, was variously described under inspiration.[43] Learn now that it was to one and the same that the most high who is Lord over all vouchsafed the words "Sit at my right hand" and "Before the morning star I have begotten you," bestowing on him, with an oath of confirmation, the unshakable and inviolable honor of the priesthood that endures, world without end: "The Lord has sworn and will not repent, 'You are a priest forever.'" Who could be the intended subject? Clearly not a mortal, or for that matter one of angelic nature, for he was born of God but made a priest for eternity. "Who but the one who also said in what went before, The Lord has made me a beginning of his ways for his works, he established me before the world, in the beginning before the mountains were set in their places, and before all the hills he brings me forth?" Now fix your mind with attention and understanding on the present psalm and the words that were juxtaposed with it in the foregoing discussion. For in this psalm the most high God appoints the second one, our Lord, as the companion of his throne, saying, "Sit at my right hand." Now in the one previously cited,[44] it was said that his throne would endure for ages of ages,

---

[41]Gal 5:17. [42]CCL 44A:197-99. [43]*Theologoumenos*—spoken of by the *theologoi*, or religious teachers of Israel. [44]Ps 44:6 at *Demonstration* 5.2.1ff.

and at the same time he was called god[45] in the words "your throne, God, is for ages of ages." Again in the text that we have in hand, he says, "The Lord will send you from Zion as a rod of power," and in the other, "A rod of righteousness is the rod of your kingdom." And again our present text says, "Sit at my right hand until I make your enemies your footstool, and you shall reign in the midst of your enemies," while the previous one says, "Your darts have been sharpened in the hearts of the enemies of the kingdom." Thus they coincide in what they say of the enemies of the one aforesaid.

Who, then, that sees with his eyes the churches of our Savior flowering in the urban centers, in villages and country places throughout the whole inhabited world and the congregations subject to his lordship and the populous multitudes of those consecrated to him, encircled as they are by enemies seen and (to humans) unseen and invisible, foes to the teaching of Christ, would not marvel at the present oracle addressed to the person of the one prophesied, "Exercise lordship in the midst of your enemies"? And since in the one previously cited, we read, "I have anointed you with the oil of gladness beyond your fellows," quite properly the text at hand pronounces him a purer priest, adding further information about him, through which it teaches that he alone is an eternal priest, excelling all that ever were. And this one cannot reconcile with any being of human nature. It says that he was made priest in succession from Melchizedek by way of contrast with the priest according to the Mosaic succession, either Aaron himself or any of his descendants, for each of these was at first no priest and was at some later time anointed by men with some manufactured unction, as it were in types and symbols. In shadow and image he became an anointed one, yet, since he was mortal, he laid down the priesthood after no long time; and he was made priest among the Jews alone, not among the other nations. Moreover, it was not by the

sworn word of God that he succeeded to the liturgy but being honored by the judgment of men and from time to time was not found worthy in their eyes of the service of God, as is written of Eli. And in addition to all this, that priest of the Mosaic succession was chosen only from the tribe of Levi, and indeed it was required that in birth he should be wholly of the line of Aaron, serving the divine with the savor and blood of irrational beasts and with bodily worship. But the one who was named Melchizedek (which means in translation "king of justice") and then king of Salem (which itself would mean "king of peace, without father, without mother, without genealogy, having according to the narrative neither beginning of days nor end of life"[46]) has nothing whatsoever in common with the fashion of priesthood that is from Aaron. For he was not exalted by people or anointed with a manufactured oil; he was not by birth one of those who previously had not existed. What is all the more remarkable, he was not even circumcised in the flesh, and nevertheless he blesses Abraham, as though he were far greater than he, though he did not perform his priesthood to the most high God with sacrifice and libations, not indeed did he carry out the liturgy in the temple at Jerusalem. How indeed could he when it did not exist? And it was properly so, since there was to be no affinity between Christ our Savior and Aaron—for as has been shown, he was not made subsequently a priest when he was not before: he did not become a priest but is.

Yes, one must pay close attention to the words "You are a priest for eternity." For he does not say, "You shall be, having not been before," or for that matter "You were before but are not now." No, it was the one who said "I am that I am"[47] who says, "You are and remain a priest for eternity." Since therefore

---

[45]Eusebius distinguishes the Father who is properly God from the Son, who is called God by derivation (see, e.g., *Demonstration* 5 proem 23; 5.4.8-12; 5.30.3). [46]Heb 7:3. [47]Ex 3:14.

Christ did not commence his priesthood in time or derive it from a tribe and was not anointed with bodily and manufactured oil, nor was he to see any end to his priesthood and was to be appointed not for the Jews alone but for all nations also—for all these reasons the text properly dissociates him from the priesthood of Aaron's type and says that he will be priest in succession from Melchizedek. And the fulfillment of the oracle is wonderful to one who considers how our Savior Jesus, the anointed one [Christ] of God, discharges his sacred functions among humanity right up to the present day through his ministers in the fashion of Melchizedek. For just as Melchizedek, being a priest of the nations, is nowhere seen to have made use of bodily sacrifices but blessed Abraham with wine and bread alone, in the same fashion first our Savior and Lord himself and then all the priests of his line throughout the nations discharge their sacred service spiritually according to the ecclesiastical precepts. By the bread and wine they represent the mysteries of his body and his saving blood, which Melchizedek had foreseen by the divine spirit, making use of images of things to come, as the Scripture of Moses witnesses, saying, "And Melchizedek, king of Salem, brought bread and wine, for he was a priest of the most high God; and he blessed Abraham."

Quite properly then it was also with an oath of adoption, and only to the one aforesaid, that "The Lord God has sworn, and will not repent, saying, 'You are a priest for eternity in succession to Melchizedek.'" Listen too to what the apostle says about this: "Wherein God, willing more abundantly to show to the heirs of his promise the immutability of his counsel, confirmed it with an oath, so that by two immutable things, in which it is impossible for God to lie, we might have a strong consolation, who have fled for refuge to lay hold on the hope set before us."[48] And to this he adds the words "And they truly were many priests, because they prevented from continuing by death; but

this man, because he continues forever, has an unchangeable priesthood. Thus he is also able to save to the uttermost those who come to God by him, living always to make intercession for them. For such a high priest became us, who is holy, blameless, undefiled, separate from sinners and made higher than the heavens."[49] . . . It is obvious to all that even now the power of our Savior and the word of his teaching give lordly protection to all those who have faith in him in the midst of their enemies and foes. PROOF OF THE GOSPEL 5.3.6-22, 26.[50]

THE PRIESTHOOD HAS NOT CEASED TO BE SACRIFICIAL. ORIGEN: Let us see now how it is that our Savior does not drink wine, until the time when he is to drink it new with the saints in the kingdom of God. Even now my Savior mourns my sins; my Savior cannot be glad so long as I remain in iniquity. Why can he not? Because he himself is the advocate for our sins as his fellow initiate John declares, saying that "if any has sinned, we have an advocate with God, Jesus Christ the righteous, and he is the propitiation for our sins."[51] How therefore can he who is the advocate for my sins drink the wine of gladness when I grieve him by my sins? How can he who approaches the altar to make propitiation for me a sinner be in gladness, when the wretchedness of my sins is always going up to him? "With you," he says, "I shall drink that wine in the kingdom of my Father." So long as we do not act in such a way as to ascend to the kingdom, he cannot drink the wine alone that he promised to drink with us. So long then as we are in error he is in wretchedness. For if his own apostle mourns certain people who have sinned previously and have not repented of what they did,[52] what shall I say of him, who is called the Son of charity, who emptied himself on

---

[48]Heb 6:17-18. [49]Heb 7:23. He then provides citations of Ps 123:4; Mt 26:42; Phil 2:8; Eph 1:20. [50]GCS 23:219-23. [51]1 Jn 2:1-2. [52]2 Cor 12:21.

account of the charity that he felt toward us, not seeking what was his own though he was equal with God but sought what pertained to us, and on this account made himself empty?[53] . . . It cannot be supposed that Paul for his part would mourn sinners and weep for delinquents, yet that my Lord Jesus would abstain from weeping when he approaches the Father, when he stands by the altar and offers propitiation on our behalf. And this is what it means to approach the altar without drinking the wine of gladness, because he still suffers the bitterness of our sins. HOMILIES ON LEVITICUS 7.[54]

YET THE CHURCH IS NOT TO SACRIFICE IN THE OLD MANNER. CHRYSOSTOM: See, we have our victim on high, our priest on high, our sacrifice on high; let us bring such sacrifices as can be offered on that altar, no longer sheep and oxen, no longer blood and fat. All these things have been done away, and there has been brought in their stead "the reasonable service."[55] But what is the reasonable service? The offerings made through the soul; those made through the spirit. ("God," it is said, "is a Spirit, and they who worship him must worship him in spirit and in truth"[56]); things that have no need of a body, no need of instruments or of special places, of which each one is himself the priest, such as moderation, temperance, mercifulness, enduring ill-treatment, long-suffering, humbleness of mind.

These sacrifices one may see in the Old Testament also, shadowed out beforehand. "Offer to God," it is said, "a sacrifice of righteousness";[57] "Offer a sacrifice of praise";[58] "A sacrifice of praise shall glorify me";[59] "The sacrifice of God is a broken spirit";[60] and "What does the Lord require of you but to listen to him?"[61] "Burnt offerings and sacrifices for sin you have had no pleasure in; then I said, 'I come to do your will, O God!' "[62] and again, "To what purpose do you bring the incense from Sheba?"[63] "Take away from me the noise of your songs,

for I will not bear the melody of your viols."[64] But instead of these "I will have mercy and not sacrifice."[65] . . .

And there are other sacrifices also that are indeed whole burnt offerings, the bodies of the martyrs: there both soul and body are offered. These have a great savor of a sweet smell.[66] You also are able, if you will, to bring such a sacrifice. For what if you do not burn your body in the fire? Yet in a different fire you can, for instance, in that of voluntary poverty, in that of affliction. For to have in one's power to spend one's days in luxury and expense, and yet to take up a life of toil and bitterness and to mortify the body, is not this a whole burnt offering? . . . This is an excellent sacrifice, needing no priest but him who brings it. This is an excellent sacrifice, performed indeed below but immediately taken up on high. HOMILIES ON HEBREWS 11.6.[67]

THE CHURCH'S OBLATION IS THE EUCHARIST.[68] HIPPOLYTUS: And then let the oblation at once be brought by the deacons to the bishop, and he shall offer thanks for the bread in the representation of the flesh of Christ; and the cup mixed with wine for the antitype[69] of the blood that was shed for all who have believed in him, and milk and honey mingled together in fulfillment of the promise that was to the ancestors, in which he said, "I will give you a land flowing with milk and honey"; which Christ indeed gave, his flesh, by which they who believe are nourished like little children,[70] making the bitterness of the heart sweet by the sweetness of his Word. APOSTOLIC TRADITION 23.1-2.[71]

---

[53]Phil 2:6-8. [54]GCS 29:374-75. [55]Rom 12:1. [56]Jn 4:24. [57]Ps 4:5. [58]Ps 50:14. [59]Ps 50:23. [60]Ps 51:17. [61]Mic 6:8. [62]Ps 40:6-7. [63]Jer 6:20. [64]Amos 5:23. [65]Hos 6:6. [66]See 2 Cor 2:15. [67]NPNF 1 14:420. [68]The following excerpts illustrate the certainty of a real presence but do little to explain the mode of presence. [69]The Greek has "antitype" where the Latin has "representation" and "likeness," according to *HTAT* 40. [70]See 1 Cor 3:2; Ex 15:25. [71]*HTAT* 40.

The Eucharist Is Efficacious. Ignatius of Antioch: Be sure, therefore, to observe a single Eucharist; for there is one flesh of our Lord Jesus Christ and one cup for union with his blood; one place of sacrifice, as there is one bishop together with the presbyters and deacons, my fellow servants. Thus, whatever you do, you are to do it for the Lord. To the Philadelphians 4.[72]

It Reminds Us That Christ Assumed Our Flesh and Blood. Irenaeus: Only outright babblers despise the universal economy of God, denying the salvation of the flesh and disowning its resurrection on the plea that it is not capable of incorruption. If in fact this were not saved, then clearly the Lord did not redeem us with his own blood, and the eucharistic chalice is not a fellowship in his blood, nor is the bread that we break a fellowship in his body. For there is no blood except from fleshly veins and from the rest of that substance that is proper to humanity, the creaturely vessel of the Word of God when he redeemed us with his blood. Thus it is that the apostle says, "In whom we have redemption through his blood and remission of sins."[73] Since we are members of him, we are also nourished through the creation. And he it is who furnishes the creation for us, making his sun rise and sending rain as he chooses.[74] The creaturely chalice he has acknowledged to be his own blood, from which he causes our own blood to flow. And the creaturely bread he has affirmed to be his own body, from which he will increase our bodies. Whenever, therefore, the mingled chalice and the created bread receive the Word of God and the Eucharist becomes the body of Christ, and in consequence the substance of our own bodies will be increased and consolidated: how can they deny that the flesh is receptive to the gift of God, which is everlasting life, when that flesh is nourished by the body and blood of the Lord and is a member of him? Against Heresies 5.2.2-3.[75]

The Eucharist Is the New Passover. Origenist Paschal Homily: The Jews celebrate an earthly Passover, having denied the heavenly one, while we, celebrating a heavenly Passover, have transcended the earthly one. The one that is celebrated by them was a symbol of the salvation of the firstborn among the Jews, when the children of the Jews were not destroyed along with those of the Egyptians, preserved symbolically by the blood of the Passover sacrifice, but the Passover that is celebrated among us is the cause of the salvation of all human beings, beginning from the first-created man, who is saved and receives new life in all. But the parts were designed as images and types of the whole, the temporal of the eternal, drawn in shadow with a view to the truth that has now dawned. And when the truth is present the type is untimely, just as when the king has taken up residence, no one neglecting the living king thinks the image worthy of worship. It is immediately apparent that the type is inferior to the truth from the fact that type celebrates the short life of the firstborn of the Jews, and the truth the unceasing life of all human beings. For it is no great thing to escape death for a while if one is to die a little later, but it is a great thing to escape death altogether, which is our lot since for us "Christ the Passover lamb has been sacrificed." And the very name of the celebration, if correctly interpreted, indicates its great superiority. For the Passover is by interpretation a passing above, for the destroyer passed above the houses of the Hebrews as he struck the firstborn, but for us it is truly a passing above the destroyer, since it passes above us once and for all when we have been raised to everlasting life by Christ. Paschal Homily 1.1-4, On the Sacrifice of the Lamb.[76]

The Worshipers Partake of the True Sacrifice. Liturgy of St. Mark: To you we

---

[72]AF 178. [73]Col 1:14. [74]See Mt 5:45. [75]SC 153:30-34. [76]SC 36:55-57.

have bent the neck of our souls and our bodies to show our condition as servants, and we beseech you to drive away from our thoughts the darkling burdens of sin and to illuminate our minds with the godly rays of the Holy Spirit, so that, being filled with the knowledge of you, we may partake of the goods before us, the unsullied body and honorable blood of your only-begotten Son, the Lord and God and our Savior Jesus Christ, pardoning us for every kind of sin on account of your great and unsearchable benevolence by the grace and mercy and humane love of your only-begotten Son, through whom and with whom the glory and the power are yours with your all-holy, benevolent and lifegiving Spirit, now and forever and to ages of ages. LITURGY OF ST. MARK.[77]

THE PASSOVER WAS BUT A TYPE OF CHRIST. ORIGEN: The lamb is sacrificed by the saints or Nazirites,[78] while the Savior is sacrificed by criminals and sinners. And if the Passover lamb is sacrificed by the saints, and if the apostle has said, "For Christ, our paschal lamb, has been sacrificed,"[79] then Christ is sacrificed according to the type of the Passover but not by the saints, and thus the Passover is indeed a type of Christ but not of his passion. It is necessary for us to sacrifice the true lamb—if indeed we have been ordained priests or like priests have offered sacrifice—and it is necessary for us to cook and eat its flesh. But if this does not take place in the passion of the Savior, then the antitype of the Passover is not his suffering; rather, the Passover becomes the type of Christ himself sacrificed for us. For each one of us first takes the lamb, then dedicates it, then sacrifices it, and thus, after roasting it eats it, and after eating it leaves nothing until the morning and then celebrates the feast of unleavened bread[80] after having come out of Egypt. To show that the Passover is something spiritual, and not this sensible Passover, he says, "Unless you eat my flesh and drink my blood, you have no life in you.[81] Are we then to eat his flesh and drink his blood in a physical manner? But if this is said spiritually, then the Passover is spiritual, not physical. ON PASCHA 12-13.[82]

---

[77]*LEW* 137. [78]On the one male lamb without blemish that is sacrificed for the Nazirite, see Num 6:14. [79]1 Cor 5:7. [80]Ex 12:5-17. [81]See Jn 6:53. [82]*OTP* 34-35.

OUTLINE OF CONTENTS

LIST OF ANCIENT AUTHORS
AND TEXTS CITED

Adamantius
Dialogues

Ambrose
Cain and Abel
Expositions on the Gospel of
  Luke
Isaac, or the Soul
On Abraham
On the Christian Faith
On the Mysteries
On the Sacraments

Ambrosiaster
Commentary on Colossians
Commentary on Ephesians

Andrew of Crete
Easter Sunday Canon

Aphrahat
Demonstrations

Apollinaris of Laodicea
Fragments

Arator
Apostolic History

Arnobius of Sicca
Against the Nations

Athanasius
Against the Arians
On the Incarnation

Augustine
Against Two Letters of the Pelagians
Confessions
Expositions of the Psalms
Harmony of the Gospels
On Eighty-Three Varied Questions
On Faith and the Creed
On the Merits and Forgiveness of Sins and on
  Infant Baptism
On the Trinity
Sermon to Catechumens, On the Creed
Tractates on the Gospel of John

Basil of Caesarea
Letters

Cassian, John
Against Nestorius

Clement of Alexandria
Answer to Tiberius
Excerpts from Theodotus
Hypotyposes
Prophetic Extracts
Stromateis
Who Is the Rich Man Who Shall Be Saved?

Clement of Rome
1 Clement

Constantine
Oration to the Saints

Cyprian
On the Unity of the Church

Cyril of Alexandria
Answer to Tiberius
Commentary on John
First Letter to Succensus
Letter to Acacius
Letter to John of Antioch
On the Creed
Second Letter to Nestorius
Second Letter to Succensus
Thesaurus
Third Letter to Nesorius

Cyril of Jerusalem
Catechetical Lectures

Dracontius
On the Praises of God

Egeria
Pilgrimage

Ephrem of Antioch
Sermon on His Being Tempted As We Are

Ephrem the Syrian
Commentary on Tatian's Diatessaron
Hymns on the Nativity
Nisibene Hymns

Epiphanius
Ancoratus
Panarion

Epistle of Barnabas

Eusebius of Caesarea
Ecclesiastical History
Onomasticon
Proof of the Gospel

Evagrius of Pontus
On Thoughts

Faustinus
On the Trinity

Gaudentius
Tractates

Gildas
Letters

Gospel of Peter

Gospel of Philip

Gospel of Truth

Gregory of Elvira
Origenist Treatise

Gregory of Nazianzus
Dogmatic Poems
Letters on the Apollinarian
  Controversy
Personal Poems

Gregory of Nyssa
Address on Religious Instruction
Against Eunomius
On the Ascension
On the Holy Spirit, Against the
  Macedonians
On the Sacred and Saving Pasch
On the Subjection of the Son
On the Three Days' Interval
Paschal Sermon

Gregory of Tours
History of the Franks

Gregory the Great
Letters

Hermas
Shepherd

Hilary of Poitiers
Commentary on Matthew
On the Mysteries
On the Trinity

Hippolytus
Apostolic Tradition
On Jacob's Blessing
On Lazarus
Paschal Homily
Refutation of All Heresies

Hymn for Compline

Ignatius of Antioch
To the Ephesians
To the Philadelphians
To the Smyrneans

Irenaeus
Against Heresies
Fragments

Jerome
Homilies on Mark
Commentary on Matthew

John Chrysostom
Homilies on Ephesians
Homilies on Galatians
Homilies on John
Homilies on Matthew
Homilies on Philippians

John of Damascus
Homily on the Nativity

Joseph's Bible Notes

Justin Martyr
Dialogue with Trypho
First Apology
Second Apology

Lactantius
Divine Institutes

Leo the Great
Letters
Sermons

Leontius of Byzantium
Pentecost Sermon

Letter to Diognetus

Liturgy of St. James

Liturgy of St. Mark

Marius Victorinus
Commentary on Ephesians
Commentary on Galatians
Commentary on Philippians

Maximus the Confessor
Fourth Century on Love
Opusculum
Questions to Thalassium
Second Century of Various Texts
Second Century on Love

Melito of Sardis
On Pascha

Methodius
Fragment, On the Cross and Passion
  of Christ
Oration on the Palms
Symposium or Banquet of the
  Ten Virgins

Minucius Felix
Octavius

Nemesius of Emesa
On Human Nature

Optatus
Against the Donatists

Origen
Against Celsus
Commentary on Genesis
Commentary on John
Commentary on Matthew

Commentary on Romans
Commentary on the Song of Songs
Dialogue with Heraclides
Fragments on John
Homilies on Joshua
Homilies on Leviticus
On First Principles
On Pascha
Philokalia

Origenest Paschal Homily

Pelagius
Commentary on Romans

Polycarp of Smyrna
Letter to the Philadelphians

Prosper of Aquitaine
The Call of All Nations
Expositions of the Psalms
Song of Ingratitude

Prudentius
Apotheosis
Daily Round
Dittochaeum

Pseudo-Dionysius
Divine Names

Pseudo-Epiphanius
Homilies

Riddles in the Apocalypse

Romanus the Melodist
Canticles

Rufinus of Aquileia
Commentary on the Apostles' Creed

Second Council of Constantinople (553)
Anathemas

Sedulius Scotus
Paschal Treatise

Sybilline Oracles

Tertullian
Against Marcion
Against Praxeas
Against the Nations
Apology
On Baptism
On Idolatry
On the Flesh of Christ

Theodore of Mopsuestia
Catechetical Homilies

Theodoret of Cyr
Eranistes
On the Changelessness of God the Word

Valentinian Treatise
Gnostic Treatise on Resurrection

Valentinus (via Hippolytus)

Venantius Fortunatus
The Blessed Cross Shines Forth
Exposition of the Catholic Faith
Hymns to the Holy Cross
On the Spectacles
Verses on the Resurrection

Author/Writings Index

Scripture Index